Recent Research in Psychology

Leslie P. Steffe Paul Cobb

With the Collaboration of Ernst von Glasersfeld

Construction of Arithmetical Meanings and Strategies

Foreword by Hermine Sinclair

Springer-Verlag
New York Berlin Heidelberg
London Paris Tokyo

Leslie P. Steffe
Department of Mathematics Education
The University of Georgia
Athens, GA 30601, USA

Paul Cobb
Department of Education
Purdue University
West Lafayette, IN 47907, USA

Ernst von Glasersfeld
Professor Emeritus
Department of Psychology
The University of Georgia
Athens, GA 30601, USA

With 9 Figures

Library of Congress Cataloging-in-Publication Data
Steffe, Leslie P.
Construction of arithmetical meanings and strategies.
(Recent research in psychology)
Bibliography: p.
1. Number concept in children—Case studies.
I. Cobb, Paul. II. Glasersfeld, Ernst von. III. Title.
IV. Series.
BF723.N8S74 1988 153.1'5 87-32297

Camera-ready copy prepared by the authors using Microsoftword.

Printed in the United States of America.

9 8 7 6 5 4 3 2 1

ISBN 0-387-96688-9 Springer-Verlag New York Berlin Heidelberg
ISBN 3-540-96688-9 Springer-Verlag Berlin Heidelberg New York

Foreword

The studies presented in this book should be of interest to anybody concerned with the teaching of arithmetic to young children or with cognitive development in general. The "teaching experiment" was carried out with half a dozen children entering first grade over two years in biweekly sessions. Methodologically the authors' research is original. It is a longitudinal but not a naturalistic study, since the experimenter-teachers directed their interaction with each individual child with a view to his or her possible progress. It is experimental in the sense that two groups of subjects were selected according to criteria derived from an earlier study (Steffe, von Glasersfeld, Richards & Cobb, 1983) and that the problems proposed were comparable, though far from identical across the subjects; but unlike more rigid and shorter "learning" or "training" studies it does not include pre- and posttests, or predetermined procedures. Theoretically, the authors subscribe to Piaget's constructivism: numbers are *made* by children, not *found* (as they may find some pretty rocks, for example) or *accepted* from adults (as they may accept and use a toy). The authors interpret changes in the children's counting behaviors in terms of constructivist concepts such as assimilation, accommodation, and reflective abstraction, and certain excerpts from protocols provide on-line examples of such processes at work. They also subscribe to Vygotsky's proposal for teachers "to utilize the zone of proximal development and to lead the child to what he (can) not yet do" (1965, p. 104). The child's actual level of development is determined by the type of problem he or she can solve without help; the zone of proximal development is determined by the dynamic possibilities of each child and evidenced by the kind of problems he or she can solve in collaboration with an adult: two children at the same actual level of development may have very different zones of proximal development. The authors also seem to agree with Inhelder who, in the context of a different type of learning study, states that "training procedures should steer the subjects in the right direction, even if this results temporarily in incorrect reasoning. Variations are possible and it is certainly not true that for each acquisition there is only one predetermined construction process" (Inhelder, Sinclair, & Bovet, 1974, p. 25). Vygotsky, by contrast, seems to see the teacher's role mostly as that of a direct guide towards the adult's conceptual construction of the new problems to be mastered.

The book provides an extremely detailed account of the different types of counting behavior of half a dozen children over two years (interview sessions were videotaped, an absolute necessity for the study of counting behavior, where gestures are as important as utterances). The data allowed the authors to reach their main goal: to document the many subtle changes in children's counting and to interpret them theoretically. At the same time, the results of their intensive study lead the authors to affirm that a major shift in the arithmetic curriculum is necessary: they have cogently demonstrated that many of the widespread presuppositions about what young children know and what they do not know are erroneous, and that better insight into how children come to "do mathematics" should greatly improve the teaching of arithmetic.

In the constructivist theory of knowledge it is assumed that new knowledge arises from new ways of asking questions and from the raising of new problems rather than from the construction of more sophisticated means of dealing with known difficulties, and that confrontation and discussion are essential for progress. From this point of view the present book is certainly constructivist: it will give rise to new problems and hypotheses, and to approbation as well as controversy. I hope that it will incite others to conduct teaching experiments along the lines pursued by the authors.

Hermine Sinclair
University of Geneva

Preface

In this book, we present the results of a teaching experiment that was carried out during the academic years 1980-1981 and 1981-1982. The term "teaching experiment" does not mean an investigation of teaching a predetermined or accepted way of operating. Instead, it is primarily an exploratory tool, derived from Piaget's clinical interview and aimed at discovering what might go on in children's heads. Because it also involves experimentation with the ways and means of influencing children's knowledge, the teaching experiment is more than a clinical interview. Whereas the clinical interview is aimed at establishing where children are, the teaching experiment is directed toward understanding the progress children make over extended periods of time. We used the methodology to investigate children's construction of (1) counting schemes, (2) uniting operations and their systems, (3) lexical and syntactic meanings of number words,[1] and (4) thinking strategies.

Theoretical Assumptions

The constructivist teaching experiment is based on two theoretical assumptions. The first is that children, when faced with problematic arithmetical situations, can develop their own solution methods. The second assumption is that any knowledge that involves carrying out actions or operations cannot be instilled ready-made into children but must, quite literally, be actively built up by them. These assumptions are based on Piaget's (1970) analysis of knowledge:

> Human knowledge is essentially active. To know is to assimilate reality into systems of transformations. . . . I find myself opposed to the view of knowledge as a copy, a passive copy of reality. (p. 15)

A recent report on education expresses a similar view:

---

[1] By "lexical meaning" we intend whatever meaning is associated with a single word, and by "syntactic meaning", those meanings that arise out of the combination of words.

> All genuine learning is active, not passive. It involves the use of the mind, not just memory. It is a process of discovery, in which the student is the main agent, not the teacher. (Adler, 1982, p. 50)

On the other hand, where mathematics teaching is concerned, we agree with Menchinskaya (1969): "Neither scientific nor everyday concepts spring forth spontaneously; both are formed under the influence of adult teaching" (p. 79). From the perspective of the two theoretical premises we have mentioned, the process of teaching in the teaching experiment took on the form of guiding the student's conceptual construction rather than attempting to impart the "correct", adult way of doing things.

There is no reason to assume that a child will interpret a given situation in the way that seems "obvious" to an adult or a teacher, nor can one assume that a child will necessarily "see" that a particular way of proceeding must result in the more standard adult's solution. We believe it is crucial to adopt this attitude for teaching mathematics in early childhood, because little commonality can be assumed between the teacher's and the children's conceptual structures. Piaget has demonstrated the difficulty of constructing operations that manifest the reversibility that is critical to an understanding of arithmetic. However, it is easy to forget that most children, when they enter school, have not yet constructed operations of this kind, and explanations or demonstrations alone are not sufficient to make the children do so.

From our perspective, the essential pedagogical task is not to instill "correct ways of doing" but rather to guide children's constructive activities until they eventually "find" viable techniques. Such guidance must necessarily start from points that are accessible to the children; in order to establish these starting-points we must first gain insight into the children's conceptual structures and methods, no matter how wayward or ineffective they might seem to us, as adults. If there is any virtue in the notion that children as cognitive organisms assimilate their experiences using structures they already possess, and accommodate these structures when their use does not lead to the expected result, it follows that the teacher will be far more successful in precipitating accommodations if he or she has gained some notion of what the child's present structures and ways of operating are.

Purposes of the Teaching Experiment

The main purposes of the teaching experiment, based on the above considerations, were to build a model of cognitive changes in children's initial, informal "number sequences" and then workable means of influencing their conceptualizations and activities. These informal number sequences took the form of counting schemes; the driving force of the teaching experiment was to investigate changes in the counting schemes of six prenumerical children in teaching episodes during their first and second grades in school.

We made no attempts to provide the participating children with an alternative to their regular school mathematics program because we used the teaching episodes as an investigative, experimental tool. The intent was to create a working model of each child's current counting scheme and then to formulate and test hypotheses about the models. We were most interested in how various components of those models might change in the context of solving problem situations.

Teaching Episodes

In a teaching episode, no simple cause-effect relationship is assumed between the teacher's acts and what the child does because experience, qua experience, is the individual's own. As teachers, we had the tasks of (1) interpreting what we saw the children doing and (2) attempting the ultimate act of decentering by imagining of our actions from the children's perspective. In this sense, the course of a teaching episode was also determined by the child. Each problem that we used in a teaching episode was designed for a particular child; our model of that child and its possible modifications constituted the rationale for each problem. We teachers were responsible for devising impromptu problems during a teaching episode after we had interpreted the child's solutions to prior problems. In fact, these spontaneously designed problems represented a major modus operandi of the teaching experiment. However, the focus was not on the problems as the adults conceived of them, but rather as they were constructed and solved by the children. Our primary objective was to give the children opportunities to abstract patterns or regularities from their own sensory-motor and conceptual activities. Guided by our current model of each child's counting scheme, we hypothesized certain patterns or regularities that it might be possible for a particular child to abstract. Activities were then initiated in the hope that the child would reflect on and abstract those patterns or regularities from his or her experiences.

As a matter of course, the teaching episodes were videotaped and this record was used for various purposes. In this book, we are concerned with the retrospective analyses at the end of the teaching experiment.

Retrospective Analyses

We have found that there is no one "best" way to present the extensive interactions among participants in a teaching experiment. Choices have to be made, based on the goals of the investigators. One choice, the children's mathematical behavior and our interpretations of it, essentially eliminates the extensive discussions that went on while the teaching experiment was in progress and the almost daily decisions we made concerning our teaching strategies and tasks. Our intention--to analyze the children's constructions rather than how we adults might have influenced them--was to study mathematical *learning* rather than mathematical *teaching*. Nevertheless, mathematical learning was observed in contexts where we teachers intervened to influence learning, examine its limits, and examine the children's generative power and flexibility.

The book contains the results of retrospective analyses that were conducted after the teaching experiment was concluded in June 1982. We had approximately 64 videotape 15-to-30-minute segments for each child, which we first analyzed in the sequence in which they were taped. During the course of the teaching experiment, we had learned a considerable amount about each child and had documented points of progress. While these proved invaluable, our interpretations often changed dramatically in the retrospective analyses.

Overview of the Book

Chapter I contains a *theoretical analysis* of the children's construction of the counting scheme and the major hypotheses we investigate in the next three chapters. Chapters II, III, and IV contain the results of our study of the children's construction of their counting schemes. Chapters II and III concern the three children who began the teaching experiment in a perceptual period, and Chapter IV concerns the three children who began the teaching experiment in a motor period.[2] Case material is presented for each child. From the extensive videotaped data, we have selected what we believe are critical protocols to document our observations and interpretations. These protocols are "snapshots" of the dynamic interactions among teachers and children over 2 years.

In Chapters V, VI, VII, and VIII, we present independent analyses of the changing meanings and strategies of the children and correlate these changes with those in the children's counting schemes. Because these analyses were conducted separately from the analyses of the children's counting schemes and independently of each other, they lend credibility to the relationships that emerged.

---

[2] The phrases "perceptual period" and "motor period" refer to the type of items the children could create and count. "Perceptual unit items" refer to those items created from visual, auditory, or tactile signals and "motor unit items" refer to those items created from kinesthetic signals.

In the chapters on meaning, the presentation of protocols established in the earlier chapters is continued. For the chapters on strategies, the focus changes from documenting the bases for our interpretations to presenting our interpretations; the emphasis on the individual children, however, is maintained. This change in style of presentation is warranted, because we refer to the protocols presented in the preceding detailed analyses of lexical and syntactical meanings.

Chapter IX contains an analysis of the cognitive changes in the counting schemes of the six children over the duration of the teaching experiment. Different types of accommodations the children made are identified, and the role of experience is clarified for each type. A new, ontogenetic model for the children's construction of the number sequence is correlated with a phylogenetic analysis of the development of the number sequence.

Any reader who has conducted videotape analyses can appreciate the amount of time involved in playing a videotape, replaying segments, transcribing protocols, correlating current observations with previous ones, and searching for behavioral indicators of certain concepts or operations. We invite readers to conduct their own analyses of the protocols, which should be stimulating and interesting and perhaps give rise to plausible competing hypotheses.

The Participating Children

The 6 participating children were selected from 20 first-graders who were interviewed in October and November of 1980. The children were from two classrooms in an Athens, Georgia, elementary school. Interviews were conducted to establish the quality of the children's number word sequences, the types of unit items they could count, and patterns they could recognize, re-present, and coordinate with counting. We selected three children in their perceptual periods--Brenda, Shawn, and Tarus. Unfortunately, Shawn left the Athens area in February 1981, and James, another child in his perceptual period, was chosen as Shawn's replacement. Three children in their motor periods--Tyrone, Jason, and Scenetra--were also selected. We taught each participant twice a week for approximately 16 weeks during the school years 1980-1981 and 1981-1982 beginning in December of each year.

Acknowledgments

The research on which this book is based was supported by the National Science Foundation under Grant No. SED 80-16562; the Department of Mathematics Education, the Institute for Behavioral Research, and the Department of Psychology of the University of Georgia. All opinions and findings are those of the authors' and are not necessarily representative of the sponsoring agencies.

Contents

LIST OF FIGURES

Chapter I

On the Construction of the Counting Scheme

Leslie P. Steffe   Ernst von Glasersfeld

Children's Counting

In an earlier publication (Steffe, von Glasersfeld, Richards, & Cobb, 1983), we presented a model of the development of children's counting schemes. This model specifies five distinct counting types, according to the most advanced type of unit items that the child counts at a given point in his or her development. The counting types indicate what children's initial, informal numerical knowledge might be like, and reflect our contention that children *see* numerical situations in a variety of qualitatively different ways. These constructs constituted the initial theoretical basis of the teaching experiment and served as a catalyst for the first year's work. Consequently, we provide an explanation of the counting types as we defined them in 1980.

Counting, as productive activity, involves the vocal production of number words in a conventional sequence and their individual coordination to units of one kind or another. In the earlier work, our observations and analyses centered on the components of this productive activity. First, there is the acquisition of the number word sequence, that is, the ability to say the number words, from "one" to "ten" or "twenty" in the right order, without omissions or repetitions. Children can and do learn to recite this sequence at an early age, rather like reciting a poem, but without any notion of the numerical meanings of the words. This has been well documented by other researchers (cf. Fuson & Richards, 1980; Ginsburg, 1977; Hatano, 1982; Piaget & Szeminska, 1941; Van den Brink, 1981).

Second, there is the isolation of the discrete experiential items to which the individual number words are coordinated. Here, our analyses uncovered a hitherto undocumented but extremely important area of conceptual development. We identified five different types of countable items in the counting behavior of children. These items were used to specify five increasingly sophisticated counting types that are characterized by an increasing independence from perceptual experience.

The third component is the ability to coordinate the utterance of each number word with one discrete experiential item among those that are to be counted. Everyone who has worked with kindergarten children has observed that this kind of coordination requires a certain amount of experience in order to be perfected.

The discrimination of the counting types was made on the basis of intensive observation of children, over periods as long as one school year, in the context of teaching experiments. These experiments were conducted for the purpose of establishing an observational base from which an experimental model of children's counting could be formulated. Such a model was produced (Steffe, Richards, & von Glasersfeld, 1978) in an attempt to organize and make sense of the experience of teaching children.

The next step in the modeling process was theoretical. On the basis of model of the construction of units and numbers (von Glasersfeld, 1981), the experimental model was reformulated into a comprehensive developmental model of counting types (von Glasersfeld, Steffe, & Richards, 1983). In devising the theoretical model, we constantly returned to the videotapes of children solving arithmetical problems for corrective feedback and stimulation. The emphasis was on conceptual analyses and the finding of a fit between them and identified behavioral regularities.

The Counting Types

Perceptual Unit Items

Children's initial ability to make countable items involves locating a collection of items in their perceptual field and taking each item as a unit to be counted. Piaget has provided a powerful model for the developmentally earlier but nevertheless complex process that results in the child's conception of objects, first as recurrent, recognizable aggregations of elements in early sensory-motor experience, and then as externalized, *permanent objects* that are considered to have an existence of their own in space and time independent of the experiencing subject (Piaget, 1937). This initial development has two consequences. On one hand, the child constructs a relatively stable conceptual structure of coordinated sensory-motor signals by empirically abstracting from experience. He or she can eventually "call up" this structure to create a re-presentation, regardless of the presence or absence of actual perceptual signals. On the other hand, the child can use that conceptual structure to recognize (assimilate) actual sensory-motor experiences as instances of the object. We call these instances perceptual items.

Piaget's observations and analyses have meticulously documented how such an object concept develops from an initially fuzzy conglomerate. Another Genevan, de Saussure, had shown before Piaget that the acquisition of language can only begin when concepts are abstracted from sensory-motor experience and "sound-images" are abstracted from the experience of spoken words (de Saussure, 1959, p. 65ff). The experiencing subject isolates groups of sensory-motor signals in the stream of experience and forms the "things" and "words" from which concepts and sound images are abstracted. That process of isolating something from the experiential continuum is an indispensable prerequisite for any conception of number. Frege (1884/1974) and Husserl (1887/1970) independently expressed the idea that cutting discrete items out of the flow of experience is the foundation for the conception of things as unitary wholes and ultimately of countable units; both researchers suggested that this is achieved by a conceptual rather than a perceptual act.

Most 2-year-olds can already do more than isolate recognizable things and label them appropriately. They can use some labels in their plural form--and that indicates a further important conceptual step. In order to use the plural of a thing-word correctly, not only must a repeatable combination of sensory signals be isolated and recorded, but this combination must also be used repeatedly in one and the same situational context. In other words, the appropriate use of a plural requires that a complex of sensory-motor signals has been abstracted and *unitized* as a specific recurrent "thing" in previous experience, and that the use of this prototypic conceptual structure be monitored so that the user can make the crucial difference between using it once and using it more than once. The construction of a plurality is a process of classification based on a conceptual prototype, an object concept that specifies a particular combination of signals and functions as a template that determines what can be recognized as a new experiential instantiation of the concept (cf. von Glasersfeld, 1981). A plurality, however, is as yet unbounded in experience, has no specific numerosity, and *must not* be mistaken for the kind of conceptual structure that might be called a set.

The operational reason for the unboundedness of pluralities lies in the conceptual process that produces them: pluralities are constructed by the repeated use of an object concept. Let us say, for example, that a child recognizes a perceptual situation as an instantiation of the concept it has associated with the word "cup". The child may utter that word and thus close the experiential episode; but the child may also continue by exploring an adjacent part of its visual field, assimilating another combination of sensory signals, and then another. If the child has kept track of the fact that its concept of cup was satisfied, not just once, but more than once, it could utter the plural, "cups". The plural indicates more than one, but not a collection, because its conceptual construction does not involve a definite beginning or end. The plurality of cups would be bounded (and thus become a collection) if and when the child perceives the table on which the cups are arrayed as a uniform background that separates them from the rest of the visual field. At that point, "the cups on the table" constitute a bounded plurality or *collection*. The items in the collection are perceptual units because each is similar to the others in terms of sensory-motor constitution. The collection is bounded by the perceptual ground constituted by the table, and because it is bounded, the collection can be counted.

Children who require actual perceptual items in order to establish units that can be counted are called counters of perceptual unit items. They know how to count but need a collection of marbles, beads, fingers, etc., in order to carry out the activity.

Figural Unit Items

One of the first manifestations of independence from immediate perception occurs when a collection of items is counted, even though it is not within the child's range of immediate perception or action. In this case, the child might attempt to count the items of a screened collection by coordinating the sequential production of number words with the sequential production of visualized images of perceptual items. The child is then said to count figural unit items.

This type of counting is exemplified by Susan's solution to a task in which the last 7 of a row of 12 checkers were hidden by a screen. Susan was asked to find how many were covered.

> Susan counted the five visible checkers in the row "1, 2, 3, 4, 5" and then continued over the screen "6, 7, 8, 9, 10, 11" fixing her gaze on and pointing to successive locations on the cloth in an attempt to find how many were hidden (there were twelve in all). She stopped when reaching the end of the row and said ten were hidden. (Steffe, Cobb, & Richards, 1983, p. 82)

Susan counted until she had "filled up" the region bounded by the cloth, a strong indication that she had counted figural unit items. Here, countable items were created by Susan's imagining the checkers she had seen, which she believed were hidden by the cloth.

Motor Unit Items

Motor acts or movements become countable items when the counter abstracts both the unitary character of the individual motor acts and their coordination with either figural or perceptual unit items. The essential feature of counting motor unit items is that the child uses the motor act as a substitute for either the perceptual item or its figural representative. This substitution provides the child, for the first time, with complete independence from its immediate perceptual world when he or she counts, because motor acts can be produced at will. In this case, unit items are created from the motor components of counting acts (e.g., pointing acts, acts of putting up fingers). This type of counting is exemplified by Tyrone's solution of a task where eight checkers were hidden beneath one cloth and three beneath another.

> The interviewer told Tyrone how many checkers were hidden under each cloth and asked him to find out how many there were in all. Tyrone uttered "1, 2, . . . 8" in synchrony with pointing over the first cloth. He then continued "9, 10, 11" while pointing over the second, the three points forming a linear pattern. A noticeable quality of his pointing activity "9, 10, 11" was that it was rhythmic. (Steffe, et al., 1983, p. 83)

Tyrone did not simply count until he filled up the region bounded by the cloth, as did Susan. Instead he stopped counting when his pointing acts completed a recognizable rhythmic pattern. The manner in which he frequently looked away from the cloth while counting the screened collections also indicates that he was counting motor rather than figural unit items. Children whose most sophisticated level of counting is to create and count motor acts as substitutes for perceptual items or figural re-presentatives are called counters of motor unit items.

Verbal Unit Items

The next step in the development of counting removes the constitution of unit items even further from the child's perceptual world. An act of counting involves the coordination of two productive activities--the production of a unit item and the utterance of a number word. When the utterance itself signifies a concomitant unit item that need not be created, it becomes a substitute for the countable item. In this case, we say that the child counts verbal unit items. In some cases, sequences of verbal items can be implied by a single number word. For example, Lexi

> solved the sentence "7 + 5 = ___" by uttering the number words "8, 9, 10, 11, 12." . . . "[S]even" referred to the . . . sequence of discrete vocal acts "1, 2, . . . 7." . . . [H]er stopping at "twelve" clearly indicates that "five" referred to a pattern. (Steffe, et al., 1983, p. 91)

Importantly, in the absence of screened items, Lexi did not attempt to create countable items by, say, putting up fingers. This indicates that her vocal productions were substitutes for concomitant unit items.

Abstract Unit Items

The transition from being a counter of perceptual unit items to a counter of verbal unit items involves the internalization of sensory-motor activity. The next step in the development of counting by one entirely divorces the creation of unit items from a necessary dependence on sensory-motor material, whether it is perceptual, figural, motor, or verbal in quality. Children who create abstract unit items can take any of the sensory-motor unit items described above as a unit that can be counted. This is indicated by Merrill's counting solution to a missing items task in which eight checkers were visible and four were screened.

> She was told how many were visible, how many there were in all, and was asked to find how many were screened. She counted "9, 10, 11, 12" before saying "Let's see, 12--9 is 1, 10 is 2--four!" Merrill counted her counting acts. She "stepped back" and took each verbal item as a countable unit, which she then counted (Steffe et al., 1983, p. 67).

Before the creation of abstract unit items, the child's counting is still dependent on sensory-motor material, either perceptual or kinesthetic. An important development occurs when the act of uttering the number words from "one" to, say, "eight" implies the presence of accompanying tangible items of some kind (counting verbal unit items). Then comes the realization that an utterance of the number word "eight" can, by itself, be taken to imply the number word sequence "one, two, . . . , eight", as well as a collection of discrete unitary items that could be coordinated with that sequence of utterances. At that point the child can be said to have, for the first time, an abstract conception of number.[1] And finally, comes the momentous realization that any sequence of counting acts can itself be counted.

Our theory distinguishes five types of counting according to the kind of unitary experiential item that the child creates. Three types of sensory-motor units--perceptual items, re-presentations thereof, and motor acts--

---

[1] We would not say that Lexi (cf. **Verbal Unit Items**) necessarily displayed all of the features for an abstract conception of number, although she did count-on.

are followed by concentration on the verbal acts and finally by awareness of the abstracted implications of number words.

Ontogenetic Analysis

We used this model of counting types to choose three children who were counters of perceptual unit items and three who were counters of motor unit items for the teaching experiment. One of our intentions was to study intensively, in carefully choreographed teaching episodes, how these children would progress. Essentially, we wanted to reformulate our theory of counting types by accounting for the children's behavior in a variety of situations and constructing a more encompassing theory--one that would supersede and extend the current theory (Bernstein, 1983; Lakatos, 1970; Toulmin, 1963). The new theory would be the result of an ontogenetic analysis of the construction of the counting scheme by all six children. For example, in the model of counting types we had formulated at the beginning of the experiment, counting perceptual, motor, and abstract unit items were considered to be major periods in the construction of counting, whereas counting figural and verbal unit items were considered to be transitional periods (Steffe, Cobb, & Richards, 1983, p. 83). We would test this conjecture with each group of children in the context of trying to establish stages in constructing the counting scheme.

Stages

The various types of items that become countable for children provides a qualitative classificatory scheme that can serve as the basis for a succession of possible developmental stages. Von Glasersfeld and Kelly (1983) make a cogent distinction between the notions of period and stage. A period designates a stretch of time and may be characterized in several different ways, but the term itself does not imply any particular characterization.

> The term "stage", on the other hand, does imply some form of progression towards an expected end state. . . . A stage is constituted by a stretch of time that is characterized by something that remains constant throughout it. This may be the presence or absence of an item (property, state, activity, or anything that can be isolated) that is considered a change because it is absent or, respectively, present in the preceding or subsequent stretch of time. . . . [T]he difference that is the constitutive characteristic of a stage . . . must have a qualitative component. (pp. 154-155)

The first criterion for stages, then, is that there be an item that remains constant throughout a period. Piaget, who focused on stages of development rather than on stages of decay, always required that an earlier stage become incorporated in the next stage. This condition is fulfilled in the case of counting, because throughout their progress to abstraction, children never lose the capacity to create and count, say, perceptual unit items. Consequently, when we speak of stages in counting theory, we adhere to this criterion of incorporation; this is the second criterion.

A third well-accepted criterion for stages is that they must form one invariant sequence. Thus, what we call stages must emerge developmentally in a constant order. It is not difficult to imagine situations where certain children might skip a particular stage in counting. The cerebral palsied child, for example, may never count motor items. While we do not investigate these special cases, we do study regularities in the emergence of the counting types in particular children.

Finally, as a fourth criterion, we accept a modified form of the feature pointed out by Flavell (1963):

> A . . . most crucial criterion is that the structural properties which define a given stage must form an integrated whole. (p. 20)

This criterion is addressed to developments that are much more general than those involving the counting scheme. The structural properties mentioned by Flavell refer to, e.g., the properties of the grouping structure, which are, supposedly, identifiable in children's reasoning in such disparate areas as classes, relations, correspondences, and spatial content. Even if all other criteria for stages are met, we would not claim that we could use the model of counting types to interpret every conceivable unit type a child might construct (e.g., units of length, area, time, etc.). Nevertheless, we do not fully abandon the structural criterion. Before we would claim that a change in counting type constitutes a stage shift, it would be necessary to justify the presence of a new organization of the counting scheme resulting from reflection and abstraction (Campbell & Bickhard, 1986, pp. 83-97).

Adaptation

Even though the current developmental model of children's counting types had an experiential basis, it had never been used to explain how a particular child might progressively modify his or her counting scheme. In such an explanation, each counting type can be considered as an adaptation--as "an equilibrium between assimilation and accommodation" (Piaget, 1950, p. 8). Generally, an accommodation in a counting scheme is any change that results either in the creation of a new or more elaborate scheme or in splitting the scheme into subschemes (cf. von Glasersfeld, 1982b, p. 82). Assimilation is the process of incorporating new experiences into the scheme where, from the perspective of the observer, certain differences might be disregarded (Piaget, 1950, p. 8). For example, certain "tasks" which are distinguishable, from the perspective of an observer, may be indistinguishable, from the perspective of a child in a particular developmental period of counting (Steffe, Thompson, & Richards, 1982).

Our interest in children's adaptation of their counting schemes is consistent with what Di Sibio (1982) pointed out as major concerns of educators:

> Still unknown are the precise conditions under which new information does or does not get assimilated to existing schemata. Even more speculative are the conditions under which existing knowledge structures change or "accommodate" to new information. (p. 172)

While Di Sibio seems to posit "information" as a given, her emphasis on assimilation and accommodation penetrated to the very core of our attempt to map the construction of the counting scheme.

Counting as a Scheme

As an activity, counting fits Piaget's (1980) characterization of scheme:

> All action that is repeatable or generalized through application to new objects engenders . . . a "scheme". (p. 24)

The view of counting as activity provides no insight into why children count--what are the intentions and goals that drive counting? Toward such an end, von Glasersfeld (1980) showed that Piaget's notion of scheme consists of three parts: first is the child's recognition of an experiential situation as one that has been experienced before; second is the specific activity the child has come to associate with the situation; and third is a result that the child has come to expect of the activity in the given situation.

The emphasis on experiential situations of a scheme does not mean that those situations are uninterpreted by the child. The seminal explication of the constructivist view of experiential situations was provided by Piaget (1964):

> A stimulus is really a stimulus only when it is assimilated into a structure and it is this structure which sets off the response. Consequently, it is not an exaggeration to say that the response is there first, or if you wish, at the beginning there is structure. (p. 15)

In the model of counting types, the focus is on the unit items a child creates while actually counting. They belong to the second part of the counting scheme and can differ in type from the elements of the interpreted experiential situation. In other words, the child can intend to count unit items of one type but actually counts unit items of another.

The First Part of the Counting Scheme

The distinction between what the child intends to count and what the child actually counts is exemplified by a child named Shawn counting the marbles in two cups. An interviewer placed the cups (one containing seven marbles and the other containing four marbles) in front of Shawn, who was sitting on a carpet, and asked him to find how many marbles were in both cups. In an attempt to count the marbles in the cup containing seven, Shawn first said, "1-2-3--4-5", while synchronously tapping on the carpet. The taps completed a row of three and a separate row of two. Realizing he had not reached "seven", he then pointed to each of the marbles in the cup, gesturing in the air over the cup in synchrony with the subvocal utterances "1-2-3-4-5-6-7".

Shawn's second count indicates that he had intended to count the marbles in the cup when he tapped on the carpet, "1-2-3--4-5". He was obviously aware of the marbles even though he could not see them. This awareness of plurality--of more than one--can be thought of as an awareness of the possibility of "running through" the collection, isolating each of its elements. The proposition that a collection is the product of an active knower was articulated by Judd in 1927:

> One recognizes a group of objects as composed of many individual items only when one points to each one or otherwise analyzes the group by reacting in succession to each member of the group. Until a person has reacted to each member of a group . . . the group will appear in his consciousness as a vague and ill-defined mass of experience. (p. 50)

We specify Judd's awareness of a "vague and ill-defined mass of experience" by adding an awareness of plurality, which requires the production of a visualized image of an item along with its repeatability, and can leave a child in a state of disequilibrium if he or she wants to specify the indefinite awareness of "more than one". A protonumerosity is formed by repeating such an item in an experiential situation if the child coordinates a number word sequence with the repetitions. This does not yet yield a numerosity in the abstract sense.

Steffe, Firth, and Cobb (l981) have experimentally confirmed the assumption that the act of recognizing perceptual things as possible items of a collection is preliminary to the act of taking them as units in counting. The second act is an operation of abstraction, in that it reviews perceptual items that have already been constituted and abstracts from them a "template"--a concept of unitariness--whose instantiation requires *some* sensory signals, but not specific ones (much like the word "thing", which conveys thinghood but no particular characteristics). The act of abstraction that yields the individual items of a plurality accounts for a child taking heterogeneous items as belonging to a collection of countable perceptual unit items, because what constitutes "common sensory content" (i.e., unitariness) is entirely of the child's own making. The "things" that are to be counted are considered only insofar as they are discrete units. When children use the concept in repeated re-presentation rather than in recognition, the child creates what we call a figural plurality or, if bounded, a figural collection.

Figural pluralities or collections that can be counted should not be confused with the conceptual structure that we call number, which requires a further mental operation. That operation, which has a composite unit as its result, was described by Joannes Caramuel in 1670:

> The intellect . . . does not find numbers but makes them; it considers different things, each distinct in itself; and intentionally unites them in thought (p. 44). (Translation by E. von Glasersfeld)

Whole numbers as composite units are considered to be the results of uniting operations. Numbers, as composite units, are therefore made by an active intellect in specific contexts to serve some purpose. We call this uniting operation integration:

> Integration is the . . . act of uniting what one may also consider distinct unitary items. (Steffe, Cobb, & Richards, 1983, p. 67)

Integrations that are carried out without words or speech are called tacit; nevertheless, they are based on material of some kind--material that could be perceptual or figural pluralities which may or may not have been specified.

In the teaching experiment, one of our main hypotheses was that the operation of integration would emerge before children could create abstract unit items. The rationale for the hypothesis was simple. The operation of taking a sensory motor unit as a unit that itself can be counted is identical to the integration operation; the only difference is the material to which the operation is applied. When the integration operation is applied to a sensory-motor item, we call it a unitizing operation.

The ontogenetic analysis of the counting schemes of the six children will include an analysis of the first part of the schemes as well as the second part. In fact, our hypothesis is that developmental changes in the first part, i.e., changes in what children intend to count, will make developmental changes in the second part possible. We will also provide an analysis of the third part of the counting scheme--the experienced results of counting. Here, we differentiate between a numerosity and a specified collection.

The Third Part of the Counting Scheme

In the preceding pages, we have outlined constructs we believe can be used to explain the conceptual structures children use to assimilate situations that lead to counting activity. The analysis, however, left an important aspect of number unaccounted for: the numerosity of a composite unit. If a child takes the results of actual counting acts as a unit, where the counted items serve as content of the integration, the resulting composite unit has a numerosity. Uniting a collection of sensory counted items into a whole "lifts" its structure to a higher mental plane. It is a process of reflective abstraction (Piaget, 1980, p. 27). The result is a numerical structure (composite unit) consisting of individual abstract unit items (Steffe, 1983).

As a matter of theoretical choice, we would not say that a collection has numerosity even after a child counts its elements. Numerosity is a property of composite units. If a child expresses a composite unit by counting sensory-motor unit items, we would say the resulting counted collection has numerosity for the child, but that is only because the child externalized the composite unit by performing sensory-motor activity in an experiential situation. In the case of a collection as a sensory-motor structure, children are aware of more than one of its elements, and this indefinite awareness can be made definite by counting. We call the collection of counted items a specified collection that has a protonumerosity to emphasize that the indefinite awareness of more than one element has been made definite by counting.

The distinction between a numerosity and a protonumerosity is based upon the reflective abstractions of which the child is capable. Children who are still limited to creating collections could not take the results of counting the collection as a unit--and could not lift its structure to a higher mental plane. They would not be able to go from the composite unit to the collection, projecting numerosity into it. They would not be "above" the collection, "looking down" on it, contemplating counting it to find out how many elements it contained. They would be aware of more than one sensory-motor item, and they could count the collection to form its protonumerosity. But the counting activity would only be introduced into the collection temporarily, and they would not be aware of the protonumerosity beyond the immediate present.

Other Sources of Numerosity

There are other experiential roots of numerosity that do not involve counting. In the following sections, we shall survey several phenomena that involve elementary experience and could be said to lead to protonumerical concepts.

Perceptual Mechanisms

Experiments by Starkey and Cooper (1980) suggest that infants around the age of 6 months are able to discriminate between two and three dots. Although these results are extremely interesting for the study of perceptual mechanisms, it should be clear that such discriminatory ability has nothing to do with number words, counting, or any kind of numerical system. At least half a dozen authoritative studies show that monkeys and apes do as well, if not better, in discriminating small arrays of perceptual items (Dooley & Gill, 1977; Ferster, 1964; Hayes & Nissen, 1971; Thomas, Fowlkes, & Vickery, 1980). It is important to note, however, that the arrays, used with the infants, were linear. "Twos" and "threes" could, therefore, *not* be discriminated on the basis of spatial patterns such as triangles. Discriminations of that kind can be accounted for by differentially tuned neurons: some that fire when they receive two successive impulses, others that fire only when they receive three. Assumptions concerning simple mechanisms like this are commonplace in neurophysiology; a wide variety of phenomena, from the "detection" of edges in the visual field to certain perceptions of motion, are usually explained in those terms. In addition, there is the well-known human (and animal) capability of recognizing and accurately recalling rhythms of one, two, and three beats in the auditory and tactual fields. This capability is habitually relied on in music, dance, and poetry, and as Bamberger (l975, 1978) has demonstrated, even young children have no difficulty transposing such rhythms into the visual mode.

If the nervous system has the built-in capability to distinguish between sequences of one, two, or three signals in various sensory modes, this ability cannot be taken as evidence of the presence of numerical concepts, even if the children have come to associate number words with the respective sequences of signals. The reason for this is simply that, given such built-in computational mechanisms, discriminating and naming the relevant events does not require the knowledge, for instance, that the event called three is a unity comprising a plurality of units. In this respect, the recognition of rhythmic configurations is analogous to the phenomenon of *subitizing*, which concerns the recognition of spatial patterns that have been associated with number words.

Spatial Patterns

There is a fundamental distinction to be made between the recognition and the re-presentation of a spatial pattern (von Glasersfeld, 1982b). The recognition of a spatial pattern refers to its actualization in perception--to its assimilation using a particular pattern scheme. A pattern may be recognized without being named. A clarifying example is provided by Fischer (1981) for a child 5 years, 4 months old. After he practiced making a square from rods in class where his teacher emphasized that there were four rods, he recognized a square pattern of four dots as "four", but then "counted" to be sure, "1-2-3-2", and said there were two! He then "re-counted", "1-3-9-10", and said there were 10 and 9! The child clearly recognized the spatial configuration as "four", but had not arrived at that result by counting--he might as well have said "square" as "four". In fact, Fisher reports that one child, 3 years, 9 months old, did recognize a square four as "a square"--and then "counted" "7-8-12-13", to find how many. So, recognition of a spatial configuration is *not* contingent on a particular semantic connection. From the observer's perspective, an utterance such as "square" (or "four") indicates recognition, but the converse does not hold.

Re-presentation of a spatial pattern refers to its actualization in the absence of specific sensory material. Using a pattern scheme, a child may re-present a spatial pattern and then count its elements. Counting can then lead to the construction of spatio-motor patterns. These patterns are characterized, from the observer's perspective, by motor activity that completes an identifiable constellation. The incentive to count re-presented spatial patterns is the desire to specify the bounded plurality consisting of the visualized elements of the pattern. Thus, spatio-motor patterns are the result of a coordination of the counting scheme and the figurative pattern schemes.

The association of spatial patterns with number words can occur in many ways. Dominoes, playing cards, and other games involve the recognition of conventional configurations of dots or other unitary elements, and in many instances these configurations have names that are number words. The work of Fischer (l981) and of Gelman and Gallistel (l978) indicates that children count perceptual patterns at a very young age to form the semantic links between patterns and number words. Through counting, they resolve the pattern into its perceptual elements and connect it with a number word. For example, Fischer (1981) reported that 70 % of the children he tested, aged 3 years, 9 months, counted to find how many dots were in a triangular arrangement of three.

In a linear two pattern, children from 3 years, 3 months, to 6 years, 6 months, rarely counted. Instead, they recognized the linear two pattern as "two". That so many of the children aged 3 years, 9 months *did* spontaneously count the triangular three does not necessarily indicate that they did not recognize it. The strongest interpretation that can be made is that they had not yet connected the number word "three" with the configuration, and that counting was their primary means for doing so.

It does not matter under what circumstances the connection between the experience of a pattern called three and the experience of counting the three components of the pattern is made. Once made, this connection will provide the first and most immediate opportunity for the revelation that the number word refers both to a unitary thing (the constellation) and to a collection of units (the elements of the constellation).

Meaning Theory

The preceding conceptual constructs are, in our opinion, crucial in any consideration of children's early numerical meanings. The few vestiges of meaning theory in current approaches to mathematics teaching hark back to two historically important schools of thought. One principal contributor to the structural school believed that "meaning is to be sought in the structure, the organization, the relationships of the subject itself" (Brownell, 1945, p. 81). The origins of the second school, the operational school, can be traced to Percy Bridgman's operational analysis of the fundamental concepts of modern physics (Bridgman, 1927). Van Engen (1949), a principal contributor to the operational school, believed that the meaning of a mathematical symbol such as "4" is "an intention to act and . . . the act need not, in itself, take place. However, if the individual is challenged to demonstrate the meaning of the symbol, then the action takes place" (p. 324). Van Engen viewed semantics as the interpretation of operational definitions. These operational definitions were taken to be universal and, therefore, identical for all children. Especially in mathematics, the main concepts seemed transparent and were expected to become "self-evident", provided they were properly explained.

Contemporary epistemology which has, since Piaget's revolutionary publications on the "Origins of Intelligence" (1936), "The Construction of Reality" (1937), and the "Formation of Symbols" (1945), tended more and more towards a constructivist view, has made us aware of the highly complex processes of abstraction that underlie "understanding" in general and mathematical understanding in particular. While a great many everyday concepts can be abstracted directly from sensory experience, this is not the case with mathematical concepts. If we believe, as did Van Engen, that the meaning of a mathematical symbol is essentially an action, it follows that mathematical concepts will be created by means of abstraction that reflects upon actions rather than upon sensory impressions. Thus, constructivism should not be confused with empiricism.

This insight, when combined with the realization that schemes can function at different levels of abstraction, makes it plausible to think of mathematical objects in terms of schemes--the experience of the object is the conceptual result of applying the scheme. It also provides a psychological interpretation for the astute statement made by Thom (1973) that "the real problem which confronts mathematics teaching is. . . . [T]he problem of the development of 'meaning,' of the 'existence' of mathematical objects" (p. 202). We agree, and interpret the "existence" of mathematical objects as psychological existence--existence as concepts in the context of schemes.

The predominant view of early meaning theorists that meaning was to be found in structural relationships and in operational definitions that were "transparent" to the adult led to classic works that emphasized standard algorithmic procedures dictated by adult conventions (Brownell, 1945; Van Engen & Gibb, 1956). Making relationships that the adult can understand transparent to children is prevalent in contemporary information processing psychology (e.g., Greeno, 1983; Resnick, 1983b; Rumelhart & Norman, 1981). In contrast, we study what children might be aware of and then try to infer their meaning of arithmetical words, numerals, and procedures. Such a meaning theory *must*, in our view, include a theory of reflection and abstraction.

Reflection and Abstraction

Adaptations of the counting scheme inevitably involve abstraction, reflection, and their conceptual products because, from the constructivist perspective, all new knowledge presupposes an abstraction (Piaget, 1980, p. 89). Re-presentation, which is inextricably involved in reflection and abstraction, is like a playback, in that one re-creates an experience of acting; one is in it and, in a very real sense, one acts again. But to re-present to oneself an activity that one has carried out is quite different from reflecting upon the results of a re-presentation and considering how that is composed. Reflecting upon the results of a re-presentation requires detachment and placing the re-presented activity at a distance in order to analyze its structure and composition.

The difficult issue of the child's awareness of his or her own perceptual or conceptual activity is woven into what Piaget generically refers to as reflective abstraction. Reflective abstraction clearly requires that the subject has something to reflect upon, that he or she takes something as a given. In general, there is nothing that could not be taken as "given" in some situation or on some level of construction. What is considered given or exogenous material for a particular activity or set of activities is itself the result of previous constructive activity. It also depends on how the subject cuts or isolates the situation, qua situation to act, from his or her stream of experience, i.e., it depends on the subject's approach or intentions. This approach is also what could be said to differentiate reflecting, reflected, and pseudo-empirical abstraction, the three kinds of reflective abstraction in Piaget's system.

In the first type, reflecting abstraction, the elements ("objects") are considered "given" (regardless of how they were constructed earlier), and what is abstracted has to do with the subject's activity of coordinating these elements in some particular way. For example, the realization that counting a collection of pebbles yields the same terminal number word, irrespective of the pebbles' arrangement in a line, a circle, or heap, is a reflecting abstraction because it is drawn from the subject's counting activity and not from the pebbles qua objects.

If the result of the reflecting abstraction is then decontextualized from pebbles or other counted objects and is turned into the higher-level abstract notion that, provided nothing is added or taken away, any collection of units will yield the same count regardless of when or how the collection is counted, Piaget refers to reflective thought, or a reflection on reflection (reflected abstraction).

By contrast, pseudo-empirical abstraction refers to any abstraction concerning an activity that the subject has isolated in previous experiential situations but whose results cannot yet be obtained without actually carrying out the activity. As an example, Piaget cites the use of beads or an abacus for beginning numerical operations (Piaget & Collaborators, 1977). The child has already abstracted a sequence of acts and therefore "knows" what he or she has to do (for example, to subtract 7 from 13), but still needs beads, pebbles, fingers, etc. in order to do it. School mathematics as it is usually taught encourages pseudo-empirical abstraction--the construction of procedures for solving narrow sets of tasks--rather than the more conceptual activity that is the product of reflecting and reflected abstraction.

Pseudo-empirical abstraction is a variation of reflective abstraction because the abstracted properties are actually introduced *into* the objects by the subject's activities. In Piaget's system, then, reflective abstraction includes pseudo-empirical abstraction, reflecting abstraction, and reflected abstraction. The results of these levels of reflective abstraction can be characterized as follows:

1. Isolates an activity as relevant in the solution of certain problems that have been encountered.

2. The ability to substitute a re-presentation of the relevant acts for their actual physical (sensory-motor) execution, provided some material is taken as given to act on and to call up the requisite acts.

3. The ability to run through the activity and produce its results in thought, i.e., without motor action and without given sensory material to act on.

The third level is a reformulation of what Piaget has already called anticipation, which "is nothing other than a transfer or application of the schema (i.e., scheme) . . . to a new situation before it actually happens" (1971, p. 195). The child anticipates the conceptual result of using a scheme. At the first level, the child can anticipate that an activity will be appropriate but has no idea why, and therefore has to carry out the activity. At the second level, the child can anticipate carrying out an activity.

All three types of reflective abstraction involve two aspects: raising abstracted elements to a new level or plane of operating, and reorganizing them on that level.

> Reflective abstraction . . . is "reflective" in two complementary senses which we shall designate as follows. In the first place it transposes onto a higher plane something it has picked up on the preceding level (. . . "reflexion"). In the second place, reflective abstraction must necessarily reconstruct on the new level B whatever it picked up on the level A from which it started; that is, it must relate the elements extracted from A with elements that are already present on level B (. . . "reflection"). Reflective abstraction, with its two components of reflexion and reflection, can be observed at all stages. . . . However, on the higher levels, once reflection is the work of thought, one still has to distinguish between its process as construction and its retroactive thematization, which then becomes a reflection on reflection, and we shall then speak of "reflective thought". (Piaget et al., 1977, p. 6; translation by E. von Glasersfeld)

The three levels of reflective abstraction have considerable explanatory power and certainly seem to fit the development of the counting scheme. As with all general theoretical constructs, it is difficult to apply them to specific situations, when the cognizing subject is not ourself but a "subject" we are observing. In practice there may be observable behavioral indications, on the basis of which levels of abstraction can be determined, but making that determination is not simple. One might say that assuming something as "given" or not is exclusively the subject's business. Hence, at best an observer can make educated guesses, taking into account--as does any experienced diagnostician--several indications collected over an extended period of observation.

Reflective abstraction, in its multifarious forms, is the mechanism of constructing mathematical knowledge. At the outset of the teaching experiment, we had two firm hypotheses concerning which level of reflective abstraction would serve as a basis for constructing each counting type. A level 3 abstraction would be necessary to account for the construction of abstract unit items, and a level 1 abstraction for the construction of perceptual unit items. Beyond these two hypotheses, it was not clear which levels would serve in the construction of the other three types of countable items. Although a level 3 abstraction did not seem to be plausible, whether levels 1 or 2 would be required was not known. One of our major goals was to document and analyze the reflective abstractions we could observe as the children participated in our teaching sessions.

Chapter II

The Construction of Motor Unit Items

Brenda, Tarus, and James

Leslie P. Steffe   Paul Cobb

In this chapter, we present the results of the teaching experiment as they pertain to the construction of motor unit items by the three children who began the teaching experiment as counters of perceptual unit items. We start with the hypothesis that adaptations of the counting scheme involve changes in the assimilatory structures of the scheme which, in turn, make possible changes in the types of countable items. We also anticipated that some of these items might never appear in the development of particular children.

The changes in the assimilatory structures of the counting scheme that might serve as a basis for the transition from counting perceptual unit items to counting motor unit items were suggested in our previous work (Steffe, Cobb, & Richards, 1983, p. 50). It was found that two children who were counters of perceptual unit items freed themselves from a dependence on perceptual items by first counting the items of a visible spatial configuration and then reenacting the same configuration as they counted over a screened collection. In other words, in the absence of perceptual items, they counted re-presented items by reproducing the preceding activity of counting a visible configuration. This observation fits with our understanding of spatial patterns as one possible experiential root of numerosity.

In general, if a child reenacts the activity of counting a spatial configuration, the motor acts involved co-occur with the isolation of elements in a visualized pattern. As motor acts are the only actual sensory items available, the child might become aware of them as unitary items long before the general capacity to use motor acts as substitutes for perceptual items or their figural re-presentatives is developed. Spatio-motor patterns of this sort might, therefore, serve the child in the transition from being a counter of perceptual unit items to being a counter of motor unit items. A number word such as "four" could, for example, lead to the enactment of a specific spatio-motor pattern if the child substitutes a visualized spatial pattern for a perceptual collection.

The spatial configurations of discrete items that are seen on dice or dominoes are only part of the experiential material that can be arranged as dyads, triads, etc. The ability to recognize sequential or rhythmic patterns in one's own activity is important when keeping track of counting activity. The distinction between recognition and re-presentation of patterns holds for sequential as well as for spatial patterns. A child might enact a sequential or rhythmic pattern by coordinating number words with the "beats" of the patterns. For example, "three" could be connected with "8-9-10". Consequently, rhythmic or sequential patterns could also play a role in freeing the child from a dependence on perceptual material.

There is one other type of pattern that is usually overlooked in discussions of the patterns children normally connect with number words: finger patterns, which are neither purely spatial nor purely motor in quality. They differ from spatio-motor patterns, in that the elements of spatio-motor patterns are produced in temporal sequence. Children usually put up fingers simultaneously to form finger patterns. In this sense, the finger patterns are motor programs whose result can appear in the visual (or tactual) field of the child. Furthermore, re-presentations of finger patterns involve spatial as well as motor features.

We studied the role these different types of patterns played in the construction of motor counting schemes by Brenda, Tarus, and James. We were particularly curious about the level of reflective abstraction that made the children's progress possible. If the children simply isolated the motor acts involved in counting the elements of a pattern, this would be the result of a level 1 abstraction. On the other hand, if the pattern was re-presented in the absence of perceptual material and prior to the children counting its elements, this would be the result of a level 2 abstraction. We were also interested in any apparent reorganizations of the children's counting scheme that occurred when they constructed the motor unit item. In fact, depending on the level of reflective abstractions involved, construction of the various types of countable items may constitute developmental stages.

In the following case material, we identify perceptual and motor periods for each child. Within each period, we record certain adaptations the children made in their counting schemes as well as the limitations of those schemes, in particular, the role of patterns in the emergence of motor acts as countable unit items. Second, we document reorganizations of the counting scheme, regardless of when they may have occurred. The limitations of these reorganizations are also documented to provide perspective on their nature. Third, we investigate the hypothesis that level 2 reflective abstraction served as a basis for the construction of motor unit items. We especially examined the role of re-presentation in the context of our study of reflective abstraction.

1. BRENDA

The first two periods that we observed for Brenda were a perceptual period (at least 7 months) and a motor period (9 months). She was classified as a counter of perceptual unit items on the basis of her performance in an interview conducted on 21 October 1980. In the teaching episode conducted on 19 March 1981, Brenda sequentially put up fingers to complete finger patterns to solve a task involving screened items. This was the precursor of her motor period, which she achieved by 5 May 1981.

The Perceptual Period

21 October 1980 Interview

Counting Perceptual Unit Items

1.01. We selected Brenda as a participant in the experiment because she could count collections of perceptual items but was stymied if some of the items were perceptually inaccessible. She could not choose her own ways of counting and required the actual presence of perceptual items in her visual field in order to count.

1.02. Brenda's inability to count unless items were in her visual field is documented in a task where four of a collection of seven squares were covered by a cloth. She was told that four squares were covered, and was asked to find out how many there were in all. After she attempted to raise the cloth but was thwarted by the interviewer, she counted the three visible squares. Her solution is presented in protocol form.

B : 1-2-3 (touches each visible square in turn).
I : There's four here (taps the cloth).
B : (Lifts the cloth, revealing two squares) 4-5. (She touches each of these squares and puts the cloth back.)
I : OK, I'll show you two of them (folds back the cloth to reveal two of the four covered squares). There's four here, you count them.
B : 1-2- . . . -5 (touches each visible square in turn).
I : There's two more here (taps the cloth).
B : (Attempts to lift the cloth.)
I : (Pulls back the cloth.)
B : 6-7 (touches the last two squares).

1.03. Brenda's attempt to lift the cloth indicates that she was aware of the hidden squares and intended to count the collection of squares. But this awareness of a figural plurality did not lead to counting because she was yet to coordinate the utterance of a number word sequence with the sequential production of figural items. She could take perceptual items as being countable, but not figural items.

Perceptual Replacements

1.04. Brenda could create and count two different kinds of perceptual items in a single counting episode. The interviewer covered six of nine marbles with his hand and asked Brenda to count all the marbles. She first counted the interviewer's five fingers and then counted the three visible marbles. The interviewer pointed out that he had six marbles beneath his hand and Brenda replied, "I don't see no six!" The accommodation of her counting scheme was contextual in that she created a collection of perceptual replacements, the interviewer's fingers, by visually scanning items in her perceptual field. Brenda's creation of a collection of perceptual replacements was a result of her search for perceptual items to count. That she took the interviewer's fingers as perceptual replacements was fortuitous; they just happened to be "there".

10 February 1981 Teaching Episode

Finger Patterns

1.05. The first major advance Brenda made during her perceptual period was to use finger patterns as replacements for perceptually inaccessible collections. This was the first step she took away from the constraints of immediate visual perception when she created countable items.

T : Now, there are five there (covers five marbles with one hand) and three there (covers three marbles with his other hand). How many altogether? Count on your fingers. Start from five and count on your fingers.

B : (Simultaneously puts up five fingers of her left hand and then simultaneously puts up three fingers of her right hand; points to each extended finger in turn with a finger of the other hand) Eight.

The teacher did not tell Brenda how to use finger patterns. She introduced them, and they quickly became a prominent feature of her counting behavior. Her flexibility had increased in that she could, in certain situations, create collections of perceptual items to count when none were immediately available.

Failure to Make Separations in Counting

1.06. Brenda's current use of finger patterns appeared to be the result of a level 1 reflective abstraction from previous occasions of counting on her fingers. Because she did not seem to re-present the finger patterns, it was not the case of a higher-level abstraction. The hypothesis that they were perceptual collections is confirmed by her failure to make appropriate separations between the fingers of two finger patterns, one for "six" and one for "three". When asked to find how many marbles were hidden beneath two cloths, one hiding six and one hiding three, she simultaneously put up five fingers of her right hand and one of her left hand. She then put up two more fingers of her left hand, forming a finger pattern for "three". Finally, she counted her eight extended fingers. Brenda failed to make a separation between the fingers she first put up when creating a collection of six items and those she subsequently put up. Her two hands formed the basis for her visual separation. The solution is typical of those in which she created two collections, one of which comprised more than five items. Further, Brenda gave no indication that her answer "eight" referred to the marbles. She seemed to be unaware of the items she had replaced by creating finger patterns. This suggests that, once she had established a finger pattern, the fingers she counted served no substitutive function. In other words, the finger patterns did not seem to refer to the hidden collections.

19 March 1981 Teaching Episode

Sequentially Putting up Fingers to Complete Finger Patterns

1.07. The second major advance Brenda made in the perceptual period was to sequentially put up fingers in synchrony with the utterance of number words. She spontaneously solved the first task of the teaching episode, where collections of three and four squares were hidden, by sequentially putting up three fingers on one hand and then four on the other, while synchronously uttering, "1-2-3--4-5-6-7".

1.08. We infer that Brenda counted her fingers rather than the acts of putting up fingers based on the analysis of the following solution:

T : (Makes the sentence 12 + 3 = ___ using felt numerals.)
B : 1-2- . . . -10 (sequentially puts up all ten fingers) 11-12 (sequentially touches two of her extended fingers) 13 (touches another extended finger).

When she reached "ten", Brenda spontaneously counted her already extended fingers; she did not close her fingers and then put them up for a second time. This indicates that she was counting fingers rather than motor acts of putting up fingers--the scheme was perceptual rather than motor in quality. Brenda actually counted what she intended to count: her fingers.

The Motor Period

5 May 1981 Teaching Episode

Counting Motor Unit Items

1.09. In this teaching episode, Brenda's spontaneous solution of the following task indicates that she counted the motor acts of putting up fingers for the first time. The teacher presented a problem: "You have 13 dolls and I have 4 dolls. How many dolls do we both have?" Brenda asked if she could count and then sequentially put up all ten fingers, closed one hand, and sequentially put up three fingers for a second time while synchronously uttering "1-2- . . . -13". She now seemed to focus on the activity of counting rather than on her global perception of the items she had counted (i.e., a finger pattern). This second accommodation gave Brenda greater generative power since she was now no longer stymied when she ran out of fingers. In particular, Brenda re-counted three fingers when she established the collection of 13. As this collection could not be bounded by scanning visually, we infer that it was bounded by the beginning and the end of the activity she performed while creating it. This is important, because it indicates she transcended visual perception. At this point, the teacher intervened and told Brenda to close her fingers before continuing, because he was aware of her reliance on finger patterns. Brenda did so and sequentially put up four fingers while synchronously uttering "14-15-16-17" to complete her solution.

1.10. The crucial feature of the solution documented in 1.09 is Brenda's spontaneous count to "thirteen". Having reached "ten", she closed her fingers and then put up three for a second time while counting "11-12-13". As she was not directed to reuse her fingers in this way, we infer that Brenda counted the motor acts of putting up fingers. The vital accommodation Brenda made was to constitute the motor component of a counting act, putting up a finger, as a countable unit item. She intended to count her fingers, but actually counted the act of putting up a finger. The major adaptations that Brenda made in her counting scheme over a 7 month period--her transition from counting perceptual unit items to counting motor unit items--have been documented. It has been noted that her scheme became increasingly flexible. However, there were definite limits to this flexibility.

14 May 1981 Teaching Episode

Lack of Reflection

1.11. Brenda was unable to complete the use of finger patterns to solve a task where eight items were screened by one cloth and ten were under both cloths. Brenda first established a finger pattern for "eight" by simultaneously putting up five fingers on one hand and three on the other. She then put up two fingers while synchronously uttering "9-10" to establish a single collection of fingers, but she did not realize that there were two items covered. To do so, it would be necessary for her to review her activity of establishing the finger pattern for ten and to re-establish the separation between the initial collection of eight fingers and those she subsequently put up. This she was unable to do even though the teacher provided several cues.

21 May 1981 Teaching Episode

Lack of a General Coordination of Patterns and Counting

1.12. Finger patterns were the only patterns that Brenda coordinated with her counting scheme. She had not developed spatio-motor patterns in spite of various interventions made by the teacher. In addition, she did not provide any indication that she could recognize patterns in her sequential motor activity and had great difficulty in recognizing any sequential or temporal pattern.

1.13. Finger patterns were still specific for Brenda. "Five", for example, referred to an open hand. It could not refer to, say, three fingers on one hand and two on the other. Moreover, she continued to rely on the visual separation of her hands when she put up fingers while counting. For example, she was asked to solve a task in which eight items were hidden beneath one cloth and five were hidden by a second cloth.

T : Eight here (points to the first cloth). Can you count eight first?
B : 1-2- . . . -8 (sequentially puts up eight fingers).
T : Eight. OK, can you now count five more?
B : 9-10 (sequentially puts up her remaining fingers and then closes her right hand) -11-12- . . . -15 (sequentially puts up five fingers).

"Five" referred to the open hand, not to two fingers on one hand and three on another.

7 November 1981 Interview

<u>**Sophisticated Finger Patterns**</u>

1.14. Until the end of May 1981, Brenda had used finger patterns for the number words for "one" through "ten". In the intervening six months, she had developed patterns for "eleven" through "fifteen".

I : (Covers 11 marbles with a cloth and then places 3 marbles on the cloth) Now there's three more.
B : Eleven (simultaneously puts up five fingers on her left hand and one on her right hand to indicate "eleven"). 1-2-3 (sequentially puts up three of her remaining fingers) fourteen.

1.15. The patterns for "eleven" through "fifteen" seemed to involve Brenda's taking an open hand as a referent for "ten". The interviewer tested this conjecture by asking Brenda to close her eyes and solve a task involving eight items under one cloth and five under another.

B : 1-2- . . . -8 (sequentially puts up five fingers on her left hand and three on her right). 1-2 (sequentially puts up her remaining two fingers) 3-4-5 (sequentially wiggles three fingers of her left hand) thirteen.

Here, Brenda recognized a pattern for "thirteen" when her eyes were shut, which indicates that she visualized the results of her counting activity. While we can never be certain that she re-presented two open hands and three more fingers, it was necessary that she at least make a record of having used the open hand that she reused.

Discussion of Brenda's Case Study

The Perceptual Period

There were two major accommodations that Brenda made in her counting scheme while she was in her perceptual period. In the 10 February 1981 teaching episode, Brenda replaced perceptual finger patterns for hidden collections and counted the fingers of her finger patterns, a modification of the first part of her counting scheme. This accommodation was essential in the re-presentation of her finger patterns we observed in the 19 March 1981 teaching episode where she sequentially put up fingers to complete finger patterns.

Spatio-motor and temporal patterns played absolutely no role in the adaptations that Brenda made in her counting scheme. She compensated for this by constructing her perceptual finger patterns which she used as perceptual replacements. Brenda's first use of replacements did not involve a reorganization of her counting scheme but instead concerned the creation of perceptual items she could count. For example, she replaced the fingers of an open hand for five hidden marbles, a pattern of three fingers for three hidden marbles, and then counted her eight extended fingers. In these situations, counting seemed to be carried out to specify the collection comprised by her two finger patterns. Her use of finger patterns was on par with the perceptual replacements she had made earlier on 21 October 1980. A limitation of her finger patterns as perceptual collections is seen in her failure to make a separation between establishing a finger pattern for "six" and one for "three".

It was not until the 19 March 1981 teaching episode (cf. 1.07) that Brenda's counting scheme changed from a perceptual scheme to a figurative scheme. Prior to this time, she always established perceptual collections before starting to count, and then counted the elements of those collections. As we have already pointed out, she could replace a finger pattern for a hidden collection of perceptual items on the basis of a semantic connection between a finger pattern and a number word. The perceptual replacements, however, served no substitutive function. We believe that she now re-presented the specific finger patterns to which number words referred and coordinated uttering number words with the sequential construction of the individual elements of those patterns (which consisted of sequentially putting up fingers).

Brenda's adaptation constituted a reorganization of her counting scheme, in that she could now establish two finger patterns by performing a single sequence of counting acts. Previously, she first established the two finger patterns and then counted the fingers of the patterns as one collection. Her intention, establishing two finger patterns, was now coordinated with her counting scheme, so that re-presented rather than actual finger patterns led to counting activity. After she had completed a finger pattern for a number word by counting, she could continue counting to complete a second finger pattern.

Brenda's re-presentation of finger patterns reflected the activity of putting up fingers in the "reflexive" sense in reflective abstraction (Piaget, l977). In other words, a re-presented finger pattern for "four" guided her activity as she sequentially put up four fingers while synchronously uttering "4-5-6-7" (cf. 1.07). The re-presented finger pattern could now imply the counting activity necessary to establish the pattern as well as the finger pattern itself. In this sense, the re-presented finger pattern embodied counting activity.

The Motor Period

Brenda soon isolated the activity of counting from that of completing finger patterns and overcame the limitations of relying exclusively on finger patterns of ten or less. Her ability to count to a number word while synchronously putting up fingers allowed her to isolate these motor acts as experiential items (cf. 1.09). Although this was not an immediate acquisition, the motor acts could now function as substitutes for figural items--for re-presentations of fingers. However, she actually counted the motor acts of putting up fingers. What she intended to count was distinct from, but was reflected by, what she actually counted.

The attainment of the motor period did not lead immediately to a structural reorganization of counting beyond that which she had already achieved when she put up fingers to complete finger patterns. The primary reason for this was her reliance on the visual separation between her hands when she attempted to establish two finger patterns. Moreover, finger patterns were still specific in that, say, "four" could not refer to any four fingers. Consequently, she could continue to count appropriately beyond one finger pattern to establish a second finger pattern only in special circumstances (i.e., beyond a pattern for "five" or "ten"). She still experienced this difficulty late in her motor period and compensated somewhat for this limitation by constructing sophisticated finger patterns to find sums greater than ten and less than sixteen.

Brenda's transition to what we have called her motor period involved a level 2 abstraction--instead of simultaneously putting up fingers to establish a finger pattern, she re-presented the finger pattern as a collection of individual elements. It was as if the re-presented finger pattern was "there" to be counted. The contention that she possessed such re-presentational capacity is consistent with her subsequent construction of sophisticated finger patterns (cf. 1.14). Brenda's motor acts of putting up or wiggling fingers were a substitute for fingers as perceptual units. This immediacy of the substitutive function of putting up fingers was manifest in the lack of separations that we observed when she continued to count beyond an already completed counting activity. The fact that she could count too many times, or not enough times (depending on the specific context), indicates that she re-presented specific patterns.

The inability to reflect on the results of counting was characteristic of Brenda while she was in her motor period (cf. 1.11). Her inability to review a completed finger pattern to re-establish the separation she had made in its establishment by counting indicates that her intention prior to counting was to complete her finger pattern for "ten", rather than to specify the plurality of the counting acts corresponding to "9-10". She was generally incapable of using her counting scheme to solve our missing addend problems and assimilated these problems only in those cases where the involved number words were connected to finger patterns. The results of her assimilations were, from our point of view, distortions. Her problem seemed to be to establish a finger pattern for "eight" and then a finger pattern for "ten". That she used the first finger pattern in the establishment of the second does not indicate that the first was included in the second.

2. TARUS

The first two periods that we observed for Tarus were a perceptual period (4 months) and a motor period (3 months). He was classified as being a counter of perceptual unit items on the basis of his performance in an interview held on 22 October 1980. In a teaching episode conducted on 3 February 1981, a novelty appeared in his counting scheme--he sequentially put up fingers when counting. This adaptation indicated that he was in transition to the motor period, which he attained by 5 March 1981.

The Perceptual Period

22 October 1980 Interview

<u>Counting Perceptual Unit Items</u>

2.01. There was a clear distinction between those situations in which Tarus counted and those in which he did not. The solution documented in the following protocol is typical. The interviewer asked Tarus to count out six marbles from a collection so that he might reenact this counting activity when the marbles were hidden. Tarus was aware of the hidden marbles and seemed to realize that "six" referred to a hidden collection.

I : (Places the six marbles Tarus had counted out by three others, hiding the six with his hand) How many do you have?
T : Six (indicating an awareness of the hidden marbles).
I : I want you to find how many marbles there are. Start over here (points to his hand).
T : (Touches the interviewer's hand, but does not count.)
I : How many are here (touching his hand)?
T : Six.
I : How many altogether?

T : Three (looking at the visible marbles).

I : (Lifts his hand from the six marbles) How many marbles on the cloth (waving his hand over all the marbles)? Find out by counting.

T : (Looking at the six marbles) One, . . .

I : (Places his hand over the six marbles after Tarus uttered "one".)

T : (Stops uttering number words and looks at the visible marbles for about 25 seconds without counting.)

2.02. Even after Tarus had been shown the hidden marbles and was allowed to start counting, he did not continue when they were again hidden. The interviewer presented a similar task with three, rather than six, marbles hidden to test whether Tarus would substitute a spatial pattern for the hidden marbles and count the elements of the pattern. However, Tarus counted only the three visible marbles. These observations serve as a basis for classifying him as a counter of perceptual unit items.

<u>Counting the Elements of Spatial Patterns</u>

2.03. During the interviews, a novelty appeared in Tarus's counting activity. After seeing spatial patterns, he re-presented them and counted their elements.

I : (Places a card in front of Tarus with two cloths on it, one covering a triangular arrangement of three squares and one covering two squares, and lifts the cloth covering the two squares.)

T : Two (immediately).

I : (Lifts the other cloth) What do you see there?

T : Three.

I : How many altogether?

T : (He slaps the cloth covering three squares, and then lifts the cloth covering two squares and replaces it. He then sequentially touches the cloth) 1-2 (He continues touching the other cloth using his other hand, where his points of contact form a triangular pattern) 3-4-5.

In an immediately preceding unsuccessful attempt, he had counted two perceptual patterns after both cloths had been removed. His behavior in the protocol above suggests that this counting activity was crucial to his reconstruction of the patterns as figurative collections whose elements could be counted.

2.04. The activity of counting covered items that occurred in patterns led in turn to counting figural items. This was indicated by his count over a cloth hiding eight squares in a subsequent task. For two reasons, we did not categorize Tarus as being a counter of figural unit items on the basis of this one solution. First, the accommodation of counting was very gradual, beginning with counting the perceptual items of two previously hidden patterns, progressing to counting the items of hidden patterns, and culminating in counting the items of a hidden collection of eight items. Second, the accommodation was highly contextual, in that it occurred as a result of carefully sequenced interventions. Counting figural items was not characteristic of his counting activity. He usually did not count when the tasks involved screened perceptual items.

3 February 1981 Teaching Episode

Spatio-Motor Patterns

2.05. The first major accommodation Tarus made in the perceptual period was to develop spatio-motor patterns. In the five teaching episodes prior to this one, Tarus solidified spatio-motor patterns for "two" and "three" and developed spatio-motor patterns for "four" and "five". He could use these spatio-motor patterns to count two hidden collections of five or fewer items if they were arranged in patterns. For example, to solve a task where three items were hidden by one cloth and four by an other, Tarus uttered "1-2-3" while synchronously tapping on the cloth (where his points of contact formed a triangular pattern). He then continued, tapping on the other cloth while synchronously uttering "4-5-6-7" (where this time his points of contact formed a square pattern).

Finger Patterns

2.06. Tarus introduced a novelty into his counting scheme that was wholly unexpected. He substituted finger patterns rather than spatial patterns for hidden perceptual collections. The following protocol captures the essence of this accommodation. Tarus was directed to tap on the carpet (on which he was sitting) to count marbles that were dropped into two cups, four in each. The teacher encouraged him to tap on the carpet in order to facilitate Tarus's use of spatio-motor patterns. To our surprise, this intervention instead led to his use of finger patterns.

I : (After reaffirming that Tarus knows that four marbles are in each cup) How many altogether?

T : (Sequentially puts up four fingers on his left hand) 1-2-3-4. (Pauses, then puts up his thumb) 5. (Sequentially puts up four fingers on his right hand) 6-7-8-9. Nine! (He intently looks at his fingers while he put them up.)

Tarus counted to complete two finger patterns. In a subsequent task involving five marbles in one cup and four in another, he asked how many marbles were in the cup containing five before he counted, even though he had recognized a spatial configuration of marbles as "five" before putting the marbles in the cup. This question indicates that Tarus substituted finger patterns for the hidden collections of marbles and that the fingers that he put up in synchrony with the utterances "1-2-3-4-5" were perceptual substitutes rather than replacements for the marbles. This is confirmed by his looking into the cup containing four before continuing to utter "6-7-8-9" synchronous with the acts of putting up fingers. Here, again, he forgot "four". In four subsequent tasks he oscillated between looking at his fingers and looking into the cups. He even attempted to count the marbles after five and then three were put into the same cup, but resorted to putting up fingers when he was thwarted by the teacher.

Failure to Make Separations in Counting

2.07. The contention that Tarus put up fingers to complete finger patterns is confirmed by his behavior in the following protocol.

I : (Places six marbles in front of Tarus) How many are there?
T : (Points to each marble) 1-2-3-4-5-6. Six.
I : (Places two more marbles in front of Tarus) How many are there?
T : Two.
I : (Places all the marbles into one cup) How many are altogether?
T : (Sequentially puts up the fingers of his left hand and one of his right hand) 1-2-3-4-5-6. (Pauses, and then puts up one more finger of his right hand) Seven.

He stopped counting after he put up the seventh finger, completing a visually separated finger pattern for two in a manner analogous to that of Brenda (cf. 1.06).

2.08. The substitution of finger patterns for hidden collections occurred when he wanted to find how many marbles were hidden in a container. When a cloth hid a spatial array, he enacted spatio-motor patterns. We do not suggest causal connections between the spatial features of the screen used to hide a collection and the type of patterns (spatial or finger) that Tarus substituted for the hidden collections. Rather, tasks that involved hiding marbles in containers were novel for Tarus in that the marbles were not arranged in patterns. He successfully concluded his search for items to count by counting the elements of re-presented finger patterns that were themselves substitutes for the hidden collections.

The Motor Period

5 March 1981 Teaching Episode

Counting Motor Unit Items

2.09. Tarus overcame some of the perceptual constraints implicit in his use of finger patterns in this teaching episode. The following solution is exemplary.

> T : (Puts eight and then four more marbles in a cup. To find how many in the cup, he sequentially puts up eight fingers) 1-2-3-4-5-6-7-8. (He then holds the three extended fingers on his left hand with his right hand while putting up his thumb and little finger. He then puts up two more fingers of his right hand) 9-10-11-12. Twelve.

2.10. There were four significant advances in this solution. First, Tarus held the three fingers of his left hand with his right hand, separating the first eight fingers from those he intended to count. Second, and as a consequence, he proceeded from one hand to the other when he made the pattern to which "four" referred in a manner that indicated he was not simply completing a specific finger pattern. Third, Tarus put up two fingers for a second time when he counted "11-12", a prime indication that he was not counting his fingers as perceptual items. These three observations lead to the inference that he took the motor acts as countable items, which is the fourth advance. In general, his counting was now more flexible, in that he could use his counting scheme to solve a broader range of tasks. In particular, he could appropriately count the items hidden by two cloths when the number word corresponding to one of the two cloths signified a pattern.

2.11. Tarus's ability to use counting as a bridge from one hand to the other indicates that his counting scheme was now a motor scheme. He recognized the thumb and little finger of his left hand and the two fingers he put up on his right hand as an array of four perceptual items--a couple of pairs. This increased mobility in the recognition of collections of four fingers as "four" indicates the presence of a motor component, introduced by counting, in his finger patterns.

2.12. The inference that Tarus counted the acts of putting up fingers is confirmed by his solution to a subsequent task where he had placed six and then five marbles into a cup. To find how many marbles were in the cup, he first sequentially put up six fingers, five on his right hand and the index finger of his left hand. After a pause, he continued to put up the fingers of his left hand and then proceeded to his right hand, putting up his right index finger to complete the pattern. In doing so, he established and maintained a separation in counting activity between the first six and the last five counting acts. As before, we infer that "five" referred to a mobile finger pattern because he used counting as a bridge from one hand to the other and reused a finger.

14 May 1981 Teaching Episode

Spatio-Auditory Patterns

2.13. The construction of a new type of pattern led to the curtailment of motor activity.

I : (Pointing to two cloths on the table) there are seven here and four here. How many altogether?

T : 1-2-3-4-5-6-7 (very quickly) --2-3-4-5-6--7 (looking up) 8-9--10-11 (looking at the cloth where four items were supposed to be hidden.)

The contention that this solution involved a curtailment of putting up fingers is confirmed by his solution of the very next task. After he was told that there were eight under one cloth and three under another, Tarus sequentially put up three fingers in synchrony with the first three utterances of "1-2-3-4-5-6-7-8", but abandoned the motor activity as he went on to quickly finish uttering the number word sequence. He again looked at the cloth supposedly hiding three items as he uttered "n-i-n-e--t-e-n--e-l-e-v-e-n", indicating a deliberate pattern.

2.14. The patterns Tarus completed for "three" and "four" in the two solutions above still contained a spatial component. This is indicated by the way in which he intently focused his gaze on the cloth as he continued to count. We call these patterns spatio-auditory because they were sequential, completed without motor activity, and seemed to be the result of abstraction. When Tarus was presented with the expression "6 + 5", he put up fingers in his solution, apparently because of lack of a spatio-auditory pattern for "five". In two subsequent solutions of the expressions

"5 + 4" and "5 + 3", Tarus sat quietly for 12 seconds and 11 seconds, respectively, before responding correctly. He appeared to be deep in thought and displayed intense concentration. We infer that he subvocally uttered the number word sequences (e.g., "1-2-3-4-5--6-7-8-9") and each time produced a spatio-auditory pattern for the second numeral. We did not yet classify Tarus as a counter of verbal unit items because his solutions were situation-specific. They were, however, harbingers of what was to come.

Discussion of Tarus's Case Study

The Perceptual Period

Tarus developed spatio-motor patterns for "two" through "five", inclusive, while in his perceptual period (cf. 2.05) as a result of his ability to count the elements of spatial patterns. Although these spatio-motor patterns were involved in a structural reorganization of counting (cf. 2.05), his counting scheme did not change from a perceptual scheme to a figurative scheme until he substituted re-presented finger patterns for perceptual collections that were hidden from view (cf. 2.06). Rather than use a finger pattern as a replacement for a hidden perceptual collection as Brenda did, Tarus substituted a finger pattern for the hidden collection. Counting his fingers as perceptual items carried the significance of counting the marbles that were hidden in the cups.

We contend that Tarus re-presented a finger pattern prior to counting and substituted this re-presentation for the hidden collection of marbles. By the manner in which he attempted to look at the marbles in the cups or asked how many were in a particular cup when he forgot a number word, he seemed to be counting a visually separated collection of marbles. His failure to make appropriate separations in counting activity (cf. 2.07), however, confirms the inference that he put up fingers to complete specific, visually bounded finger patterns. Tarus's counting scheme had developed into a figurative scheme, but what he actually counted corresponded to what he intended to count--fingers. This development was the result of a level 2 reflective abstraction because Tarus substituted a re-presentation of a finger pattern for the activity of actually establishing the finger pattern.

As a result of this level 2 reflective abstraction, Tarus had an opportunity to isolate the motor act of putting up a finger as an experiential item. When he eventually made this construction, motor acts functioned as substitutes for hidden perceptual items. He now had two motor counting schemes--one that involved putting up fingers and one that involved the pointing acts that he carried out to complete spatio-motor patterns (cf. 2.08).

The Motor Period

Tarus's isolation of the act of putting up a finger as a motor unit item led to a further structural reorganization of his motor counting scheme. He could make and maintain separations between counting acts he had performed and those that he intended to perform when counting the items of two hidden collections (cf. 2.09). The manner in which he proceeded from one hand to the other when he continued to count was made possible by the mobile finger patterns he abstracted from the activity of counting to establish finger patterns. He could now, for example, utter four number words and coordinate them with the activity of putting up any four fingers. He could double use fingers. His intention before continuing to count was not to establish a particular finger pattern but to count four more times.

Tarus subsequently began to curtail the motor activity of his two motoric counting schemes when he enacted the patterns that he coordinated with both counting schemes. Specifically, he curtailed the motor activity of triangular and square spatio-motor patterns and the motor component of his mobile finger patterns. These curtailments were observed in the 14 May 1981 teaching episode (cf. 2.13), when he put up fingers to count covered spatial arrangements and also in synchrony with only the first three utterances of "1-2-3-4-5-6-7-8--9-10-11" (cf. 2.13). The seeds for future adaptations in his counting scheme had been sown, as the spatio-motor patterns and the mobile finger patterns were being displaced by spatio-auditory patterns.

3. JAMES

The first two periods for James were a perceptual period (observed for 2 months) and a motor period (2 months), separated by about 6 months. He was classified as being a counter of perceptual unit items on the basis of his performance in interviews held on 25 and 26 March 1981, and remained in the perceptual period for the rest of the 1980-1981 school year. James counted motor unit items in an interview held on 7 December 1981.

The Perceptual Period

25 March 1981 Interview

Finger Patterns

3.01. The first scheme we discuss involved replacing finger patterns for hidden collections and then counting the fingers as perceptual unit items as exemplified by the following protocol. James was shown five marbles arranged in a domino five pattern, which he immediately recognized as "five". He was then shown two other marbles, which he recognized as "two".

I : (Covers the marbles with his hands) How many altogether?
J : (Sequentially touches his lips with the fingers of his right hand) 1-2-3-4-5. (Continues touching his lips with the fingers of his left hand) 6-7-8-9-10!
I : Ten? How many are here (the five)?
J : Five.
I : How many are here (the two)?
J : Two.
I : How many are altogether?
J : (Sequentially touches his lips with the fingers of his open right hand) 1-2-3-4-5. (Continues, touching his lips with two fingers of his left hand) 6-7.

Initially, he counted the fingers of each of his two open hands, indicating that his finger patterns replaced the hidden collections of marbles. He was searching for perceptual items to count and changed from counting marbles to counting fingers. This is on a par with Brenda's use of finger patterns as perceptual replacements (cf. 1.05).

3.02. When James counted the fingers of his open hand, he characteristically touched his lips while synchronously uttering number words. We believe that what he counted were tactual perceptual items. However, his intention seemed to be to count visual perceptual items--his fingers--because he first established finger patterns.

Perceptual Replacements

3.03. James also made perceptual replacements by using items other than his own fingers. The following protocol contains one such example.

I : (Places five marbles on the table and covers them with his hand. Four other marbles were visible.)
J : (Points to each visible marble) 1-2-3-4. (Points to each side of the interviewer's hand) 5-6 (Touches specific places on the interviewer's hand) 7-8-9-10.
I : Count these first (moves his hand).
J : (Points to each finger on the interviewer's hand covering the marbles) 1-2-3-4-5. (Points to each visible marble) 6-7-8-9.

The directive "count these first" led James to count the interviewer's fingers as perceptual replacements for the marbles, also on a par with Brenda (cf. 1.04).

Counting Figural Unit Items

3.04. Before he counted the interviewer's fingers as perceptual replacements, James counted figural unit items, as indicated by his attempt to see a marble under each side of the interviewer's hand when he uttered "5-6". He was constrained to the location of the visible marbles and went on, touching specific places on the interviewer's hand. Even though James counted figural unit items on this occasion, he did not usually do so. In fact, we view his momentary advance as a source of subsequent development of his counting scheme because it led to counting pointing acts.

Counting Pointing Acts--A Momentary Advance

3.05. James made a highly contextual temporary advance and counted his pointing acts as substitutes for hidden marbles when he was not allowed to count any perceptual items by the interviewer. In the following protocol, James had previously counted the five marbles in a cup, beside which there were three visible marbles.

I : How many marbles altogether (has his hand over the cup)?
J : (Points to each visible marble) 1-2-3.
I : Count these first (moving the cup).
J : (Points to a finger of the interviewer's hand over the cup) 1--.
I : (As James points to his finger, the interviewer removes his hand. James then points into the cup) 1. (He then points at the interviewer's moved hand) 1-2-3. (He then grabs the cup and starts pointing to the marbles.)
I : (Takes the cup from James) Don't count them! Don't count my fingers, either! (Covers the cup with a cloth) How many altogether?

J : Places his hand in the air over the cloth and points sequentially to the same location 1-2-3-4-5. (Points to each visible marble) 6-7-8.

James wanted to count perceptual items. He counted his pointing acts only after being prevented from counting the marbles and the interviewer's fingers. We infer that his acts of pointing at the interviewer's hand while uttering "1-2-3" led James to isolate his pointing acts--to the novelty of counting motor items. Immediately after this task, James analogously pointed over the aperture of a cup containing eight marbles and then went on to count three visible marbles. Although he did not carry over the advance of counting his pointing acts when similar tasks were presented, this demonstrates that James's search for sensory items to count could lead to his making the motor acts that were auxiliary in locating perceptual items into countable items.

26 March 1981 Interview

Two Distinct Counting Schemes

3.06. Two distinct counting schemes were observed in this interview. The general task format was to present James with two arrays of squares glued onto a card, each covered by a cloth. James was asked to count the squares of the arrays whose protonumerosities he did not immediately recognize when the cloths were temporarily removed. After James had found how many squares were in each array, they were again hidden and he was asked to find how many squares were hidden under both cloths. The first scheme involved sequentially touching his lips with his fingers while synchronously uttering number words. He rarely replaced the appropriate finger pattern for the second covered collection. Rather, he simply continued to touch his fingers on his lips as he said number words and lost track of his counting activity.

3.07. On one occasion, James experienced conflict when he attempted to count hidden arrays of seven and five squares. Before they were hidden, he had counted the seven squares and had recognized the five squares as "five". After they were hidden, to find how many squares there were, he sequentially touched his lips with his fingers while synchronously uttering "1-2-3-4-5-6-7". He did not continue even though he understood that he had not counted the five squares. He was stymied because he had only three fingers left to count. In this case, it was crucial that he had enough fingers in his visual field to establish a finger pattern for "five".

3.08. His awareness that he had not counted all the squares was indicated in part by what he did next. He started again, and attempted to count the seven hidden squares by pointing to locations on the cloth, but pointed only four times, his points of contact forming a square pattern. Clearly, he re-presented a spatial pattern, used it as a replacement for the hidden array, then counted the elements of this figural pattern. This second counting scheme differed from the first in the material that he re-presented prior to counting.

3.09. Although we classify James as a counter of perceptual unit items, the rather erratic use of finger patterns and the re-presentation of spatial patterns for hidden collections provided James with new possibilities in counting. Coupled with the temporary advance he made as he counted pointing acts, he seemed to be in transition to the motor period.

31 April 1981 Teaching Episode

Curtailment of Pointing Acts in Spatio-Motor Patterns

3.10. Since James could re-present spatial patterns and use them to replace hidden arrays, the focus of the first three teaching episodes after the 25 and 26 March 1981 interviews was on his production of spatio-motor patterns. The goal was to provide James with opportunities to isolate and count the motor acts of pointing but he went beyond this and curtailed the motor acts involved in the enactments of spatio-motor patterns.

3.11. James merely uttered number words as he enacted spatial patterns immediately after he had solved five tasks using spatio-motor patterns, indicating that he had curtailed his pointing acts. The sixth task involved the three numerals "5", "3", and "5", where "3" was placed on the middle of the three cloths. James quickly uttered "1-2-3-4-5" while looking at the left cloth and then "6-7-8-9" while looking at the middle cloth. He realized that he had made a mistake, returned to the left cloth and again quickly uttered "1-2-3-4-5". This time he nodded his head while uttering "6-7-8", as if visually scanning a triangular pattern. He then continued over the right cloth while uttering "9-10-11-12-13", again nodding his head as if scanning a domino five pattern.

3.12. We would not say that James was a counter of verbal unit items based on his above activity, any more than we would say that he was a counter of motor unit items when he enacted spatio-motor patterns. Both were results of level 1 reflective abstractions. Nevertheless, the curtailment of motor activity was a significant advance because it marked the emergence of spatio-auditory patterns.

19 May 1981 Teaching Episode

<u>Lack of Reflection</u>

3.13. The apparent lack of conflict in the following protocol indicates that James did not reflect on already completed counting activity.

T : (Places the numerals "9" and "3" on two cloths which James was told hid cookies and asks James to find how many cookies.)
J : (Utters) 1-2- . . . -9. (Touches the second cloth in four places and utters) 10-11-12-13.
T : Oops! Three (points to the numeral "3").
J : (Touches the cloth in three places and utters) 13-14-15.

This episode may seem to be trivial--just a misinterpretation of the teacher's intention, but to us it is a valuable indicator of an apparent lack of conflict in counting over the second cloth for a second time, "13-14-15". His behavior fits the interpretation that he enacted spatio-motor patterns upon hearing number words because he did not seem to reflect on what he was going to count. Instead, he just counted.

The Motor Period

7 December 1981 Interview

<u>Counting Motor Unit Items</u>

3.14. During the initial interviews in the second year of the teaching experiment, it became obvious that James had made progress. In a single counting episode, he counted both the acts of putting up fingers and of moving his hand. The task involved 14 blocks hidden by a cover and 4 more hidden by the interviewer's hand; James sequentially put up all 10 fingers while synchronously uttering "1-2- . . . -10" and then simultaneously moved both open hands while uttering "11-12-13-14". To complete his solution, he touched the interviewer's hand in four places while uttering "15-16-17-18". His acts of simultaneously moving both hands were a modification of counting the motor acts of putting up fingers and strongly indicate that he was a counter of motor unit items because they demonstrate that he could flexibly create countable items.

But James's failure to put up four fingers for a second time when he counted beyond "ten" suggests that he still experienced the perceptual constraint of the finger pattern for "ten"--he could not reuse his fingers. His ability to overcome this by creating a somewhat innovative motor act is a strong indication that he could make an impromptu adaptation in the middle of counting and create a novel countable item that he did not initially intend to count.

Lack of Re-presentation of Counting

3.15. James's inability to re-present counting activity was manifested when he attempted to specify a hidden portion of a collection. His most sophisticated solution is presented in the following protocol.

J : (Sequentially places four marbles in a tube) 1-2-3-4.
T : (Takes the tube from James) Okay, I am going to put some more in. (Holds up his closed hand) If I put these marbles in there, there would be seven. How many are in my hand?
J : Three!
I : How do you know that?
J : (Holds the interviewer's closed hand) Because there's two right here and one right here (pointing to the interviewer's fingers).

In the next task, he again counted the interviewer's fingers as perceptual replacements for marbles, this time arriving at an inappropriate result. To find how many marbles were in the interviewer's hand, he counted perceptual replacements. However, he did not anticipate that he could solve the task by finding how many times he counted over the interviewer's hand.

Discussion of James's Case Study

The Perceptual Period

At the time of the first interview, James was a counter of perceptual unit items. However, in specific situations initiated by the interviewer, James created and counted figural unit items (cf. 3.04) or motor unit items (cf. 3.05). Those two instances did not typify James's characteristic counting behavior even when he attempted to count hidden collections (cf. 3.01 and 3.03). They were a consequence of James's search for sensory material from which he could create countable items in highly contextual situations and, as such, constituted temporary modifications of his counting scheme.

While in transition to his motor period, unlike Brenda and Tarus, James counted touching his fingers to his lips, a tactual perceptual item. He also realized for the first time that he could produce a number word sequence until he reached a particular number word. The latter level 1 abstraction was based on his repeated use of spatio-motor patterns. He curtailed the motor acts and reenacted spatial patterns by just uttering number words (cf. 3.11), resembling Tarus's use of spatio-auditory patterns to decide when to stop counting.

The Motor Period

The first observations we made when James entered the motor period (cf. 3.15) indicated that he had reorganized his counting scheme in two important ways. First, he used two different types of motor acts in one counting activity. Second, he could continue to count beyond already completed counts until he completed either a spatio-motor pattern, a mobile finger pattern, or a number word (spatio-auditory) pattern (he also stopped after he completed finger patterns). This was more encompassing than the reorganizations accomplished by either Brenda or Tarus in the same period.

Unlike Tarus and Brenda, James counted pointing acts, movements of his hand, and the acts of putting up fingers. This suggests that while finger patterns and spatial patterns played a crucial role in the development of his counting scheme, he isolated his pointing acts as experiential items in contexts other than those of counting patterns (cf. 3.05).

PERSPECTIVES ON THE THREE CASE STUDIES

The question of whether the construction of motor unit items constituted a stage shift can be answered in the affirmative. There is solid justification for claiming that the emergence of the motor unit item indicates a shift from a perceptual stage to a figurative stage in counting. Each of the four criteria for stages will be discussed in turn.

Period Criterion

There was a stretch of time when each child was observed primarily counting perceptual unit items and another period when each was observed counting motor unit items as well as perceptual unit items. The emergence of motor unit items involved a change in the first part of the children's counting schemes, in that they all established the elements of re-presented finger patterns as countable items. The prominent role played by finger patterns in the children's transition to the motor period can be partially accounted for by accessibility. In the context of their search for perceptual material, it seemed quite natural for the children to use their fingers as countable perceptual items.

There is a further reason why finger patterns played this important developmental role. The semantic connections that the children had established between these patterns and the number words "two", "three", "four", and "five" were the result of counting. Consequently, "four" could refer to a finger pattern as well as to the activity of counting fingers to complete the pattern. The counting acts that were implicit in the finger patterns were eventually externalized as countable items. The isolation of these motor acts implicit in the patterns is similar to Piaget's pseudo-empirical abstraction (i.e., level 1).

> Reflective abstraction . . . in its elementary forms, is accessible to the subject only when it is embodied in external objects . . . the embodiment is merely a matter of temporary characteristics, introduced and imposed upon the objects by the subject himself. (Piaget, 1980, p. 92)

The difference resides in the internalization of the finger patterns through their re-presentation (a level 2 reflective abstraction). The level 1 reflective abstraction involved in isolating putting up fingers as countable items was preceded by the level 2 reflective abstraction of re-presenting finger patterns.

The absence of a distinct period when the children counted figural unit items does not lessen the importance of the role played by the figural item in the development of counting. First, all three children were observed counting figural unit items in specific situations while they were in the perceptual period. Second, all three children sequentially put up fingers as they counted motor unit items. On one occasion, Tarus put eight and then four more marbles in a cup. To find out how many were in the cup, he first sequentially uttered "1-2-3-4-5-6-7-8" as he put up eight fingers, then continued "9-10-11-12" while putting up his two remaining fingers, and then two other fingers for a second time. Tarus did not first simultaneously put up fingers and then count them; instead, he put up fingers as he went along. This indicates that counting in these situations was possible because of the re-presentation of a plurality of fingers. The manner in which he put up two fingers for a second time indicates that he actually counted motor unit items and he was not stymied when he ran out of fingers as perceptual items. Thus, his ability to re-present a plurality of fingers enabled him to count motor unit items. The other two children were also able to re-present pluralities of fingers. These re-presentations gave them an opportunity to isolate the motor acts of putting up fingers as discrete experiential items or things.

Figural pluralities other than pluralities of fingers played a secondary role in Brenda's and Tarus's transitions to the motor period, but were primarily involved in James's transition. He often replaced or substituted spatial patterns for hidden collections, and he was the only child who prominently used both spatial and finger patterns as assimilatory structures.

The Incorporation and Invariant Sequence Criteria

The incorporation criterion seems to be satisfied by the role of figural unit items. Since the motor acts were substitutes for corresponding perceptual unit items, whether fingers or other perceptual items, the perceptual items were implicitly implied by the motor unit items. Nevertheless, the children still counted perceptual items per se on occasion. The "reflexive" aspect of reflective abstraction provides a basis for understanding the steps in the construction of these various unit items. The figural unit item, being a re-presentation of the perceptual unit item, reflects the perceptual unit item. The motor unit item signifies both because it is isolated in the context of counting perceptual unit items or their figural re-presentatives.

The invariant sequence criterion seems to be satisfied by all three children. Even though James started the teaching experiment in a transitional period, it was enough like the transitional periods of the two other children to conjecture that there was a length of time when he was a counter of perceptual unit items. This inference will become especially plausible when we consider the verbal periods of the children in the next chapter.

The Reorganization Criterion

While in the motor period, all three children were able to count two collections by performing a single sequence of counting acts. This advance indicates that they had coordinated their counting scheme with spatial, spatio-auditory, or finger patterns and had associated number words with specific patterns that they could re-present before they counted the second collection. We call solutions of this type intuitive extensions. The word "extension" emphasizes continuing beyond the activity of counting the first collection and "intuitive" is used because the children completed figural patterns when they counted the second collection. In the absence of such patterns, they were not certain where to stop or, on occasion, where to start counting. But the children did not reflect on their activity and then devise a novel means of keeping track of their counting activity. They knew that something had gone wrong, but were unable to resolve their problematic situation.

These behaviors strongly indicate that the children did not intentionally decide to use a particular pattern before they started to count--they did not have an overall plan of action. Instead, they re-presented a particular pattern once they had counted the first collection. In other words, the re-presentation was established only within the context of on-going counting activity. The construction of the intuitive extension scheme is but an example of the aspect of reflective abstraction that involves "mental reorganization: necessarily so, since reflection culminates on a higher level, where it is a matter first of all of reconstructing what has been abstracted from a lower level" (Piaget, 1980, p. 90). Such reorganization is involved in level 2 reflective abstractions.

Chapter III

The Construction of Verbal Unit Items

Brenda, Tarus, and James

Leslie P. Steffe Paul Cobb

We have argued that the shift in counting type from perceptual to motor unit items constituted a stage shift in the counting scheme, and we have called these stages the perceptual and the figurative stages. Re-presentation was the vital mechanism in the children's progress; however, the material they re-presented was predominantly restricted to finger patterns. The children could coordinate re-presented finger patterns and their counting schemes because their finger patterns came to embody the counting activity that was used to establish the patterns. In this chapter, we continue the investigation of the role of re-presentation and its material as the children made the transition to their verbal periods. Our initial hypothesis--that the verbal period is a transitional period in the same sense that counting figural unit items was for Brenda, Tarus, and James--will be thoroughly tested.

To count verbal unit items, the child must curtail the production of sensory-motor countable items that accompany the uttering of number words in sequence. At the outset, we could imagine no mechanism of curtailment other than reflection on the results of a re-presentation. However, we could not make the material of such re-presentations explicit through conceptual analysis alone although re-presentation of the results of counting provided us with an excellent candidate. We thought the form those results would take might be patterns, but that was not certain, because it seemed possible for a child to re-present the records of the activity--a specified collection.

In the case studies, we document the situations in which we first observed the children counting verbal unit items. Because one of our primary interests is to investigate whether this shift in counting type constituted a stage shift, we will also document the children's use of counting in problem-solving situations. The reorganization criterion will be investigated in the context of the children solving problems because any reorganizations that occurred should be manifested in that context.

Toward this end, we investigate the construction of counting-on, which can sometimes be a behavioral indication of the uniting operation of integration.

1. BRENDA

1 February 1982 Teaching Episode

<u>Counting Verbal Unit Items</u>

1.16. Brenda curtailed the coordination of motor acts and number word utterances when she counted the first of two hidden collections in this teaching episode.

T : Do this one, fifteen plus nine.
B : (Utters) 1-2-3- . . . -15. (Simultaneously puts up all ten fingers)--16-17- . . . -24 (while sequentially folding down nine fingers).

The initial count "1-2-3- . . . -15" was performed without any accompanying motor activity. The accommodation Brenda made was to substitute her vocal acts of uttering number words for acts of folding down fingers. She seemed to have abstracted the number word utterances from acts of counting that involved coordinating such an utterance with folding down a finger. She used this verbal scheme consistently when the first number word of an additive expression was after "ten", but if it preceded "ten", she used her finger pattern scheme. This suggests that she was aware of the limitations of her finger patterns.

1.17. To explore the possibility that Brenda had made a major reorganization of her counting scheme, the teacher asked her to do 15 take away 3, first by counting forward and then by counting backward. But, Brenda continued to used her sophisticated finger patterns.

T : OK, do fifteen take away three. Do it out loud--1-2-3-4-- like that.
B : 1-2-3- . . . -15 (counting verbal unit items).
T : Take away three.
B : (Simultaneously puts up five fingers of her right hand) 1-2-3 (Sequentially folds down three fingers)--12?

Brenda's open hand was, for her, a finger pattern for "fifteen". She closed three fingers and then hesitatingly recognized the remaining two fingers as a pattern for "twelve". Brenda explained her solution as follows:

B : I did fifteen (simultaneously puts up all ten fingers). I counted like this--14 and then 13 (sequentially folds down two fingers), like that.

1.18. Clearly, Brenda attempted to comply with the teacher's requests in her explanation. However, she did solve a subsequent task by counting backward.

T : OK, do twenty-four take away six like that. Do it out loud.
B : 1-2-3-. . . -24.
T : Take away six.
B : Twenty-four (simultaneously puts up five fingers on one hand and one on her other hand)--24-24-23-22-21 (sequentially folds down three fingers).
T : Twenty (a prompt).
B : 20-19 (sequentially folds down two fingers).
T : Eighteen (a prompt).
B : Eighteen (folds down the remaining finger).

Aided by the teacher's prompts, Brenda made a modification. The scheme discussed in 1.17 was limited to the range of her patterns and she could not create a pattern for "twenty-four". The modification she made was to utter the forward number word sequence, which she had just produced, in the reverse direction. Having counted to "twenty-four", she had an *immediate prior* experience that she could re-present and a starting place from which to utter number words backward. She coordinated these utterances with her finger pattern for "six".

1.19. This analysis is corroborated by her solution to a subsequent task. She solved the sentence "17 - 4 = ____" in a similar way after she had counted from "one" to "seventeen". These were the only two occasions where she made this contextual modification. During the rest of the teaching experiment, all the solutions she produced in subtraction situations involved her finger pattern scheme. For example, on 20 April 1982, she used sophisticated finger patterns to solve story problems corresponding to "18 - 3" and "15 - 3". However, she said that she could not solve story problems that corresponded to "30 - 4" and "27 - 3". As the teacher did not direct her to count from "one", she did not produce a forward number word sequence that she could then re-present as immediate past experience. In other words, she could produce a completed counting activity in the reverse direction, but she could not *anticipate* counting to, say, "thirty", and then actually produce four backward counting acts.

8 March 1982 Teaching Episode

Solving Our Missing Addend Situations Using Finger Patterns

1.20. Solving what were to us subtraction situations by counting backward presents a particular difficulty, even for children who have constructed abstract unit items. Consequently, we used missing addend situations to further explore the possibility that Brenda had made a major reorganization in her counting scheme. She solved some situations of this type by using her sophisticated finger patterns. For example, she solved the sentence "12 + ___ = 14" with apparent ease by putting up seven fingers (a finger pattern for "twelve"), putting up two more fingers to complete a finger pattern for "fourteen", and then answering "two". This solution indicates that Brenda was able to review her activity of creating a finger pattern for "fourteen" and maintain the separation she had made.

1.21. Despite the advances Brenda had made since entering the verbal period, her schemes were still quite limited. The teacher presented the sentence "14 + ___ = 19", but Brenda could not use finger patterns because "nineteen" was beyond their current range. Instead, she counted "14-15-16-17-18--sequentially putting up fingers as she did so, and answered "eighteen". The teacher asked her to try again and she repeated this count, again answering "eighteen."

1.22. When Brenda used sophisticated finger patterns, she created a perceptual record of the entire activity, which could then be used to review her activity. However, she did not create a perceptual record of the counting acts implied by "fourteen" when she attempted to solve her problem in paragraph 1.21. Her termination of counting activity at "eighteen" and her answer "eighteen" both indicate that her task was to count from "fourteen" to "nineteen." There was no indication that she intended to find how many times she counted. She stopped at "eighteen" rather than "nineteen" because she did not have a sophisticated finger pattern for six extended fingers.

31 May 1982 Teaching Episode

Lack of Anticipation Before Counting

1.23. Brenda's most sophisticated solutions of what to us was a missing addend situation occurred in this teaching episode.

T : Makes the sentence 40 + ___ = 50 using felt numerals) Forty plus how many more makes fifty? Can you do that one? I bet you can do that one . . . go ahead.

B : 41-42- . . . -50 (sequentially closes all ten fingers).
T : What did you find?
B : . . .
T : How many times did you count?
B : (Sequentially wiggles each finger) Ten.

After she counted, Brenda did not give an answer, indicating that she had completed her solution. Presumably her task was to count to "fifty", but again, there was no indication that she intended to find the protonumerosity of the counting acts that she performed before she began to count. However, when the teacher asked "How many times did you count?" Brenda reviewed her past activity and counted the fingers that she had folded down.

1.24. Brenda frequently counted subvocally once she had entered the verbal period and often seemed to focus inwardly rather than outwardly on her counting activity. In general, her behavior appeared to be more reflective than that exhibited while she was in the motor period. It should be stressed, however, that Brenda reflected only on immediate past and current experience. She did not reflect on activity that she could carry out in the future.

Discussion of Brenda's Case Study

Brenda's sophisticated finger patterns seemed to play a crucial role in her curtailment of the motor component of counting activity. These patterns, which she initially established by counting, became perceptual records of the results of counting. Consequently, "fourteen" eventually referred to a sophisticated finger pattern that she could substitute for counting (cf. 1.20).

The developmental role played by these finger patterns is indicated by the way in which she coordinated her two addition schemes. If the first number word or numeral of an additive expression was after "ten" (e.g., 15 + 9), Brenda uttered number words, starting with "one", until she reached the first number word. Then she established a finger pattern for the second number word (or numeral) and counted the pattern (cf. 1.16). She clearly anticipated that she would end up beyond "fifteen", the range of her sophisticated finger patterns. So, rather than substitute a pattern for the activity of counting to "fifteen" and then count nine more, she made an adaptation--she uttered number words to "fifteen". This particular adaptation was possible because her sophisticated finger patterns embodied the result of counting. The contention that her activity of uttering "1-2- 3- . . . -15" involved curtailing the production of motor unit items is indicated by the manner in which she sequentially folded down nine fingers as she continued, "16-17- . . . -24" (cf. 1.16). Her coordination of number words with the acts of folding down fingers in the continuation indicates that each of the number words "one" through "twenty-four" carried the significance of a countable unit item.

The reorganizations that Brenda seemed to make in her counting scheme were limited. We did observe contextual modifications that were made possible by her sophisticated finger patterns and by her newly found ability to take the patterns as given in reflection. She could also count from one number word to another in an attempt to solve a missing addend problem. However, there was no general reorganization of her counting scheme. She did not anticipate finding how many times she could count nor did she keep track of how many counting acts she could perform in any general and systematic way.

2. TARUS

17 December 1981 Interview

Counting Verbal Unit Items

2.15. Tarus was a counter of verbal unit items at the time of this interview. The following protocol typifies the advance in his counting scheme.

I : (Presents Tarus with nine marbles hidden beneath one cloth and six beneath another) There are nine here and six here. Can you work that out?
T : (After 12 seconds of sitting silently) fifteen! (He uttered "fifteen" immediately after clenching his fist and moving his index finger.)
I : How did you do that?
T : I count.
I : Tell me what you counted.
T : (Sequentially puts up fingers while synchronously uttering) "1-2-3- . . . -15".

Tarus's slight finger movements to complete a finger pattern for "six" is an especially strong indication that he had curtailed the motor component of counting activity because he reenacted counting by putting up fingers synchronously with uttering number words.

2.16. There are various reasons why we do not infer that Tarus had reorganized his counting scheme. Tarus started counting from "one" in the protocol above and in a preceding task that involved hidden collections of nine and eight marbles. Then, as he solved the preceding task, Tarus sat silently for sixteen seconds before uttering "seventeen". He completed a finger pattern for "eight", again by only slightly moving his fingers. Finally, he used the abbreviated motor activity to complete a finger pattern when making an intuitive extension.

2.17. By itself, the observation that Tarus always started to count from "one" would not be sufficient to rule out a possible reorganization of his counting scheme. The crucial question is whether Tarus intended to keep track of how many times he was going to count prior to making an extension in counting. Because there is no indication of such an intention in 2.15, we turn to other task solutions. We first seek an indication of whether Tarus was aware of how he counted to solve addition situations.

Lack of Awareness

2.18. Although Tarus was able to reenact his solution in the protocol of 2.l5 when questioned, other solutions indicate that he was not aware of exactly how he had counted.

T : (When finding how many marbles were hidden under two cloths, one hiding seven and one four, Tarus looks to his left for four seconds and then shifts his gaze to the right for three seconds, his left corresponding to the seven and his right to the four) Eleven!
I : That's correct. Can you explain it?
T : (No response.)
I : Did you count?
T : (Shakes his head "yes".)
I : What did you say when you counted?
T : Ten.
I : Where did you start counting? Did you start from one or did you start somewhere else?
T : (No response.)

We assume that Tarus did count. It seems plausible that he uttered "1-2-3-. . . -7" when he looked to his left and "8-9-l0-11" when he looked to his right. Regardless of how he counted, he did not provide any indication that he was aware of starting with "one". This lack of awareness is a second reason why we reject the hypothesis of a reorganization of his counting scheme.

Lack of Anticipation of Counting

2.19. The quality of Tarus's solutions to our missing addend situations constitutes the major reason we believe he did not reorganize his counting scheme. We presented several such situations in an attempt to find one that Tarus could solve; however, he simply guessed.

2.20. In a search for a problem situation in which he would count, we next presented two tasks involving a collection separated into a visible and a hidden portion, where Tarus was told how many blocks were hidden. In both cases, Tarus first counted the visible blocks, continued by sequentially putting up fingers, and then answered appropriately. Next, we presented the task described in the following protocol.

I : (The interviewer uncovers seven blocks) How many have you there?
T : (Counts the blocks) Seven.
I : (Covers the seven blocks and places some more with them) Now we have eleven. How many more did I put under there?
T : Two more.
I : No. There are eleven altogether now. There were seven before. How many extra ones did I put under there?
T : (Sits up straight when the interviewer uttered "eleven", indicating that "eleven" had become significant. After a 20-second pause) Four!
I : How did you do that?
T : I count!
I : How did you count?
T : I go "1-2-3-4-5-6-7 (rapidly)--8--9--10--11".
I : Did you use your fingers?
T : No.

At this point, exactly why he counted was unknown. It seems that there were two crucial conditions: first, he actually counted the seven blocks before they were hidden, and second, the extra blocks were hidden under the same cloth, so that when the interviewer said "there are eleven altogether now", "eleven" may have led to a realization that he was to *complete* the activity of counting eleven blocks. His explanation confirms this because he rapidly uttered "1-2-3-4-5-6-7", indicating that this was a reenactment of an immediate past experience. The separation of this counting activity from its continuation is also quite significant. It is taken as an indication that he was aware he had to complete the activity of counting all the blocks. We speculate that it was this awareness that finally led him to count.

2.21. The solutions to the next two tasks show how important it was that he had counted the initial collection before it was covered. In the first task, he counted 11 blocks before they were covered. Extra blocks were added and he was told that there were l6 covered. It took him l7 seconds to respond "five". He said that he counted and reenacted his solution "1-2- . . . -17", but without a pause. Nevertheless, this is a solid indication that he recognized a spatio-temporal pattern for "five", which was important to his solution. When he solved the second task, he did not count the initial twelve blocks of a collection of 17, and guessed "ten". It was not sufficient that "seventeen" referred to one collection. For "twelve" and "seventeen" to refer to number word sequences, there had to be an utterance of a number word sequence in his immediate experience. He could then reenact this sequence by uttering number words, say, to "twelve" and then continue to "seventeen".

2.22. Tarus's capacity to reenact and complete number word sequences is similar to that attributed to Brenda when she solved subtraction tasks (cf. Brenda, 1.18 and 1.19) during her verbal period.

2.23. We emphasize that Tarus did not independently count to solve our missing addend situations. Even when he did count part of a collection, had it not been for the interventions of the teacher, Tarus would not have solved the situation. Because of the contextual nature of these solutions, we do not claim that Tarus made a general reorganization of his counting scheme. Rather, he seems to have made a contextual modification. He could not separate, in his thoughts, the activity of counting the two subcollections before he counted the first; it was only after he reenacted counting the first subcollection that he separated his activity. Also, Tarus did not appear to anticipate that he could complete a specific pattern to find how many blocks had been added. Recognition of the pattern was fortuitous and occurred only after he had completed counting.

22 April 1982 Teaching Episode

Counting-on

2.24. Tarus eventually became able to substitute a re-presentation of counting for the activity itself. This is indicated by his behavior in the following protocol.

I : Pretend you put fifteen Hershey bars in a basket. But we want more candy bars than that! So, I will put three Baby Ruth candy bars in there. How many are in there?
T : (After three seconds) Eighteen! (No overt signs of counting.)

We assume that Tarus silently uttered "16-17-18". In a preceding task corresponding to "7 + 3", Tarus was led to count "7--8-9-10". These two solutions show that Tarus could curtail the activity of uttering the first of the two number word sequences.

Local Anticipations of Counting Backward

2.25. Tarus counted backward to solve subtraction situations only in very specific contexts.

I : (Places a container in front of Tarus) This time you put eight Snickers bars in the basket.
T : (Enacts placing candy bars in the container in one bunch.)
I : You take two out.
T : (Enacts taking two out, one at a time) 1-2.
I : How many are left in there?
T : Um, seven--six!

Following this, Tarus acted out putting 12 candy bars in and then pretended to take 3 out, one at a time, responding "nine". But when he acted out putting 12 in and taking 6 out, he guessed "five" and never counted backward. The first two solutions show that the action patterns of two or three physical acts led him to utter number words backward. Uttering "seven--six" was a reenactment of the physical acts of taking two candy bars out of the basket. He did not utter number words backward on the last task because he did not recognize his six acts as a pattern. Generally, he did not display anticipation of counting backward.

Discussion of Tarus's Case Study

There were behavioral indications that Tarus's utterances of number words carried the significance of a curtailed production of motor unit items. The observation that he sometimes slightly moved his index finger as he subvocally uttered number words was particularly significant in this respect (cf. 2.15). Moreover, his reenactments of counting involved sequentially putting up fingers while synchronously uttering number words. There is no reason to believe, however, that the emergence of the verbal unit involved substituting a re-presentation of counting activity for the actual performance of that activity.

Instead, it would seem that verbal unit items emerged when Tarus re-presented the records of counting perceptual unit items in his immediate past experience by uttering number words (cf. 2.20). This reflective abstraction involved stripping away the production of countable items and their coordination with number words--a level 2 abstraction--and allowed Tarus to produce highly contextual solutions to missing addend tasks (cf. 2.20). His inability to run through the solution in thought before actually carrying it out is a strong indication that he had not reorganized his counting scheme.

He made another level 2 abstraction in the 22 April 1981 teaching episode, when he substituted a re-presentation of counting for actual counting activity and counted-on (cf. 2.24). In the same teaching episode, his attempts to solve a carefully sequenced series of subtraction situations indicate that he could not make level 3 abstractions. He could utter number words backward to reenact action patterns, but when it was necessary that he reflect on what he was going to do before carrying out counting activity, he resorted to guessing.

3. JAMES

25 January 1982 Teaching Episode

<u>Counting Verbal Unit Items</u>

3.16. In earlier teaching episodes, James curtailed the motor component of counting--pointing acts--when he counted the first of two collections of hidden items that he thought were arranged in patterns (cf. 3.11). We did not take this contextual advancement as an indication that he had counted verbal unit items, because it was limited to the situations in which we made the observation. In other, more complex situations, he resorted to counting his motor acts as much as 8 months later (cf. 3.14). In this teaching episode, James curtailed the motor component of counting--pointing acts--when he counted the first of two collections of hidden items. This is a more solid indication that James was entering a new period in counting.

T : (Places checkers under two cloths) OK, James, I have fifteen here (touching one cloth) and five here (touching the other cloth). How many altogether?

J : (Shuts his eyes and whispers number words) 1-2-3-4-5- . . . -15. How many you got here (pointing to the cloth covering five)?

T : Five.

J : (Touches the table where the points of contact form a domino five pattern) 1-2-3-4-5. (Slaps the cloth covering the fifteen) Fifteen right here. (Subvocally utters, tapping the table in synchrony with the first two utterances) 1-2-3-4-5-6-7-8-9-10-11-12-13-14-15. (Pauses, and then touches the table where the points of contact form a domino five pattern while subvocally uttering) 16-17-18-19-20. Twenty.

After he had counted to "five", James reenacted his prior counting activity, first recounting the collection of 15, then continuing as he counted the collection of five. But he still needed to start counting at "one". "Fifteen" was not an index of the number word sequence "1-2-. . . - 15"--that is, he could not substitute a re-presentation of counting to "fifteen" for the actual counting activity.

3.17. On the very next task, where collections of 19 and 5 were hidden, James shut his eyes and subvocally uttered "1-2-3- . . . -19", paused, and then continued, deliberately uttering "20-21-22-23-24". He did not perform motor acts as he made the intuitive extension.

2 March 1982 Teaching Episode

Construction of Counting-On

3.18. The teacher made a concerted attempt to help James count-on. James was asked to write numerals in a sequence of circles, each numeral three beyond the preceding one.

T : (Points to the initial numeral in the sequence) Three and three more.

J : (Simultaneously extends three fingers on his left hand) Three. (And then three more on his right hand) Three more. (Immediately) Six.

T : Six. Right.

J : (Writes "6" in the second circle, puts up five fingers on one hand and the index finger on his other hand) Six. (Puts up three more fingers sequentially) Nine! (Writes "9" in the third circle.)

J : N-i-n-e. (Puts up nine fingers. He then puts up the one left and sits quietly. He finally utters), ten!

T : Put nine fingers up. Put those fingers in your head!

J : (Simultaneously puts up nine fingers) N-i-n-e. (Closes his eyes and presses all nine fingers on his forehead) Nine--(sequentially puts up two fingers) 10, 11.

T : I said three more!

J : Twelve! (Writes "12" in the fourth circle. He then presses his open hands on his forehead) T-w-e-l-v-e (sequentially puts up three fingers in synchrony with subvocal utterances), fifteen!

J : (Presses one hand on his forehead) F-i-f-t-e-e-n. (Sequentially puts up three fingers) 16-17-18--19-- (Shakes his head "no") Eight (Writes "18".).

J : (Continues in this manner until reaching "27".)

The major accommodation that James made in his counting scheme was to take a number word as signifying a plurality of figural items--re-presented fingers. This is indicated by the manner in which he pressed his fingers to his forehead after he had closed his eyes. In other words, he substituted the re-presented perceptual result of counting--a counted collection of fingers--for counting activity.

31 May 1982 Teaching Episode

Counting in Our Missing Addend Situations

3.19. James's most sophisticated solutions to our missing addend situations occurred in this teaching episode. His solutions were a direct consequence of his capacity to re-present an already completed counting activity.

T : (Presents the sentence "32 + ___ = 43") Put thirty-two in your head and count (after James had guessed "three more").
J : (Places his hand on his forehead) Thirty-two. (Sequentially puts up all 10 fingers, putting up two simultaneously on two different occasions) 33-34-35-36-37-38-39-40 (nods his head as if scanning a row of three dots), 41-42-43. (Sits quietly as if he is done).
T : How many?
J : (Puts up all 10 fingers and moves his head as if scanning a row) Thirteen.

James originally intended to count until he reached "43" and had to be directed to recount to find out how many counting acts he had performed. His ability to do so indicates that he could re-present the result of his prior counting activity. He apparently counted "10--11,12,13", completing a pattern for "three" beyond a finger pattern for "ten". (Remember that we are investigating conceptual processes and not teaching arithmetic; "wrong" results are often far more illuminating for us than "correctly" solved problems.)

3.20. James's advancements and limitations are captured in the following protocol. This was his most sophisticated observed solution.

T : (Pushes a transparent container toward James) You put in thirty Snickers bars.
J : (Pretends to place candy bars into the container.)
T : Now, I am going to put some more in there (enacts putting candy bars into the container). I am going to count them all

(enacts counting the Snickers bars). Do you know how many are in there? Forty-six! You put in thirty and I put in some more. Now there are forty-six. You figure out how many more I put in.

J : Thirty (sequentially puts up fingers), 31-32- . . . -40 (nods his head as if scanning a row of dots), 41-42-43-44-45-46. Five more!

T : How many?

J : (Puts up all ten fingers) Forty, (Closes his hands and sequentially puts fingers) 41-42-43-44-45-46. Six more!

T : What about those others you counted?

J : (Puts up all ten fingers and again nods his head as if scanning a row) 40-41-42-43-44-45-46. Forty-six.

T : How many more?

J : Sixteen!

James arrived at his last answer, "sixteen", after he had put up all 10 fingers and re-presented six fingers. However, we do not claim that James had generally reorganized counting because he never anticipated that he could keep track of how many counting acts he would perform before he counted. He never seemed to reflect on his counting activity before he carried it out.

Discussion of James's Case Study

James initially created verbal unit items when he counted the first of two hidden collections. He was yet to substitute a re-presentation of counting for actual counting. Reenactments of counting collections and counting patterns seemed to be major sources for the curtailment of pointing acts.

James did not count-on for more than a month after he was first observed counting verbal unit items. This was the case even though he was taught twice a week in one-half-hour sessions and was given repeated opportunities to curtail counting activity. In these sessions, we varied what was to us the first or second addend while holding the other constant in repeated tasks. These attempts only led to momentary curtailments of the count of the first collection. We finally asked James to repeatedly count three more, starting at "three" (cf. 3.23). Upon reaching "nine and three more", he experienced difficulty because he ran out of fingers. As a consequence, he did not have to count his fingers a second time; "n-i-n-e" referred to the perceptual result of counting, enabling him to continue to count. In this case, counting-on did not constitute a reorganization of his counting scheme because of its contextual nature and because of his substitution of a finger pattern for counting. In the case of his solution of missing addend tasks, however, a contextual reorganization of counting seemed to occur.

PERSPECTIVES ON THE CASE STUDIES

In Chapter II, we hypothesized that figural patterns might play a prominent role in the attainment of the motor period. Although that hypothesis was not corroborated in the way we expected, we have seen how both finger and spatial patterns contributed to the emergence of the figurative stage. These patterns embodied the result of counting--they were specified collections.

Patterns also played a role in the children's transition to the verbal period. James and Tarus used spatio-auditory patterns to keep track of counting activity when they made an intuitive extension and Brenda's sophisticated finger patterns provided her with items to count. We have seen that these patterns contributed to the spontaneous curtailment of motor activity in counting. A second primary source of the children's progress to the verbal period involved the reenactments of the activity of counting perceptual collections (e.g., 2.20).

The Verbal Period as a Subperiod in the Figurative Stage

Upon the emergence of the verbal unit items, the curtailment of actually producing countable items introduced a new period in the development of the counting scheme. The children could now simply utter number words to count the items of hidden or visible collections. They often focused inwardly on their utterances as they counted, indicating an awareness of a new role of number words in counting. The number words were signifiers of other countable items, and uttering a number word constituted an act of counting. Although the first three criteria for stages--the period criterion, the incorporation criterion, and the invariant sequence criterion, were all satisfied by the emergence of the verbal item, no reorganizations of counting were initially introduced. The children still started counting from "one" and made intuitive extensions if the second hidden part of a collection was associated with a number word that was, in turn, associated with a pattern for them.

The primary reason intuitive extension was considered to be a reorganization of the counting scheme in the motor period is that there was a change in the assimilating structures from perceptual collections to figural collections. This change was manifest in the way the children constructed intuitive extensions independently of the interventions of the teacher and, in some cases, even in spite of those interventions. There were no similar changes in the first part of the counting scheme when the children entered the verbal period.

Because we are able to explain the initial changes in the children's counting behavior without appealing to the appearance of new assimilating structures, we see no rationale for considering the early verbal periods of the children to be a stage apart from their motor periods. Nevertheless, re-presentation was a critical mechanism for constructing verbal unit items.

Counting-On

We found that the children initially learned to count-on beyond the re-presentation of a specified collection of fingers. Curtailment of the production of countable items made this possible, and we seriously considered that the appearance of counting-on might indicate a structural reorganization. Its nonspontaneous appearance, however, implies that the children had not constructed the operation of integration and no new assimilating structures were incorporated into the counting scheme.

Counting-on seemed to occur in situations that were familiar to the children. It was easy to pose problems in which the children should have counted-on to find a solution, had counting-on been indicative of the uniting operation of integration, but didn't. The contextual nature of counting-on was revealed in missing addend tasks. The children simply counted from one given number word to another without intending to find how many times they counted. Further, they did not seem to reflect on their completed counting activity and create a new result--the numerosity of the collection of counting acts. Instead, their intentions seemed to be to say number words until they reached one of the two given number words. At the time of the emergence of counting-on, a seemingly novel mechanism--substitution--appeared. The children substituted a pattern for counting activity. In retrospect, however, substitution had been "there" all along. Only its use was novel, not the mechanism. A similar change in the use of re-presentation served as a basis for the children's progress to their motor periods. In this case, the accommodation was that the children took the elements of re-presented patterns as countable. The material to which the unitizing operation was applied changed from perceptual to figural in quality. The adaptation that occurred with the emergence of counting-on was to substitute a composite whole--a pattern--for an activity rather than for another composite whole. This was possible because the pattern embodied the activity and so the activity could be abstracted from the patterns in the form of a number word sequence.

Initially, counting-on was the result of the children substituting a finger pattern for counting, a level 2 abstraction. Eventually, when the children substituted a re-presentation of counting for the activity--when a number word became an index for its associated number word sequence--a reorganization of the counting scheme occurred because a new assimilating structure appeared--a number word sequence. Interestingly, this reorganization was introduced by the children independently of our interventions.

We consider the children's ability to count-on as the beginning of a subperiod of the verbal period, but we do not take it as a marker for a new stage. However, if it is inferred that a child substitutes a re-presentation of counting for the activity, the inference that the child reorganized his or her counting scheme is justified, although this advance is made possible by a level 2 reflective abstraction. The apparent lack of generative power that would be expected of a child in the abstract stage, however, prohibited us from making the inference that any of the three children had attained this stage.

Chapter IV

The Construction of Abstract Unit Items

Tyrone, Scenetra, and Jason

Leslie P. Steffe Paul Cobb

We now turn to the three children who entered the teaching experiment as counters of motor unit items: Tyrone, Scenetra, and Jason. These three children had already reached the figurative stage of their counting scheme at the beginning of the teaching experiment, in that they could count their motor acts as substitutes for countable perceptual or figural items. One of our primary interests at the outset was to study the assimilatory structures of their counting schemes. Although we do not make unwarranted historical extrapolations, if patterns were a prominent feature of the children's counting activity, we would hypothesize that the patterns had played a role in their development of the figurative stage. This hypothesis would be plausible because of the role patterns played in Brenda's, Tarus's, and James's development.

A second major interest was to study the periods in the development of the three children's counting schemes. One of our original hypotheses (Steffe et al., 1983), that the figurative and verbal periods would be transitional periods and the perceptual, motor, and abstract periods would be major periods, was not confirmed by the case studies of Brenda, Tarus, and James. Further investigation of this hypothesis was warranted because there was no a priori reason to expect that the developmental itineraries of Tyrone, Scenetra, and Jason would replicate those of Brenda, Tarus, and James. We did hypothesize that there would be structural similarities in the ways that Tyrone, Scenetra, and Jason made progress. Although those similarities could not be specified in advance, we did speculate that the periods observed would emerge in an invariant sequence on the basis of certain adaptations we expected in the assimilatory structures of the counting scheme.

We hypothesized that the assimilatory structures of the counting scheme would change to include the uniting operation of integration. Toward the goal of testing this hypothesis, we investigated any observed reorganizations of counting in an attempt to infer the level of reflective abstraction that seemed to be involved. If a level 3 reflective abstraction could be inferred, we studied the occasion to ascertain if it was necessary to posit a constructive mechanism other than re-presentation and substitution--namely, new ways of operating. The need to introduce a novel constructive mechanism would be especially compelling if reorganizations of the counting scheme occurred in the context of patterns and went beyond the reorganizations of Brenda, Tarus, and James.

The stage shifts that we observed for Brenda, Tarus, and James were based on re-presentation and substitution in the context of patterns. If the reorganizations that we observed for Tyrone, Scenetra, and Jason occurred in the context of specified collections whose elements did not co-occur in patterns for the children, we would be inclined to appeal to reflection on the results of a re-presentation as an explanatory constructive mechanism. However, conscious reflection requires an object to reflect on, so reflection alone would not circumvent the necessity of analyzing the involved objects any more than it did in the context of patterns. For example, if the children reflected on potential counting activity and separated it into two or more parts, it seemed to us it would be necessary to posit the conceptual uniting operation of integration as an explanatory construct to account for the conceptual separation. In this case, counting would be numerical in quality and we would speak of making numerical rather than making intuitive extensions.

The most clear-cut case of making a numerical extension is when a child double counts, say, three more than 5--"6 is 1; 7 is 2; 8 is 3". Here, the child intends to count how many counting acts he or she performs before making the extension. In some cases, however, the child might not actually double count, but instead record (or tally) each counting act by, say, putting up a finger. The child ends up with a recognizable pattern, or else spontaneously counts the records after completing the counting acts. In this case, there can be a conflation between numerical and intuitive extensions. The crucial aspect in distinguishing between a numerical extension and an intuitive extension is the reflective awareness of the child as he or she carries out counting activity. If there is a reason to believe that the child intended to find how many counting acts he or she was going to perform and was aware of making records while making them, the extension would be considered numerical. Otherwise, it would be intuitive.

We now present protocols of the three children who were initially counters of motor unit items to document some of their progressive adaptations. In particular, we document the emergence of counting abstract unit items and the possible changes in the assimilatory structures of the counting scheme that made this emergence possible. Second, we document any reorganization of the counting scheme, regardless of when it might have occurred. Finally, we relate the analysis to the levels of reflective abstraction.

4. TYRONE

The periods that we observed for Tyrone were a motor period (2 months) and an abstract period (17 months). He was classified as being a counter of motor unit items on the basis of his performance in interviews held on 15 October 1980. He was still in the motor period in early December 1980, but was observed counting verbal unit items in a teaching episode held on 15 December 1980. He completely reorganized his counting scheme over the Christmas holidays. In the teaching episodes held on 22 January 1981 (our first observation of Tyrone after 15 December 1980), he spontaneously counted backward to solve our subtraction situations. It was clear that Tyrone had entered a new period.

The Motor Period

15 October 1980 Interview

<u>Counting Motor Unit Items</u>

4.01. The counting episodes that we used to classify Tyrone as a counter of motor unit items were somewhat ambiguous because it was difficult to decide whether he was counting figural items or whether he substituted pointing acts for the figural items and counted those pointing acts. Our interpretation turned on his reflective awareness while counting. We inferred that Tyrone first counted figural items and then isolated his pointing acts (motor items) as substitutes for hidden perceptual items in a continuation of counting figural items. In the continuation of counting, he did not put up fingers to establish finger patterns but continued counting until he completed a linear spatial pattern.

I : (Places a card covered by two cloths in front of Tyrone) There's eight here (touches one of the cloths) and three here (touches the other cloth).

Ty : 1-2- . . . -8 (looks at and synchronously touches the first cloth) -9-10-11 (looks at and synchronously touches the second cloth, his points of contact forming a linear pattern)--11.

Tyrone's activity of looking at and touching the first cloth in distinct locations each time he performed a counting act indicates that he intended to count the screened items. He seemed to be aware of the squares of a hidden collection and counted to specify this collection. But because he looked intently at the cloth that covered perceptual items as if trying to see through it, we believe that he counted figural items.

4.02. Tyrone did not continue to count until he reached an edge of the second cloth, indicating that he did not attempt to fill the region bounded by it with imaginary squares. Instead, he counted until he completed a linear spatial pattern for "three", which indicated that he focused on the motor component of his counting acts, the act of touching the cloth. Our interpretation is supported by his performance on two other tasks where he looked away from the cloths while he counted. This is important because it indicated that he was aware of and could monitor his pointing acts. We take his pointing acts as substitutes for the screened items in the latter two tasks. These solutions also indicate that Tyrone had coordinated linear spatial patterns with his counting scheme.

Lack of Level 3 Abstraction

4.03. Tyrone did experience difficulty when he attempted to count to solve certain tasks. On one occasion he was asked to find out how many squares were covered by one cloth, given that seven were under another cloth and there were ten in all. Initially, Tyrone answered "five". The interviewer then asked Tyrone to count and he did so, counting to "seven" over the appropriate cloth and then continuing until he completed a linear spatial pattern for "five" over the second cloth. The remainder of Tyrone's solution is presented in protocol form.

I : How many in all on the card?
Ty : Ten.
I : Ten. So, start over again.
Ty : 1-2- . . . -7 (sequentially touches the cloth covering the seven visible squares), -8-9-10 (synchronously touches the other cloth, his points of contact forming a linear pattern)--11 (places his hand on the cloth) -12 (taps the cloth with a finger).
I : How many under there?
Ty : . . . Six.

Tyrone did not anticipate that he could find out how many squares were screened by keeping track of how many times he counted. He did not "run through" counting prior to counting, but instead complied with the interviewer's directives ("So, start over again") and counted the collection of ten squares under both cloths. When he reached "ten", he hesitated before continuing "11-12". He seemed to know that he had counted all ten squares, but he did not know how many were covered, even though he was capable of recognizing a linear spatial pattern for "three". This indicates that he did not review his completed counting activity and maintain the experiential separation he made between counting over the first and second cloths. His failure to do so further indicates that he did not take the two collections hidden by the cloths as material for integrations before counting. Had he done so, their separated results could have served as a guide for his experiential separation. However, the experiential separation occurred as he made the transition from one cloth to the other and seemed to be completely outside of his awareness.

15 December 1980 Teaching Episode

Curtailing the Motor Component of Counting

4.04. Tyrone was sensitive to the teacher's directives and made accommodations in counting that required level 2 abstractions. The teacher presented a sequence of tasks by pointing to two distinct locations on a felt board and telling Tyrone how many imaginary items there were at each location. He was asked to find out how many imaginary items there were in all. He solved the first three tasks by sequentially touching the board in the appropriate location as he counted. He hesitated after the teacher had presented the fourth task (eight and six imaginary items), so the teacher told him that he did not have to point if he did not want to. Tyrone looked away from the board and uttered "1-2-. . . -8--9-10-11-12-13", presumably stopping when he thought he had completed a pattern for "six". Tyrone also counted without pointing to solve the remaining two tasks presented. These solutions are significant in that they indicate that Tyrone could now substitute his vocal productions for the imaginary items. This major accommodation of his counting scheme involved curtailing the coordination of pointing acts with the utterance of number words.

Flexibility of Linear Patterns

4.05. A second notable feature of Tyrone's performance in this session was the apparent flexibility of the patterns he completed as he counted. For example, one pattern he completed for "five" was a linear spatial pattern of three pointing acts followed by two pointing acts. Tyrone produced this pattern when he solved a task early in the session. However, he also produced two utterances followed by three utterances when solving a later task. A marked pause after he had produced the first two of these utterances indicated that two utterances followed by three utterances was not his standard "five" pattern, suggesting that he had inadvertently produced two rather than three utterances. However, instead of re-counting, he reflected on his utterances and seemed to realize what he needed to do to complete a pattern for "five". This spontaneous modification of a linear pattern was an indication that Tyrone could reflect on and reorganize his activity of producing a pattern while he solved a task. Tyrone's reflective awareness was beyond anything we observed in the cases of Brenda, Tarus, or James while they were in their motor periods. In retrospect, it was a harbinger of Tyrone's entry into the abstract stage.

<u>Failure of a Counting Act to Serve Two Functions</u>

4.06. In presenting a task involving imaginary items, the interviewer told Tyrone that there were six imaginary items at one location, some more at a second location, and that there were seven in all. Tyrone was asked to find out how many there were at the second location. Tyrone answered "seven". He knew that "seven" was the immediate successor of "six", but did not realize that the corresponding counting act could serve as a count of the second (in this case, unitary) collection as well as the last act of a count of the collection of all the imaginary items. This indicates that a counting act did not serve two functions for him. He made sense of the task by inferring that the interviewer had meant to say that there were seven items at the second location. This is an indication of a lack of level 3 abstraction.

The Abstract Period

22 January 1981 Teaching Episode

<u>Reorganization of the Counting Scheme</u>

4.07. Tyrone demonstrated that he could modify his counting scheme to solve missing addend tasks in this teaching episode. We asked Tyrone to complete several arithmetical sentences. When the sentence "4 + ___ = 12" was presented, Tyrone sequentially put up five fingers on one hand and three on his other hand and wrote "8" in the blank. He also counted-on to solve our missing-addend story problems in this teaching episode. These independent solutions indicate that he anticipated finding how many counting acts he would perform before he started counting. He put up fingers while counting to create records of his counting acts. In contrast to Brenda, Tarus, and James (cf. 1.23, 2.20, and 3.19), Tyrone did not have to be prompted to find how many times he counted. Consequently, we interpret Tyrone's continuation of counting as a numerical rather than as an intuitive extension. His reorganization of counting involved a level 3 reflective abstraction because he could "run through" or anticipate the results of counting before actually carrying it out.

Forming Composite Units

4.08. Tyrone also counted backward to solve our subtraction situations. For example, he paused for several seconds and then wrote "8" as his answer to "12 - 4 = ___". He explained his solution as follows:

Ty : Twelve take away four. . . I counted backwards four to eight.
I : From where, from where did you count?
Ty : 12-11-10-9 equals four.

The statements "I counted backwards four to eight" and "12-11-10-9 equals four" are prime indications that Tyrone could make integrations. The statements also indicate that Tyrone was aware of how he was going to count before counting, a prime indication of a level 3 abstraction. We infer that Tyrone re-presented counting backward before counting and that the involved number words referred to composite units.

Separating Counting Activity into two Composite Units

4.09. In the protocol of 4.08, we infer that Tyrone actually segmented the contents of the composite unit to which "twelve" referred into two separate composite units. His solution of the following protocol contains a more dramatic instance.

T : Suppose you have thirteen marbles and I take seven of them away?
Ty : Seven.
T : How can you tell for sure? Suppose you can't remember. How could you find out?
Ty : (Sequentially puts up seven fingers) Six.
T : . . . Do it aloud so we can hear your words.
Ty : I had thirteen and I went 13-12-11-10-9-8-7 (in synchrony with putting up fingers).

Tyrone's initial answer "seven" did not seem to be just a guess. It was a response that he believed was plausible. His eventual method of solution--counting backward--was not suggested to him. Because of this spontaneity, we infer that "thirteen" denoted the backward number word sequence "13-12-11-10-9-8-7-6-5-4-3-2-1". He actually separated this number word sequence into "13-12- . . . -7" and into "6"--which we infer denoted "6-5- . . . -1", the number word sequence he would utter if he continued to count. "Seven" seemed to refer to a finger pattern he used to keep track of uttering "13-12- . . . -7". He seemed to understand the difference between counting backward seven times (which he did in his justification) and how many more times he would count if he were to continue (which was his answer, "six").

11 February 1981 Teaching Episode

Counting Already Counted Unit Items

4.10. There is a subtle, yet important, difference between the ways in which Tyrone and James (cf. 3.19) solved our missing addend tasks where the missing addend was greater than ten.

T : (Covers 14 of 20 squares with a cloth) This time, there are twenty altogether.

Ty : 1-2- . . . -6 (in synchrony with touching the visible squares). 7-8-9- . . . -20 (in synchrony with putting up fingers. After putting up all ten fingers, he closes his hands and sequentially puts up four fingers of his right hand for a second time. He then touches his lips with each of his four extended fingers) Fourteen under there.

When James attempted to solve a similar task with 16 as the missing addend, he focused on the immediate perceptual result and said, "Six more"! In contrast, Tyrone counted-on to find how many counting acts he had performed. The manner in which he independently counted the fingers that he had put up to record his counting acts beyond "seven" indicates a constructive mechanism other than re-presentation and substitution. We infer that he took the records of counting acts as material of an integration and counted further to specify its numerosity.

Double Function of Counting Acts

4.11. In 4.10, Tyrone separated his counting activity into two parts--counting to "six" and continuing to count to "twenty". Each counting act beyond "six" served two functions. First, it was one of the counting acts of counting to "twenty" and, second, it was one of the counting acts of counting the hidden collection. Although he did not explicitly double count--e.g., "seven is one"--the act of putting up a finger and uttering "seven" implicitly served two functions because he spontaneously counted the records of these acts. The awareness of what he was doing while he was doing it is a strong indication of level 3 abstraction and confirms that Tyrone could construct abstract units from sensory-motor units.

Discussion of Tyrone's Case Study

Based upon our observation of Tyrone in the 15 October 1980 interview (cf. 4.01-4.03), it is plausible to argue that the isolation of motor acts as countable items occurred in the context of re-presented patterns. Tyrone at first seemed to be aware of the hidden squares, and his pointing acts were carried out to locate a place where a square might be hidden. He became aware of his motor acts when he attempted to keep track of his counting acts in a continuation of counting. However, linear spatial patterns rather than finger patterns were the source of his progress.

A dramatic reorganization of Tyrone's counting scheme occurred over the Christmas holidays. Before the Christmas holidays, we had not observed him counting-on or solving missing addend tasks in that or any other way. Nevertheless, our observations of Tyrone's problem solutions during the 15 December 1980 teaching episode strongly indicated that reorganizations were under way. He had curtailed the production of countable items and counted to solve tasks by uttering number words. Taken alone, this indicated a level 2 abstraction; but coupled with his modification of producing a linear spatial five pattern (cf. 4.05), it could be interpreted as a level 3 abstraction. That is, we attribute to Tyrone the ability to reflect on a re-presented linear pattern. Certainly the manner in which Tyrone paused after producing the two number words and modified his subsequent activity indicates that he could substitute a re-presentation of a linear spatial pattern for counting activity and could compare the pattern formed by his two completed counting acts with that linear pattern.

We infer that Tyrone's ability to reflect on the re-presented five pattern was possible because he applied the uniting operation of integration to the pattern. The attribution of a uniting operation to Tyrone in this isolated case is plausible because he could hold the five pattern "at a distance" and choose his own ways of operating. Such reflection indicates number (Davydov & Andronov, 1981, pp. 17-18).

Tyrone reorganized his counting scheme independently of our and his classroom teacher's interventions. When we next taught him on 22 January 1981, Tyrone appeared to be a totally different child with regard to his solutions of arithmetical tasks. His counting scheme was now numerical rather than figurative in quality and he repeatedly made level 3 abstractions. He could now anticipate finding how many counting acts he was going to perform when he solved our missing addend tasks by counting-on (cf. 4.07) and subtraction tasks by counting-off-from (cf. 4.08). Moreover, he exemplified awareness of reversibility of counting (Steffe, Cobb, & Richards, 1983, p. 103). He realized that the counting acts he could carry out if he were to count backward, "8-7-6-5-4-3-2-1", would be the self-same counting acts that he would carry out if he were to count forward from "one" to "eight" (cf. 4.08 and 4.09 for substantiation).

5. SCENETRA

The three periods that we observed for Scenetra were a motor period (3 months), a verbal period (2 months), and an abstract period (14 months). She was classified as a counter of motor unit items on the basis of her performance in the interviews held on 16 October 1980. She had entered her verbal period by 20 January 1981 and her abstract period by 9 March 1981. She had also completed a reorganization of her counting scheme by the latter date and spontaneously counted-on to solve a missing addend task.

The Motor Period

16 October 1980 Interviews

Counting Motor Unit Items

5.01. Finger patterns were a prominent feature of the counting episodes that we used to classify Scenetra as a counter of motor unit items. Initially, it was difficult to decide whether Scenetra was counting her fingers as perceptual unit items or her motor acts of putting up fingers or folding down fingers. However, several solutions indicated that she had isolated the motor act of putting up fingers. In one task, for example, seven squares were visible and eight were hidden by a cloth. The interviewer did not tell Scenetra how many visible squares there were, but did tell her that eight were hidden.

> S : 1-2- . . . -8 (sequentially puts up five fingers on her left hand and three on her right hand, touching each finger as she puts it up. She pauses and then counts the visible squares. She then continues by sequentially touching two fingers on her right hand and all five fingers on her left hand for a second time) Fifteen.

Scenetra's pause to count the visible squares indicates that she intended to count the hidden squares and that her fingers were substitutes for them. She pointed to each finger as she put it up, indicating that she intended to count her fingers as substitutes. Scenetra's double use of fingers when counting seven times beyond eight, however, indicated that the motor acts of putting up fingers were salient. Had she simply been counting her fingers as perceptual items, upon reaching "ten" she would have had nothing left to count and, hence, would have stopped there.

Lack of Level 3 Abstraction

5.02. In another task, two of five squares were covered by a cloth and Scenetra was asked to find how many squares were covered. Initially, Scenetra did not attempt to solve the task. The interviewer intervened and she eventually counted "1-2-3" while pointing at the visible squares and then continued "4-5" while synchronously moving a finger. Because she did not know how many squares were covered, the interviewer asked her to count again. She sequentially put up fingers while counting "1-2- . . . -5" and then said four were covered. Because Scenetra did not independently count in her attempt to solve the task, we infer she could not "run through" counting activity in re-presentation. When she counted, her intention seemed to be to count the single collection of five squares, because she did not separate her activity into counts of two collections. A counting act seemed to serve only one function for her.

The Verbal Period

20 January 1981 Teaching Episode

Counting Verbal Unit Items

5.03. Scenetra curtailed the motor acts that accompanied her number word utterances in this teaching episode.

T : (Covers 7 of a collection of 11 squares with a cloth) Scenetra, I have some squares here (points to the visible squares). How many?
S : Four.
T : And I have seven under here.
S : (Utters) 4--5--6-7-8-9--10-11--12.

Scenetra uttered number words beyond a spatial pattern for "four", indicating that she counted verbal unit items. She organized these utterances into a pattern for "seven", which seemed to be a composition of a four pattern, a two pattern, and a singleton, even though she made an error in completing the pattern. "Seven" referred to a sequential pattern--to a spatio-auditory pattern.

Solving Missing Addend Tasks Using Finger Patterns

5.04. Given that Scenetra had entered her verbal period, we used missing addend tasks to explore the possibility that she could reorganize her counting scheme. She could use finger patterns to solve our missing addend tasks whenever ten or fewer perceptual items were involved (cf. Brenda, 1.26).

T : (Covers six of a collection of ten squares with a cloth) How many do we have there? (Points to the visible squares.)
S : (Without counting) Four.
T : How many do you think we have altogether (waves his hand over the visible and covered squares)?
S : I don't know.
T : I'll tell you, ten.
S : Ten under there (points to the cloth)?
T : No, there are four there (points to the visible squares) and there are ten altogether (waves his hand over the visible and covered squares). Here are four of the ten (points to the visible squares), so how many are under here (points to the cloth)?
S : (Simultaneously puts up all ten fingers and then simultaneously wiggles four fingers of her left hand) Six (recognizing the open right hand and the left thumb as a finger pattern for "six").

Scenetra's finger pattern for "ten" was a substitute for the squares because her partition of the pattern corresponded to the partition of the squares. She could reflect on her completed finger pattern, separate it into two parts, and substitute those parts for the perceptually separated parts of the collection of squares. This did not constitute a reorganization of her counting scheme. Rather, it represents new possibilities for using her finger patterns and seemed to be the result of a level 3 abstraction.

Separating Counting Activity

5.05. In the next task, the interviewer covered 5 of 11 squares with a cloth. Initially, Scenetra said she could not solve the task because she did not have enough fingers.

T : Can you think of another way to do it?
S : I think I know a way.
T : You have another way?

S : 1-2- . . . -6 (synchronously points to each of the visible squares) -six. How many are under there (points to the cloth)?

T : There are eleven altogether (waves his hand over the visible and covered squares). You have to find how many are under here (points to the cloth). Six here (points to the visible squares) and eleven altogether (waves his hand over the visible and covered squares).

S : (Simultaneously puts up all ten fingers) Six-six. (Shakes both hands and closes her fingers) Six--7-8- . . . -11 (sequentially wiggles the extended fingers of her left hand), there's five under there.

T : How did you know that?

S : 'Cause I counted with my fingers.

T : What did you count? That was very good indeed.

S : I hold six in my head, I put six in my head, and then count-on five.

T : And what did you count to?

S : I count to eleven.

When Scenetra shook both hands and closed her fingers, we infer that she changed her way of operating. She could no longer use her finger patterns as perceptual collections that she could reflect on for the simple reason that she did not have 11 fingers. Instead, we infer she re-presented the six visible squares she had counted. The activity of counting all the squares could then be separated experientially into those she had counted and those she was yet to count. Consequently, she was able to complete the activity of counting to "eleven", which referred to all of the squares.

5.06. This solution indicates that Scenetra's counting scheme was more flexible now that she had entered her verbal period. Although the modifications she made were contextual, her solution was carried out with only minimal suggestion from the teacher. After she put up all ten fingers, she spontaneously changed her way of operating in a manner that strongly suggests the numerical operation of integration. As she could not re-present a pattern for "six", we infer the number word "six" she uttered when she began to count referred to a composite unit whose content was the counted squares--the material to which she applied the integration operation. This spontaneous curtailment is in stark contrast to the elaborate interventions the teacher had to make before James counted on. Even so, Scenetra did not appear to anticipate, prior to counting, that she could count her own counting acts.

26 January 1981 Teaching Episode

Contextual Records of Backward Counting Acts

5.07. A novelty appeared in Scenetra's counting scheme in this teaching episode. She intentionally recorded her counting acts when she counted backward over a cloth for a second time.

T : (Covers the first three of a row of nine squares with a cloth) There are some of them under here (runs his finger over the cloth). You can't see them. Altogether, there are nine (runs his finger over the covered and visible portions of the row). Can you count backward starting from here (points to the visible square at the end of the row to Scenetra's right)? There are nine altogether.
S : 9-8- . . . -4 (synchronously pointing to each visible square, moving to her left towards the cloth as she does so). (Looks at the interviewer.)
T : Can you count the other ones under the cloth?
S : 3-2-1-zero (synchronously touching the cloth, moving along the cloth away from the visible squares as she does so).
T : Very good. Do you know how many are under the cloth?
S : Two?
T : Count again and see if you can find out. Count backward, though.
S : 9-8- . . . -4 (synchronously pointing to each visible square, moving towards the cloth as she does so)--3 (touches the cloth) -3 (touches the cloth for a second time in the same location and wiggles an extended finger of her other hand) -2-1 (synchronously touching the cloth, each time wiggling an extended finger of her other hand; looks at the fingers she had just wiggled) three.

5.08. Scenetra intentionally wiggled her fingers to record her backward counting acts. However, she made these records only after she had already counted over the cloth once. She did not anticipate that she could record her counting acts before she counted for the first time.

5.09. Once Scenetra reached the cloth for the second time, she did reflect on her potential counting activity. This level 3 abstraction was highly contextual, in that her re-presentation was supported by a review of her first count over the cloth and would not have occurred without the teacher's interventions. Although this solution gives some indication of a possible source of the integration operation and suggests that she was making the transition to the abstract stage in counting, its contextual nature does not allow us to classify Scenetra as a counter of abstract unit items.

The Abstract Period

9 March 1981 Teaching Episode

<u>Reorganizations of the Counting Scheme</u>

5.10. For the first time, Scenetra spontaneously modified her counting scheme to solve our missing addend tasks. She solved the sentence "7 + ___ = 10" as follows:

S : 1-2- . . . -7 (sequentially touches five fingers of her left hand and two fingers of her right hand to her lips)--8-9-10 (sequentially touches three fingers of her left hand to her lips and then picks up the felt numeral "3").

She solved a subsequent sentence "8 + ___ = 12" by uttering "9-10-11-12", and then picked up the felt numeral "4". These independent and spontaneous solutions indicate that Scenetra could anticipate finding out how many counting acts she was going to perform before she started counting. She could reflect on a re-presentation of potential counting activity and separate it, in thought, into two parts; one corresponding to the first numeral of the sentence and the other to the counting acts she would perform to count to the other numeral.

<u>Forming Composite Units</u>

5.11. Scenetra's solution to the following task indicates that she could now take completed counting activity as material to which the integration operation could be applied.

T : (Makes the sentence "8 + ___ = 12" using felt numerals) What about that one?
S : One (touches her lips with the thumb of her left hand). Eight (simultaneously puts up all five fingers of her right hand and then looks at her hand for several seconds)-9-10-11-12 (sequentially touches her lips with four fingers of her right hand; picks up the numeral "4").

There is no indication that Scenetra actually counted to "eight". We infer that she at least intended to, because she uttered "one". These counting acts were left implicit in her solution. We infer that "eight" referred to a finger pattern that embodied these counting acts. Moreover, after completing her count to "twelve", Scenetra counted the fingers she had already counted, indicating that she formed the goal of specifying their numerosity. This is in contrast to Brenda (cf. 1.23) and James (3.19) when they were in their verbal periods. To explain the difference, we attribute the integration operation to Scenetra. That is, she applied the integration operation to the four fingers she counted "9-10-11-12".

15 April 1981 Teaching Episode

Segmenting Composite Units

5.12. Scenetra rarely counted backward to solve subtraction problems because she had constructed other, to her more familiar, schemes; but she did count backward on several occasions. The following protocol is one such instance.

T : What is nineteen take away four? Say out loud how you do it.
S : (Puts up the thumb of her right hand) N-i-n-e-t-e-e-n (puts up her index finger), e-i-g-h-t-e-e-n (puts up her middle finger), s-e-v-e-n-t-e-e-n (puts up her ring finger), sixteen (puts up her little finger and pauses)--five--fifteen!

Scenetra was very deliberate when she counted four backward and displayed obvious concentration on what she was doing, indicating reflection on counting backward. Her independent use of counting backward indicates that "nineteen" could denote the backward number word sequence that she segmented into "19-18-17-16" and into "15"--which denoted "15-14- . . . -2-1". "Four" referred to the numerosity of the composite unit she apparently made from "19-18-17-16".

5.13. The question of whether "fifteen" denoted a numerosity is not clear. "Fifteen" could refer to a number word sequence. If the integration operation was applied to that sequence, then the resulting composite unit would have a numerosity. There was no way of knowing if Scenetra made this integration.

5.14. Scenetra's awareness of what she was doing while she was doing it (cf. 5.12) is a prime indication that she had made a level 3 reflective abstraction; she could anticipate counting backward nineteen times. Moreover, a backward counting act served two functions. First, it was one of the counting acts of the sequence "19-18-17- . . . -2-1". Second, it was one of the four backward counting acts that she intended to perform, starting at "nineteen".

Discussion of Scenetra's Case Study

Based upon our observations in the 16 October 1980 interview (cf. 5.01-5.02), it is plausible to infer that Scenetra isolated the motor acts of putting up fingers as countable items in the context of re-presented finger patterns. However, her patterns were more varied than finger patterns (cf. 5.03) and included spatio-auditory patterns. Even so, there are indications in both Scenetra's (cf. 5.03) and Tyrone's (cf. 4.04) case studies of curtailment of motor activity on a par with the level 2 abstractions made by Brenda, Tarus, and James when they entered their verbal periods. However, Scenetra produced several novel modifications once she had entered her verbal period. These modifications indicate the emergence of the uniting operation of integration.

The first modification occurred when she solved a missing addend task by using her finger pattern scheme (cf. 5.05). She re-presented counting six visible squares and continued counting to eleven, thus making an intuitive extension. This adaptive behavior occurred when her usual ways of operating--using finger patterns--did not work because she did not have enough fingers. Her reflective attitude and her independent modification both indicate the uniting operation of integration. These were qualities that we did not observe in the cases of Brenda, Tarus, and James.

Six days later (cf. 5.07), Scenetra was asked to count a row of nine items backward to find how many of the row were screened from view (the first three). First, she counted the visible items backward, and then pointed to specific locations on the cloth as she uttered "3-2-1-0", but she did not know how many squares were covered. She was asked to try once again. After recounting the visible items backward, she introduced a novelty--double counting. She sequentially put up fingers of one hand while synchronously pointing to the cloth with her other hand as she uttered "3-2-1". She then answered "three". She intentionally coordinated two counting acts--putting up a finger as a record of pointing at the cloth--in order to find how many times she counted backward. The attribution of a unitizing operation to Scenetra is especially plausible because she counted her pointing acts.

When contrasted with Tyrone's fleeting verbal period, Scenetra's verbal period was quite long. Nevertheless, it was a transitional period to her abstract period. We emphasize that its transitional character is indicated by Scenetra's ability to apply the uniting operation in very specific experiential situations.

The major reason that Scenetra's verbal period was longer than Tyrone's seemed to be a lag in the application of the uniting operation of integration to the results of counting. She could make a composite unity as long as there was some sensory or figurative material available that she could take as a given and to which she could apply her uniting operation (e.g., a finger pattern). Making composite units whose constituent unit items only signify counting makes anticipatory solutions of missing addend tasks possible. Scenetra was unable to do this until she attained the abstract stage, 6 weeks later.

6. JASON

The three periods that we observed for Jason were a motor period (7 months), a fleeting verbal period, and an abstract period (12 months). He was classified as a counter of motor unit items on the basis of his performance in the interviews held on 18 October 1980. His motor period lasted at least until 11 May 1981. He then rapidly progressed to the abstract period, which he entered by 21 May 1981.

The Motor Period

18 October 1980 Interview

<u>Counting Motor Unit Items</u>

6.01. Jason used a pointing scheme to count partially hidden collections and a scheme that involved putting up fingers if all the items of a collection were hidden by two screens. Patterns were not a prominent feature of his two motor counting schemes. For example, given a collection of marbles, six visible and four covered by the interviewer's hand, he counted as follows:

> J : 1-2- . . . -6 (points to each visible marble in turn), -7-8 (wiggles the index and then the middle finger of his right hand over the interviewer's hand), -9-10 (again, wiggles the index and then the middle finger of his right hand over the interviewer's hand).

Clearly, Jason counted to specify the collection of marbles. His repetition of two pointing acts when he counted the covered marbles indicates that he used an action pattern for "two" to know when to stop counting. He completed two of these action patterns to make a pattern for "four". This observation is important because it indicated that he counted motor rather than figural unit items.

6.02. This was the most sophisticated action pattern Jason produced when he counted hidden perceptual items. On one occasion, he did produce a spatio-motor pattern for "four" after he had arranged four marbles into a square pattern before they were covered. But he did not substitute a spatial pattern for a hidden collection. Jason was yet to coordinate spatial patterns with the counting scheme that involved the motor acts of pointing (called his pointing scheme).

6.03. Jason used a different scheme if both collections were covered. For example, the interviewer held six marbles in one hand and five in his other hand and asked Jason to find how many he had in both of his hands.

J : 1-2- . . . -5 (sequentially puts up five fingers of his left hand), -6 (closes and then puts up the thumb of his left hand), -7-8 (puts up two fingers of his right hand).

Jason's double use of a finger when he counted to "six" indicated that he was counting the acts of putting up fingers and not the outstretched fingers as visual entities. This scheme was motor rather than perceptual in quality. He stopped counting when he had performed two more counting acts, which is a recurrence of the action pattern for "two" observed in the protocol of paragraph 6.01. This was typical. He could complete action patterns for "two" and "four" when he counted the second of two hidden collections. He put up fingers when solving several other tasks, but he did not continue to count until he completed an appropriate finger pattern. He had not coordinated finger patterns with this counting scheme (called his finger pattern scheme) and so could not make an intuitive extension that involved putting up more than two fingers.

21 January 1981 Teaching Episode

Spatio-Motor Patterns

6.04. Jason had previously isolated his pointing acts and used them as substitutes for visual perceptual items when he continued to count a hidden portion of a collection (cf. 6.01). Our goal in teaching was to encourage him to isolate his pointing acts as countable items before he began to count. Toward this goal, one of our primary objectives when working with him in November and December of 1980 was to help him coordinate spatial patterns with his pointing scheme. Frequently, we asked Jason to count a collection of visible items. The teacher would then cover the items and ask Jason to count them again (i.e., to re-enact previous counting activity). This procedure was successful only in that

Jason now coordinated spatial patterns for "three", "four", and "five" with his pointing scheme. For example, he solved a task in which five squares were visible and four were covered by counting the visible squares and then continuing "6-7-8-9" while tapping on the cloth, his points of contact forming a square pattern.

Use of Finger Patterns When Finding Sums

6.05. We also worked with Jason on developing finger patterns. But he still used his pointing scheme to count a partially screened collection. If both portions of the collection were covered, he no longer attempted to use his finger extension scheme because he had developed finger patterns up to "ten". For example, he solved a task in which five marbles were in one cup and three were in another by simultaneously putting up five fingers on one hand and three on his other hand before answering "eight" without counting. He also attempted to use finger patterns to solve a subsequent task that involved collections of seven and four marbles in cups but failed, explaining "I don't have enough fingers". At this time, Jason appeared to have regressed to a perceptual period.

9 February 1981 Teaching Episode

Use of the Pointing Scheme to Count Two Hidden Collections

6.06. For the first time, Jason used his pointing scheme to count two hidden portions of a collection. We placed him about two meters from two cups containing marbles, seven in one and four in another. To count the marbles, Jason uttered "1-2-3- . . . -7" while synchronously pointing in the direction of the first cup, and then continued "8-9-10-11" while pointing in the direction of the second cup. This represented progress because Jason recognized four pointing acts as "four" without there being a spatial component.

18 March 1981 Teaching Episode

Re-presentation of Finger Patterns

6.07. In the teaching sessions that intervened between this and the session conducted on 9 February 1981, Jason re-presented his finger patterns. Jason and the teacher pretended that ten cookies were beneath one cloth and four were beneath another. Jason was asked to find how many cookies there were altogether.

J : 1-2- . . . -10 (sequentially putting up all ten fingers and then closing his right hand), -11-12-13-14 (sequentially putting up four fingers on his right hand).

The teacher had anticipated that Jason would use his pointing scheme. Instead, he sequentially put up fingers until completing a pattern for "four". This was a surprise to us because Jason previously had used his finger patterns as a perceptual adding scheme (cf. 6.05). Behaviors that had appeared to indicate a regression now provided him with material to re-present.

23 March 1981 Teaching Episode

Re-enactments of Counting to Resolve a Conflict

6.08. Jason's attempt to solve a task where four of a row of ten poker chips were hidden by a cloth constitutes one of the first occasions where he re-enacted counting to resolve a conflict. First, Jason counted the visible chips and then continued "7-8-9-10" while synchronously pointing over the cloth. The remainder of the solution is presented in protocol form.

T : How many are under here (the hidden chips)?

J : 1-2- . . . -6 (points to each of the visible chips), -7-8-9-10. (Points over the cloth, his points forming a linear pattern, but not recognizing the pattern, he utters) 1-2-3- . . . -6--7-8-9-10 (sequentially putting up fingers), five (holds up an open hand).

This solution is important because it provides one of the first indications that Jason was aware that the results of counting did not provide an answer to his question. It should be stressed that his awareness was situational. Nevertheless, this observation of productive, purposeful behavior marked the beginning of his future progress.

Creating Verbal Unit Items

11 May 1981 Teaching Episode

6.09. In the teaching episodes conducted between 23 March 1981 and 11 May 1981, the teacher encouraged Jason to count-on and to coordinate linear patterns with his counting schemes. However, when left to his own resources, Jason continued to count from "one". Until this teaching episode, he had only coordinated a spatial pattern for "three" with his counting scheme except in those cases where he counted covered rows of perceptual items. Consider, in contrast, his spontaneous solution to a task in which he and the teacher pretended that eight items were hidden beneath one cloth and seven beneath a second cloth.

J : 1-2- . . . -8 (looking at the first cloth),--9-10 (synchronously points over the second cloth)--9-10-11-12-13-14-15 (synchronously touches the second cloth, his first six points of contact forming a linear pattern).

Jason stopped counting when he completed a linear spatial pattern for "seven" (which was a linear pattern for "six" and one more).

6.10. This solution also indicates that Jason had made another important advance. His initial count to "eight" did not involve motor activity such as pointing or putting up fingers. The accommodation Jason had made in his counting scheme was to substitute his vocal productions for covered or imaginary items. He could now count verbal unit items.

The Abstract Period

21 May 1981 Teaching Episode

Reorganization of the Counting Scheme

6.11. Jason's solution in the protocol of paragraph 6.09 indicates that he was in the process of reorganizing his counting scheme. His use of a linear spatial pattern was encouraging. Jason's solutions in this teaching episode indicated that he had made further reorganization of his counting scheme. The teacher and Jason pretended that cookies were hidden under cloths. In one task, the teacher told Jason that nine cookies were hidden under one of two cloths and fifteen were under both cloths. Jason was asked to find out how many were hidden under the second cloth.

J : Nine plus (sequentially puts up five fingers on one hand and then looks at his other hand while making subvocal utterances) six. (Points to the appropriate cloth.)

This spontaneous solution indicates that Jason anticipated that he could find how many counting acts he was going to perform when he counted beyond "nine" to "fifteen". He could count-on to solve a missing addend task.

Forming Numerical Composites

6.12. Jason now seemed to apply the integration operation to the unit items he created while counting--he could form composites of already counted units. This is also indicated by his spontaneous solutions of subtraction tasks. For example, on one occasion he was asked how many marbles were left in a cup after five of nineteen marbles had been removed. Jason counted backward "19-18-17-16-15" while sequentially putting up five fingers, and then said, "There's fourteen in there" as he looked at the cup. This solution is analogous to that of Tyrone (cf. Tyrone, 4.08). Jason did not explicitly state that he counted backward five times to fourteen. But he seemed aware of what he was doing while he was doing it. This is strongly indicated by his comment, "There's fourteen in there" and by his stopping after putting five fingers up and recognizing the finger pattern.

14 December 1981 Interview

Separating the Content of Composite Units

6.13. In the solution described in 6.12, we infer that Jason separated his counting acts into two parts. His solution of the following protocol contains a more dramatic instance because he paused after he counted backward 8 times from 17 before answering "nine".

I : (Places "17 - 8" in front of Jason) What would that be?
J : 17-16-15-14-13-12-11-10 (in synchrony with putting up fingers to form a pattern for "eight"), that would be (pauses)--nine.
I : It *would* be nine! That is really beautiful!

His pause before saying "nine" indicates that he took stock of where he was--he had uttered eight number words backward and, based on this counting activity, he had to find how many times he was yet to count to reach "one". He segmented counting activity into a composite of eight number words and the remainder. The manner in which he coordinated number word utterances with the acts of putting up fingers indicates that his intention was to say eight number words backward. He now took his number words as countable and could separate his number word sequence into distinct segments. This represents a profound reorganization of his counting scheme.

Double Function of a Counting Act

6.14. Jason's awareness of what he was doing while he was doing it in the protocol of 6.13 is a prime indication of a level 3 abstraction. Each backward counting act he performed served two functions. It was one of the counting acts of the backward number word sequence denoted by "17" as well as one of the first eight that he intended to perform. This double function was manifest by the way he put up a finger to record his utterances. Each utterance served as one of the elements of the number word sequence "17-16-15-. . . -1" and putting up a finger served as one of his first eight counting acts.

Discussion of Jason's Case Study

On the basis of our observations of Jason in the 18 October 1980 interview (cf. 6.01-6.03), his action pattern for "two" did play a role in isolating pointing acts as countable items that could be substituted for hidden perceptual items. Although re-presentations of past counting episodes played a critical role in his progress, we have no basis for claiming that the material of re-presentation was a pattern. It is possible that he re-presented a spatio-motor pattern, but the fact that his counting activity was not organized into patterns argues against this possibility.

Jason's use of his finger extension scheme (cf. 6.03) did not seem to involve the re-presentation of finger patterns simply because he had not established any finger patterns that we could observe. An act of putting up a finger seemed to be a substitute for an item of a figural collection of marbles. He seemed to re-present a collection of marbles and then count to specify the collection. His search for sensory material he could use to make tangible items to count led him to isolate the motor act of putting up fingers. Re-presentation was critical, but the material of re-presentation was not a figural pattern of marbles. Rather, he seemed to be aware of a plurality of marbles. This was similar to the way in which Tyrone isolated his pointing acts (cf. 4.01-4.02).

There seemed to be several reasons for Jason's rather long (7 months) motor period. First, upon development of finger patterns, he independently substituted finger patterns for hidden collections and counted his fingers as perceptual items. This substitution provided Jason with a perceptual adding scheme that he could use to solve the presented tasks. It also impeded his progress, because it was essentially a regression to counting perceptual items. The availability of a perceptual adding scheme circumvented the need to make adaptations in his counting scheme in order to solve the presented tasks. We have seen that Scenetra also used finger patterns whenever possible even though she had more sophisticated means of solving the problems. When Jason finally began to re-present his finger patterns, his progress to the abstract stage was rather rapid, taking about two months. Had Jason developed finger patterns earlier, we feel his progress to the abstract stage would have been even more rapid. Our decision to introduce finger patterns, in retrospect, may have been inappropriate. It is possible that Jason could have developed integrations in the context of re-presented collections.

There was also a significant difference between Tyrone's and Jason's motor pointing schemes. Tyrone abstracted pointing acts as countable in the contexts of re-presented collections and linear spatial patterns that he used when making intuitive extensions. Once Tyrone made the abstraction, pointing acts were experiential items in their own right and could easily be used as countable items when the need arose. Jason, on the other hand, first abstracted his pointing acts as countable items when he actually counted the visible perceptual items. It was not until the 9 February 1981 teaching episode that Jason abstracted his pointing acts as countable items in the same sense as had Tyrone in the 15 October 1980 interviews (cf. 4.01). When he attempted to count two hidden collections, Jason finally isolated his pointing acts to solve the problem of counting a re-presented collection of perceptual items. Moreover, although he displayed an action pattern for "four" in the initial interview, he failed to develop action patterns as part of his finger extension scheme until rather late in his motor period.

Like Tyrone, Jason essentially had no verbal period. He was observed counting verbal unit items (cf. 6.09), but we would not classify this as a period. In retrospect, we were witnessing the emergence of the uniting operation of integration. The linear pattern for "seven" (6.09) provides some indication of what it means for a child to "strip away" the sensory motor material involved in counting and thus create abstract unit items. We infer that the linear pattern was an expression of a numerical composite of numerosity seven because of its linearity and its novelty. Our interpretation is corroborated by the reorganizations of counting that we observed ten days later (cf. 6.11-6.12) when Jason counted to solve missing addend and subtraction tasks. These novel adaptations of his counting scheme require constructive mechanisms beyond re-presentation. To explain them, we attribute to him the mental operation of integration.

PERSPECTIVES ON THE CASE STUDIES

Our analysis of the children's construction of the counting scheme is compatible with Piaget's concern with the ontogeny of every kind of know-how and knowledge, irrespective of the knower's awareness. That implies that Piaget intended to bring that ontogeny within the observer's domain of conscious knowledge, regardless of the fact that neither his nor anyone else's introspection was able to investigate and apprehend the steps in the ontogeny of his own knowledge. Consequently, he observed children and constructed models of how they might come to do whatever intelligent things (and "mistakes") he observed them doing. Any such model that satisfactorily fits a sufficient number of children, so that it can be generalized for a particular developmental level, becomes the model of what he called the epistemic subject. The changes that may have to be made in the epistemic-subject-model when children are observed over extended periods determine different levels of development and, ultimately, the generalized development of the epistemic subject, i.e., a theory of cognitive constructions. Somewhere in that ontogeny, however, there is the development of the individual subject's awareness of knowing, the development of conscious knowledge.

Piaget has mentioned a "psychological subject" as counterpart to the epistemic one, and has said that it is "centered on the conscious self" and plays "an incontestable functional role" (Beth & Piaget, 1966, p. 329). But the psychological subject does not crop up frequently in his writings. It is not explicitly mentioned in the two more recent consecutive volumes, *The Grasp of Consciousness* (l974a) and *Success and Understanding* (1974b). Nevertheless, it is in these two books that one finds such hints as Piaget has given about the ontogeny of the conscious knower. "The grasp of consciousness consists essentially in conceptualization" (1974a, p. 261) and "a conceptualization proper is the transformation of action schemes into notions and operations" (1974b, p. 6).

This transformation is precisely the one we are concerned with as the children become able to take the sensory-motor results of their counting acts as material for further operating. In the abstract period, the children could reflect on results of counting and deliberately segment them as the need arose to resolve problematic situations. While they were in their motor periods, they were capable of specific accommodations, but they were never able to take the results of counting as a given, as something to be operated on. Rather, counting was a function they carried out to reach another goal. Even though what a child is aware of can only be inferred by an observer, the transformation of the counting scheme from an action scheme to an operative scheme that involves abstract unit items can take place only after the action scheme has been used successfully.

> The subject does not manage to "see" certain quite "observable" characteristics that assure the action's success but are precluded from conceptualized comprehension because they are unconscious or not registered by consciousness. (Piaget, 1974b, p. 6)

This ability to "see" is brought about in the case of counting by the emergence of the integration operation.

Stages

We did not observe the perceptual periods of these three children because they had already entered their motor periods when we started to work with them. In the case studies, our analyses of stages had to start with changes observed in and after the motor period, and consequently, we can only speculate about periods preceding the motor period. Our hypothesis that re-presented patterns might have played an important role in development as the children shifted from their perceptual periods to their motor periods was only partially confirmed.

Scenetra (cf. 5.01) provided the strongest indication that she re-presented her finger patterns. Jason and Tyrone, however, seemed to re-present collections whose elements did not co-occur in patterns and then searched for sensory material they could use to make countable items. Tyrone seemed to generate pointing acts and Jason the acts of putting up fingers as appropriate sensory material. If we accept these inferences as the basis for a working hypothesis, it changes our view of the role of patterns in the development of counting schemes. Re-presentation is the crucial constructive mechanism that, for some children, is first applied to patterns (most likely, finger patterns). It is then generalized to include possible bounded pluralities beyond the range of patterns. In other cases, re-presentation does not seem to be subject to that initial restriction.

We focus now on the incorporation and reorganization criteria because all three children made progress from their motor periods to their abstract periods.

Incorporation Criterion

There were several indications that the motor unit items the children counted signified perceptual unit items or their figural representatives. One indication occurred when the children first counted visible perceptual items and then screened items as one collection in the same counting activity. Tyrone's activity of touching distinct locations on a cloth that he took as covering perceptual items provides a second indication (cf. 4.01). A third indication was observed when Scenetra looked at seven visible squares and then proceeded to utter "9-10-11-12-13-14-15" as she put up fingers (cf. 5.01). Her intention was to count the squares, but she actually counted her motor acts of putting up fingers. A fourth indication was documented when Jason, sitting about two meters from two cups, pointed at the cups as he synchronously uttered number words (cf. 6.08). All of these indications provide substance to our claim that the motor acts signified perceptual items or their figural representatives. In other words, the latter two types of items were incorporated into the motor counting schemes of the children.

Transition to the Abstract Period

We understand the children's curtailment of their motor acts as an interiorization of these motor acts. This is quite different in nature from the curtailments we observed in the case studies of Brenda, Tarus, and James, who internalized rather that interiorized their motor acts. As they re-enacted counting, for example, these three children isolated their number word sequences as being relevant to the solution of tasks, a level 2 reflective abstraction made possible by re-presentation without the operation of integration. Interiorization of motor acts requires that the unitizing operation be applied to the records of the motor acts.

Our analysis of the interiorization of motor acts in counting fits our observation of Jason (cf. 6.09) as he produced a linear pattern for "seven". This phenomenon occurred in the counting episode where he spontaneously curtailed the motor component of counting activity. His use of the linear spatial pattern and the fact that Brenda, Tarus, and James never produced patterns of this type indicated to us that he had applied the integration operation before he counted. Taken alone, however, these indications would not be strong enough to justify inferring that motor acts had been interiorized. However, the inference becomes more convincing when placed in the context of his attainment of the abstract period only ten days later.

Scenetra's problem-solving behavior provided valuable indications of the progressive interiorization of her motor acts when she was in her verbal period. She substituted a re-presentation of counting for the actual counting activity (cf. 5.05) and split a counting act into two co-ordinated parts (cf. 5.07). These novel adaptations were accompanied by a temporal pattern that still contained a motor component. Her solution of a missing addend task by counting-on from six to eleven and then spontaneously reviewing her perceptual records also strongly indicates the presence of the integration operation. She clearly separated "holding six in her head" and "counting-on five" (cf. 5.05). In fact, Scenetra was the only child of the three who could be said to experience a verbal period. It was, however, quite different from those of Brenda, Tarus, and James. For them, re-presentation and substitution were the basic developmental mechanisms and their verbal periods were much longer than Scenetra's. Her verbal period marked the emergence of the uniting operation of integration and she made rapid progress to her abstract period.

In Tyrone's case (cf. 4.04), a suggestion from the teacher was enough for him to curtail his pointing activity. In contrast, Brenda, Tarus, and James repeatedly failed to curtail their motor activity despite numerous interventions by their teachers. Moreover, Tyrone could run through an auditory pattern for "five" in thought and reconstitute it as a sequence of two beats followed by three beats, a reversal in the order of these two subpatterns. These adaptations of his counting scheme presaged the reorganizations that he would make over the next two weeks of the Christmas holidays.

The children's interiorization of motor acts involved the application of the integration operation to records of motor items in order to create abstract unit items. The counting solutions discussed in the next section demonstrate extensive use of the motor units during the abstract period. However, the three children used motor acts in ways that were not possible when they were in their motor period.

The Reorganization of Counting

The reorganizations of counting made by Tyrone and Jason when we observed them creating verbal unit items involved using auditory or linear spatial patterns to decide when to stop counting. For Scenetra, the reorganizations also included the substitution of a re-presentation of the results of counting for actual counting activity, a substitution that was manifest as counting-on (cf. 5.05, 5.09). Counting verbal unit items marked the children's transitions to their abstract periods and was the result of the emergence of the uniting operation of integration. We explain the relatively long verbal period for Scenetra as a lag in the interiorization of counting. The mental operation of integration had developed, but its application was restricted to patterns.

Our observations of the children in their abstract periods provided various indications of the integration operation (cf. 4.10, 5.12, 6.13). Tyrone (cf. 4.10) made a numerical extension by sequentially putting up 14 fingers in synchrony with uttering "7-8-9- . . . -20". After completing two open hands, he closed both hands and then proceeded to put up four fingers as he uttered "17-18-19-20". As such, counting was carried out to specify a numerosity. However, he had not double counted nor did he recognize a pattern. What convinced us that he could unite his results of counting into a composite was the spontaneous, independent way he counted his records of counting. The decision to operate further on the records of counting was his own.

We believe that certain records of counting acts eventually become contained in the individual unit items of the numerical composite that is produced by applying the integration operation. In that case, if a child re-presents the contents of the numerical composite, some minimal reconstruction of counting acts is what is re-presented. So, while re-presentation remains a critical mechanism of change, the emergence of the conceptual uniting operation of integration broadens its material to include sensory-motor counting acts, and the children become able to re-present counting and segment it to "fit" problematical situations. They are in control of their actions and can plan procedures that were lacking in the earlier stages.

The double function of a counting act, such as putting up a finger, is a good indication that the motor acts have been interiorized. There are several behavioral indications of this double function, the most illustrative being counting backward to solve subtraction tasks (cf. 4.09, 5.12, 6.14). Tyrone (cf. 4.09) explained his solution of a verbally presented subtraction problem by saying, "I had thirteen and I went 13-12-11-10-9-8-7" (in synchrony with putting up fingers). Most importantly, Tyrone's solution was independently initiated without any direct suggestions from the teacher. While we do not investigate all of the mental operations involved here, an integration operation corresponding to "thirteen" is indicated by the comment "I had thirteen". From Tyrone's perspective, he was at "the end" of 13 with the intention of counting backward toward one, an intention that is indicated by his actually counting backward.

The separation of backward counting activity to solve subtraction tasks requires interiorization of a number word sequence, in the sense that we have discussed the interiorization of motor acts in counting. This interiorization leads to "operative" sequences that could be used flexibly in the solution of arithmetical tasks. The concomitant reorganizations of the counting scheme manifested by the double function of a counting act, together with the interiorizations, justify our contention that the abstract period constituted a stage in the development of the counting scheme (as did the motor period).

Chapter V

Lexical and Syntactical Meanings

Brenda, Tarus, and James

Leslie P. Steffe

In Chapters II and III, we focused on changes in the unit items that Brenda, Tarus, and James created and counted over the two-year duration of the teaching experiment. Knowledge of the periods in the development of the three children's counting schemes, however, only partially specifies the possible lexical and syntactical meanings they gave to number words or combinations of number words while they were in the various periods. In this chapter, we consider lexical and syntactical meanings within each period of development of the counting scheme. As will be seen, these meanings changed as the children changed from one counting type period to another.

Because of its importance in the decimal numeration system, we made a special effort to investigate the meaning of "ten" for the three children when they were in their verbal periods. The instructional activities involving "ten" that we devised during their perceptual and motor periods resulted only in the children establishing finger patterns or spatial patterns as meanings of the word. When the children were in their verbal periods, we designed problem situations that are somewhat novel from the perspective of school mathematics. Using these novel problem situations, we were able to foster the children's construction of several types of units for "ten" beyond finger or spatial patterns. Our work with these units for "ten" with the children was, from their standpoint, particularly important because they were in their third year in school during their verbal periods and were expected to learn standard two-digit addition and subtraction algorithms.

In general, the children's counting schemes, finger pattern schemes, and spatial pattern schemes were their primary sources of meaning for number words. We took whatever aspect of those schemes they seemed to be aware of as constituting their meaning. This view of meaning is broad enough to incorporate Van Engen's (1949) opinion that meaning is an *intention* to act and Bridgman's (1934) belief that meaning is found in *activity*: "The meaning that I ascribe to 'beautiful', for example, I find in the operations which I perform, or more simply, in what I do" (p. 104). We found it necessary to go one step farther and consider the experiential results of activity as another aspect of meaning. In the case of "beautiful", for example, despite Bridgman's view, it is very difficult to be aware of the operations that can be applied in any particular context. Nevertheless, what an individual takes as being beautiful in a particular context can be known to that individual because he or she can consider the results of operating as the meaning of the term. Similarly, it would always seem to be possible for the results of counting activity to be what the child takes as the meaning of a number word or numeral.

Our focus on meaning as being *what the child is aware of* highlights the fact that meaning is related to "where the child is at". For example, if a number word is a symbol for counting activity, then the activity would not have to actually be carried out in order for the number word to have meaning. The counting activity could be carried out, of course, and the child would be aware of this possibility. In this case, the meaning would be an intention to act.

A child can also find meaning in counting activity if the child is "above" actual counting activity "looking down" on it--e.g., recording how many times he or she counts. There is also the possibility that the child might find meaning in the *structure* of the activity, which can be distinguished from the activity. Reflecting on the activity is essential if the child is to find meaning in its structure.

A more primitive case is that in which a number word or numeral only signifies counting. Although counting activity would not necessarily be produced upon hearing the number word spoken or seeing the numeral, the activity of counting would be used to give meaning to the number word or numeral. The essence of the child's meaning in this case would seem to be the results of the activity rather than the activity itself, because the activity serves as a means to an end. The child would not find meaning in the counting activity any more than he or she would find meaning in an act of pointing to a red object when asked to indicate the red item.

Considering the results of counting as one possible meaning of number words is particularly important because after a child counts to solve a task, the number word uttered prior to counting may have a new meaning as a result of counting. For example, a child may be told there are eight marbles hidden prior to counting and then say "eight" last when counting. The child's meaning of "eight" in this case might be found in his or her intentions prior to counting, in the activity of counting, in the results of counting, or in some combination of these. In the latter case, a child might then be told there are three marbles hidden in another location. If the child counts all of the marbles, he or she would say "eleven" as the last number word said and the child's meaning of "eleven" in this situation would, by necessity, be based on the results of counting. There are other instances to consider, such as when a child counts to solve a missing addend task. In each case, we look at all three parts of the children's counting scheme in our attempts to understand their meanings.

This analysis of meaning would be incomplete without considering the nature of items of awareness. In fact, the purpose of this chapter is to explicate, as precisely as possible, both the items of awareness within each period of the counting scheme and the changes in these items across the periods. In the course of the analysis, we found it useful to make a distinction between a concept and a preconcept. In our analysis, the meaning of a number word or a combination of number words must involve a re-presentation of some type for the word or words to refer to a concept. A spatial pattern might, for example, be re-presented in visualized imagination when the child hears a number word spoken. In this case, the visualized pattern is an example of a concept and the intention to count its elements could be the meaning of the number word. While a child would not normally be aware of the activity involved in constructing the re-presentation, the results of this activity--the particular constellation of figural items--would be within the child's awareness, and that result would be an essential part of the meaning of the number word. In general, we reserve the term "concept" for any conceptual structure that can be re-presented in the absence of perceptual material (von Glasersfeld, 1982b, p. 194). Its construction is the result of a level 2 or 3 abstraction.

On the other hand, we found that the children could initially recognize but not re-present spatial patterns. That is, upon seeing a particular constellation, the children were able to utter an appropriate number word in recognition but were not able to re-present the pattern in visualized imagination when they heard the number word spoken. The children were aware of the pattern in the here and now, but "three", for example, had no pattern meaning apart from the immediate visual experience. In this case, we call the pattern a perceptual preconcept. More generally, a preconcept is any conceptual structure whose use requires perceptual material of some type. Its construction is the result of a level 1 abstraction.

The major goal of the chapter is to investigate the concepts and the preconcepts to which number words (or phrases or sentences involving number words) referred for Brenda, Tarus, and James. Numerical concepts, however, do not concern us here, for the simple reason that we found no behavioral indicators that would warrant imputing numerical operations to the three children--in other words, we found no indication of a level 3 abstraction. We will continue the case study format of Chapters II and III and the numbering scheme for the convenience of cross reference.

1. BRENDA

The periods in Brenda's construction of the counting scheme that we documented in Chapters II and III are summarized in Figure 1. Starting on 21 October 1980 (cf. 1.01), Brenda's perceptual period lasted until 5 May 1981, when we observed her counting the acts of putting up fingers for the first time (cf. 1.09). On 1 February 1982, well into the second year of the teaching experiment, we observed a curtailment in putting up or folding down fingers when she counted to "fifteen" while solving a task (cf. 1.16). Her vocal acts of uttering number words now signified those motor acts.

Figure 1

Periods in Brenda's Construction of the Counting Scheme

```
VERBAL      |                                       ******
PERIOD      |
            |
MOTOR       |                       *************
PERIOD      |
            |
PERCEPTUAL  |  ***********
PERIOD      | .___________.______________.______.

          10/80        5/81            2/82   6/82
```

The Perceptual Period

21 October 1980 Interview

During the initial interview that was used to select the children, one of our intentions was to investigate their ability to recognize spatial patterns. We momentarily showed the children a dot pattern drawn on a card and asked how many dots they saw. If the children were unable to respond, they were again shown the pattern for a length of time that seemed appropriate. There was no predetermined time interval for exposure of the dots. If the children were not able to recognize the pattern, they were finally allowed to count the dots.

Spatial Patterns as Perceptual Preconcepts

1.25. Brenda could recognize triangular and linear arrangements of three items as "three" and any two items as "two" after seeing the arrangements only for a moment. When a square arrangement of four dots was shown, she had to count the dots before she could say "four". There was no indication that she could re-present the arrangement of four dots and count its elements in re-presentation. Moreover, she did not recognize a row of four dots as "four", nor did she recognize a domino five arrangement of dots as "five". Without actually counting these arrangements, she could not say how many dots they contained.

An Enactive Preconcept for "Two"

1.26. We searched for some indication that Brenda could re-present a two or a three pattern. While there was no indication in either case, "two" seemed to have a special meaning for her. Brenda could complete a two pattern when she counted two hidden tiles in a row of eight tiles.

I : (Points to the tiles) This is number one, number two, number three, and there are two under here. How many tiles are in the row?

B : (Touches the cover synchronously) Number four, number five (continuing over the visible tiles), number six, number seven, number eight.

Brenda touched the cover twice as she uttered "number four, number five". We attribute an *enactive preconcept* of "two" to Brenda because she could recognize a pair of counting actions. The reason that we did not attribute a figurative concept of "two" to Brenda is that she seemed to recognize two counting acts as she actually performed them rather than counting a previously re-presented pattern for "two". This inference is based on the specificity of the observation and its uniqueness. Her completion of two counting acts in this task was the sole indication of anything beyond a perceptual preconcept at the time of the interview. She was unable, for example, to solve an analogous task where there were three tiles covered.

10 February 1981 Teaching Episode

Finger Patterns as Perceptual Preconcepts

Given the status of Brenda's spatial patterns, our hypothesis was that her finger patterns would be also perceptual preconcepts. The task of analyzing her finger patterns was more difficult than analyzing her spatial patterns, however, because of the covert way in which she sometimes used her finger patterns. There was an ambiguous case where Brenda *seemed* to re-present finger patterns and their elements. This led us to establish criteria for distinguishing between finger patterns as perceptual preconcepts and as figurative concepts. We first present the ambiguous case and our interpretation.

1.27. Brenda used finger patterns for the number words "three" and "four" without actually forming the finger patterns in her visual field.

T : (Places three marbles in front of Brenda) Brenda, how many marbles do we have there?
B : Three (immediately).
T : How many marbles do we have there (places four marbles in front of Brenda)?
B : (Touching each marble) 1-2-3-4.
T : (Places cups over each collection) Let's cover those up. How many do we have altogether?
B : (Stares straight ahead for about 25 seconds with her hands resting in her lap) I hope it's seven!
T : It's seven alright! How did you get that?
B : I counted on my fingers!

Brenda looked straight ahead while she apparently established two finger patterns, one for "four" and one for "three". Obviously, the finger patterns were not in her visual field. We take them as being in her tactual and kinesthetic fields because Brenda said, "I counted on my fingers". Although this comment can be interpreted in more than one way, we infer that she actually took the fingers of her finger patterns as countable perceptual items. Our interpretation is consistent with the manner in which she established finger patterns in the protocol of paragraph 1.06. In that case, she *simultaneously* put up five fingers for "five" and then three fingers for "three". There, the finger patterns were established in her visual field and the number words "five" and "three" signaled their establishment. Our inference is also consistent with Brenda's solution of an analogous task involving five and four marbles. Brenda performed similarly and did not establish finger patterns in her visual field. This time, however, she explained how she arrived at nine by opening her left hand, opening four fingers on her right hand, and then counting all nine fingers by touching each one as she uttered a number word. We take this as corroboration of the inference that she actually established finger patterns in her tactual and kinesthetic fields and that she did not re-present them and count their elements.

1.28. In the protocol of paragraph 1.27, Brenda stared straight ahead for about 25 seconds. During this time, she displayed intense concentration and seemed to be aware of what she was doing with her fingers as they rested in her lap. She seemed to reflect on the activities of establishing finger patterns in her tactual and kinesthetic fields and counting the elements of those patterns. Her reflection on this sensory-motor activity indicates that her re-presentation of finger patterns was at least beginning. In fact, the manner in which she established finger patterns was a harbinger of what was to come in the 19 March 1981 teaching episode. The following protocol is another example in which we see the beginnings of Brenda's subsequent ability to re-present her finger patterns. She first recognized spatial patterns for three and two, but when the spatial patterns were hidden from view, she resorted to using finger patterns.

T : How many do you see (three marbles)?
B : Three (immediately).
T : How many are there (places two marbles by the three)?
B : Two.
T : Now try (covers the marbles).
B : (Sits silently for 12 seconds and then simultaneously puts up three fingers on one hand and two on the other. She then touches each finger) 1-2-3--4-5. Five.

We take the 12-second pause as an indication that Brenda searched for something tangible she could use to give meaning to "three" and "two". That she finally used her finger patterns is quite remarkable and is consistent with her solution in the protocol of paragraph 1.27. Her use of finger patterns shows that, although certain number words referred to at least two types of patterns, her finger patterns were the more accessible. In fact, they were her only possible way of proceeding because she could not re-present her spatial patterns. If she did re-present her finger patterns, and that is a distinct possibility, she established them in her visual field in order to create perceptual items to count. Parenthetically, it was not desirable for us, as teachers, to discourage her use of finger patterns as perceptual preconcepts.

19 March 1981 Teaching Episode

Finger Patterns as Figurative Concepts

1.29. The behavioral criterion we use to infer that a child re-presents finger patterns prior to counting is that the child completes *two* finger patterns by putting up fingers *sequentially* rather than *simultaneously* (cf. 1.07). We feel justified in adopting this criterion because the ability to sequentially put up fingers for this purpose made a limited reorganization of counting possible. Before the current teaching episode, Brenda established two finger patterns by simultaneously putting up fingers and then counting her fingers as perceptual items. We now confirm that she could re-present the finger patterns and coordinate the utterance of number words with acts of sequentially putting up fingers.

T : (Displays four squares) See those?
B : (Nods her head "yes".)
T : (Hides the four squares and displays three squares) See those? (Hides the three squares.)
B : Three.
T : OK?
B : (Simultaneously puts up four fingers) Four. (Closes her hand and sequentially puts up the same four fingers) 1-2-3-4 (continues sequentially putting up fingers on her other hand), 5-6-7.

The act of simultaneously putting up four fingers while uttering "four" and then sequentially putting up the same four fingers while uttering "1-2-3-4" is a strong indication that Brenda re-presented the finger patterns and then counted the elements of the re-presented patterns. In other words, "four" (and "three") could refer to a re-presented unitary whole comprised of figural elements that could be sequentially isolated and counted. This criterion clarifies the ambiguous cases noted in paragraphs 1.27 and 1.28. Nevertheless, these cases are important because they serve as indications of her future progress.

1.30. It is especially significant that Brenda could coordinate the implementation of a finger pattern for "three" with her utterances "5-6-7". This shows that "three" referred to a re-presented finger pattern whose elements could be coordinated with any three number words in sequence. "Three", then, referred to a specified figural collection--the re-presented finger pattern. She made similar coordinations for finger patterns associated with "two", "three", "four", and "five". Her ability to re-present these finger patterns in order to keep track of counting activity provides the necessary basis for calling them figurative concepts.

Re-presented Collections of Fingers as Figurative Concepts

1.31. Remarkably, Brenda soon gave meaning to number words beyond the range of her finger patterns by re-presenting a plurality of fingers. In the following protocol, our first inclination was to infer that the activity of counting to "fifteen" constituted her meaning of the number word. However, a more viable interpretation is that she counted to specify a collection of fingers that she re-presented before she counted. The particular manner in which she counted to "fifteen" provides the justification for this interpretation.

T : (Makes the sentence 15 + 3 = using felt numerals.)
B : 1-2-3- . . . -10 (sequentially puts up all ten fingers) --11-12-13-14-15 (sequentially touches the fingers of her open right hand). 16-17-EIGHTEEN (touching three fingers of her left hand, enunciating "eighteen" to indicate that was the answer).

Her activity of continuing to count beyond "ten" to "fifteen" by touching five fingers that she had already used is a particularly strong indication that a plurality of fingers was active in re-presentation.

The Motor Period

7 November 1981 Interview

Sophisticated Finger Patterns as Figurative Concepts

1.32. The question of whether the collections of fingers that Brenda specified by counting in 1.31 were significant for her can be at least partially answered by reconsidering the sophisticated finger patterns that she developed in the intervening 6 months for the number words (or numerals) "eleven" through "fifteen" (cf. 1.14, 1.15). We believe that these figurative concepts were derived from her awareness of the visual records she created by counting within contexts like that of 1.31. In that episode, for example, the visual record of counting from "one" to "fifteen" was an open hand. This later became one of her sophisticated finger patterns for "fifteen".

The Verbal Period

1 February 1982 Teaching Episode

Dual Meanings of Number Words

There is also the question of whether Brenda found a meaning for number words in the activity of counting itself. This question can be partially addressed by considering solutions produced when she was in her verbal period. We argue below that her sophisticated finger patterns were connected to counting. Number words signified uttering number word sequences as well as establishing sophisticated finger patterns.

1.33. The following protocol suggests that "fifteen" referred to the activity of uttering "1-2-3- . . . -15", and that an open hand and two fingers were recognized as "twelve" by Brenda.

T : Do fifteen take away three. Do it aloud.
B : (Utters) 1-2-3- . . . -15 (Opens both hands and closes her right thumb, index finger, and middle finger) 1-2-3. (Immediately) Twelve.

Her utterance of the number words from "one" to "fifteen" after she heard "fifteen" indicates that producing this sequence provided her with a necessary sensory-motor experience that constituted her meaning for the number word. She could not take the number word sequence as a given--she could not substitute a re-presentation of the number word sequence for the activity of producing it. Counting was still an enactive preconcept. Nevertheless, the activity of uttering the number word sequence seemed to be one of two experiential sources of her meanings. The other was her sophisticated finger pattern of two open hands. We see in the protocol that after she uttered the number word sequence she opened both hands, which was her other meaning of "fifteen". So, "fifteen" could refer to the activity of uttering number words up to and including "fifteen" as well as to the finger pattern of two open hands, an abbreviation of three open hands. In this case, the activity of uttering number words was linked to her sophisticated finger pattern, and both were experiential meanings for "fifteen".

1.34. We now investigated the meaning that Brenda gave to number words beyond the range of her sophisticated finger patterns. Our hypothesis was that the activity of counting would be her primary meaning of those number words (cf. 1.18).

T : Do twenty-four take away six.
B : (Utters) 1-2- . . . -23-24.

It seemed essential that Brenda produce this number word sequence in order to give meaning to "twenty-four". She did not substitute a re-presentation of counting to "twenty-four" for the activity at this point in the teaching experiment, as indicated in the following section. There was, however, some indication that "twenty-four" could also refer to a plurality of fingers. In the very next task, Brenda counted to "seventeen" by coordinating acts of putting up fingers with number words, indicating that the hypothesis that "twenty-four" referred to a re-presented plurality of fingers is plausible. But "twenty-four" (and "seventeen") did *not* refer to specific finger patterns.

2 February 1982 Teaching Episode

Mobile Finger Patterns as Meaning of Number Words

1.35. Brenda's awareness of her counting activity is clarified in the following protocol. This awareness manifested itself in her construction of mobile finger patterns. Her solution to the first task of the teaching episode involved counting to find "eight plus five".

T : Can you tell me what eight plus five is?
B : (Sequentially puts up eight fingers) 1-2-3-4-5-6-7-8. (Continues putting up the two remaining fingers and five more, after a pause during which she looked disconcerted) 9-10-11-12-13-14-15--fifteen.

During the pause, Brenda looked puzzled and was prompted by her teacher to continue. Her puzzlement suggests that she was aware of a conflict between "five" referring to an open hand and having two fingers on her left hand yet to count. Even though she did not establish a new finger pattern for "five" by using these two fingers, her conflict indicates that, for her, "five" might have referred to the activity of counting five times beyond "eight" as well as to an open hand--she was aware of how she was going to count. This inference was corroborated by a solution in which she established an open hand and an index finger for "six". She easily "broke" the specificity of this finger pattern as seen in the next paragraph.

1.36. It was quite difficult for Brenda to establish new finger patterns for "five" as she counted, because her open hand was a strong finger pattern. An open hand and an index finger for "six" was not as strong.

T : Can you tell me what eight plus six is?
B : (Sequentially puts up eight fingers) 1-2-3-4-5-6-7-8. (Continues ticking off the two remaining fingers and four more on her other hand after a pause) 9-10-11-12- 13-14.

Brenda's finger pattern for "six" was mobile in that it could be implemented by any six fingers. She also displayed a mobile finger pattern for "four". She could now establish a finger pattern by coordinating acts of putting up or ticking off fingers with number words. "Four" could refer to any four fingers that she focused on to know when to stop counting. A "finger pattern" now consisted of a specific sequence of finger movements bounded by the activity of counting them. We call them finger patterns because a collection of six fingers was a result of the activity. The fact that number words had two meanings for her (counting and pattern) was essential to her development of the mobility of her patterns.

9 February 1982 Teaching Episode

Counting Beyond a Sophisticated Finger Pattern

1.37. The issue of whether Brenda could substitute a re-presentation of counting for the activity is clarified by analyzing her meaning of number words that could refer to finger patterns. Our hypothesis was that her sophisticated finger patterns might lead her to curtail the activity of producing number word sequences in additive situations. In the following protocol, upon suggestion by her teacher, Brenda continued to count beyond "twelve" without first counting to "twelve".

T : Can you do twelve plus five?
B : (Long pause. Sequentially puts up three fingers) 1-2-3- . . .
T : (Gestures over Brenda's fingers, interrupting) could you not count to twelve at all? You have twelve plus five.
B : (Nods her head "yes". Sits silently in deep concentration, then sequentially puts up five fingers) 13-14-15-16-17.

Brenda clearly intended to count to "twelve". The teacher's suggestion led Brenda to reflect, and she proceeded to coordinate the number words "thirteen, fourteen, . . . " with acts of putting up fingers to complete the finger pattern for "five". Our inference is that her sophisticated finger pattern for "twelve" was a substitute for counting activity. We do not believe she reflected on possible counting activity; rather, she reflected on her sophisticated finger pattern that embodied it and that would be the result of counting (cf. 1.20-1.22).

The Meaning of "Ten"

When Brenda was in her perceptual period, she could coordinate the number word sequence "1-2-3-4- . . . -10" with an appropriate collection of perceptual items. As a result of doing this, the collection of items she had counted constituted a meaning of the number word "ten" for Brenda. Perceptual collections of ten had one thing in common for her: the auditory item "ten". Although these collections of counted items temporarily embodied her counting activity, they were bounded perceptually (e.g., by location or spatial configuration). Other than these counted collections and her perceptual and figurative finger pattern for "ten", our work involving "ten" with her was essentially unproductive in the perceptual and motor periods. It was more productive during the last part of her verbal period, although there were important limitations. Beyond her construction of a finger pattern for "ten" as a figurative concept, what the meaning of "ten" could be for her at this time was not clear, nor was the nature of the items of which she might be aware.

17 May 1982 Teaching Episode

"Ten" as an Index of Counting

1.38. The distinction between a perceptual collection (i.e., a perceptual preconcept) and an enactive concept as a meaning of "ten" is illustrated in the following protocol. The teacher called centimeter cubes "candies".

T : Brenda, would you put ten of these candies in a row?
B : (Aligns, one by one, ten cubes in a row that extends approximately 18 inches from her left to her right.)
T : Here is a bag of candies. How many candies are in here?
B : Ten (Brenda had already counted the cubes in a similar bag).
T : And how many candies are in the row (placing the bag by the row)?
B : Ten.
T : If you had those candies to eat, would you rather have the candies in the bag, the candies in the row, or would it make a difference (hereafter called the comparative question)?
B : (Runs her finger along the row, indicating she would rather have those "candies".)
T : You would rather have the candies in the row?
B : (Nods "yes").
T : Why? Would there be more to eat?
B : (Vigorously nods her head "yes".)
T : (Casts doubt on Brenda's answer) Tell me why you would rather have them?
B : (Looks disconcerted and stares blankly into space for approximately 15 seconds. She then turns in her chair and obviously becomes mentally active. After about 10 seconds, she looks at the teacher) They would be both the same!
T : They are both the same (again casts doubt on Brenda's answer)?
B : (Nods her head "yes".)
T : (Asks the comparative question.)
B : It would make no difference!

We believe that the row of ten and the bag of ten were initially perceptual collections for Brenda. This is strongly indicated by her comparison of the row of cubes and the bag of cubes without regard to the results of counting, even though "ten" referred to both. Her act of running her finger along the row is a strong indication that she made a gross quantitative comparison (Piaget & Szeminska, 1941). When she reconsidered, she did not look at the row or the bag. The 25 second time lapse before she declared, "They would be both the same!" indicates that she was trying to solve a problem. Our inference is that she re-presented past counting activity to solve her problem.

1.39. If Brenda did re-present prior counting activity, she would be able to view the collections of centimeter cubes from a novel perspective and compare them in terms of the result of the re-presented counting activity (which could be indexed by the number word "ten"). Her ability to take "ten" as an index of the number word sequence "1-2- . . . -10" that now implied counting apparently allowed her to introduce mobility into the perceptual collections. She could establish their equivalence regardless of their location or perceptual configuration. These abilities characterize a child in the verbal period who can count-on.

18 May 1982 Teaching Episode

<u>Counting by Ten</u>

1.40. Although "ten" had a counting-by-one meaning, we had little idea what her counting-by-ten scheme might be like. Our initial hypothesis was that her counting-by-ten scheme would be, in its development, somewhat similar to her counting-by-one scheme. The next few protocols illustrate the role that her counting-by-one scheme played in the construction of her counting-by-ten scheme. In the following protocol, Brenda substituted the act of closing a finger for the contents of figurally re-presented collections of ten.

T : How many little blocks are in this bag?
B : Ten (without counting).
T : (Places five cellophane bags, each containing ten blocks, in front of Brenda) How many bags are there?
B : (Counts the bags) Five.
T : (Covers the bags with a cloth) Can you count, using your fingers, to tell me how many little blocks are in those bags?
B : (Points to the cloth) Five.
T : There are five bags. But, if you counted the little blocks in each one of those bags, how many little blocks would you get?

B : (Opens the fingers of both of her hands and looks intently at them. She then wiggles each finger of her right hand with no visible indication of uttering number words.)
T : Count out loud so I can hear you.
B : (Sits back in her chair and looks disconcerted.)
T : You did it right!
B : Fifty!
T : How did you do that?
B : (Closes the fingers of her open hand) 10-20-30-40-50.

After the teacher asked Brenda how many little blocks there were, she produced her finger pattern for "ten". We believe that this finger pattern led her to utter "10-20-30-40-50" and to coordinate those utterances with closing fingers.

1.41. It was not clear what "fifty" referred to nor what an act of closing or wiggling a finger signified. Our initial interpretation that "fifty" referred to the blocks was corroborated by her solution to the next problem. Eight bags were hidden and she counted by ten, this time uttering the number words "10-20-30-40-50-60-70-80" aloud as she closed eight fingers. When she was asked whether there were 80 bags or 80 blocks, she said 80 blocks. She also answered that there were eight bags.

1.42. We believe that Brenda substituted a re-presented finger pattern for the blocks in a bag. What was common to the finger pattern and the covered bags was their protonumerosity--if she were to count their elements, there would be ten. "Ten", then, referred to a substitute (finger pattern) for the blocks in a bag. The act of putting down a finger seemed to signify counting that substitute by one.

1.43. We now had the problem of determining whether Brenda could consider the bags of centimeter cubes as discrete entities while simultaneously maintaining their protonumerosity. The following protocol shows how Brenda experienced difficulties. She was unable to keep track of her counting acts when she made an intuitive extension by counting by ten. Above all, making an intuitive extension requires that the items the child intends to count be unit items of some type so that they can be taken as the elements of a re-presented pattern.

T : (Places six bags in front of Brenda) How many bags do you have there?
B : (Points to each bag) Six.
T : (Covers the bags) How many bags do you have here (places two more bags in front of Brenda)?

B : Two.
T : Can you count those bags by using your fingers?
B : (Sequentially puts down six fingers in synchrony with subvocal utterances) 10-20-30-40-50-60. (She then sequentially puts down three more fingers in synchrony with subvocal utterances and looks disconcerted.)
T : (Uncovers the bags) How many bags are here?
B : Six.
T : And how many are here (pointing to the cloth)?
B : Two.
T : (Urges Brenda to count them again.)
B : (Sequentially puts down six fingers in synchrony with uttering) 10-20-30-40-50-60. (Pauses, and puts down one more finger) 70. (Sits and stares, indicating she realizes she is not done.)
T : Seventy?
B : (Puts down two more fingers) 70--90-100!

Brenda's difficulty when she tried to keep track of counting by ten could have been a recurrence of the difficulties she had previously experienced when she attempted to keep track of, say, performing three counting acts (by one) beyond six (cf. 1.06). There, she initially included the lone finger she had put down on one hand as one of the next three that she put down. This resulted in her putting down eight rather than nine fingers. However, Brenda counted to solve a subsequent task where three bags were covered by one cloth and four by another by sequentially putting down nine fingers in synchrony with the utterances "10-20-30- . . . -90". Because Brenda could have recorded four counting acts on one hand and three on her other hand, the reason she counted to "ninety" seems to be something other than failure to make a separation between two finger patterns and confirms our interpretation that her difficulty in the task of the protocol was not due to proceeding beyond six fingers. Her difficulty seemed to be that she focused on the counted elements of the collection of ten. Consequently, she could not re-present the bags as elements of a pattern she could use to keep track as she made an intuitive extension by counting by ten.

1.44. To test this interpretation, a task where three pennies were covered by one cloth and four by another was presented. To find how many pennies were covered, Brenda sequentially extended three fingers of her left hand in synchrony with "1-2-3". She paused and then made an intuitive extension. She put up the two other fingers of her left hand as she uttered "4-5" and then proceeded to her right hand. She put her thumb down, looked at her remaining fingers and exclaimed "seven". Here, she could focus on the pennies as singleton units and she could re-present them as elements of a pattern that she used to keep track of her counting acts. Brenda then made a decisive advance.

T : Seven! You did it! (Takes away the cloths and pennies.)
B : If you do it the other way . . .
T : Tell us the other way (this was suggested by a witness).
B : (Sequentially puts up three fingers) 10-20-30 (proceeds to her other hand and sequentially puts down four fingers), 40-50-60-70.
T : That's right (in surprise)!

This is a critical protocol because Brenda had just attempted to keep track of her counting acts when counting by ten, but failed and so counted to "ninety" rather than to "seventy". Brenda apparently became aware of how she counted when counting by one. She transposed the resulting structure into her counting by ten scheme, thus resolving her past conflict. But this reflective abstraction was made without the distraction of re-presenting collections of ten.

1.45. A new task was presented to test the limits of Brenda's reorganization. Would she now take the bags as singleton units and re-present them as elements of a pattern, keeping track of her counting acts as she made an intuitive extension?

T : (Places three bags under one cloth and four bags under another) Can you find out how many little blocks there are altogether (note that "three" and "four" were carried over from the task using pennies)?
B : (Sequentially puts down seven fingers in synchrony with uttering) 1-2-3-4-5-6-7.
T : Seven. Seven what, seven . . .
B : Seventy.
T : Can you count by ten to find out? Seventy is right. Can you prove it to me by counting by ten?
B : Uh-huh (yes). (Sequentially puts down five fingers on her left hand) 10-20-30-40-50 (sequentially puts down three more fingers of her right hand in spite of the teacher's statement that there were only four bags under the first cloth)--60-70-80.
T : Eighty? (The teacher had Brenda re-count. This time she stopped at "forty" when she counted the bags under the first cloth. But then she put down all five fingers of her right hand, proceeding to "ninety".)

Brenda initially viewed the bags as singleton units to be counted and counted them by one, making an intuitive extension while doing so. This novelty was a direct result of her previous reflective abstraction. She now realized that she could count the bags. Her response "seventy" was encouraging, and it was taken as an occasion for her to verify that it actually referred to the seventy blocks. However, she experienced the same difficulties that we had previously observed when she attempted to make an intuitive extension while counting by ten. So, we have no recourse but to infer that an act of putting down a finger when counting by ten was a substitute for a specified collection of ten.

1.46. It was difficult for Brenda to re-present a collection of bags as a pattern as she focused on the items in the bags (i.e., re-presented collections of ten). That she could re-present four bags as a pattern is amply demonstrated when she counted them by one. In this case, she focused on the bags as figural units of one rather than on their contents. Had Brenda viewed the bags as singleton units for "ten", she should have been able to make an intuitive extension when she counted by ten. But then the last number word uttered ("seventy") would refer to the bags rather than to the blocks. Brenda seemingly failed to "pack" the items to which "ten" referred into composite units. She could, however, re-present counted collections in a highly contextual situation when they were not actually in her immediate visual field and substituted a finger (or the act of putting down a finger) for these re-presentations.

Discussion of Brenda's Case Study

The parts of Brenda's schemes of which she was aware changed dramatically as she progressed through the periods in the development of her counting scheme. Her construction of patterns and her reorganizations of counting were manifestations of the adaptations she made in her schemes over the duration of the teaching experiment.

The Perceptual Stage

At the beginning of the experiment, the only meanings Brenda had for number words aside from counted perceptual collections were the spatial patterns for "two" and "three", and possibly an action pattern for "two". Although these results cannot be taken as confirmation of Starkey and Cooper's (1980) finding that infants are able to discriminate between two and three dots, they are compatible with the assumption that the nervous system has the built-in capacity to distinguish between spatial patterns of "twos" and "threes". We categorized these patterns as perceptual preconcepts because Brenda could recognize (but not re-present) them by saying the appropriate number word.

The criterion we used to classify a spatial pattern as a preconcept is that it be a specified perceptual collection experientially connected to some number word for the child. There is justification for this criterion. If a child counts the elements of a pattern "1-2-3", connecting the specified collection with the last number word said is a level 1 act of reflective abstraction. Without this abstraction, the pattern could not be a specified collection that constitutes the meaning of "three". If a child isolates a spatial pattern in his or her visual field on some future occasion, the assimilation could lead the child to utter the number word "three" without the intervening counting activity. In general, when the connection has been made by means of abstraction, the counting activity can be curtailed because the pattern embodies its results. Essentially, the child takes the pattern as being counted because the result of counting, were it to be carried out, is known.

Brenda initially established both her finger patterns and their connections to number words by counting. Certain features of the finger patterns, however, cannot be attributed solely to the results of counting. A pattern provides an opportunity for the child to construct the dual meaning of the result of counting--unitary and, at the same time, composite. Brenda could count out 12 blocks, but the resulting collection was not recognized by Brenda in the way that a pattern comprised by her index finger, middle finger, and ring finger could be recognized as "three". The specified collection of 12 blocks could be the meaning of "twelve" only after Brenda had counted them. The specification was temporarily introduced by counting, and the collection could not be recognized as "twelve" apart from that activity. The collection always had to be specified by counting unless it constituted a recurrent pattern.

Brenda did not seem to find meaning in counting activity per se while she was in the perceptual period. She was aware of counting in much the same way that she was of, say, skipping rope. Counting was, like skipping rope, a sensory-motor activity in which she engaged. Skipping rope could not be a meaning of "three", but if "1-2-3" was coordinated with skips, the result could be a meaning of "three". However, knowing that one engages in an activity and taking the records of the experience of engaging in the activity as a unitary whole *when there are no perceptual records of the experience* are very different. Brenda would have to take the records of counting activity as a single entity before the activity could be taken as the meaning of a number word for her. Consequently, she was limited to patterns in her construction of perceptual concepts as meanings of number words.

We found the distinction between a finger pattern as perceptual preconcept and as figurative concept important in understanding how Brenda counted two separate collections by starting with "one" and performing a single sequence of counting acts (i.e., making an intuitive extension). When her finger patterns were perceptual preconcepts, she first established two finger patterns by simultaneously putting up fingers and then counted to specify the collection of all the fingers she had put up. Each act of simultaneously putting up fingers to establish a pattern was an abbreviation of the counting activity that she had previously carried out to establish them.

When her finger patterns were figurative concepts, Brenda could complete two finger patterns as well as specify the single collection composed of their elements by performing a single sequence of counting acts. Her ability to re-present a finger pattern was the result of a level 2 reflective abstraction. She could now anticipate the perceptual result of counting in those cases where the number words referred to re-presented finger patterns. Her figurative concepts of "four" and "three" made it possible for her to experience the dual meaning of the result of counting at the level of re-presentation. These figurative wholes, when juxtaposed, provided her with an awareness of an unspecified figural plurality that she could specify by counting.

The unspecified collection comprised by the juxtaposed figurative wholes, coupled with its specification by counting, apparently allowed Brenda to establish meaning for number words beyond the range of her finger patterns. The first few of these number words came to refer to a figurative plurality of fingers. This was her most advanced meaning of number words while she was in her perceptual stage.

The Figurative Stage

The Motor Period

Brenda's figurative concepts gave her the opportunity to isolate the acts of putting up fingers as countable items. The activity of counting by putting up (or folding down) fingers in turn led to her subsequent construction of sophisticated finger patterns as figurative concepts that embodied counting activity. These patterns played the same role as her more elementary finger patterns. To the extent that they embodied counting, they also had the status of specified collections. The sophisticated finger patterns played a role in her subsequent abstraction of number word sequences as enactive preconcepts and led to the dual meanings she gave to number words--uttering a number word sequence and re-presenting a finger pattern.

The Verbal Period

The number word sequence introduced mobility into Brenda's finger patterns in that any four fingers could, for example, be a finger pattern that she could recognize when she counted. Although we do not claim that Brenda re-presented these mobile finger patterns before she counted to establish them, we do infer that she re-presented the specific finger patterns that she used to establish them. For example, we infer that Brenda re-presented specific patterns when she counted four more times and stopped when she recognized three fingers of one hand together with one finger on her other hand as "four" (cf. 1.36).

Number words beyond the range of her sophisticated finger patterns had a dual meaning late in her verbal period. They referred to a plurality of fingers that could be bounded by the activity of counting them as well as to a number word sequence that she actually uttered. Eventually, a number word became an index of its associated number word sequence, and the sequence then became an enactive concept.

Brenda's developing meanings of "ten" can be understood in the context of the developing meaning of other number words. In the verbal period, "ten" came to refer to an enactive concept--re-presenting ten number words in sequence as a substitute for counting a collection. Counting by ten, however, remained problematic for her. Although she made progress and substituted a motor act for a finger pattern for "ten", she could not transform her finger patterns for "ten" into numerical composites. That is, she could not focus on the perceptual collections as one item while simultaneously maintaining their protonumerosity. When she made an intuitive extension by counting by ten, she invariably lost track of counting and did not know when to stop. We took this as an indication that Brenda focused on the individual unit items when she counted by ten.

2. TARUS

The periods in Tarus's construction of the counting scheme that we documented in Chapters II and III are summarized in Figure 2. Starting on 22 October 1980 (cf. 2.01), Tarus's perceptual period lasted until 5 March 1981, when we observed him counting the acts of putting up fingers for the first time (cf. 2.09). On 17 December 1981, the beginning of the second year of the teaching experiment, we observed a curtailment in putting up fingers (cf. 2.15) when he counted to "fifteen" when reenacting the solution of a task. His vocal acts of uttering number words now signified motor acts. As indicated in Figure 2, there is an uncertainty about whether Tarus should be classified as being in the motor period or in the verbal period from 6/81 to 12/81, because he was in his verbal period at the time we first observed him during the second year of the experiment. Our best estimate is that he entered his verbal period sometime during the fall of the 1981-1982 school year, because he was still in his motor period when he left the first grade. However, exactly when he entered his verbal period is not a major issue in the teaching experiment because he did not enter an abstract period during the second year.

Figure 2

Periods in Tarus's Construction of the Counting Scheme

```
VERBAL      |                                   *********
PERIOD      |
            |
MOTOR       |              *****
PERIOD      |
            |
PERCEPTUAL  |  ********
PERIOD      | .________.______._________.__________.

           10/80     3/81  6/81     12/81       6/82
```

The Perceptual Period

22 October 1980 Interview

<u>**Spatial Patterns as Perceptual Preconcepts**</u>

2.26. In the initial interview that was used to select the children, Tarus recognized a wider range of patterns than did Brenda. He recognized any two items as "two", various triangular and linear arrangement of three items as "three", square arrangements of four items as "four", and a domino arrangement of five items as "five". Other than domino patterns, Tarus had difficulty recognizing patterns for "four" and "five". He recognized a diamond four on the second trial but did not recognize a row of four items as "four", nor did he recognize a random arrangement of five items as "five". Moreover, he had to count to find how many marbles were in piles of four and five.

2.27. There was no indication that Tarus had constructed an enactive preconcept for "two" as Brenda did (cf. 1.26). Moreover, even though he could re-present a triangular three (cf. 2.03), we do not attribute a figurative concept of "three" to him because he could not count the three items of a hidden collection unless he first saw them (cf. 2.03). He had to see the patterns before he could re-present them and this was different from our observations of Brenda. Therefore, we classified his spatial patterns for "two" and "three" as *figurative preconcepts* at the time of the interview. They were also perceptual preconcepts because Tarus *could* recognize them, as indicated by his saying the respective number words. But they were not figurative concepts because he could not re-present the patterns upon hearing the number words "two" or "three".

10 February 1981 Teaching Episode

<u>**Spatio-Motor Patterns as Enactive Preconcepts**</u>

2.28. Tarus had constructed spatio-motor patterns as enactive preconcepts for the number words "two" through "five" in previous teaching episodes. However, his use of spatio-motor patterns to solve problems was restricted to the situations in which they were initially constructed. The following protocol documents one of our attempts to have Tarus generalize their use. Our hypothesis was that since "five" and "three" were connected to spatial patterns, Tarus would substitute these patterns for the marbles he had placed into a cup and then use his spatio-motor patterns to specify the collection formed by the juxtaposed patterns. His use of spatial patterns reveals their function.

T : (Places a cup and a collection of marbles in front of Tarus) Put five marbles in here.
Ta : (Places marbles one by one into a domino five pattern and then puts them into the cup.)
T : Put three more in there.
Ta : (Places marbles one by one into a triangular three and then puts them into the cup.)
T : How many do you have in there? (Places his hand over the aperture of the cup.)
Ta : (Attempts to look through the side of the cup to see the marbles, but does not count.)
T : Do you know how many are in there?
Ta : Five--three.
T : Can you count them?
Ta : (Sequentially puts up fingers on his left hand and then continues, sequentially putting up three fingers on his right hand synchronous with subvocal utterances) Eight.

The way in which Tarus made domino five and triangular three patterns indicates that these patterns were his meanings of the corresponding number words. However, even though he had well-developed spatio-motor patterns corresponding to the spatial patterns, he used his finger patterns to count the hidden marbles. Our hypothesis was not confirmed.

While spatio-motor patterns constituted one meaning of the number words, it was a meaning restricted to the context of counting the items of screened patterns.

Finger Patterns as Figurative Concepts

2.29. The reason Tarus used his finger patterns in 2.28 seemed to be that the spatial patterns he had made were destroyed when he put the marbles into the cups. They were no longer "there", and he did not seem to be able to re-present them and count their elements. He overcame this difficulty by using his finger patterns for "three" and "five" when he counted. He had first been observed using finger patterns as figurative concepts 6 days earlier (cf. 2.06).

The Emergence of Counting as an Enactive Preconcept

2.30. We did not call counting an enactive preconcept for Brenda until early in her verbal period. It was not until then that we could justify the inference that counting was carried out to specify a figural plurality of fingers. Tarus, however, provided several indications that he was becoming aware of the distinction between the items that he intended to count (e.g., marbles) and the items that he actually counted (e.g., fingers) late in his perceptual period. The following protocol suggests that counting was carried out to specify a figural collection of marbles.

T : Take seven marbles.
Ta : (Coordinates selection of marbles with uttering) 1-2-3-4-5-6-7. (Takes them in one hand and places them in a cup.)
T : Take two more.
Ta : (Again coordinates selection of marbles with uttering)1-2. (Places them in the same cup.)
T : How many in there?
Ta : (Sequentially puts up fingers, five on his left hand and two on his right) 1-2-3-4-5-6-7. (Continues, sequentially putting up fingers on his right hand) 8-9.

Tarus seemed to count to specify the collection of marbles that he placed into the cup. We infer, however, that Tarus re-presented collections of fingers before he counted and substituted these for those of hidden marbles because he sequentially put up fingers to complete finger patterns. He *substituted* rather than *replaced* collections of fingers for the collections of marbles in the cup and reenacted counting the marbles by counting his fingers. This was possible because "seven" could refer to the activity of counting a collection of items until he reached the number word "seven". In this sense, a collection of seven fingers and seven marbles could be "the same". Counting was still a preconcept, however, because he did not re-present counting and substitute that re-presentation for the activity. Nevertheless, we believe that Tarus was beginning to find meaning for "seven" in the activity of counting.

The Motor Period

Mobile Finger Patterns and Spatio-Auditory Patterns

2.31. The most significant conceptual structures that Tarus constructed while he was in his motor period were mobile finger patterns (cf. 2.11, 2.12) and spatio-auditory patterns (cf. 2.13, 2.14). The former were produced by counting motor unit items while making an intuitive extension of counting. They were specified sequences of finger movements that were bounded by the activity of producing them. We infer that he re-presented finger movements before he counted. We do not mean by this that he visualized a finger movement; instead because the finger movements were embodied in his finger patterns, he could re-present the movements by re-presenting a plurality of fingers. We classify his mobile finger patterns as figurative concepts with an enactive component. They could be also called enactive concepts, but we feel that calling them figurative concepts more adequately emphasizes the necessary figurative component of re-presentation.

The motor activity was curtailed when he produced the spatio-auditory patterns that he had abstracted from the mobile finger patterns. He implemented his spatio-auditory patterns by saying three or four number words in sequence. His lack of a spatio-auditory pattern for "five" strongly indicated that a specified collection of items was active in re-presentation when he made an intuitive extension by saying three or four number words. Had he simply recognized having uttered three or four number words, he would probably have recognized saying five number words as well. Consequently, his spatio-auditory patterns for "three" and "four" were classified as figurative concepts.

The Verbal Period

The extent to which counting served as a meaning of number words for Tarus while he was in his motor period is at least partially clarified by the counting solutions he produced early in his verbal period. One issue that we investigated was whether he could reflect on the results of counting--was he aware of how he counted? Was he aware, for example, of the number word he said first? To specify a plurality of marbles comprised by collections of nine and six, Tarus silently uttered number words (cf. 2.16). But, when he was finished, he could not say whether he started with "one" or with some other number word, nor could he explain how he knew when to stop counting (2.18). Like Brenda (cf. 1.13), he could not reflect on his preceding counting activity.

He could, however, reenact the activity of counting perceptual unit items by uttering a number word sequence (cf. 2.19-2.23). In the reenactment, his countable items (saying number words) were substitutes for the perceptual items he had already counted, and counting was removed one step from the collection he intended to count. In this instance, the number word utterances constituted the aspect of counting within his awareness (cf. 2.15, 2.22). We therefore infer that the activity of counting could be the meaning of a number word for Tarus if he had just counted out a collection of perceptual unit items. However, he could not take counting as a given prior to counting and substitute a re-presentation for the actual activity. Consequently, he did not give meaning to a number word in terms of counting activity before he started to count. Instead, a number word signified counting for him. For example, upon hearing a number word spoken, he could count the acts of putting up fingers. To the extent that he was aware of his acts, he could find the meaning of the number word in the activity once he had started to count. But the activity was carried out as a means to an end--to specify a collection that constituted his initial meaning of the number word.

Re-presented Collections of Fingers as Meanings of Number Words

2.32. In his verbal period, Tarus did not need perceptual items, screened or otherwise, in order to count. A number word, or a numeral, could now refer to a figural collection of fingers that he specified by counting (cf. 2.15, 2.16). For example, Tarus justified counting a collection of 15 marbles hidden under two cloths, nine under one and six under the other, by uttering "1-2-3-4-5-7-8-9-10-11-12-13-14-15" as he put up fingers. Tarus did not take counting as a given and count-on, because he still could not substitute a re-presentation of counting for the activity itself. For example, he counted from "one" to solve "20 + 4", "20 + 5", and "20 + 6," even though they were presented in sequence. He failed to isolate the activity of counting to "twenty" as a common feature of his counting solutions.

Dual Meaning of Number Words

2.33. Tarus constructed dual meanings of number words, but they were distinctly different from those constructed by Brenda (cf. 1.33). Even though Tarus did not develop sophisticated finger patterns, "eleven" could both signal the activity of uttering the number word sequence "1-2- . . . - 11" as well as refer to a partially specified collection of blocks (cf. 2.21).

However, number words acquired this dual meaning only if he had counted at least part of the collection before it was hidden. He could then re-present a partially specified collection of blocks and become aware of the unspecified part. This separation of the figural collection into two parts--the part he had already counted and the part he was yet to count--indicates that the dual meanings Tarus constructed were context-specific. Unlike Tarus, Brenda had a "permanent" figural concept of "eleven" that embodied counting: her sophisticated finger pattern. Consequently, she did not need to count a perceptual collection first so that a number word would have a dual meaning.

22 January 1982 Teaching Episode

The Emergence of Counting as an Enactive Concept

2.34. The issue of whether number words could be indices of associated number word sequences for Tarus in the teaching experiment is a difficult one to resolve. Some clarification is found in this teaching episode. Tarus found how many tiles of a row were covered when he was told which tile was number nine.

T : Close your eyes (covers the first 6 tiles of a row of 12). OK. Open your eyes. Number one is right down there (pointing to the spot on the cloth that covers the first tile of the row). This one is number nine. How many are under the cloth?
Ta : I don't know! Six!
T : (Surprised) How did you do that one!?
Ta : Cause. I count backward. I say nine, then eight, seven (pointing to the appropriate tiles), six (pointing to the spot on the cloth that covers the sixth tile).
T : That's really smart.

Tarus's solution raises the possibility that, for him, "six" referred to the number word sequence "6-5-4-3-2-1". The interpretation turns on what "six" referred to when Tarus pointed to the edge of the cloth. If it referred to all of the covered tiles, then it could also have referred to the number word sequence. On the other hand, it might have referred just to the particular tile under the edge of the cloth.

2.35. To test which interpretation was more plausible, the teacher presented a new task. The row of tiles constituted a "structured" task, in that the row was arranged linearly. Tarus was told the location of the items that corresponded to the first and last number words of a possible sequence (i.e., "one" and "nine"). Moreover, he had already counted the row of tiles and was not required to organize the tiles linearly, either in action or in placement. In the new task, the teacher presented a cylindrical tube open at one end. A marble would just fit into the tube.

T : Could you put some marbles in here? Count them as you put them in.
Ta : 1-2-3- . . . -11 . . .
T : OK. That is enough. Give me your hand. I am going to give some of these to you (pours three marbles out of the tube into Tarus's hand). How many have I given you?
Ta : Three.
T : How many did you put in here? Do you remember? (Tarus doesn't) Eleven. You put eleven in here. Then I give you three. How many are left in the tube?
Ta : (Buries his head in his arms and plays with the three marbles) Ten.
T : How did you get ten?
Ta : (After a long pause) I count.
T : How did you count?
Ta : (No response.)

The teacher presented two more tasks of this type in which Tarus remembered how many marbles he put into the tube before taking out two. But, on each occasion, he guessed how many marbles remained in the tube. There was no indication that he had counted and, on one occasion, he said that he had not counted. The critical difference between these tasks and the task involving the row of tiles (cf. 2.34) was that Tarus would be required to to produce a backward number word sequence when no cues as to the location of the items corresponding to the first and last number words of the sequence were given. Tarus simply played with the three marbles that he was given. The inability to produce a number word sequence in this situation makes plausible the interpretation that number word sequences were not yet enactive concepts for Tarus.

22 April 1982 Teaching Episode

Counting as an Enactive Concept

2.36. One of the best indications that number words finally became indices of number word sequences occurred in the 22 April 1982 teaching episode (cf. 2.25). To find how many Snickers bars would be left in a basket if two or three were taken out, Tarus started with the given number word that referred to the Snickers bars and said two (or three) number words in the backward direction to find how many were left. He did not have to first utter the number word sequence forward in order to establish an experiential meaning for "eight" and "twelve"--he could take his forward number word sequence as a given. It was as if he had already produced the forward number word sequence, which is to say that it was active in re-presentation, in sharp contrast to his earlier behavior (cf. 2.35).

13 May 1982 Teaching Episode

The Meaning of "Ten"

2.37. When Tarus was in his verbal period, "ten" could refer to an enactive concept in the same way as any other number word could (cf. 2.36). In the following paragraphs, we investigate the types of wholes Tarus could count when he used his number word sequence "10-20-30-40- . . . ". Tarus, like Brenda, could take perceptual collections of ten as being countable. That is, he could coordinate the number word sequence "10-20-30-40- . . . " with specific perceptual collections of ten items. But counting by ten had specific limitations that became apparent when the collections were screened from view.

2.38. There were circumstances in which Tarus produced his number word sequence "10-20-30- . . . " when only one collection of ten was in his visual field. For example, after the teacher had asked Tarus to make a tower of ten blocks, Tarus stacked blocks one by one as he uttered "1-2-3- 4- . . . -10". He was then asked to pretend to make another tower of ten blocks on top of the one he had just made. He said there would now be 20 and went on, saying there would be 30 if ten more were put on top of the 20, etc. Once he had counted up to "ten", he proceeded to utter his number word sequence "10-20- . . . ". This is similar to the situation in which Brenda counted by ten (cf. 1.41). We believe, however, that his utterances beyond "ten" did not refer to anything. He was simply reciting his number word sequence.

2.39. The narrow scope of Tarus's seemingly creative counting behavior was demonstrated in the next task. The teacher put a stack of four blocks by the stack of ten and Tarus immediately said that there were 14 blocks. But when the teacher asked Tarus to pretend to make another stack of ten, Tarus said there would be 15. The teacher went on, directing Tarus to count ten more. After he had helped Tarus to count-on from "fourteen", Tarus put up fingers as he uttered "15-16- . . . -24". When the teacher then asked Tarus to pretend to count a stack of ten more blocks, Tarus again had to be helped by the teacher to count-on from "twenty-four".

Tarus's failure to begin counting the stacks of ten blocks by one on his own indicates that he did not re-present a collection of ten blocks. Had he done so, he could have counted the elements of the re-presented collection. A second indication occurred when he was asked how many blocks there would be if ten more were added immediately after counting "25-26-27-28- . . . - 34" (with the help of the teacher). He responded by saying "thirty-five". However, when he was presented with four bags of ten blocks and four more individual blocks, Tarus counted "10-20-30-40; 41-42-43-44", indicating that he could discriminate between perceptual units of ten and perceptual units of one.

2.40. When Tarus believed that ten hidden items were part of the larger collection he was counting, he did manage to continue counting by folding down his fingers as he produced a number word sequence, say, "24-25- . . . -33". In this situation, he could create re-presentations of specific collections that he believed were "there". However, he was not able to create the figural collection in the absence of given (but hidden) perceptual material.

Discussion of Tarus's Case Study

The Perceptual Stage

Early in his perceptual period, Tarus could re-present spatial patterns for "two" and "three" that he had isolated in his visual field. His difficulty in re-presenting these patterns and then counting their elements supports our contention that children can first establish the connections between spatial patterns and number words by counting patterns that are in their visual field. Tarus's ability to recognize but not re-present domino patterns for "four" and "five" also supports this contention (cf. 2.26).

When a child reenacts a previously recognized spatial pattern by counting, the reenactments might lead to a connection between the appropriate number word and a visualized image of the pattern. In this case, upon hearing the number word spoken, the child could re-present an appropriate spatial pattern and then count its elements. In Tarus's case, this hypothesis was not confirmed because he developed spatio-motor patterns as enactive preconcepts. He used them only in situations similar to those from which they had been abstracted. Tarus had to believe that the perceptual collections were arranged in patterns before he would use his spatio-motor patterns to find how many items were in two hidden collections regardless of hearing the number words spoken (cf. 2.28.). There was little assimilating generalization. In retrospect, it seemed as if Tarus had developed a context-specific scheme that did not contribute to his subsequent progress.

Tarus's finger patterns spontaneously emerged as figurative concepts and he used them as substitutes for hidden perceptual collections when he solved a broad range of additive tasks. This is in contrast to Brenda, whose finger patterns as figurative concepts seemed to stand only for themselves; they were replacements rather than substitutes.

The Figurative Stage

The Motor Period

After Tarus's finger patterns had emerged as figurative concepts, there was a period when he counted his fingers as perceptual items (indicated by his prolonged use of specific finger patterns). Upon the achievement of his motor period, Tarus developed mobile finger patterns and used them to make intuitive extensions. In contrast, it was not until Brenda achieved her verbal period that she developed mobile finger patterns. One possible reason for this difference is that Tarus appeared to re-present a wider variety of perceptual collections. Tarus independently and spontaneously introduced finger patterns as figurative concepts and those finger patterns referred to hidden collections. Brenda's finger patterns, however, were replacements rather than substitutes for hidden collections. In fact, Brenda used her finger patterns as replacements for over a month before we inferred that she could re-present them. Even then there was little reason to believe that her finger patterns stood for anything other than themselves.

Because Tarus's goal was to count hidden items, he isolated his acts of putting up fingers more rapidly than did Brenda and overcame the perceptual constraints of specific finger patterns. He established a specified collection of fingers rather than a specified finger pattern when he made an intuitive extension. At about this time, mobile finger patterns emerged for "two", "three", "four, and "five". He used these mobile finger patterns to bridge from one hand to the other as he made an intuitive extension. Spatio-auditory patterns also emerged for "three" and "four" but not for "five".

Tarus's mobile finger patterns served as a basis for the development of figural pluralities as meanings for the number words through and beyond the second decade. "Twenty", for example, could now refer to a figural plurality of fingers that he specified by counting. He seemed to be aware of his motor acts when he was actually counting and these motor acts could refer to the items of a hidden collection.

Like Brenda, the aspects of counting within Tarus's awareness changed dramatically with the emergence of a novel type of countable item. Also, collections other than finger patterns played an important role in his progress, in contrast to Brenda's almost total reliance on finger patterns. During our work with Tarus, we felt he would make much faster progress than Brenda but that did not turn out to be true.

The Verbal Period

Early in his verbal period, Tarus recognized that a pattern was established by saying four or five number words such as "eight-nine-ten-eleven" and "twelve-thirteen-fourteen-fifteen-sixteen". There was good indication that he organized these utterances into recognizable patterns as he went along. Encouraged by this behavior, we expected Tarus to enter his abstract period soon. However, he failed to make substantial progress other than developing counting as an enactive concept.

Number words that he heard spoken led Tarus to subvocally utter number word sequences early in his verbal period, and he seemed to focus inwardly on his utterances. He was totally consumed with uttering number words and he seemed to find meaning in the activity. In other situations, he appeared to create meaning by re-presenting counted collections and then reenacting counting (cf. 2.33). Dual meanings emerged when he reenacted counting. His re-presentation of the specified collection was the source of his dual meaning--a specified figural collection and a number word sequence.

Eventually, number words seemed to become indices for number word sequences for Tarus (cf. 2.36). In particular, "ten" could refer to the number word sequence "1-2-3- . . . -10" and he could substitute "ten" for the activity of uttering the sequence. Moreover, "ten" could refer to a specified figural collection if he believed that there were ten items hidden from view. However, he could not create a figural collection and count its elements to extend an immediately preceding counting activity when there were no hidden collections available that he could take as givens. He could re-present and reenact immediately prior experiences, but he could not create new experiences in the realm of re-presentation without the immediately prior experience.

3. JAMES

The periods in James's construction of the counting scheme that we documented in Chapters II and III are summarized in Figure 3. On 25 March 1981 (cf. 3.01), James was well into his perceptual period when we interviewed him as a possible candidate for the teaching experiment. At the beginning of the second year of the teaching experiment on 7 December 1981, James was in his motor period. Because of his temporary advances at the beginning of the teaching experiment, it is indeed quite likely that James entered his motor period during the fall of 1981. In any event, his motor period lasted until 25 January 1982, when we observed curtailment of pointing acts when he counted to "fifteen" (cf.

3.16). His vocal acts of uttering number words now signified motor acts, and he remained in his verbal period for the remainder of the teaching experiment.

Figure 3

Periods in James's Construction of the Counting Scheme

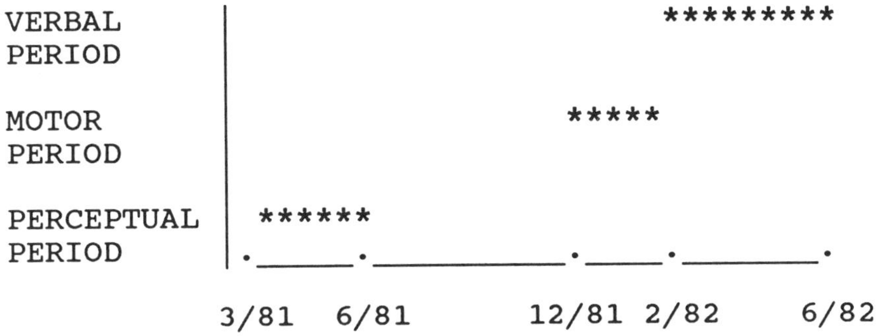

The Perceptual Period

5 March 1981 Interview

James's ability to recognize spatial patterns at the time of his entry into the teaching experiment was on a par with Tarus's (cf. 2.26). James could recognize rows of two, three, and four marbles, a triangular arrangement of three marbles, a square arrangement of four marbles, and a domino arrangement of five marbles without counting. To say how many marbles there were in a rectangular six pattern, however, he had to count the two rows of three marbles.

3.21. As with Tarus, there was no indication that James could give meaning to a number word by re-presenting a spatial pattern. However, if he saw the pattern before it was hidden, he could re-present it. For example, James recognized a triangular arrangement of three items as "three" and a row of two items as "two" before they were hidden. To count the hidden items, he pointed in the air over the respective cloths as he said, "one, two, un-three, un-four, un-five". He also re-presented a spatial pattern for "four" and counted its elements after seeing it (cf. 3.13).

Finger Patterns as Perceptual Preconcepts

3.22. James used his finger patterns to count two previously hidden arrays of squares glued onto a card after he was shown the arrays. Had he substituted his finger patterns for the hidden arrays, we would have called his finger patterns figurative preconcepts because he simultaneously put up fingers. In paragraph 3.25, we will see that by the middle of May, finger patterns emerged for James as figurative preconcepts and then became figurative concepts. This is an important distinction, because James's use of finger patterns is typical. In the initial interview, James counted the elements of his finger patterns by touching his fingers to his lips as he uttered number words. Although this might seem to indicate that number words signaled a re-presentation of finger patterns, his capricious use of finger patterns argues against that interpretation. In the following protocol, James had just counted five squares and recognized three squares as "three" before both collections were hidden.

T : How many altogether?
J : (Sequentially touches fingers to his lips) 1-2-3-4-5-6-7-8-9-10. Ten.

There were no pauses that might indicate that James's counting activity carried the significance of counting the hidden squares. He did not even pause when he went from one hand to the other. He seemed to be counting the fingers on his two open hands as replacements for the hidden items. On other occasions, however, pauses did indicate separations in counting activity that corresponded to the visual separations of the cloths (cf. 3.01). In these cases, there is no reason to believe that the finger patterns were substitutes for the collections that were hidden from view. He seemed to use his finger patterns as replacements rather than as substitutes for the hidden collections.

14 April 1981 Teaching Episode

Spatio-Motor Patterns as Enactive Preconcepts

3.23. In two previous teaching episodes (31 March 1981 and 8 April 1981), James developed spatio-motor patterns for the number words "two" through "six". In the following protocol, the teacher placed two cloths in front of James and asked him to pretend that there were chocolate chip cookies under each.

T : (Lifts the two cloths) There are three under here (the cloth to James's right) and five under here (the cloth to James's left). How many cookies are under both cloths?

J : (Points to specific spots on the left cloth where the spots form a domino five) 1-2-3-4-5 (points to specific spots on the right cloth where the spots form a square four), 6-7-8-9.

James's completion of a domino five pattern cannot be taken as a solid indication that he re-presented a spatial pattern, because he may have completed a motor pattern. We have to look at how he counted over the second cloth. There, he enacted a spatio-motor pattern for "four" that he had already completed when he solved an immediately preceding task. The previous experience rather than the word "three" seemed to be significant to him. He filled the "void" created by not having three countable items in his visual field with a reenactment of an immediate past experience. As such, we infer that the production of the spatio-motor pattern did not involve a re-presentation of the spatial pattern that had served in its construction. In this sense, the spatio-motor patterns were enactive preconcepts. They were something that James did to create meaning (the completed spatial patterns) for certain number words in situations similar to those from which they (the spatio-motor patterns) had been abstracted.

3.24. There were no indications that James re-presented the spatio-motor patterns because, like Tarus (cf. 2.28), he used them only in situations similar to those from which they had been abstracted. For example, after he put six blocks into one cup and five into another, he found how many blocks there were in both cups by proceeding as follows.

J : (Slaps the cup containing six blocks) Six. (Touching his lips with fingers) 1-2-3-4-5-6. (Slaps the other cup) You got five.

James failed to proceed because he did not have five more fingers. To solve the task by completing a spatio-motor pattern for "five" he would at least have to re-present and count the elements of a spatial pattern. His inability to do so serves as a basis for inferring that his spatial pattern for "five" was no more than a figurative preconcept. The issue of whether James could re-present his spatio-motor patterns is resolved, because he did not even re-present the spatial patterns on which they were based.

5 May 1981 Teaching Episode

Spatial Patterns as Figurative Concepts

3.25. In an earlier teaching episode, James began to curtail the motor acts of his spatio-motor patterns (cf. 3.11, 3.13, 3.14). In this teaching episode, we inferred that James re-presented spatial patterns for the number words "two" through "five" and counted their elements. The behavioral indication was that James nodded his head as if scanning spatial patterns when he counted the screened collections. Although there were occasions when he did complete a spatio-motor pattern, his curtailment of the motor component seemed to result from his re-presentation of the spatial patterns because he could focus on the elements of the re-presented spatial patterns and count them without producing motor activity.

19 May 1981 Teaching Episode

Finger Patterns as Figurative Preconcepts

3.26. We tested the hypothesis that James could re-present spatial patterns that he saw before they were hidden and use his spatio-motor patterns to specify the collection formed by two juxtaposed spatial patterns. However, our hypothesis was not confirmed. James used his finger patterns even though his spatial patterns were now figurative concepts.

T : (Places five blocks into a domino pattern) James, how many blocks are there?
J : (Immediately) Five.
T : (Places three blocks into a triangular pattern) How many blocks are there?
J : (Immediately) Three.
T : How many blocks are there altogether (hides the blocks with his hand)?
J : Five--three (simultaneously puts up five fingers on his right hand and three fingers on his left hand. He then touches his lips with each extended finger, uttering) 1-2-3-4-5-6-7-8. Eight.

His failure to use spatio-motor patterns indicates their context-specific nature and suggests they were connected to number words and numerals rather than re-presentations of spatial patterns. This phenomenon is similar to the one we observed in Tarus's case study (cf. 2.28). Too, James's utterance of "eight" in the protocol above seemed to indicate a specified collection of blocks as well as fingers. This was also indicated by his solution to the subsequent task in which the interviewer hid a triangular pattern of three blocks and two additional blocks. When asked how many blocks there were altogether, James responded "five" immediately, without using his finger patterns. The observation that "five" clearly referred to the blocks provides justification for the inference that, in the above protocol, James used his finger patterns to specify how many blocks were hidden. Because the finger patterns were substitutes for the blocks, we call them figurative (as well as perceptual) preconcepts.

The Motor Period

7 December 1981 Interview

Counting as an Enactive Preconcept

3.27. In the protocol of paragraph 3.26, James was obviously aware of his spatial patterns and finger patterns. Moreover, "eight" seemed to refer to a specified collection of fingers as well as to blocks when he finished counting. The issue of which aspects of counting were within his awareness, however, has yet to be resolved. Other observations suggest that James was particularly unaware of how he counted: the results of counting were not items of reflection, and he did not notice conflicts that were implicit in his counting activity. Counting seemed to be nothing more than a sensory-motor activity that he carried out. In this interview, James appeared to become aware of his motor acts as countable items while he was counting, but he still needed actual engagement in some activity to give meaning to number words beyond the range of his finger patterns. To find how many blocks were under two cloths, one covering 14 and the other 5, James sequentially put up fingers until he reached "ten" and then simultaneously moved both hands as he continued, "11-12-13-14". Although he could not re-present counting to "fourteen" in this way, he did use counting for constructing a specified collection to give experiential meaning to "fourteen".

Because he was momentarily aware of his motor acts as countable items, we infer that counting up to a given number word was an enactive preconcept. James found meaning for "fourteen" in the experience of counting as well as in the specified collection of motor acts bounded at the ends by the initiation and termination of counting. It is important to remember that the distinct motor acts actually signified corresponding blocks and thereby acquired a re-presentational function. This is essential for counting to be considered an enactive preconcept.

The Verbal Period

2 February 1982 Teaching Episode

Finger Patterns as Figurative Concepts

3.28. James used his finger patterns in this teaching episode in a way that we did not observe in the case of the other two children. The adaptation that he made was completely unexpected.

T : (With the help of James, places the sentence "9 + 4 = " on the table) Teach me how to do this problem.
J : (Puts up three fingers) 1-2-3- . . . It's thirteen!
T : It's thirteen (surprised)!
J : (Sequentially puts up fingers while looking at his hands) 1-2-3-4-5-6-7-8-9. (Puts up five fingers on his left hand and four on his right hand and continues, putting up his thumb, his index finger, his middle finger, and his ring finger while looking at his right hand) 10-11-12-13.
T : It is thirteen!

The inference that James re-presented his finger patterns prior to counting is solidly indicated by his exclamation, "It's thirteen!" after he had put up only three fingers. Once he had started to count the elements of his finger pattern for "nine", he anticipated the results of counting to complete both finger patterns. He could apparently "see" that his finger pattern for "four" would be separated into a finger pattern for "three" and one element that he could add to his finger pattern for "nine", making two open hands. This hypothesis is confirmed by the way in which he put up four more fingers after completing a finger pattern for "nine".

3.29. "Nine" referred to his open left hand and to the finger pattern on his right hand consisting of his index, middle, ring, and little fingers. When he continued to count, he put up his index, middle, and ring fingers, and his thumb. The act of putting up his thumb indicates that he had previously separated a finger pattern for "four" into three fingers and another finger that completed two open hands. This solution demonstrates that he could re-present his finger patterns before he counted their elements and recombine them to form new finger patterns. Counting introduced a new mobility into his finger patterns and led to a re-presentation of the results of the activity without the activity actually being carried out.

Dual Meanings of Number Words

3.30. James's solution of a subsequent task indicated that a number word had a dual meaning--it could refer to the activity of uttering the standard number word sequence up to and including the given number word, as well as to a figural collection of fingers.

T : OK, James, make another hard problem!

J : (Assembles the sentence "33 + 5 = ___" and utters) 1-2-3- . . . -22-23-24 (spontaneously puts up fingers) 25-26-28-29-31-32-33 (sits back in his chair, changes from his left hand to his right hand, and continues putting up fingers), 34-35-36-38-39.

The way James spontaneously started putting up fingers when he reached "twenty-five" strongly indicates that uttering a number word carried the significance of putting up a finger, regardless of whether the actual motor act was carried out. Uttering the number word sequence 1-2- . . . -33 (even with its omissions) was a curtailment of the activity of putting up fingers, and "thirty-three" referred to the specified figural collection of fingers spanned by the number word sequence. We infer that the activity of counting to "thirty-three" was the meaning he gave to the number word because he seemed to be aware of his utterances. But the number word sequence was still a preconcept in that it had to actually be uttered, and James could not take it as a given.

2 March and 31 May 1982 Teaching Episodes

Dual Meanings in Counting-On

3.31. Counting-on emerged for James in much the same way as it did for Brenda. An intervention made by the teacher played a critical role in James's progress and led him to substitute a re-presented finger pattern for the activity of counting. This substitution was made possible by the dual meaning that he had established for number words (cf. 3.18, 3.19).

18 May 1982 Teaching Episode

Counting by Ten

3.32. The introduction of a motor act into his counting by ten scheme occurred when James attempted to count hidden perceptual collections of ten. The following protocol documents James's first reorganization of counting by ten.

T : Would you take ten little blocks, James?
J : (Takes a handful of blocks and counts out ten.)
T : Now, I am going to give you these (places four bags of blocks with James's pile of ten). How many little blocks do you have now?
J : 10-20-30-40 (pointing to each bag as he utters number words), f-i-f-t-y!
T : OK. Let's put all of those under this cloth (covers the blocks). How many little blocks under that cloth?
J : Fifty.
T : Under this (another) cloth, I am going to put five bags (covers five bags). How many blocks are under both cloths?
J : (Touches the cloth covering the four bags and the pile of ten little blocks. He then touches the other cloth in distinct places in synchrony with uttering) 60-70-80-90 (looks up), hundred (covers his eyes and mumbles number words, indicating that he is not sure of when to stop).
T : Keep track for sure.
J : (Places his hand over the first cloth and utters) 10-20-30-40-50- . . .
T : How many are under here (pointing to the other cloth)?
J : (Abruptly sits back in his chair and sequentially puts up fingers on his left hand in synchrony with uttering) 10-20-30-40-50-60-70-80-90-100.

The request to count the little blocks led James to count the four bags of blocks and the pile of ten blocks by ten. Screening the five counted and the five uncounted perceptual collections did not stop James from proceeding. He clearly viewed the uncounted perceptual collections of ten as belonging with the counted perceptual collections, even though they were hidden beneath a different cloth. We believe that, initially, a common element was that if each was counted, the same number word sequence would be produced. This homogeneity of countable perceptual collections of ten was a crucial feature of the initial extension of counting by ten that James made--the five bags of cubes were added after James had just counted "10-20-30-40-50"; from his perspective, then, the task was to continue to count bags of cubes.

3.33. On his first attempt to count the hidden bags, James touched the cloth covering the five bags at specific locations. This indicates that he coordinated the sequential production of number words with the sequential production of visualized images of a bag of cubes--he counted figural items.

3.34. James wanted to keep track of how many times he counted over the second cloth, but had no means to do so. In his search to find a way, James extricated himself from the context of counting visualized images of hidden bags and introduced a novel countable item (putting up a finger) into his counting activity. This countable motor unit did not correspond to the pointing acts he had produced in his immediate past counting experience. Instead, its source was the motor counting scheme for one that he had constructed earlier in the same school year. It was quite natural for him to use finger patterns to know when to stop counting even though he was now using a different number word sequence. We understand the modification of his counting by ten scheme as taking each bag of blocks as a singleton rather than as a collection of ten items. This assimilation led to his putting up fingers, because he was essentially coordinating singleton units with uttering the number words "10-20- . . .".

3.35. The nature of the items that were signified by acts of putting up fingers remains to be analyzed. Their nature is indicated by James's solution of a subsequent task where three bags were hidden by one cloth and five by another. After he counted by ten as he put up fingers, James insisted that there were eighty bags, even though the teacher asked him whether there were eighty or eight. He also said that there were ten blocks in a bag, but he never said that there were eight bags and eighty blocks. This did not seem to be a linguistic difficulty. The act of putting up a finger was a substitute for a bag taken as a singleton without regard to the items it contained, even though he knew that "ten" would be the last number word that he would utter if he counted the blocks in a bag. However, the act of putting up a finger was not a substitute for a specified collection of blocks but for a single bag. This analysis is supported by James's failure to discriminate between counting by ten and by one when both bags of ten and individual cubes were hidden. If he started to count by ten, he did not shift to counting by one in the same counting episode. It was as if he were counting by one but using a different number word sequence.

Discussion of James's Case Study

The Perceptual Stage

Of the three children, we had the most difficulty interpreting James's behavior because he seemed to use his schemes differently. But, in its broad outlines, his progress was neither faster nor slower than either Tarus's or Brenda's. Nevertheless, the differences in the conceptual structures that he used to give meaning to number words must be documented because they could easily be given alternative interpretations.

We make a distinction between finger patterns as perceptual preconcepts and as figurative preconcepts. As perceptual preconcepts, Brenda used her finger patterns only as replacements for hidden collections. They served no re-presentative function. James's use of finger patterns, even though self-generated, initially seemed to be on a par with Brenda's. Finger patterns were a result of his search for perceptual items to count. From James's perspective, the items that he found--his fingers--just happened to occur in certain patterns.

As figurative preconcepts, James used his finger patterns as substitutes for specific spatial patterns. He seemed to re-present the spatial patterns prior to substituting a finger pattern for them. In essence, he substituted a perceptual finger pattern for a figural spatial pattern. In this sense, the finger patterns signified the spatial patterns, and counting the fingers of the patterns carried the significance of counting the elements of the spatial pattern.

For James as well as for Tarus, spatio-motor patterns functioned as context-specific schemes that were used in situations similar to those from which they had been abstracted. They were primarily enactive preconcepts before James curtailed the motor activity involved in the patterns. At this time, he did not first re-present the associated spatial pattern, but instead carried out the motor activity to create the spatial pattern. He subsequently abstracted the spatial patterns and became able to re-present them as he uttered sequences of number words (e.g., 9-10-11-12). These spatio-auditory patterns were associated with the number words through "five" for James (and "four" for Tarus) and were used prominently while he was in his verbal period.

The Figurative Stage

The Motor Period

In the motor period, James's counting scheme became an enactive preconcept (cf. 3.28). He had isolated the motor activity while he was engaged in counting activity, as indicated by the way he changed from putting up fingers to moving both hands when counting to "fourteen". It is critical to note that moving his hands was a "natural" extension of putting up fingers because he had all ten fingers extended and could not double use fingers. He had been moving his hands when putting up fingers, so those motor items were in his immediate experience.

The Verbal Period

James's finger patterns emerged as figurative concepts (cf. 3.37) in a rather dramatic way. He demonstrated an ability to reorganize two re-presented finger patterns, one for "nine" and one for "four", to form a single finger pattern. The figural join was made possible by the mobility that counting activity introduced. He could jump to the results of counting two finger patterns because he could rearrange their elements in re-presentation and complete two open hands for "ten" and a pattern of the remaining three fingers. This forward reorganization was possible because he had started to count. Dual meanings for number words emerged at the same time that James figurally joined two re-presented finger patterns. In fact, it is possible to interpret this reorganization as a consequence of dual meanings of number words. Since the finger patterns embodied counting, which he had abstracted from the finger patterns in the form of a number word sequence, he could anticipate the results of counting.

James's counting by ten scheme was essentially a counting by one scheme. He constructed a countable motor unit for "ten" when he attempted to count five hidden bags of blocks by continuing the activity of counting by ten to "fifty" (cf. 3.32). This motor unit seemed to be a part of his counting by one scheme, because when James made an intuitive extension by counting by ten, each counting act seemed to refer to a perceptual unit of one. He seemed to "lose" the protonumerosities of the collections of blocks and could not shift from counting by ten to counting by one in the same counting episode.

PERSPECTIVES ON THE CASE STUDIES

The Perceptual Stage

When the children were in their early perceptual periods, they acted much as the children that Fischer (1981) observed at the age of 3 years, 9 months. Although they could recognize certain spatial patterns, there was little indication that they could re-present the patterns unless they saw them before the patterns were hidden. If they could recognize the patterns but could not re-present them under any circumstances, we called the patterns *perceptual preconcepts*. If they could re-present the patterns only after they saw them, we called the spatial patterns *figurative preconcepts*. We took the recognition of a pattern by saying the appropriate number word as a minimal criterion for calling the pattern a preconcept connected to the number word. We acknowledge that the children may have been nonverbally aware of a pattern they gave no indication of recognizing. But we did not call these patterns preconcepts because we are concerned with the meanings they gave to number words.

The elements of spatial patterns can appear to co-occur for children, thus providing them with a dual experience of a number word--unitary and, at the same time, composite. The children specified the composite experience--a collection--by counting the elements of the pattern. They introduced counting into the spatial patterns and its results were embodied in the patterns. In this way, the children were able to say the appropriate number word when they recognized a pattern.

Finger Patterns

Finger patterns for the number words from "one" up to and including "six" were also perceptual preconcepts for the three children early in their perceptual periods. They could establish finger patterns in their tactual and kinesthetic fields as well as in their visual field upon hearing a number word spoken. From our perspective, it was very difficult to observe what the children were doing when they established finger patterns in their tactual and kinesthetic fields. They were secretive about their methods and seemed not to want us to know that they used their fingers.

As perceptual preconcepts, Brenda and James used their finger patterns as *replacements* for hidden perceptual items. As replacements, a finger pattern did not signify other perceptual items; rather, it was used for its own sake. Whenever we could infer that the children could use their perceptual finger patterns as *substitutes* for hidden items (i.e., remaining aware of the hidden items) we called them *figurative preconcepts*. In each case (replacement and substitute), the children simultaneously rather than sequentially put up fingers to establish their finger patterns. In substitution, there is at least a minimal re-presentation of the pattern of hidden perceptual items. The number word, being connected to the finger pattern, served as a connecting link between the perceptual finger pattern and the re-presented spatial pattern.

The Figurative Stage

A behavioral indication that children re-presented finger patterns before counting is putting up fingers one after another to complete finger patterns. We feel that this behavioral indicator is justified because sequentially putting up fingers led to a reorganization of counting. After the reorganization, the children could count a partially hidden collection by first counting the visible part and then continuing to count without starting from "one" again. They started with "one" only once, beginning the count of the hidden portion with the number word that was the successor of the number word said last when counting the visible portion.

The number word that referred to the hidden portion led to a re-presentation of a composite whole--a finger pattern; had it not, the children would have become lost in counting, and would not have known when to stop.

The children could also count the items of a collection that was hidden by two cloths. We took the children's ability to count beyond an already completed count (sequentially putting up fingers to complete a finger pattern) as a good sign that the finger pattern embodied the records of counting.

Mobile Finger Patterns

Mobile finger patterns emerged in the figurative stage and consisted of a specified collection of finger movements. The result of counting was that any five fingers could be a finger pattern for "five"; the children used the pattern to keep track of counting. The children could also double use fingers in a continuation of counting--they could count by putting up fingers they had already used. Although Brenda did not develop mobile finger patterns until she was in her verbal period, Tarus and James both developed the patterns while they were in their motor periods. We believe that this difference can be attributed to the re-presentations the children created to give meaning to number words before they counted. Brenda always seemed to re-present collections of fingers--she counted what she intended to count: her fingers. The two other children could re-present collections of perceptual items other than fingers--marbles, checkers, etc. These collections were often arranged in spatial patterns and the two children re-presented these patterns and substituted finger patterns for the spatial patterns. Acts of putting up or folding down fingers then became substitutes for figural items of the re-presented collection.

The ability to substitute a finger pattern for a spatial pattern provided the children with a basis for their subsequent development of mobile finger patterns. For example, if they were counting the second hidden part of four items of a collection of twelve items, they would have only two unused fingers after they counted the first hidden part of eight items. In this situation, they might re-present a spatial pattern for "four", count its elements by putting up the two unused fingers in synchrony with saying "nine", "ten", and then continue to put up two more fingers for a second time in synchrony with saying "eleven", "twelve". They could do this because, in their past experience, they had put up fingers as substitutes for the elements of spatial patterns. Now, rather than re-present a specific finger pattern for "four", the children simply put up fingers as substitute countable items. This observation provides a solid rationale for including spatial patterns as well as finger patterns in the early experiences of perceptual children, for we believe that Tarus and James were more typical of other children than was Brenda. Nevertheless, Brenda provides an interesting contrast, allowing us to assert that there is more than one path to the development of mobile finger patterns and to the construction of motor and verbal items as countable items.

We believe that James (and perhaps Tarus) eventually re-presented mobile finger patterns prior to counting (or at least before continuing to count). This inference is based on observations made when James was in his verbal period. Brenda, however, seemed to recognize but not re-present a mobile finger pattern in a continuation of counting. If so, then what did she re-present before she continued to count? Surely she could not have counted six more times beyond counting to eight (completing a finger pattern for "eight") unless she re-presented something that could guide her counting activity.

We take that "something" as an awareness of a plurality of fingers, just as we do with the two other children; however, there is an important difference. James and Tarus could re-present any four fingers as a mobile finger pattern that seemed to be a composite whole whose items co-occurred. It seemed as if the boundaries of Brenda's specific finger pattern were "dropped out", leaving an unbounded plurality (a true plurality) of re-presented fingers. This inference is consistent with her development of sophisticated finger patterns. In fact, we believe that Brenda had a unique motor period. Her motor items were always substitutes for items of like kind (i.e., motor acts of putting up fingers were substitutes for fingers) and she seemed to see little reason to work with other perceptual items. This made it particularly difficult for us as teachers to find activities that would interest her.

Sophisticated Finger Patterns

Brenda developed sophisticated finger patterns while she was in her motor period. These patterns were abstracted from the results of counting by putting up fingers and confirm that Brenda re-presented collections of fingers before she counted to give meaning to number words.

Spatio-Auditory Patterns

For Tarus and James, spatio-auditory patterns seemed to be abstracted from the activity of substituting finger patterns for figural spatial patterns. They curtailed their results of putting up fingers and re-presented and counted the associated spatial patterns by scanning their elements as they made intuitive extensions. This development provided the two children with one avenue of progress toward the verbal period.

Eventually, all three children seemed to re-present collections of fingers and count to any reasonable number word by coordinating their standard number word sequence with acts of putting up fingers. A number word like "twenty-three" could now be given meaning by counting, and the children seemed to find meaning in the counting experience as well as in the results of counting.

Dual Meanings of Number Words

The dual meanings of number words constructed by the three children in their verbal periods were subtle and yet differed in substantial ways. In retrospect, they played an important developmental role in the overall progress of the children. Tarus became aware that a number word could refer to both the number word sequence that he uttered when counting a perceptual collection and to a re-presentation of the counted collection. He was attempting to solve a problem when he first became aware of the dual meaning. This is encouraging because it provides us as teachers with some confidence that our interventions contributed to Tarus's progress. It was extremely difficult to find situations that would foster an awareness of their activity in the three children.

The dual meanings of number words that we inferred from James's problem-solving behavior were observed in a context where he created and solved his own problems and was highly motivated to do so. For James, re-presented pluralities of fingers within and beyond the range of his mobile finger patterns seemed to be a primary source of meaning. He was confident that he could specify these collections by counting, which was now curtailed to uttering number word sequences. The meaningfulness of his counting activity when he used number words beyond the range of his mobile finger patterns resulted from his awareness of an unspecified plurality before counting and his awareness of uttering number words to specify it.

Brenda's sophisticated finger patterns seemed to embody records of counting. As she had abstracted counting from the patterns and reduced it to uttering number words in sequence, counting could refer to these sophisticated finger patterns, and vice versa. She used them interchangeably, and a number word could lead to either activity--counting or establishing a finger pattern. In the case of number words beyond her finger patterns, counting was her primary source of meaning. But there seemed to be an awareness that counting could also refer to a plurality of fingers.

Counting as the Meaning of Number Words

Eventually, number words became indices of number word sequences and counting was categorized as an enactive concept for all three children. The dual meanings of number words constructed earlier in the verbal period seemed to be the origin of the ability to re-present counting. Because number words had a counting meaning and a specified collection meaning, we found that re-presentations of counting initially involved re-presenting a specified collection that embodied records of counting. Although we did not observe it while we worked with the children, we believe in retrospect that the children would soon have become numerical. Their failure to construct the integration operation was the major disappointment of the teaching experiment.

Summary of the Types of Preconcepts and Concepts

Figure 4 contains a summary of the preconcepts and concepts that the children used to give meaning to number words during the teaching experiment as they progressed from one period of their counting scheme to an other. The entries indicate periods in the development of counting.

Figure 4

Summary of the Types of Preconcepts and Concepts

Structure Type	Finger Patterns	Spatial Patterns	Counting
Perceptual Preconcept	P	P	
Figurative Preconcept	P,M	P,M	
Enactive Preconcept			M,V
Figurative Concept	P,M,V	P,M,V	
Enactive Concept			V

Meanings of "Ten"

The meanings of "ten" that the children created are outlined below. The first three are not "countable units" and are merely restatements of the meanings of any other number word. The next two are distinguished from the first three by their function in the children's counting by ten scheme.

1. Specified collection. Any counted collection of ten perceptual items.

2. Figural pattern. Any specified collection of ten counted items that can be re-presented and where items seem to co-occur.

3. Enactive concept. Any specified collection of ten items that is framed by a re-presentation of counting.

4. Countable figural unit. Any figural pattern or enactive concept of ten that is coordinated with a number word of the sequence "10-20-30-40-50- . . . ".

5. Countable motor unit. Any motor act that is coordinated with a number word of the sequence "10-20-30-40-50- . . . " and that constitutes a substitute for a figural unit of ten.

Ten as an Enactive Concept

When the children were in their verbal periods, they could re-present the counting activity embodied in a specified collection and use the re-presentation to compare two collections. This introduced "perceptual mobility" into the collections in that the counting activity was abstracted from its particular experiential context. While the counted perceptual items were within the child's awareness, any two specified collections of ten could be viewed as having a common feature because if they were to be counted, "ten" would be the result. The specified collections were thus "framed" by counting activity, even though the child still viewed them as comprising individual items. Specified perceptual collections are initially akin to what Herscovics (1983) has identified as a unit in a physical sense: "The bag of candies is clearly discrete and experiential and remains a unit until the bag is broken" (p. 18). However, an enactive concept of ten is not constrained by such physical boundaries.

Ten as a Countable Figural Unit

Attributing the ability to re-present counting activity to the children allows us to explain what Brenda saw as being common to a finger pattern and covered bags of ten items and what James saw as being common to unbagged and bagged collections of ten items each: if they were to count the items in the collections, there would be ten. In other words, these specified collections, covered or otherwise, had a property of "tenness" for the children--a protonumerosity.

A countable figural unit of ten is derived from the dual meanings of number words--a counting meaning and a pattern meaning. "Ten" could refer to a specified figural collection or to the re-presented number word sequence. These countable figural units and their "tenness" triggered counting by ten. Before they put up fingers as countable motor items, Brenda and James both counted figural units of ten.

Ten as a Countable Motor Unit

We have seen that both James and Brenda could coordinate the act of putting up (or closing) fingers with their number word sequence "10-20-30- 40 . . . ". They could use this motor scheme to find how many bags of ten were covered by two cloths, provided they focused on the bags as singleton units corresponding to one. If they focused on the contents of the bags, they lost track of how many times they counted in a continuation. In other words, these children could not re-present a specified perceptual collection of ten as a singleton (as a "bag of candy") and maintain its tenness.

Adding Schemes

In many cases we asked the children to solve problems that were, from our perspective, additive situations. The children's interpretations of these situations depended on the meaning they gave to number words. Generally, it can be said that they interpreted the tasks by first acting to establish meaning for one of the two number words and then to establish meaning for the other. If the number words referred to preconcepts, the children established meaning for the second of the two number words independently of the first word. Addition was either a perceptual or a figurative preconcept depending on the involved number words.

In the following paragraphs, we characterize adding schemes by the periods in the development of countable items. Various distinctions and overlaps are omitted for clarity of presentation, such as addition as a figurative concept late in the perceptual stage.

The Perceptual Stage

There was no indication of addition as a joining operation while addition was a preconcept, although joining actions were observed. When the children simply counted out perceptual items to establish two collections and then counted the items of both collections, addition was a perceptual preconcept.

Finger Pattern Adding Scheme

Brenda first established two finger patterns when she used her finger pattern adding scheme. Since the elements of the patterns were in her visual field, she could experience them as a bounded plurality that she counted to specify. The taking of two finger patterns as an experiential whole was the adding action. Upon further analysis, her finger pattern adding scheme can be seen to involve the coordination of two subschemes. The first subscheme successively established two finger patterns and took them as a whole; the second subscheme specified the resulting collection by counting. The only advance that James made when he used finger patterns as figurative preconcepts was to substitute finger patterns for hidden collections. His resulting finger pattern adding scheme can be characterized in the same way as Brenda's.

Spatio-Motor Pattern Adding Scheme

James and Tarus often used what we call a spatio-motor pattern adding scheme when they did not recognize small collections of items before they were hidden. The children counted the elements of each re-presented pattern, where their counting acts completed two spatial patterns. In this case, addition was a figurative preconcept, but this scheme was very situation-specific.

The Figurative Stage

Intuitive Extension Adding Scheme

When finger patterns were figurative concepts, it was possible for the children to accomplish two things by performing one sequence of counting acts. They could complete a finger pattern for the second of the two number words by continuing the count to complete a finger pattern for the first of the two number words--an intuitive extension of counting. In this case, the children sequentially rather than simultaneously put up fingers. Addition was was now a figurative concept rather than a preconcept, because the children successively re-presented the two finger patterns before counting, resulting in two juxtaposed figural patterns.

Addition still involved giving meaning to first one number word and then the other, but this took place in re-presentation rather than in perception. The children gave meaning to the two number words by successively re-presenting two finger patterns. Although they did not intend to join the patterns before they put up fingers, the result was two re-presented, juxtaposed composite wholes whose elements were salient. This is analogous to what happened in visual perception when addition was a preconcept. The join the children made was supported by the common elements of the two separate composite wholes. The children then counted to establish and specify this unspecified collection--the second subscheme.

Sophisticated Finger Pattern Adding Scheme

Brenda's sophisticated finger pattern adding scheme was a generalization of her previous finger pattern adding scheme. Addition was now a figurative concept rather than a perceptual preconcept. For example, to find the "sum" of nine and three, Brenda simultaneously put up nine fingers, then counted three more, "1-2-3", as she put up the remaining finger and two fingers of her other hand. Her now open hand and two fingers signified "twelve."

One of the most elucidating examples of addition as a figurative concept occurred when James reorganized, in re-presentation, mobile finger patterns for "nine" and for "four" into two open hands and three more fingers. This ability to reorganize two re-presented finger patterns and recognize the resulting finger pattern is on a par with Brenda's sophisticated finger patterns. If the children counted here, it was to specify the collection of elements of the figurally joined finger patterns.

Addition as an Enactive Preconcept

Occasions when counting was not the second subscheme of the adding scheme occurred primarily when counting was an enactive preconcept, and the meaning the children gave to a number word was counting to specify a figural collection to which the number word referred. Thus, in order to solve "15 + 4 = ___", the children might coordinate putting up fifteen fingers with the standard number word sequence up to and including "fifteen" (or just utter the number words). Because the children were engaged in counting activity, they could simply continue counting if "four" referred to a re-presented pattern. "Addition", to the child, meant to continue counting four more times; we call this an enactive preconcept.

Addition as an Enactive Concept

Finally, we have the situations in which the children counted-on. Initially, addition was a figurative concept, because the number word that the children started with referred to a figural collection. When the children finally re-presented counting activity in the context of counting-on, addition became an enactive concept.

Comments on Prenumerical Children

The changes that we observed were remarkably consistent in all three children. Although it is not possible to "factor out" the influence of our contributions as teachers (as well as interpreters) of the children, we quickly learned that we could not *cause* a child to change in a particular way. However, without our interventions, we believe that the children would not have constructed a concept of ten beyond a figural pattern. Our basis for this conviction is that the children constructed ten as an enactive concept, as a countable figural unit, and as a countable motor unit in the context of solving our problems. We can confidently say that ten as a countable motor unit was the most advanced concept of ten that the children constructed. Its prenumerical nature, however, precluded them from spontaneously using it in the context of finding how many tens were in a certain two-digit number in their mathematics classroom. Consequently, the most advanced unit of ten they could use to give meaning to numerals like "52" was ten as a figural pattern. This unit is very limited and cannot serve as an adequate conceptual basis for mathematics learning, especially in the area of numeration. The children were particularly unsuccessful in learning addition and subtraction paper and pencil algorithms in their mathematics classrooms and we believe that these failures can be traced directly to the prenumerical nature of the units of ten they constructed.

Of course, the meanings the three children gave number words in general were prenumerical, and because the meanings they gave to addition were based on the meanings they gave to number words, their meanings of addition were prenumerical as well. As educators, we believe that the educational problems posed by the prenumerical child are identified but not solved. We have a better understanding of how the children might modify their number word meanings, but this knowledge does not constitute a blueprint for their mathematical education.

Their enactive concept of addition was the most advanced concept they constructed in the context of solving our problems. It was not used in their mathematics classroom to give meanings to sums. The children used their paper and pencil algorithms to complete exercises like the following:

$$\text{(a)}\quad \begin{array}{r} 24 \\ +\underline{\ 55} \\ 79 \end{array} \qquad\qquad \text{(b)}\quad \begin{array}{r} 36 \\ +\underline{\ 24} \\ 510 \end{array}$$

They simply found the sum of the vertically aligned numerals, using their prenumerical adding schemes (other than addition as enactive concept) to find sums they didn't already know. From their point of view, they were successful in learning arithmetic. From our point of view, their prenumerical concepts and schemes were totally inadequate to give meaning to the sums in (a) and (b) above.

Chapter VI

Lexical and Syntactical Meanings

Tyrone, Scenetra, and Jason

Leslie P. Steffe

With the collaboration of Paul Cobb

The integration operation emerged in the context of patterns for Tyrone, Scenetra, and Jason in contrast to its emergence for Brenda, Tarus, and James. We are therefore obliged to add numerical concepts to those explained in Chapter V. When the elements of a spatial pattern serve as material of an integration operation, we call the resulting pattern numerical. In Chapter V we saw how the elements of a figural spatial pattern can embody the records of counting. The constituent unit items of a numerical pattern can similarly contain records of counting, and in that case, we say counting is contained in the pattern, in that an item of the pattern can signify a counting act--the numerical pattern implies counting and becomes an assimilating or first part of the counting scheme.

The previously documented reorganizations of Tyrone's, Scenetra's, and Jason's counting schemes (cf. Chapter IV) strongly indicate that their counting schemes evolved as numerical concepts in contexts other than patterns. In fact, these documented reorganizations were followed by further changes that we chronicle in this chapter. To account for the initial reorganizations, we contended that the assimilating structures of the scheme changed from re-presented collections and patterns to composite units. These changes were accounted for by attributing the uniting operation of integration to the children. In this chapter, we will argue that a *system of integrations* subsequently emerged in stages as an assimilatory structure of the counting scheme and that the children's adaptations with respect to the system accounted for their further progress. The argument is based on a retrospective analysis of the teaching episodes, beginning with those in which we first observed the emergence of the integration operation.

The problem-solving situations that we used during the teaching experiment were chosen for a variety of reasons. First, we posed situations we thought the children could assimilate and solve using their currently available concepts and operations. These situations were quite demanding and, when solved, often led to the construction of a conceptual object that closed the solution episode for the involved child. Second, we posed situations we thought the children could assimilate if they constructed a currently unavailable concept, such as a particular numerical finger pattern for "eleven". Third, we posed situations we thought the children could assimilate using their currently available concepts but could not solve unless they made an adaptation in their available conceptual operations. In the latter case, we intentionally posed situations where the hypothesized adaptation might have been within the realm of possibility for the child. Finally, we posed situations that we believed would require a major adaptation if the child was to be successful. From our perspective, each situation presented one or more new elements that we had reason to believe were not present in the knowledge of a particular child at a given point in the teaching experiment. They represented our attempts to provide opportunities for the children to make progress.

SYSTEMS OF INTEGRATIONS

Integrations

Our focus in Chapter IV was on documenting that Tyrone, Scenetra, and Jason did construct the integration operation. In this chapter, we investigate what we observed to be the children's first integrations in an attempt to isolate the conceptual material of this developing operation. Our hypothesis at the outset was that spatial patterns might serve as this material. Our reasoning was as follows: when the children reorganized counting, they could count-on to solve missing addend problems and count-off-from to solve subtraction problems (cf. 4.09; 5.11-5.12; 6.11-6.12). Both of these counting solutions appeared concurrently, indicating that the elements of their composite units might be linearly ordered. At the same time, the composite units maintained their function as recognizable patterns. Both Jason and Scenetra (cf. 6.11 and 5.03) appeared to re-present linear patterns after they curtailed the motor components of their counting activity. In order to be recognized as patterns, however, linear arrangements of elements must contain a rhythmic component (cf. von Glasersfeld, 1982b). Consequently, it would seem that with the emergence of the integration operation, the children became able to transform or "straighten out" two-dimensional spatial patterns into a one-dimensional linear pattern that could be recognized by its rhythmic characteristics.

Sequential Integration Operations

Subsequent to the reorganizations of counting that we documented in Chapter IV, we explored the operations the children used to give meaning to various problem situations. During the first few months, we continually tested the viability of our hypothesis that the children applied the integration operation sequentially to create two juxtaposed numerical composites. To illustrate *sequential integration operations*, we use Tyrone's solution of a subtraction problem in which he counted-off-from (cf. 4.09). When Tyrone segmented the backward number word sequence "13-12- . . . -1" into "13-12- . . . -7" and "six" by counting 7 off from 13, we attributed to him the ability to apply the integration operation sequentially. Before counting, we infer that "thirteen" implied an integration operation whose contents were--"13-12- . . . -1". Moreover, because Tyrone started counting at "thirteen" and kept track of how many times he counted, we infer that the numerical composite corresponding to "seven" had as its material the indefinite number word sequence starting at "thirteen", going downward, and ending with the seventh number word that would be uttered. In our view, then, his counting acts were made possible by symbolized mental operations he could use before counting.

In addition to exploring the children's use of the sequential integrations, we also investigated the viability of our hypothesis that the children focused on the *contents* of the composite units--on their constituent unit items--but not on the composite unit as one entity. We call these initial composite units that are the product of applying the integration operation *numerical composites* to distinguish them from the more sophisticated composite units the children subsequently constructed.

Progressive Integration Operations

As the retrospective analysis progressed, we explored whether the children might become able to take the result of applying the integration operation (a numerical composite) as one thing. For example, a numerical pattern of numerosity ten (ten ones) might be transformed into one ten. Observations indicated that the children could make transformations of this sort, and we reasoned that a new system of operations should be attributed to them because they could take the results of prior operating (a numerical composite) as one thing. During the teaching episodes, we observed the children make progress in the range of problems they could solve and in the methods used to solve the problems. Consequently, we had a sound experiential basis from which to hypothesize a reorganization of sequential integration operations that we call progressive integration operations. *Progressive integration operations* can perhaps most appropriately be characterized by considering their results. After counting to ten, say, a child might take that as one thing and then proceed to count four more times. In this example, the integration operation was applied to the numerical composite of ten that was itself constructed by applying the integration operation. Thus, the progressive integration system involves a second application of the integration operation to the results of a first application. "Fourteen" would then refer to a specified numerosity structured as "one ten and four more ones".

Part-Whole Operations

The progress the children eventually made in solving problems indicated they had made another reorganization. A more complete system of operations is indicated when a child can take the four individual units discussed above as one thing and then apply the integration operation to the two component units, one of numerosity ten and one of four. The construction of *part-whole operations* involves applying the integration operation to the results of the progressive integration operations. When the system of part-whole operations emerged, the children gave every indication that they could extract a composite unit from a containing unit while at the same time leave it "in" the containing unit. For convenience, we call this operation the *disembedding operation*. It is an act of reflective abstraction that was indicated both by new flexibility when solving problems and by anticipatory planning of solutions heretofore impossible. We looked for such flexibility and planning in the retrospective analysis as indicators of the disembedding operation. Let us now turn to the case studies.

4. TYRONE

The periods in Tyrone's construction of the counting scheme that we documented in Chapter IV are summarized in Figure 5. Starting on 15 October 1980, Tyrone's motor period lasted until 22 January 1981, when we observed him for the first time counting-on to solve missing addend sentences like "4 + ___ = 12" (cf. 4.07). This latter date was our first teaching episode with him after the Christmas holidays. He could now anticipate finding how many counting acts he would perform before he started counting to solve such sentences, and independently kept track of how many times he counted by one.

Figure 5

Periods in Tyrone's Construction of the Counting Scheme

```
ABSTRACT  |          ****************************
PERIOD    |
          |
MOTOR     |   *****
PERIOD    |  .____.________________________________.

        10/80 1/81                                6/82
```

The Emergence of the Integration Operation

In contrast to Brenda, Tarus, and James, Tyrone used linear spatial patterns to keep track of counting when he was in his motor period (cf. 4.01 - 4.05). Because of his rather rapid advancement to the abstract stage, we tested the viability of the hypothesis that these linear patterns were the results of applying the integration operation. In the initial interviews held on 15 October 1980, Tyrone recognized the domino patterns, a triangular three, rows of four and five items, and various arrangements of five items as "five". He could also recognize two-through-five evenly spaced drum beats. Tyrone had made connections between number words and auditory patterns as well as between number words and visual patterns. He had an extensive repertory of patterns available, but he used linear spatial patterns when solving problems.

15 October 1980 Interview

<u>Monitoring Counting Activity Using Linear Patterns</u>

4.12. When Tyrone extended counting an initial hidden portion of a collection to count a second hidden portion of two, three, or four perceptual items, he completed linear spatial patterns by pointing over the second cloth (cf. 4.01) and recognized the patterns as "two", "three", or "four". We inferred that Tyrone monitored his activity of completing these patterns. This inference is confirmed in a case where he attempted to count a collection of items hidden by two cloths, one hiding seven and one five squares.

I : Tyrone, there are seven here (pointing to one cloth) and five here (pointing to the other).

Ty : (Touches the first cloth seven times while whispering) 1-2-3-4-5-6-7. (Tyrone's points of contact form no identifiable pattern. He continues touching the second cloth six times in a row while whispering) 8-9-10-11-12-13.

Ty : (Realizes he doesn't know how many times he touched the second cloth, so he starts over without suggestion. In the midst of touching the second cloth, he loses track, so he starts over once again. This time he deliberately touches the second cloth five times in a row, while looking intently at his points of contact) 8-9-10-11-12 (looks up), 13-14. Fourteen!

Tyrone monitored how many times he touched the cloth. His reflection on what he was doing while carrying out the activity indicates that he tried to recognize a completed pattern after each touch; he tried to keep track of how many times he counted.

4.13. The act of recognizing a row of five dots does not require an intentional monitoring of the activity that produces the pattern. When he was producing a pattern consisting of points of contact of his finger on a cloth, Tyrone had to recall what pattern he produced after each touch, because there were no visible traces. The way in which he uttered "13-14" in the protocol of 4.12 indicated that he wasn't sure whether he had just completed a pattern for "five". The interviewer then asked Tyrone how many there were hidden under the second cloth. Tyrone said "five" and proceeded to count one more time.

Ty : (Touches the first cloth and utters) 1-2-3-4-5-6-7, (continues touching the second cloth five times in a row, but this time stares into space) 8-9-10-11--(looks at the interviewer), twelve!

His continuation of counting indicates that he isolated a linear five pattern in his counting acts. His conviction that he was to stop at "twelve", coupled with staring into space, again indicates intentional monitoring of counting activity using a linear pattern. Tyrone's efforts to organize his continuation of counting in the protocol of 4.12 apparently led to his abstraction of a linear rhythmic pattern for "five". At this point, he seemed to re-present the pattern and use it in his efforts to recognize when he had completed five counting acts. We infer that the five counting acts he performed and combined formed a numerical composite.

3 December 1980 Teaching Episode

Using Nonlinear Spatial Patterns to Monitor Counting

4.14. Tyrone's use of spatial patterns soon encompassed more than the linear rhythmic patterns he displayed earlier. Situations that encouraged him to re-present spatial patterns were posed in two previous teaching episodes. As a consequence of these experiences, he could keep track of performing five counting acts more flexibly.

T : (Presents three visible squares and five hidden squares to Tyrone) Can you count to find out how many altogether?
Ty : (Points to each visible square) 1-2-3. (Points in the air twice, moving his hand laterally) 4-5. (Pauses and continues pointing twice more) 6-7. (Points once more) eight.

He seemed to re-present a domino five and count its elements. In a later task, he counted five more by completing a linear three and then a linear two pattern.

15 December 1980 Teaching Episode

A Return to Linear Spatial Patterns as Numerical Composites

4.15. Even though he had solved tasks that involved nonlinear spatial patterns, Tyrone returned to using rhythmic spatial patterns almost exclusively. Their dominance for "two" through "five" was highlighted when additive problems were presented by using a blank felt board rather than covered collections (cf. 4.04). Tyrone completed linear spatial patterns for "three", "four", and "five", stopping correctly on each occasion. As before (cf. 4.13), his knowing when to stop counting indicates that he recognized the patterns. The last pattern that he completed in the session was a number word pattern for "five" (cf. 4.05). All of these behavioral indications might be taken to indicate that his patterns were figurative concepts. However, his reflective awareness, his self-corrections of counting activity, his monitoring activity, and his subsequent entry into the abstract stage (cf. 4.07) together indicate that they were numerical composites. These four qualities were *not* observed in the cases of Brenda, Tarus, and James. Although the children used patterns to keep track of counting, these were always patterns that they had previously established. While the children were in their motor periods, the completed patterns always involved visible traces and, as such, served as perceptual records of a continuation of counting. There was no indication that they intentionally monitored counting, as did Tyrone. We believe that Tyrone's patterns had changed from figurative to numerical, and we account for this change by imputing the uniting operation of integration to him.

The Period of Sequential Integration Operations

8 January 1981 Teaching Episode

<u>The Counting Scheme as a Numerical Concept</u>

4.16. Tyrone's use of counting in this and a preceding teaching episode (cf. 4.07, 4.08, and 4.09) provides the basis for our inference that his counting scheme was a numerical concept. Tyrone modified the activity of counting in the following protocol to fit his interpretation of the task.

T : (Presents nine visible squares beside a cloth) Tyrone, you have sixteen squares altogether. Some of them are there (pointing to the visible squares). So, how many are there (pointing to the cloth)?
Ty : (Points to each visible square, subvocally uttering number words. He then rests his head on his hand while looking into space) Eight!
T : Why did you say eight?
Ty : Because there's nine there and nine and eight makes sixteen!
T : How did you know for sure?
Ty : (Sequentially puts up seven fingers while subvocally uttering number words) Seven!

Initially, "sixteen" was the only number word available to Tyrone. It seemed to refer to the activity of counting, an activity that he partitioned into the first nine counting acts and those necessary to continue counting to "sixteen". We infer that after counting the visible squares, he subvocally uttered "10-11-12-13-14-15-16" without keeping track of his utterances when he was resting his head on his hands looking into space. This inference is based on his actually counting-on to "sixteen" when asked how he knew for sure.

4.17. We also infer that Tyrone applied the integration operation sequentially to the counted visual items and to the records of subvocally uttered number words, creating two numerical composites. This interpretation is supported by his estimate "eight" and by his saying "Because there's nine there and nine and eight makes sixteen!" It wasn't until after he counted that this sentence evolved and had meaning.

Tyrone seemed to reduce the task to what might be called a "direct addition" task.

4.18. Tyrone estimated the numerosity of the numerical composite containing the records of counting "10-11- . . . -16" and eventually counted-on to specify this numerosity. However, he did not interpret the problem situation as a missing addend task prior to counting. It was simply a counting problem where "sixteen" implied counting the visible as well as the covered squares. He was "above" counting "looking down" on his own counting actions, actions that were under his control. In this sense, counting was a numerical concept.

Creating Juxtaposed Numerical Composites

4.19. We emphasize that Tyrone's estimate "eight" provides a basis for imputing to him the ability to juxtapose two numerical composites, one corresponding to "nine" and one of unspecified numerosity, hold them "side-by-side", and estimate the unspecified numerosity that could be specified by counting from "nine" to "sixteen". As we try to decenter and contemplate what Tyrone was aware of, it seems plausible that he was more aware of the elements in the two numerical composites than of the numerical composites as one thing, although there are no behavioral indicators that we can point to in the protocol. Consequently, we look to other problem solutions for indications of the nature of the elements within his awareness.

Finger Patterns as Numerical Concepts

4.20. The power that we attributed to Tyrone (cf. 4.15) to create a linear spatial pattern "on the spot" by abstracting from his counting activity is confirmed in this teaching episode. He could also create a finger pattern "on the spot" to keep track of his counting activity. This provides corroboration of his inferable ability to apply the integration operation sequentially and clarifies the elements within his awareness.

T : (Presents eight visible squares beside a cloth) Eight there (pointing to the visible squares) and there are eleven under the cloth.

Ty : Seventeen.

T : Why don't you see if that is right?

Ty : (Touches each visible square while subvocally uttering number words. He then sequentially puts up fingers) 9-10--. (Returns to subvocally uttering number words until ten fingers are extended. He then emphatically puts up one more and shakes his head as if confused.)

T : There are eight here and eleven here!

Ty : (Starts over, sequentially putting up ten fingers as he whispers number words) 9-10-11- . . . - 18 (Pauses, then closes his hand and puts up one more finger) Nineteen!

Tyrone's answer "seventeen" seemed to be an estimate rather than a wild guess. It is consistent with the contention that he could juxtapose two numerical composites of specific numerosity and estimate the numerosity of the result.

4.21. Tyrone's last attempt to count is a solid indication that the finger pattern for "eleven" was created on the spot. The first time he counted, he seemed to have no confidence that the result was "right", possibly because it conflicted with his estimate. After the teacher said, "There are eight here and eleven here!" Tyrone paused when he completed two open hands and displayed intense concentration. During the pause, he created a finger pattern for "eleven" as two open hands and one more finger; he made a similar finger pattern for "fourteen" in a later teaching episode (cf. 4.10).

4.22. Tyrone knew that he had to count 11 more times starting with "nine", but he did not have a finger pattern that he could use to keep track of how many times he counted. We believe the finger pattern that he created was a numerical composite because he displayed intense concentration each time he constructed it and monitored his counting activity both times. Also, on his first attempt, he apparently experienced conflict between the result of counting and his estimate. He seemed to be explicitly aware that he had produced two different number words. These characteristics of his solution argue for the interpretation that the finger pattern he created for "eleven" was numerical. It was not simply a figurative concept because he did not re-present the finger pattern and then count its elements because he did not have a finger pattern for "eleven" prior to the solution. Moreover, he did not first count 11 fingers to establish a finger pattern and then use that in his solution. Although he may have re-presented a plurality of fingers prior to counting, we still believe he established his finger pattern as a numerical composite because of his monitoring activity.

30 March 1981 Teaching Episode

<u>Numerical Composites</u>

4.23. The analysis of whether Tyrone was aware of the fingers in his numerical finger pattern for "eleven", or of the pattern as one thing, or of both, could not be decided solely on the basis of his solution in the protocol of paragraph 4.20. We do believe that he was aware of the numerosity of his juxtaposed numerical composites symbolized by "eight" and "eleven" as indicated by his response "seventeen". He could anticipate the results of counting without actually counting. The conjecture that Tyrone was aware of his fingers rather than of the pattern as one thing is supported by his solution of the task in the following protocol.

T : (Places two cloths in front of Tyrone side by side, and the numeral "12" at the upper edge of the cloths) There are twelve altogether and six under here (places the numeral "6" on top of the cloth to Tyrone's left). How many would be here?

Ty : (Immediately) Six!

T : (Places the two numerals "6" and "6" above "12") Now find another that makes twelve.

Ty : (After sitting silently for about ten seconds while he was in deep concentration, selects "0" and "12".)

T : (Suggests that Tyrone now try "7".)

Ty : (Sequentially puts up five fingers while subvocally uttering number words, and selects "5".)

T : What is the next one?

Ty : (Selects "5". Sequentially puts up seven fingers while subvocally uttering number words, and selects "7".)

T : What is the next one?

Ty : (Selects "10". Then subvocally utters number words and selects "2".)

T : What is the next one?

Ty : (Selects "3". Sequentially puts up nine fingers while subvocally uttering number words, and selects "9".)

There are two places in the protocol where Tyrone could have generated the second addend based on his previous selection. However, on both occasions he had to count to find what the missing second addend would be. He also failed to use previous results earlier when similar activities were presented. These are strong indications that it was his intention to find how many individual units it would take to complete 12 units. Had "5" and "7" been symbols for single entities, it seems plausible that Tyrone would have selected "7" after choosing "5" without counting. Throughout the task, Tyrone's behavior is consistent with our hypothesis that he was aware of the individual units in 12. He seemed to partition the individual units and to reflect on the contents of the resulting numerical composites rather than on them as individual entities.

5 April 1981 Teaching Episode

Partitioning to Solve Subtraction Tasks

4.24. Tyrone's solutions of subtraction tasks, coupled with the contention that he focused on the individual unit items of a numerical composite, indicates to us that he could partition the unit items. We have seen that Tyrone used counting-off-from to solve subtraction tasks (cf. 4.08 and 4.09). This solution would be implausible if he did not first make a numerical composite corresponding to the minuend, and take these items as being linearly ordered. The linear ordering hypothesis is plausible because we have already documented the linearity of his numerical composites regarding patterns. Besides, as signifiers of counting, the individual unit items could inherit their order from counting. For instance, "thirteen" could denote the backward number word sequence from "thirteen" down to "one" (cf. 4.09). Tyrone could then produce this number word sequence and use it as material for making two numerical composites--one corresponding to "seven" and the other to the number words that he would say, were he to continue counting down to "one".

Failure to Construct Subtraction as the Inversion of Addition

4.25. If Tyrone did indeed focus on the individual unit items of numerical composites, he would not be able to transform the backward number word sequence discussed in paragraph 4.24 from "backward" to "forward" because he could not take the sequence as material of an integration operation. The realization that counting from "six" to "thirteen" would yield a numerosity of seven, after he had counted backward and without actually counting forward, would seem to require that the two parts of 13 he constructed--seven and six--be viewed as entities composing 13. On one occasion Tyrone *did* construct subtraction as the inversion of addition but, in contrast to his overall solutions, it was a very specific case. The teacher had asked Tyrone to find out how many cookies there would be in all if 15 were under one cloth and 6 were under another. Tyrone counted-on to solve the task, saying "twenty-one" as his answer. The teacher then removed the cloth that he and Tyrone had pretended covered six cookies and pretended to push the cookies under the cloth covering 15.

T : I've got twenty-one under this cloth. Now watch me very carefully. I'm going to take six away (lifts the cloth and pretends to remove six cookies). How many are left?

Ty : (Immediately) Fifteen!

T : How do you know that?

Ty : 'Cause when I counted to twenty-one and you took. . . and that was six and I counted to twenty-one, and take away six equals fifteen, 'cause plus and take away, they're the same thing.

T : Plus and take away are the same thing, is that right?

Ty : If you take away something . . . if you plus something and then take away, it would still be the number that you came from and went to it from the plus.

The language that Tyrone used in his justifications indicates that he was referring to the involved numerical composites as objects or entities. Other tasks were posed that involved 34 and 9 cookies and then 43 take away 34 cookies; 11 and 7 cookies and then 18 take away 7 cookies; and 19 and 8 cookies and then 27 take away 8 cookies. Tyrone solved each of these subtraction tasks independently of his immediately preceding solution of the addition task. As opposed to what he did in the tasks that he did relate, the teacher did not pretend to add and then to remove cookies from the same collection. Tyrone counted-on to solve the addition tasks and counted-off-from to solve the subtraction tasks (he counted backward the number of times indicated by the subtrahend).

4.26. Given the clarity of Tyrone's language in the protocol of paragraph 4.25, there is little alternative but to interpret his number words as referring to numerical composites taken as one thing in this instance. It was important, however, that he could re-present compensating actions that occurred in his immediate past experience. He did not appear to have internalized these actions or to have reconstituted them as conceptual operations.

The Period of Progressive Integration Operations

December 1981 Interview

<u>Counting by Ten and by One</u>

4.27. We have seen in the protocol of paragraph 4.26 that Tyrone could take a numerical composite as a unit in specific contexts at the end of May in the 1980-1981 school year. In the initial interview on 15 October

1981, there was every indication that Tyrone had modified his counting-by-one scheme to incorporate *abstract composite units of ten*--units that are the results of taking numerical composites of ten as one thing. One indication that he made abstract composite units of ten was his ability to keep track of how many times he counted by ten and by one in the same counting episode.

T : (Places two dimes in front of Tyrone) How many pennies would one dime make?

Ty : Ten.

T : How many pennies would you count out to make two dimes?

Ty : Twenty pennies.

T : Shut your eyes. (Places two dimes on the table and hides three dimes and three pennies) Altogether, there are 53 cents. How many dimes are under here (taps on the cloth)?

Ty : (Places his left thumb and forefinger on the two visible dimes and puts up three fingers on his right hand, inaudibly uttering number words. He then closes his right hand and sequentially puts up three fingers, again inaudibly uttering number words) Three dimes under there and three pennies.

T : That's right! How did you do that?

Ty : I counted 10-20, and then (sequentially putting up fingers) 30-40-50, and then (sequentially putting up the same three fingers) 51-52-53!

When Tyrone made the numerical extension "30-40-50-51-52-53", he discriminated between the dimes as units and the pennies as units. His use of the decade names to count dimes indicates that he viewed one dime as being a substitute for ten pennies. This is especially plausible because he flexibly shifted from counting by ten to counting by one.

4.28. It could be debated that the presence of hidden dimes enabled Tyrone to count by ten and by one in much the same way as having pennies covered enabled Brenda to count by ten as she made an intuitive extension (cf. 1.44). Here is a protocol where Tyrone did keep track of counting by ten to solve a task involving hidden strips with ten squares per strip.

T : Shut your eyes (places five strips in front of Tyrone and covers three others). Open them. Altogether, there are eighty little squares. How many strips are under there (pointing to the cloth)?

Ty : (Sequentially touches the visible strips and then sequentially puts up three fingers) Three.

T : Tell me how you did that.

Ty : I went 10-20-30-40-50- (touching the visible strips), 60-70-80 (putting up three fingers).

Tyrone's ability to keep track of how many times he counted by ten indicates that he focused on the unit structure of the numerical composite ten. In both protocols, Tyrone took a numerical composite of ten as a countable unit. An act of putting up a finger in synchrony with uttering, say, "forty", was an act of counting an abstract composite unit. His finger served as a record of that act. In this example, we call each act of putting up a finger a *symbolic motor unit* of ten.

4.29. The distinction Tyrone made between an act of counting that involved a dime and an act of counting that involved a penny demonstrates that a dime and a penny were not homogeneous countable items for him. Nevertheless, he took both as countable items in the same counting activity. To do this, the numerical composite, ten, and the unit, one, had to be objects of reflective thought. In other words, the two units of different ranks were equivalent from the perspective of their unity but were distinct from the perspective of their numerosity.

4.30. Tyrone's ability to take a numerical composite as a unit is an act of abstraction beyond that of applying the integration operation to discrete unit items. It involves applying the integration operation to the results of a prior integration--an integration of an integration. We have called its results an *abstract composite unit of ten*.

Ten More

4.31. On one occasion, Tyrone counted in such a way that indicated he constructed a unit that we call "ten more". Tyrone segmented the activity of making a numerical extension by counting by one and, in a review of the activity, took each segment of ten as a countable unit.

T : (Places three strips in front of Tyrone and hides two strips and two more squares) How many are there here (the three strips that are visible)?

Ty : Thirty.

T : If I put these (hidden strips and squares) with them, there would be fifty-two. How many would be under here? How many little squares and how many strips?

Ty : (Sequentially puts up twenty-two fingers in synchrony with subvocal utterances. He then says, after a crucial pause where he appeared to be deep in thought) There would be two of these (slaps the strips) and two of them (gesturing toward a pile of squares).

T : How did you figure that out so well?

Ty : I counted, 10-20-30 (in synchrony with moving strips); and then 40-50; and then 51-52.

Tyrone's answer that two strips and two squares were hidden indicates that he intended to find how many strips of ten he could make. Tyrone counted by one until completing a unit of "ten more"--he segmented counting by one into numerical composites of ten counting acts as he went along. After reaching "fifty-two", he reviewed his past activity. The way in which he did this is strongly indicated by his explanation, "I counted 10-20-30; and then 40-50; and then 51-52". Although this is not what he *actually* did when counting by one, it was the *meaning* of what he did, and is a strong indication that he took each numerical composite of ten as one thing.

4.32. It was essential that Tyrone at least believe there were strips covered. We believe that he re-presented a strip of ten before he counted. Obviously, he substituted his numerical finger pattern of ten for this abstract composite unit and could count ten more times, starting at any point in his number sequence. His review and reconstruction of his past counting activity implies the emergence of *progressive integration operations*. Without these operations, it is unlikely that Tyrone could have organized counting 22 times beyond 30 into two abstract composite units of ten and two more units of one.

4.33. Tyrone's solution in 4.31 indicates a certain interpretation of the problem. We infer that "fifty-two" referred to the number sequence (a numerical composite whose elements signify counting) 1-2-3- . . . -52 that he segmented into two parts--10-20-30 and 31-32- . . . -52--before counting. Although "thirty" seemed to refer to 10-20-30, which in turn was an abbreviation of counting from "one" up to and including "thirty", there was no indication that he unpacked this meaning of "thirty" in his solution. Instead, he seemed to focus on the remainder of the number sequence, 31-32-33- . . . -52. We further infer that he used "thirty" as a symbol for the results of counting and that he re-presented the rest the number sequence before he counted, because he seemed to be "above" his counting activity, "looking down" on it. His review of counting by one corroborates our inference that he re-presented the remainder of the number sequence before he counted.

In any event, he shifted flexibly from units of one to the units of ten that contained them, and took the first numerical extension of ten (uttering 31-32- . . . -40 synchronous with putting up fingers) as one thing. He then proceeded to make a second abstract composite unit of ten more and seemed to realize that he could not make a third before he reached "fifty-two". The important feature of his solution is that he could "step back" and take each segment of ten counting acts as one thing--as a countable unit of ten--while simultaneously maintaining its numerosity (i.e., its "tenness").

Because of these available operations, we infer that Tyrone constituted his number sequence 52 as the initial segment, 30, and the remainder as juxtaposed, component units. But we have no reason to believe that he took the number sequence 52 as an abstract composite unit, although we do think it was the source of the necessary material of operating. Tyrone had definitely made progress in interpreting and solving missing addend situations, in contrast with his interpretation and solution approximately ten months earlier (cf. 4.16). He could now take the two parts (i.e., the addends) as single entities (abstract composite units) while maintaining their numerosity, and flexibly shift from the abstract composite units to the elements they contained, and vice versa.

Ten as a Repeatable Unit

4.34. In the protocol of paragraph 4.31, Tyrone knew that there were strips under the cloth and that there were ten squares on each strip. Consequently, he could re-present the strips as abstract composite units and focus on their unit structure. His solution carried the significance of counting the squares on the strips. In the following protocol, we see his limitations:

T : (Presents a bag of centimeter cubes) There are one hundred thirty-four blocks in this bag. Take out a row of ten.
Ty : (Makes a row of ten, using blocks from the bag.)
T : I would like to know how many rows of ten you could make like that.
Ty : One hundred and thirty-four?
T : There are one hundred-thirty four little cubes. I would like to know how many rows of ten like that you could make.
Ty : (Sequentially puts up fingers and sits quietly for approximately 25 seconds. He then begins to sequentially put up fingers) 10-20-30-40-50-60-70-80-90-100--10-20-30-40-50-60-70-80-90-100--110-120-130-131-132-133-134--seventeen!

Tyrone's decision to count by ten seemed to be influenced by the row of ten that he made. He appeared to realize that he could repeat the action of making a row of ten, and that keeping track of counting by ten could be used to find out how many such rows of ten he could make. However, his answer of "seventeen" indicates that he failed to distinguish between records of counting by ten acts and counting by one acts. The primary difference between this task and the task of the protocol in paragraph 4.32

is that preformed rows were (from our perspective) used to present the latter task. Consequently, the contention that a counting by ten act was a symbolic substitute for a row of ten in the current protocol is not supported. He seemed to lose whatever composite quality led him to count by ten, and he took all his counting acts as acts of counting individual entities. He essentially lost the meaning of counting by ten, and counting was reduced to co-ordinating the production of a number word sequence with acts of putting up fingers.

9 February 1982 Teaching Episode

Progressive Integrations in Subtraction

4.35. Tyrone provided another indication of progressive integrations in this teaching episode when he solved subtraction tasks. In previous episodes, he counted the subtrahend off from the minuend (cf. 4.25). In the following protocol, we see that Tyrone could now count from the minuend down to the subtrahend:

T : (Presents the sentence "22 - 17 = ") Can you tell me what twenty-two take away seventeen is?
Ty : (Sits silently for about six seconds. Sequentially puts up fingers while subvocally uttering number words. Selects the numeral "5".)
T : How did you know that so fast?
Ty : I took seventeen away from this.
T : And how did you do it? What did your mind say?
Ty : (Sequentially puts up fingers) 21-20-19-18-17.
T : That was really a clever way to do it. Can you think of another way to do that one by counting?
Ty : (After placing "17" under "22", the teacher asks Tyrone if he could think of a way to do it by counting forward. Tyrone shakes his head "no".)

His activity of counting from 22 down to 17 is a strong indication that "22" was a symbol for an abstract composite unit comprising a number sequence, which consisted of an initial segment symbolized by "17" and the remaining individual unit items of the sequence. Tyrone could "unpack" 22 into these two constituent abstract composite units. Because "17" symbolized the initial segment of the number sequence, the numerosity of the remainder of 17 in 22 could be specified by counting down to "17".

4.36. A possible reason why Tyrone could not think of another way to solve the problem by counting forward is that he had reached his goal of specifying the numerosity of the remainder of 17 in 22. The minuend and the subtrahend were taken as givens in the problem, and he actually produced the remainder when he specified its numerosity. To then take his result as a given and to consider the given minuend as a *result* of operating would seem to require that he re-establish 22 by combining the given initial segment and the resulting remainder in a new synthesis. These reversible mental operations did not seem to be available to him at this time.

4.37. In our view, this solution involved the same operations that made his solution of the missing addend problem possible (cf. 4.31). We infer that an additional integration operation was indicated in the subtraction task because the minuend would have to be constituted at least as an abstract composite unit. Of course, a child might take the sum in a missing addend situation as one thing, but that was not indicated by Tyrone's solution.

The Period of Part-Whole Operations

9 March 1982 Teaching Episode

Disembedding Numerical Parts from a Numerical Whole: Subtraction

4.38. There is a certain ambiguity associated with the operations that might be imputed to a child who solves a subtraction task by counting from the minuend down to the subtrahend. In the protocol of 4.35, for example, Tyrone took the records of counting as completing his solution. He had done what he had set out to do--specify an unspecified numerosity. A child who is capable of carrying out more complicated part-whole operations would, in all likelihood solve the subtraction tasks exactly as Tyrone did. Tyrone's inability to think of another way to solve the task by counting forward, however, indicated that he did not recombine the two parts into a whole. This requires that the child "rise above" the initial given part and the part whose numerosity is specified by counting and take them both as material for further operating--as given in a new part-part combination to yield the whole. The role of the whole would have to be seen as changing from a given to a result. In other words, the child would have to reverse his initial partitioning of the given whole into parts and synthesize the parts to form the whole. Nevertheless, Tyrone had taken a necessary step in the construction of part-whole operations in that he could include a given part (seventeen) as a unitary item in a given numerical whole (twenty-two). In this teaching episode, Tyrone's problem-solving activity indicated that he could now extract the included given part from the whole. A part of a whole could now serve two functions--as a unit in its own right and as a part of the including unit. In the following protocol, we see that Tyrone could now count by ten and by one from the minuend down to the difference to find a missing subtrahend. There was also some indication of a dawning awareness that he could choose the direction of counting as it suited his purpose.

T : (Places the sentence "71 - = 39" in front of Tyrone) We have seventy-one take away a number and that leaves us with thirty-nine.

Ty : (Sequentially puts up three fingers on his left hand) 61-51-41. (He then puts up a finger on his right hand and pauses) 41--40!--39. (He then places "32" in the blank space).

T : (Removes "32" from the blank space) Let's pretend we don't know the answer to that one. Could you find that answer by counting forward?

Ty : (Sequentially puts up three fingers on his right hand) 49-59-69--69--69. (Shifts to his right hand and sequentially puts up three fingers) 70-71-72 (looks into space as if he is aware of a mistake).

T : (Intervenes, suggesting that Tyrone has "71", not "72". Tyrone goes on to work out the mistake.)

Although Tyrone's solution was not free of mistakes and his count forward was not made independently, both are indicators of mental operations that use the results of progressive integrations as material, because his choice to count backward by ten and by one in the absence of perceptual material was made independently.

4.39. Tyrone apparently viewed 39 as a segment of 71--the unit comprising the first 39 individual units. His goal was to specify the numerosity of the remainder. Counting backward to find the subtrahend indicates an explicit realization that 39 and its remainder were units composing 71, and that these two units were extracted from their inclusions. That is, to assimilate the missing subtrahend problem using his counting-down-to scheme, 39 would have to be viewed as being included in 71. But, this inclusion expresses the sentence "71 - 39 = ___", not the missing subtrahend problem. In that problem, 39 is the result of counting--the third part of the scheme. Consequently, there has to be an identical element between the assimilating structure of the counting-down-to scheme and the result of applying the scheme. This identical element is only possible if 39 is extracted from its inclusion and is viewed as a number in its own right as well as being part of 71. Our discussion implies that Tyrone should have been able to transform his counting-down-to scheme into a counting-up-to scheme as an internal necessity.

However, Tyrone's attempt to count forward at the teacher's request only partially indicates reversibility between the two schemes. Had Tyrone counted forward without error, the indication would have been stronger. As it was, he did not seem to realize that counting forward, when carried out, would yield the same answer as when counting backward. This seems to say that directionality in counting introduces an obstacle to be overcome before the two schemes are interchangeable in their application. It is necessary to have flexibility in the direction of counting or an indication that the child understands that counting forward and counting backward will yield the same result before inferring a fully elaborated system of reversible part-whole operations.

Ten as an Iterable Unit

4.40. Tyrone had reorganized his counting schemes for adding and subtracting that he had used to include the unit of ten while he was in the period of sequential integrations. Counting-on and counting-off-from by one were now reorganized to include counting-on by ten and one, counting-off-from by ten and one, and counting-down-to by ten and one. For example, his activity of counting backward by ten to 41 and then counting "40, 39", and his answer "32", indicate that each counting by ten act referred to ten individual unit items--counting backward one ten decremented by ten ones. Sixty-one, for example, was ten less than 71. Ten was an iterable unit in the backward direction that he coordinated with counting backward by one to specify the numerosity of the remainder of 39 in 71. Solutions that involve iterating by ten seemed to require the ability to disembed ten from a numerical whole of unspecified numerosity.

4.41. Tyrone could count forward as well as backward by ten and one. To solve the sentence "42 + 59 = ____ ", he proceeded as follows:

Ty : (Sequentially puts up fingers) 52-62-72-82-92--93-94-95-96-97-98-99--100-101-102 (completing two open hands when he counted by one).

T : OK. That is really good. I have another way to do it. Can I show you another way? 42-52-62-72-82-92 (putting up fingers). That's five tens. One hundred two would be six tens (putting up another finger). But I want to go nine (pointing to "9" of "59"). So, it's one hundred one. Is that a right way to do it? Could you do it my way?

Ty : (After a long pause) I get a hundred one, too!

T : You do! Can you show me out loud?

Ty : (Repeats his original solution with a correction in counting.)

Tyrone counted forward by ten and one to solve the sentence. Taking his solution of the missing minuend sentence of 4.40 into account, we infer that he used ten as an iterable unit--a forward counting act by ten incremented by ten ones. It was hoped that Tyrone would view the teacher's solution as an alternative, but there was no indication that solution was significant for Tyrone. Instead of attempting to modify his original solution, he seemed to focus on and try to resolve the conflict between the results of the two solutions.

Lack of a Reversible Coordination Between Ten and One

4.42. To reversibly coordinate ten and one, Tyrone would have to realize that he could count on 59 by counting forward 60 and backward once. He would have to take the last unit of ten he produced as material for further operating--as a given before he counted--in order to construct the reversible coordination.

18 May 1982 Teaching Episode

Reflecting on Units of Ten

4.43. Tyrone made the decision to count by ten when only individual unit cubes rather than strips were hidden by a cloth.

T : (Places two cloths in front of Tyrone) I am going to pretend that we have forty-eight pieces of candy under this cloth (places a handful of cubes under the cloth), and pretend that we have twenty-six more pieces of candy under here (places a handful of cubes under the other cloth). How many candies would that be altogether?

Ty : (Places his hand on top of the cloth covering the "forty-eight candies" and sequentially puts up fingers emphatically) Forty-eight--58-68--69-70-71-72-73-74.

The teacher did not indicate to Tyrone that he should count by ten and then by one. Counting by ten and then by one seemed to be a quick way for Tyrone to count the individual cubes. In the very next task, five bags of ten were hidden under one cloth, and three bags of ten and three individual cubes were hidden under the other cloth. To find how many individual blocks were hidden, Tyrone uttered "50--60-70-80-81-82-83" as he put up fingers. A counting by ten act symbolized the activity of counting ten individual blocks in both cases.

4.44. The most convincing example that a counting by ten act referred to the activity of counting ten individual blocks occurred when

Tyrone solved a missing addend task by counting by ten. To find how many bags of ten blocks per bag were hidden under a cloth, after he was told that another cloth covered 39 little blocks and that 89 little blocks were hidden, he counted by ten and said "five". He then volunteered that there were fifty little blocks under the cloth as well, and justified his answer by explaining, "There are five bags and if you took them out of the bags, there would be fifty". This demonstrates that he could "unpack" his units of ten into their constituent unit items--he could reflect on units of ten he created while counting and recover the units that were symbolized by his counting acts. Here, he took the units of ten as given after he had counted. In contrast, he would have to take units of ten as given before he counted in order to reversibly coordinate tens and ones.

Discussion of Tyrone's Case Study

The Emergence of the Integration Operation

While Tyrone was in his motor period, number words that did not refer to patterns referred to collections. "Seven", for example, referred to a figural collection rather than to a pattern (cf. 4.12). Tyrone did not visualize it as a unitary whole whose elements seemed to co-occur. To specify the involved protonumerosity, Tyrone had to count from "one". He had to make countable items from actual sensory motor experience and coordinate the items with number word utterances. Because these motor items were substitutes for other countable items, counting had a re-presentational function and was therefore an enactive preconcept. But he could not yet re-present counting activity and take it as a given.

The operation of integration emerged when Tyrone used patterns to keep track of his counting activity. This conclusion is based on the way he used spatial patterns (cf. 4.12). Their linear aspect fits the theoretical assumption that the unit items of a numerical composite are arranged in an order of succession. Other indications that he applied the integration operation to his figurative patterns were found in his reflective awareness, his self-corrections of counting, and his monitoring activity (cf. 4.15). When left to his own resources, he spontaneously produced linear spatial patterns and appeared to be aware of what he was doing while he was doing it. The contention that he had applied the integration operation to re-presented patterns in December of 1980 is corroborated by the reorganization that occurred in his counting scheme over the Christmas holidays (cf. 4.07 and 4.16). This reorganization is consistent with the emergence of the integration operation. Although Tyrone occasionally counted verbal unit items, we could not identify a verbal period in the development of his counting scheme.

The Period of Sequential Integration Operations

Tyrone could now take counting as a given--number words were now symbols for the activity or could refer to numerical composites. They could be substitutes for counting starting from "one" and proceeding to a particular number word (cf. 4.16), or they could be substitutes for counting starting from a particular number word after "one" and continuing until reaching another (cf. 4.16). In fact, "nine" referred to the specified numerosity of a numerical composite that was juxtaposed with another numerical composite of unspecified numerosity that he estimated as "eight".

Counting was, therefore, a numerical concept in that the elements of the composite units that Tyrone re-presented could signify counting acts. Our best indication is his estimation of how many times he counted beyond nine to reach sixteen and his justification of his estimate "eight" by actually counting from "nine" to "sixteen". The estimate was the result of mental activity--activity that we take to be reflection on completed counting activity.

Tyrone's solution in the protocol of paragraph 4.20 further demonstrates that he could reflect on re-presented counting activity. After he estimated that 8 and 11 would be 17, he counted to see if it was right. However, he did not have a finger pattern for "eleven" that he could use to record counting 11 more times beyond 8, but he resolved the difficulty by creating a finger pattern as he counted. His reflection obviously indicates that he constructed a conceptual object to use as he monitored his counting activity. We take this object to be a numerical composite. Tyrone could, therefore, anticipate the results of counting activity that could be carried out when he re-presented a numerical composite, because the numerical composite symbolized the counting activity. This is not to say that Tyrone actually "saw" 11 unit items in visual re-presentation. It is only necessary that he create figurative material that could symbolize counting activity, a symbolization that made reflection possible. The ability to estimate an unspecified numerosity is a first step toward the construction of an unknown, an idea that is not often attributed to a child as young as Tyrone. We believe that the idea had its origins in Tyrone's construction of linear patterns as he attempted to keep track of counting activity.

There was every indication that Tyrone could perform integration operations sequentially and that these sequential operations constituted his meaning of what were addition, subtraction, and missing addend tasks from our perspective. In the case of the missing addend tasks, he seemed to work with the elements of the numerical composite that we consider to be the sum. In the case where the sum was 16 (cf. 4.16), Tyrone created a numerical composite of numerosity nine that corresponded to the visible squares. His task was then to specify the numerosity of the numerical composite that he made using the records of continuing to count subvocally to "sixteen". We call the act of making this second numerical composite tacit because it was not symbolized by a heard or spoken number word or by a numeral. Although the teacher did say "some of them are there" to refer to the hidden squares, Tyrone had to make a numerical composite and specify its numerosity by whatever means were at his disposal. There was no number word or numeral available that would symbolize that activity.

We believe that Tyrone worked with the elements of the numerical composites that he made rather than with them as one thing. His failure to use one partition of a numerical composite to make a related partition (cf. 4.22) and his failure to conceptualize subtraction as the inversion of addition (cf. 4.25) are both strong indicators that he focused on the elements of the numerical composites. It was as if he were inside the numerical composites that he made, working with their elements.

The Period of Progressive Integration Operations

In the second year of the teaching experiment, Tyrone became able to apply the integration operation to the results of prior integrations and, for the first time, he could take a numerical composite as one thing (cf. 4.27, 4.31). This new meaning of a number word eventually was manifest in his subtracting schemes. He became able to take 17 away from 22 by counting from the minuend down to the subtrahend (cf. 4.34). His comment "I took seventeen away from this" and then counting "21-20-19-18-17" to justify his answer "five" provides the necessary basis for interpreting "22" as a symbol for a number sequence that he took as an entity, "17" as a symbol for the initial segment of the number sequence, the remainder of 17 in 22 as an abstract composite unit, and his meaning of subtraction as separating the initial segment from the remainder.

Once Tyrone was capable of making abstract composite units, he could include such an abstract unit within another and eventually use them as material for another integration operation. But he was yet to disembed numerical parts from a numerical whole, indicating that he had not completed the construction of the system of part-whole operations.

The Period of Part-Whole Operations

In early March of the second year of the teaching experiment, we first observed indications that Tyrone's number words now symbolized more complete part-whole operations (cf. 4.37). He became able to count from the minuend down to the difference to establish the subtrahend in a subtraction problem. To solve 71 - ___ = 39, for example (cf. 4.38), Tyrone could take 71 as a symbol for an abstract composite unit that comprised two other abstract composite units, the subtrahend and the difference. He could disembed these abstract composite units from their inclusion in 71 and work with them as units in their own right while simultaneously leaving them in 71--as constitutive component units. This was the beginning of reversible part-whole operations. But, although he did change the direction of counting on the suggestion of his teacher, his part-whole operations seemed not to be fully reversible. He could start with a symbolized number sequence and partition it into two abstract composite units. However, after he expressed one of the two parts by counting backward, he seemed to take that part as a result and could not reconsider it as a given and the initial number sequence as a potential result. To do so would require that the two schemes, counting-down-to and counting-up-to be synthesized into one reversible scheme.

Unit Types of the Unit of Ten

Tyrone could work with ten as a numerical composite when he entered the abstract stage. By November of the second year of the teaching experiment, he could work with ten as an abstract composite unit. Abstract composite units are made by applying the integration operation to a numerical composite of ten individual unit items. Because this is nothing other than a progressive integration, it is not surprising that the construction of ten as an abstract composite unit seemed to be correlated with the emergence of counting-down-to in subtraction.

Abstract composite units of ten led to the unit that we called "ten more" (cf. 4.31). The unit "ten more" was based on applying the integration operation to the results of counting ten times beyond a completed count. Thus, "ten more" was based on an abstract composite unit of ten that guided counting, on the number sequence, and on the integration operation being applied progressively. "Ten more" and the abstract composite unit of ten differ in terms of their figural content but not in terms of the system of operations they express.

Ten emerged as an iterable unit when Tyrone could disembed a numerical part from a numerical whole. A counting-by-ten act could now signify incrementing by one ten times, and Tyrone no longer needed perceptual material (hidden or otherwise) to construct units of ten. This was indicated by his ability to coordinate counting by ten and counting by one in both forward and backward directions to specify the numerosity of a composite unit in a complex subtraction situation (cf. 4.37).

5. SCENETRA

The periods in Scenetra's construction of the counting scheme that we documented in Chapter IV are summarized in Figure 6. Starting on 16 October 1980, Scenetra's motor period lasted until 20 January 1981, when we observed a curtailment in the motor acts she had previously coordinated with producing a number word sequence (cf. 5.03). Her verbal period lasted until 9 March 1981, when we observed her counting-on to solve missing addend sentences (cf. 5.10). She could now anticipate how many counting acts she would perform before she started counting to solve such sentences and independently kept track of how many times she counted by one.

Figure 6

Periods in Scenetra's Construction of the Counting Scheme

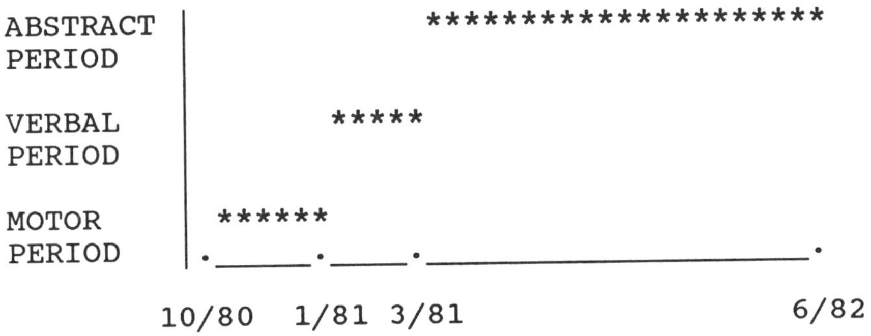

Recognition and Re-presentation of Patterns

At the beginning of the teaching experiment, Scenetra's ability to re-present patterns exceeded anything we observed for Brenda, Tarus, and James. We formulated and tested the hypothesis that her patterns were numerical (i.e., the result of applying the integration operation) but our tests were inconclusive until the 20 January 1981 teaching episode. The intentional monitoring carried out by Tyrone (cf. 4.12) was not observed for Scenetra, and we were unable to attribute the integration operation to her early in the teaching experiment.

16 October 1980 Interview

<u>**Spatial Patterns**</u>

5.15. Scenetra could recognize the domino patterns, a triangular three, rows of four and five items, and a diamond four. After seeing various other arrangements that she did not recognize, she re-presented them and counted their elements.

T : (Presents a pattern consisting of a square four and two dots arranged to complete a rectangular six. The pattern was only momentarily shown to Scenetra.)
S : (Whispering) 1-2-3-4-5-6. Six.

Other patterns that Scenetra re-presented and then counted were a rectangular arrangement of six, a triangular arrangement of six, a random arrangement of five, and two square fours.

Finger Patterns

5.16. Scenetra displayed flexibility in her use of finger patterns. She could establish finger patterns for the number words through "seven" by simultaneously putting up fingers, but counted to establish a finger pattern for "eight" in the following protocol.

T : (Presents a cardboard rectangle covered with two cloths) There are eight here and three here.
S : (Opens her left hand and touches each finger with her right index finger) 1-2-3-4-5. (Continues, touching three fingers of her right hand with her left thumb) 6-7-8. (Starts over, and asks how many are covered after reaching "six". Upon being told, she starts over again and proceeds as before. This time she continues touching three more fingers after reaching "eight", the remaining two on her right hand and her left thumb) 9-10-11. Eleven.

Although there is no indication in the protocol that Scenetra re-presented a finger pattern for "eight", it seemed that any three fingers could be a finger pattern for "three". Another solution indicated that "two" could also refer to such a finger pattern.

5.17. In 5.16, Scenetra used finger patterns to keep track of how many times she counted as she made an intuitive extension. She could also re-present finger patterns for "five" and for "six" and modify her use of them. This indicated that she was becoming aware of how she used her finger patterns, a realization that involves more than their simple re-presentation.

T : (Presents a cardboard rectangle covered with two cloths) This time there are five here and six here (pointing to the cloth on Scenetra's left and then on her right).
S : (Opens her left hand and touches each finger while whispering) 1-2-3-4-5 (touches her right little finger while

whispering), 6--6 (places both hands on her face in puzzlement), six! (Whispers "five" and "six" while touching each respective cloth. Opens her left hand and touches her left thumb) Five. (Continues, touching each finger of her right hand, and then her left thumb to her lips while whispering) 6-7-8-9-10-11. Eleven.

The place in the protocol where Scenetra seemed to re-present finger patterns for "five" and "six" was when she touched both cloths and whispered the number words. Before this, she had established a finger pattern for "six" in her immediate visual field, but did not have enough fingers to establish a pattern for "five", and experienced conflict. The way she changed the original finger pattern from six to five indicates that she had reflected on her activity and made a deliberate choice. However, this may indicate a functional change rather than a result of applying the operation of integration--an open hand could be marked by putting up a thumb, which could also be used as part of her finger pattern for "six". This double use of her thumb was a key to her success, and our interpretation was that she was quite unaware of why it worked, an inference consistent with her failure to make as rapid progress toward her abstract period as Tyrone. Nevertheless, her resolved conflict involved a use of her finger patterns that was more sophisticated than anything we observed for Brenda, Tarus, and James while they were in their motor periods.

The Emergence of the Integration Operation

20 January 1981 Teaching Episode

Spatial Patterns

5.18. Previously, Scenetra had used finger patterns to keep track of how many times she counted. Activities in which she re-presented spatial patterns in two previous teaching episodes (24 November 1980 and 1 December 1980) led her to use spatial patterns to keep track of how many times she counted.

T : (Places four squares beside a cloth, asks Scenetra how many are visible, and then tells her that five are covered.)
S : (Looks at the visible squares) Four. (Looks into space and utters) 5-6--7-8--9.

The manner in which Scenetra looked into space while she uttered number words indicates she was counting the elements of a spatial pattern she could "see". She performed similarly with patterns for "four" and "six", in which case she said "eight", "nine"--"ten", "eleven"--"twelve", "thirteen" in a rhythmic manner. For seven hidden squares (cf. 5.03), she uttered eight rather than seven number words.

5.19. Scenetra also produced a rhythmic pattern for "six" when counting two hidden collections of squares, one of five and the other of six. After counting to "five" by sequentially pointing to one place while uttering "one", "two", . . . , "five", she continued by pointing in pairs while uttering "six", "seven"--"eight", "nine"--"ten", "eleven". Her rhythmic pattern for "six" indicates that she at least re-presented a spatial pattern for "six" and counted its elements.

5.20. The discussion in paragraphs 5.18 and 5.19 could lead to the inference that Scenetra's spatial patterns were, like her finger pattern (cf. 5.16-5.17), figurative concepts. Her solutions to other tasks suggest, however, that her spatial patterns were numerical in quality.

T : (Presents four squares beside a cloth in no particular order) We have four here. Altogether there are six (waving his hand over the visible squares and the cloth). How many are under here (pointing to the cloth)?
S : (Stares into space) Two!
T : How do you know?
S : 'Cause there would be six. And make a line like this (makes a row of three squares) and add two more under there, there would be another line like this (places the remaining visible square by the first square of the line of three that she made and runs her hand down the row, indicating another line) and that makes six!

"Six" referred to a re-presented rectangular pattern whose elements she recomposed. First, she created a subpattern that corresponded to the visible squares. Then she completed the pattern for "six" and understood that the resulting subpattern corresponded to the covered squares.

5.21. The mobility that Scenetra displayed indicates that her rectangular pattern for "six" was an object of reflection. She not only re-presented it but she operated with its elements and recomposed them into subpatterns that she took in unitary wholes. This analysis is consistent with the way in which she uttered number words rhythmically to complete patterns for "four" and "six".

5.22. The operations that Scenetra applied to the figural pattern for "six" were similar to those that Tyrone applied when he made linear spatial patterns. She could also use her finger patterns in a similar way (cf. 5.04). She applied the integration operation to finger patterns in her immediate visual field as well as to re-presented spatial patterns.

Limitation of Integration to Patterns

5.23. Our hypothesis was that the material of Scenetra's integration operation was limited to visible or re-presented patterns. First, we observed that the solution in the protocol of paragraph 5.05 was contextual and depended on Scenetra's re-presentation of a counted spatial pattern for "six". As a composite whole, this pattern could be used in an experiential partitioning of the collection of 11 squares. That is, after re-presenting a pattern for "six", she could continue to count, because the numerical pattern signified the counting acts that she had just carried out. She could then focus on the figural items of the hidden part of the collection and count them by counting her motor acts of wiggling fingers.

5.24. The importance of re-presenting the pattern for "six" was demonstrated in the very next task, where the teacher placed eight squares next to a cloth and told Scenetra that there were 15 altogether. Scenetra started counting from "one" and attempted to separate her counting activity into two parts, but she lost track of when to stop counting and continued past "fifteen". Because she pointed to the visible squares when she counted them and then wiggled her fingers when she continued to count the hidden squares, it was possible for her to keep track of counting the hidden squares. However, her inability to keep track of counting indicates that she did not take the collection of eight counted visible squares as a numerical composite. We see in paragraph 5.21 that when she created a numerical composite for "six", she could keep track of counting the hidden portion of the collection. In that case, she could make numerical composites using patterns and substitute those numerical composites for counted collections. But she did not seem to apply the integration operation to the counted collections per se.

5.25. The conclusion that she could only apply the integration operation to patterns is further substantiated when the teacher reposed the task in paragraph 5.24. This time Scenetra drawled "e-i-g-h-t" as she simultaneously put up eight fingers. She closed her hands and continued counting, sequentially wiggling fingers synchronously with uttering "9-10-11-12-13-14-15". Then she reviewed her fingers and said, "seven". After establishing a finger pattern for "eight", her intention seemed to be to establish another by counting. She was in a finger pattern context and counting was meaningful to her. So, if Scenetra applied her integration operation here, it was restricted to patterns.

The Period of Sequential Integration Operations

5 March 1981 Teaching Episode

<u>A Number Word as an Index of a Number Word Sequence</u>

5.26. Scenetra's behavior in this protocol provides a basis for interpreting what number words and numerals in the decades might have meant to her. In the following protocol, she spontaneously counted-on from "forty-three" to solve an addition task.

T : (Touches two cloths that he and Scenetra are pretending cover cookies) You have forth-three here and six here. So, how many are there altogether?
S : (Touches the cloth "covering" forty-three) Forty-three. (Sequentially puts up fingers as she utters) 44-45-46-47-48-(emphatically) 49!

The act of touching the cloth and saying "forty-three" indicates that Scenetra understood that if she were to count the imaginary cookies, the result would be "forty-three". But at this point, there is no basis for deciding whether the number word referred to a figural plurality, to a number sequence, or to a result of counting.

5.27. Scenetra's subsequent behavior indicated that "forty-three" referred only to what the results of counting would be if it were to be carried out.

T : Very good! You know what would happen if I moved these around like this (interchanges the cloths)?--I moved the cookies around--Now there are six here and there are forty-nine altogether. How many are here?
S : I don't know!
T : Could you find out?
S : Yes. How many do you have here (points to the cloth covering the six)?
T : Six. And there are forty-nine altogether. Can you find out how many I have here?
S : (Counts-on) Six--(sequentially puts up fingers) 7-8-9- . . . -14-15 -- (laughs). How many have you got here (points to the cloth covering 43)?

Scenetra's failure to simply say "forty-three" is a strong indication that this number word did not refer to a number sequence. When she attempted to count on beyond six, she obviously did not realize there were 43 imaginary cookies under the other cloth. "Forty-three" seemed to serve as an index for a number word sequence starting with "one" and proceeding up to "forty-three", which is a result of counting. It did not seem to refer to a composite unit. It may have pointed to a figural plurality, but she did not seem to produce it. Her failure to produce a signified object would explain why she forgot "forty-three" so rapidly. In her solution to a similar task in the following protocol, she did produce a numerical composite as a signified object.

Counting as a Numerical Concept

5.28. Scenetra's behavior in the following protocol suggests that counting was emerging as a numerical concept and that she could apply the integration operation sequentially.

T : (There are two cloths placed side by side) There are nine there and we have sixteen altogether (waving his hand over both cloths). How many are under there (looks under the appropriate cloth)?

S : (Points to the cloth covering nine and puts up her thumb) Nine (continues sequentially putting up fingers) 10-11-12-13-14-15-16. That's eight!

T : (After Scenetra wrote "9 + 8 = 16" on the board) I've got eight here (touches the cloth that Scenetra said covered eight) and sixteen cookies altogether (waving his hand over both cloths). How many cookies are here?

S : (Points to the cloth covering eight) eight. (Continues sequentially putting up fingers) 9-10-11-12-13-14-15-16. You have eight!

T : What do you think it should be?

S : Puts up nine fingers.

T : Why do you think it should be that many?

S : I don't know!

The difference between this solution and the solution in the protocol of paragraph 5.27 was that "nine" seemed to refer to a particular numerical composite, whereas "forty-three" did not. Scenetra's act of putting up nine fingers in response to the teacher's query, "What do you think it should be?" indicates that her act of putting up her thumb as she said "nine" signified a finger pattern for "nine". "Nine" referred to a numerical finger pattern, whereas "forty-three" in paragraph 5.27 was an index of a number word sequence. There, counting-on was essentially used as a number word procedure she had abstracted from her solutions of tasks like those in this paragraph. Here, counting-on was meaningful because her numerical finger patterns embodied counting. She could re-present counting when she re-presented her numerical finger patterns and, as such, it was a numerical concept.

5.29. Scenetra's solution should not be taken to indicate that she viewed 8 and 9 as being abstract composite units included in 16. Simply reposing the task emphasizing "eight", the number word that she had just established by using counting-on, led to Scenetra counting-on again rather than using what she already had established.

18 May 1981 Teaching Episode

Partitioning a Numerical Finger Pattern for "Ten"

5.30. Scenetra seemed to focus on the elements of her numerical finger patterns rather than on the patterns as one thing. This claim is corroborated by the way in which she partitioned ten in this teaching episode.

T : (Places "9" on one of two cloths that are placed side by side and "10" above the cloths) Let's pretend there are ten altogether. How many are under here?
S : One.
T : I want you to arrange the cookies under here so that you make all the numbers that add to be ten. What would be two more that would be different?
S : (Selects "8" and "2".)
T : All right! Find two more numbers that make ten.
S : (Selects "5" and "5".)

From a pile of numerals, Scenetra went on to select "7" and "3"; "4" and "6"; "6" and "4"; and "3" and "7". She used a finger pattern to generate "3" after selecting "7"; counted-on to generate "6" after selecting "4"; and counted-on to generate "7" after selecting "3". "Eight" just happened to be next to "9" when she removed "9" from the cloth and searched for another numeral. The only time where she seemed to base her selection on a previous selection was in the case of "6" and "4". Her strategy was to scan the available numerals rather than to use what she had just chosen. Nevertheless, she used the numeral she chose as a guide to partition her finger pattern for "ten". These activities indicate that it was her intention after selecting a numeral to find how many individual units it would take to complete her finger pattern for "ten". There was no sign that Scenetra took her finger pattern for "ten" as one thing. At best, she focused on the fingers of the finger pattern.

Lack of a System of Progressive Integrations

5.31. There was no indication that Scenetra could use the results of an integration as material for another integration more than two months after she had entered her abstract period (cf. 5.10). Her performance in the following task provides our strongest indication that she continued to focus on the constituent items of numerical composites.

T : (Shows Scenetra three checkers and hides them beneath a cloth) Count ten more and put them here (by the cloth).
S : (Counts out ten checkers and places them by the cloth.)
T : If you took all of those ten and put them with these (the three), how many would you have?
S : (Counts the visible checkers starting from "three") Thirteen.
T : (Places the checkers under the cloth and places the numeral "13" on the cloth) Take ten more.
S : (Counts out ten more, placing them by the cloth.)
T : (Places the ten checkers under the cloth with the 13) Now how many do I have? There are thirteen and ten more.
S : (Puts her hands under the table and counts ten more, using her fingers) Twenty-three.
T : Twenty-three! Take ten more. (Replaces the numeral "13" with "23".)
S : (Counts out ten more and places them under the cloth. Upon being asked how many were under there, Scenetra said "thirty".)
T : Thirty what?
S : Thirty-one?
T : You had twenty-three and added ten more.
S : Twenty-three--twenty-nine--thirty! (After the teacher re-posed the problem and encouraged Scenetra to count, she sequentially put up fingers while uttering) twenty-three--24-25-26-27-29-30-31-32-33.

The teacher then asked Scenetra to pretend to put ten more under the cloth on four different occasions. She counted-on ten each time. After reaching "seventy-three", the teacher asked Scenetra to say how many ten more would be without counting. Scenetra said she didn't know.

5.32. Scenetra tried to generate the next number word that would be ten more than "twenty-three" but could only say "thirty". Her strategy was to add ten to twenty, not to twenty-three. The reason for her apparent failure to reflect on the results of counting ten more beyond 23 is provided in the 10 December 1981 interview discussed below. The decade names were semantically linked with patterns for "ten", and a ten pattern could be put with two patterns of ten to make "thirty". In this particular case, her patterns for ten seemed to consist of re-presentations of material she used in her classroom, such as multibase longs (a rectangular stick 1 cm by 1 cm by 10 cm). This essentially prevented her from using the results of an integration in a subsequent integration, an operation that we believe she could perform (cf. Chapter VIII).

The Period of Progressive Integration Operations

10 December 1981 Interview

Partitioning Numerical Composites into Tens and Ones

5.33. The interviews that were held at the beginning of the second year of the teaching experiment indicated that Scenetra had developed highly figurative linguistic rules for separating the contents of the numerical composites associated with two-digit numerals into so many tens and so many ones. In these cases, "ten" seemed to refer to a particular pattern, depending on the context.

T : (Presents Scenetra with a cellophane bag of centimeter cubes) How many blocks do you think would be in there?
S : About ninety-nine!
T : That is too many. I counted them and there are forty-six. If you take those blocks out and make rows of ten, how many rows could you make?
S : Forty-six!
T : Rows of ten!
S : Hm! I could make six rows.
T : How many!?
S : Forty and six blocks.
T : OK. And how many rows of ten could you make?
S : Four!
T : And why would that be?
S : Because, forty, and you add a zero and that would be four rows of ten!

The teacher then presented a cellophane bag with 57 centimeter cubes in it. Scenetra thought there would be five rows of ten and that seven blocks would be left over. However, when 100 blocks were presented, Scenetra displayed no method for finding how many rows of ten there would be, even after she had actually made six rows. The activity of making rows of ten did not suggest counting to her and her only method of solution was suggested by the interviewer--actually make the rows! "One hundred" had no meaning as so many units of ten.

5.34. The decade numerals--"20", "30", "40", etc.--were clearly semantically linked with a pattern of so many singletons, just as the numerals corresponding to the digits were semantically linked with spatial or finger patterns. We currently interpret the elements of her patterns as singleton units (e.g., a multi-base long interpreted as a stick) rather than as numerical composites, because Scenetra displayed no indications of integration operations to generate these patterns of ten. Interestingly enough, she could use linguistic rules as a guide for generating the patterns, but these rules were limited in scope. For example, after Scenetra "decomposed" the symbol "46" into the two symbols "40" ("Because, forty, and you add a zero . . . ") and "6", "40" then triggered the pattern of four "rows" of ten. There had to be four of something, where "something" comprised a re-presentation of a "row" of ten. The numeral "100", however, could not be decomposed and Scenetra was left without a guiding linguistic rule. Counting by ten was not relevant to her, given the way in which she interpreted the task. Our problem now was to decide whether Scenetra could take her re-presentation of four rows of ten and six blocks as material for more complex operating.

11 December 1981 Interview

Taking Numerical Composites as Units

5.35. In the first few subtraction tasks Scenetra solved in this interview, there was an indication that she worked with ten as a numerical composite. She seemed to work with the individual units, in contrast to the protocol in paragraph 5.33.

I : (Presents a rectangular tube into which marbles will just fit. Scenetra places 16 marbles into the tube) How many do you want to take away?
S : Eight.
I : (Removes eight marbles and asks Scenetra to verify that eight have been taken out) How many are in there?
S : (Opens both hands while muttering. Folds eight fingers) Six, 7-8 (closing the remaining two fingers).
I : How did you do that?
S : Six in my head (touches her forehead and opens both of her hands), take away eight (folds eight fingers), six; 7-8.

Scenetra partitioned 16 into two parts -- the part that referred to those she "put in her head" and the part that referred to the finger pattern for ten. This partitioning could be done without focusing on ten as one thing. She had ten fingers in a pattern, just as she had six fingers "in her head".

5.36. In the task immediately following, Scenetra took 6 blocks away from 23 that were under a cloth. This time she put ten in her head, ten on her fingers, and then folded six fingers. After counting "ten; 11-12-13-14" she said that 14 were still covered. In subsequent probes, it became apparent she could not include the three she had left out, even though she became aware of them. She repeatedly solved the problem the same way, even after she realized that when she put ten on her fingers there would be 13 of the 23 left.

5.37. In a later task, Scenetra seemed to change the way she worked with ten.

I : (Presents 23 pennies in two stacks of ten and three individual pennies. After covering them with a cloth) Reach under there and take six.
S : (Removes six pennies, one at a time) 1-2-3-4-5-6.
I : How many are left under there?
S : (After sitting silently but moving her fingers) Seventeen!
I : How did you do that?
S : (Places her hand on her forehead and then extends her ten fingers) Thirteen take away six (folds six fingers). Three; 4-5-6-7 (sequentially folding her four extended fingers), and then add ten and have seventeen!

Although it is not indicated clearly in the above protocol, Scenetra "put ten in her head" as before. However, this time she separated 13 into her finger pattern for ten and three more. This last partition indicates that Scenetra might have focused on the finger pattern as a single entity while maintaining its composite structure. In other words, she seemed to take a numerical composite of ten as one thing and construct an *abstract composite unit* of ten.

17 December 1981 Teaching Episode

5.38. Our inference that Scenetra could treat ten ones as one ten is substantiated by the algorithm she displayed in the following protocol.

T : (Presents the sentence "62 - 7 = ") Are you ready for this? What is sixty-two take away seven?
S : (Sits silently for about 40 seconds) Fifty-five!

T : How did you get fifty-five?
S : I took two away from sixty (removes "2" from"62") and I took five away from sixty.
T : How did you take five away from sixty?
S : (Opens her hands) I had five tens (pointing to her head) so I had--take five away (folds one hand). I went five away from one of the tens.

Putting five tens in her head is a strong indication that she now viewed each ten as an individual unit. Her language is also indicative--"I had five tens" and "five away from one of the tens". The way she put up ten fingers also shows that each abstract composite unit of ten retained its composite quality.

12 March 1982 Teaching Episode

<u>Applying Integrations to Re-presented Counting Activity</u>

5.39. Scenetra's primary algorithms for finding differences have been illustrated in the preceding protocols. Although she could create abstract composite units by applying the integration operation to numerical composites of ten, the abstract composite units were limited to the patterns she produced by applying her linguistic rules. Her use of these algorithms did not facilitate the application of the integration operation to re-presented counting activity. She could apply the integration operation to numerical composites of ten as early as 17 December 1981, but she seemed not to construct one number as a segment of another as Tyrone did (cf. 4.34). Her behavior in the following protocol shows that she was capable of doing so.

T : (Presents the sentence "48 - 37 = ___") Can you do that one by counting?
S : (Nods her head "yes" and ticks off fingers) 47-46-45-44-43-42-41-40-39-38-37--eleven.
T : Beautiful! Let's do another one! (Presents the sentence "53 - 12 = ___") Can you do that one by counting?
S : (Ticks off fingers) 52-51-50-49-48-47-46-45-44-43-42 (Scenetra passed over her thumb and thought she had ticked off 12 fingers rather than 11).

The teacher asked Scenetra to count, since she usually used her algorithms to solve subtraction tasks (cf. 5.35-5.38). In this case, Scenetra did not partition the two involved numbers into tens. Rather, she gave meaning to the numerals solely in terms of the unit of one. Because there was no indication from the teacher concerning how Scenetra was to count, counting 12 off from 53 and counting from 48 down to 37 confirm that she could make appropriate decisions concerning when to count-off-from and count-down-to. These decisions strongly indicate that Scenetra used at least the system of progressive integration operations as an assimilating structure of her counting scheme.

Failure to Disembed a Numerical Part from a Numerical Whole

5.40. The question of whether Scenetra could extract numerical parts from a numerical whole and treat them as units in their own right is not clearly indicated by her counting solutions of the above protocols. However, when coupled with an inability to compare two-digit numbers, demonstrated in the following protocol, there is indication that she was yet to disembed a numerical part from a numerical whole. This in turn indicates that she had not yet constructed the system of part-whole operations. The teacher intentionally selected numbers that were in different decades so Scenetra would be unlikely to use her algorithms to find the differences between the numbers.

T : How much "bigger" is forty-four than thirty-five?
S : One.
T : Do you think it's one bigger?
S : I don't know.
T : Start at thirty-five and see how many times you count.
S : (Sequentially puts up fingers) 36-37- . . . - 44; nine.

Scenetra's answer "one" indicates that she compared either "5" and "4" or "3" and "4". In either case, she did not seem to view 35 as an initial segment of 44. Even if she compared 4 tens and 3 tens, she did not have to include 35 in 44 to make the comparison. In fact, her lack of spontaneity in counting from 35 up to 44 is a strong indication to the contrary. Later in the teaching episode, the teacher asked Scenetra how much "smaller" 47 was than 53. Scenetra counted backward to find out only after it was suggested. Too, she did not know how many times she would count if she were then to count forward. Although Scenetra counted appropriately after the teacher prompted her, we do not infer that she included the lesser of the two numbers in the other. She seemed to view the two numbers to be compared as separate entities having no possible inclusion relation.

8 April 1982 Teaching Episode

Ten as a Repeatable Unit

5.41. The way in which Scenetra used the unit of ten changed dramatically in this teaching episode. She previously constructed units of ten by using her linguistic rules to partition two-digit numbers. She could now count by ten to find how many piles of ten pennies she could make from 100 pennies.

T : (Holds a dollar bill in front of Scenetra) Do you know how many pennies this would buy?
S : A hundred!
T : (Places a pile of pennies in front of Scenetra) Could you make a pile of ten pennies?
S : (Counts out ten pennies and places them in a stack.)
T : How many piles of pennies could you make like that if you had this many pennies (holds the dollar bill in front of Scenetra)?
S : Oh--(Sits silently for about ten seconds) A hundred--ten!
T : How did you know that?
S : I put up my fingers when I counted to a hundred!
T : Do that for me.
S : (Sequentially puts up fingers) 10-20-30-40-50-60-70-80-90-100.
T : Put up a finger. (Scenetra puts up her index finger) How many piles does that stand for?
S : One.

Scenetra independently counted by ten in the above protocol--counting was not suggested by her teacher. This indicates that her unit of ten may have been iterable. To make this inference, it would be necessary to have some indication that each counting by ten act could symbolize an increment of ten ones. We will see in subsequent protocols that such an inference is implausible.

5.42. It is elucidating to separate Scenetra's counting by ten scheme in the protocol of paragraph 5.41 into its three constituent parts. First, there was the situation as understood by Scenetra; second, there was the counting activity; and third, there was the result of the activity. We focus on the second part and on Scenetra's spontaneity in order to make inferences about the first part. Our primary question is whether Scenetra disembedded a unit of ten from one hundred prior to counting. This will allow us to decide whether she applied the disembedding operation. The fact that she correctly kept track of counting suggests that she might have done so. However, her solutions to other tasks make it more plausible to suggest that her curtailment of counting by one was influenced by her prior counting activity of making a pile of ten pennies. We argue below that although she could take that pile of ten pennies as a unit, she could not yet disembed a unit of ten from a unit of one hundred.

5.43. We now focus on the result of counting to make inferences about the nature of the units of ten she counted and, correspondingly, about her disembedding operation. In 5.41, after Scenetra counted by ten to 100, she looked at her fingers and said that she had counted ten times. In another similar task, she counted to 150 by ten and then paused to review her records of counting before saying that she counted fifteen times. In both cases, she seemed to rely on finger patterns to know how many times she had counted by ten. Although there is every indication that she took the records as one thing, there is no indication that she incremented the counted units. We therefore turn to a later teaching episode in an attempt to investigate this question.

15 April 1982 Teaching Episode

<u>Failure of a Counting by Ten Act to Increment Ten More Ones</u>

5.44. The most viable inference concerning the nature of the countable unit items that Scenetra created and counted in the protocol of paragraph 5.41 is that she coordinated symbolic motor units of ten with number words rather than incremented ten more ones. This inference is based on her performance in the following protocol.

T : (Places four pennies under a container and a dime on top of the container) If I put a dime on top of there, how many pennies--how many cents would that make?
S : Fourteen.
T : (Repeatedly places another dime on top of the container and each time Scenetra says a number word) And another dime?
S : (Utters) 24-34-44-54- . . . -94-104-114--(After the teacher suggests that she count by one) 115-116- . . . -124--134- . . . -214-224.
T : Very good! (Uncovers the four pennies.)
S : I want to count it! (Proceeds, counting the dimes by tens and the pennies by ones.)
T : (Holds up a dime) Two hundred and fourteen of what? Of these?
S : No.
T : Two hundred fourteen what?
S : I don't know!

T : Suppose I gave you pennies instead of dimes? How many pennies would you have altogether?
S : I don't know.

Scenetra genuinely did not know. Once she detected a pattern in the number word sequence "4-14-24- . . . ", she was able to generate succeeding number words quite fluently. Importantly, counting ten more by one had to be suggested by the teacher when she reached "one hundred fourteen" and could not continue the number word pattern. Our observation indicates that saying a number word did not imply incrementing ten more ones. This inference is consistent with her failure to understand that there would be 214 pennies, and her need to count the money after she had just "counted" it. Counting by ten, then, was an activity that resulted from her construction of an abstract composite unit of ten. Even though each motor unit she counted in the protocol of paragraph 5.41 might have been a symbol for making an abstract composite unit, these abstract composite units did not seem to be easily accessible during her counting activity. She seemed to forget that putting up a finger was a substitute for ten items, and she treated her counted units as singletons. Making motor units was repeated and formed an experiential chain. Also, she seemed to take her records of counting (a collection of fingers) as a unit only after she completed counting. Consequently there would be no reason for her to know how many pennies there were when she finished counting. She only knew how many times she counted.

22 April 1982 Teaching Episode

Lack of a Decade Concept

5.45. Scenetra's performance in this teaching episode confirms that she did not increment ten more ones when she counted by ten, because she did not realize that each decade comprised ten units of one.

T : (Presents a long, narrow card with the numerals "21" to "30", inclusive, written on it. Each numeral was placed below a dot and the dots were connected by line segments) Scenetra, what is this (points to "21")?
S : Twenty-one.
T : (Points to "30") What is this?
S : Thirty.
T : (Turns the card over, face down) I want you to tell me how many dots (the teacher said both "dots" and "numbers" to clarify his intentions) are on that card.

S : (Points at each place on the back of the card that she takes as hiding a dot with her left hand and synchronously puts up a finger as she says) 21-22-23-24-25-26-27-28-29-30. (She loses track, making a coordination error, so she starts over and repeats counting in the same way) Ten!!

In a subsequent task, the teacher presented a similar number card with the numerals from "31" to "40", inclusive. Scenetra again counted in an analogous fashion and, after getting "ten" as a result, said, "I knew all the time!" She then thought there would be 11 numbers from 91 to 100, inclusive. She counted to find out for sure and produced "ten", said "ten", gesturing with one hand, and then "ten", gesturing with her other hand, as if that was always the result. This was her first realization that each decade comprised ten units of one. In confirmation, she emulated a "solution" by the teacher where he double counted to emphasize the correspondence between the number words in the decades and the digits. This double counting activity seemed to validate Scenetra's new discovery.

23 April 1982 Teaching Episode

<u>Abstracting from Ten More</u>

5.46. Scenetra's insight that each decade comprises ten unit items did not immediately lead to the realization that counting by ten also increments by ten. Instead, there seemed to be intermediary steps.

T : (Presents two number cards to Scenetra and places "65" above "55") How many more numbers would you have to count on to get to sixty-five?
S : (Sequentially puts up fingers) 56-57-58-59-60-61-62- . . . --ten!

In the midst of counting, Scenetra anticipated the result, ten. This abstraction from counting activity led her to say "ten" when the "70's" decade card was added because, if she were to count ten more, she would be in that decade.

5.47. The teacher then asked Scenetra how many she would have to count to get from 51 to 61 and from 58 to 68. Scenetra answered "ten" immediately both times. So the teacher added a "40's" decade card and asked her how many it would take to get from 42 to 62. The three decade cards were aligned one above the other, with the "40's" on top. Scenetra said "twenty" immediately. The teacher then added the "30's" decade card and Scenetra said "thirty" before he could ask any questions.

T : Prove it to me!
S : (Starts at "34", touching each dot in synchrony with putting up fingers) 34-35-36- . . . -42-43. (The teacher interrupts.)
T : How many did you get right there?
S : Ten.
T : (Points to "53") How many more would you count if you counted down to here?
S : Ten.
T : (Points to "63") And what about here?
S : Ten.
T : So altogether you would have?
S : Thirty!

After she counted by one, Scenetra seemed to be quite confident of "thirty". She even counted "10, 20, 30" as she pointed to "43", "53", and "63" in verification.

5.48. The teacher presented Scenetra with a new task to break the pattern of saying the next decade name after adding one more decade card. He placed the "80's" card below the "20's" and "60's" cards.

T : (Points to "23") How many would you count if you start at twenty-three and go to eighty-three (pointing to "83")?
S : (Sequentially puts up fingers as she says) 33-43-53-63-73-83. Six.
T : That makes six tens. How many ones?
S : Eighty-three!

Subsequent probes indicated that Scenetra truly did not know how many ones she had counted. She could not "unpack" the six tens into 60 ones, apparently because she did not count ten more by ones prior to counting by ten from 23 to 83. Counting by ten, if it was not abstracted from the activity of counting by one, still consisted of repeating counting acts. Even if these acts referred to abstract composite units of ten, she could not "unpack" them into their constituent units.

7 May 1982 Teaching Episode

<u>**Abstracting Counting by Ten from Counting by One**</u>

5.49. Scenetra's knowledge that there were ten units of one between two numbers in adjacent decades that were, in fact, ten units apart was contextual and limited to the time and situation in which it was abstracted. Its situational nature is demonstrated in the following protocol.

T : (A row of blocks is partitioned into two rows of ten. Points to the eighth block of the first row) How many blocks do you think are up to here?
S : (Simultaneously extends ten fingers and folds two) Eight.
T : Where is number 18?
S : (Points to the correct block after scanning the second row of ten.)
T : (Covers the ten blocks from number 9 to number 18, inclusive) How many are covered?
S : (Moves her fingers as she whispers) Ten! (Expresses surprise.)

She did not use ten, the result of counting from 9 to 18, to interpret the problem situation. The assimilating operations of her counting scheme apparently were not connected to the operations that enabled her to partition two-digit numbers into tens and ones and thus "see" 18 as one ten and eight. These latter operations belonged to a separate scheme.

5.50. After Scenetra had abstracted ten as a record of counting, the teacher extended the problem situation in an attempt to lead Scenetra to give meaning to the problem in terms of this unit.

T : Let's put another row of ten on there (continues the row of blocks by placing another ten). Where is number twenty-seven?
S : Where is number twenty-seven? (After a pause, touches the correct block.)
T : How did you know that was 27?
S : Because, this right here was twenty (gesturing over the first two rows) and (touching each of the first seven blocks of the third row) 1-2-3-4-5-6-7.
T : (Covers the blocks from 8 to 27, inclusive) How many are covered up? (Scenetra knew the first seven were visible).
S : (Ticks off fingers) 8-9-10- . . . -26-27. Twenty!
T : Can you think of a way that Marva could do it (Marva was an observer that Scenetra knew well)?
S : She could count by tens!
T : Go ahead and do it!
S : She went ten (placing her hand on the first row)--seven!--ten-17-27--is that right? She went SEVEN, SEVENTEEN, TWENTY-SEVEN! (Synchronously placing her hand along the cover.)
T : How many tens did you get?
S : Two.
T : How many are two tens?

S : Twenty.

The tactic of encouraging Scenetra to find another way to do the problem led to a seemingly novel insight--that she could find how many individual blocks were hidden by counting by ten. Even though the blocks were arranged in rows of ten, she seemed to reorganize what she put into the situation--counting 20 times by ones--before realizing that she could have solved the problem by counting by ten. At least momentarily, she understood that counting by ten also incremented by ten individual units. The possibility that she could take ten as a given before, rather than after, she counted by one was tested in a subsequent teaching episode.

20 May 1982 Teaching Episode

<u>Numerical Extension Using the Counting by Ten Scheme</u>

5.51. Scenetra used the unit of ten in this teaching episode to solve a missing addend task so that it was possible to impute to her the ability to take ten as a given prior to counting, if there was perceptual material to make an abstract composite unit of numerosity ten.

T : (Places a cloth in front of Scenetra) Let's pretend that I put forty-seven pieces of candy under this cloth. I am going to put some bags of candy under this cloth (Scenetra understood that each bag held ten candies).
S : How many?
T : That is what I want you to find out. Altogether, there are eighty-seven pieces of candy.
S : (Ticks off fingers) 57-67-87 (Makes a coordination error) Three.
T : Scenetra, could you do that again?
S : (Again ticks off fingers) 57-67-77-87. Four!
T : How many candies are under there?
S : Hm--87--I mean, forty!
T : How did you get that?
S : I don't know.

Scenetra's use of her counting by ten scheme is analogous to how she used her counting by one scheme to solve missing addend tasks when she was in the period of sequential integrations. As long as she believed there were bags with ten candies per bag, she could count-on by ten and unpack the units of ten that she counted into their constituent unit items. The assimilating operations of her counting by ten scheme now seemed to involve the system of sequential integrations applied to given figural collections of ten.

Counting-Up-To to Solve a Subtraction Problem

5.52. Scenetra now spontaneously counted to solve subtractive situations. However, she still could not extract a numerical part from a numerical whole, as indicated in the next protocol. Moreover, she counted-up-to by one in situations where she might have counted by ten.

T : (Places candies under a cloth) There are sixty-three candies under there. (Takes out some of the candies) I took out 21. How many are still under there? Can you count backward to do it?

S : (Shakes her head "no". . Ticks off 42 fingers while subvocally uttering number words) It's forty-two!

T : How did you get that? Did you start at twenty-one?

S : (Nods her head "yes" and starts ticking off fingers again) 22-23-24- . . . .

T : Can you find another way to do it? Can you start at sixty-three and count down to twenty-one?

S : (Shakes her head "no".)

Starting at 21 and counting up to 63 by one indicates that Scenetra assimilated the problem using her counting-by-one scheme. Although she may have disembedded 21 from 63, there is little reason to infer that Scenetra did so, because progressive integrations were sufficient to allow her solution of the task in the given context. Apparently, the assimilating operations of her counting scheme included this latter system of integrations. This solution of the protocol constituted progress in her counting-by-one scheme, although she still did not make decisions about when to count-down-to or count-up-to, an ability that seems to require reversible part-whole operations.

Discussion of Scenetra's Case Study

The Emergence of the Integration Operation

Early in her motor period, most of Scenetra's number words (and numerals) corresponding to the digits referred to patterns, or else she quickly established a pattern meaning. These number words could have a counting meaning as well as a pattern meaning--a dual meaning (cf. 5.17 for a dual meaning of "six"). But, prior to the emergence of the integration operation, she only re-presented patterns. Counting was re-presented to the extent that it was embodied in patterns.

When Scenetra could take the elements of patterns as material for integrations, she curtailed the motor activity in counting (cf. 5.03) primarily because the patterns embodied counting and the elements of a pattern could now signify counting acts. She simply uttered number words in a rhythmic manner while she continued to count, without coordinating those utterances with motor activity (cf. 5.20). Nevertheless, because her integrations were restricted to patterns at this time, her counting scheme was still primarily an enactive preconcept.

The Period of Sequential Integration Operations

Scenetra partitioned numbers signified by a two-digit numeral into so many tens and so many ones by using linguistic rules that she had learned in her classroom. The decade numerals--"20", "30", etc., were semantically linked with so many "tens". She separated a numeral like "46" into "40" and "6", and then translated "40" into "four tens", by re-presenting a visual pattern for "ten" that depended on the situation (cf. 5.33). Eventually, there was every indication that these re-presentations carried the significance of numerical composites of ten (cf. 5.38).

When Scenetra did not partition numbers using her patterns of ten, number words like "forty-three" served as indices for number word sequences and counting-on could be an abstracted number word procedure (cf. 5.26). The number words corresponding to the digits could refer to counting backward the number of times indicated (cf. 5.12). For example, "five" could refer to counting backward five times, starting with "nineteen". Because she kept track of her number word utterances, "five" referred to a numerical composite whose elements were of a rather arbitrary nature--a composite whose elements could be specified because there would be five of them. In this sense, she had taken a step similar to Tyrone's toward the construction of an "unknown". Also like Tyrone, she focused on the contents of the numerical composites that she had made (cf. 5.30 and 5.31) early in her abstract period.

Scenetra could apply the integration operation sequentially in the context of solving what, to us, were missing addend problems (cf. 5.28), subtraction problems (cf. 5.12), and direct addition problems upon entry into the abstract stage. These sequential applications constituted her meaning of these numerical "operations". In each instance of sequential application, she made juxtaposed numerical composites. However, she seemed genuinely unable to use the results of a prior integration--a numerical composite--as material for further operating during this period and generally viewed each new task as being unrelated to previously solved tasks.

The Period of Progressive Integration Operations

Because Scenetra partitioned numbers referred to by two-digit numerals into so many tens and so many ones, and used her rather ingenious algorithms to solve addition and subtraction problems (cf. 5.37), she generally did not view these numbers as comprising an ordered series of units of one. However, her solution of subtraction tasks by counting backward indicates that she was capable of viewing numbers in this way (cf. 5.12) in April of 1981, when she could apply the integration operation sequentially. However, she preferred to use her algorithms to solve addition and subtraction problems, and counted only when she was specifically requested to do so. We did not observe her applying the integration operation progressively, except on rare occasions, one of which occurred in March of 1982 (cf. 5.39). She could, like Tyrone when he could apply the integration operation progressively, make decisions whether to count off from or to count-down-to while solving subtraction problems. Scenetra's algorithms definitely constrained the development of part-whole operations and made it especially difficult to work with her on the construction of the unit of ten as iterable. As documented (cf. 5.35), she could take her finger pattern for "ten" as one thing as early as December of 1981, and her algorithms were based on ten as an abstract composite unit. It was not necessary for ten to be iterable for Scenetra to use her algorithms.

A great deal of work was done with Scenetra during the months of April and May of 1982 to encourage her to construct ten as an iterable unit. As a by-product, Scenetra seemed to change her preferred ways of doing subtraction problems (cf. 5.52). In the protocol of paragraph 5.52, Scenetra seemed to be quite flexible, and independently counted from 21 up to 63 by one to solve the problem. This was not an isolated instance. Scenetra had modified her concept of subtraction to include her counting-up-to scheme. In fact, we inferred that Scenetra had modified the first part of her counting by one scheme to include the system of progressive integrations. While counting, accurately keeping track of her counting acts was an impressive performance that Scenetra undertook herself. She seemed to be explicitly aware of 21 as the numerosity of an abstract composite unit, of the as-yet-uncounted candies that were hidden as another abstract composite unit of unspecified numerosity, and of 63 as comprising these two units. The behavioral indications would be stronger had she also independently counted, say, 21 off from 63 as a matter of choice. But Scenetra had a particular aversion to counting backward, even though she could do it (cf. 5.39).

Unit Types of the Unit of Ten

Scenetra could create ten as a numerical composite soon after she entered the abstract stage in March of 1981 (cf. 5.10 and 5.31). In December of 1981, she operated with ten as an abstract composite unit (cf. 5.38) in the context of her subtraction and addition algorithms. From 12 March 1982 to 20 May 1982 we presented problems to Scenetra with the intention of helping her construct ten as an iterable unit. When Scenetra could apply the integration operation progressively, she counted by ten in an attempt to partition a collection of one hundred pennies (cf. 5.39 and 5.40). This was possible because a pile of ten pennies were in her visual field and she could take them as material for making an abstract composite unit. But she seemed to "lose" her re-presentation of the abstract composite unit of ten while she counted, and simply repeated the acts of counting by ten as though she were counting by one. The result of counting by ten was a finger pattern that she took as referring to individual units -- "fifteen tens" meant that she had put up fifteen fingers. Although each act of putting up a finger was originally a substitute for an abstract composite unit of ten, her results of counting did not signify so many units of one. We called this unit of ten a repeatable unit.

Tyrone abstracted ten as an iterable unit from his activity of solving addition and subtraction problems by counting by ten and by one (cf. 4.37). Other situations had to be devised for Scenetra because of her reliance on algorithms. We illustrated two of these situations (cf. 5.51 - 5.53 and 5.54 - 5.55) that resulted from our search for situations where Scenetra would use her progressive integration operations rather than partitioning operations as assimilating operations. Scenetra's abstraction of a unit of ten more is illustrated in the protocol of paragraph 5.50. The salient feature of solution is that she used the records of counting from seven up to twenty-seven by one as material for further operating. She reflected on her records of counting by one, and tried to find another way to solve the problem. Her other way was to organize the twenty units that she had produced when counting by one into abstract composite units of ten that she could then count by ten. In a later teaching episode, she finally realized that counting by ten could be used to find how many units of one (cf. 5.51). She could apply the integration operation sequentially to figural collections of ten. This represented progress in her counting by ten scheme because, prior to this time, her assimilating operation for this scheme was essentially a single integration operation. This novel counting by ten scheme was yet to be synthesized with her counting by one scheme and its more advanced assimilating operations. Scenetra never constructed a system of part-whole operations during the teaching experiment because there was no indication whatever that she could disembed a numerical part from a numerical whole. Moreover, we could find no indication that Scenetra had constructed ten as an iterable unit.

6. JASON

The periods in Jason's construction of the counting scheme that we documented in Chapter IV are summarized in Figure 7. Starting on 18 October 1980, Jason's motor period lasted until 11 May 1981, when we observed him creating verbal unit items (cf. 6.09). He essentially had no verbal period, since we observed him counting-on to solve missing addend sentences on 21 May 1981 (cf. 6.11). His spontaneous solutions in this teaching episode indicated to us that Jason anticipated that he could find how many counting acts he was going to perform before he counted. He also independently kept track of how many times he counted.

Figure 7

Periods in Jason's Construction of the Counting Scheme

```
ABSTRACT  |                     **********************
PERIOD    |
          |
MOTOR     |   ***********
PERIOD    | .___________.______________________.

        10/80         5/81                    6/82
```

Recognition and Re-presentation of Patterns

In Chapter IV, we documented that patterns played only a minor role in Jason's progress to his motor period. The most sophisticated patterns that he used to make intuitive extensions were action patterns for "two" and "four" (cf. 6.01-6.02). While in his motor period, he developed a repertory of finger and spatial patterns. Like Tyrone and Scenetra, the integration operation emerged in the context of these patterns. At the very outset of the teaching experiment, Jason could spontaneously re-present complex spatial patterns and count their elements. This indicates a power of re-presentation that exceeded anything we observed for Brenda, Tarus, and James and is consistent with his more rapid progress. Unlike Tyrone, Jason did not intentionally monitor his activity of counting to make patterns as Tyrone did (cf. 4.12), and we were unable to attribute the integration operation to him early in the teaching experiment.

16 October 1980 Interview

Spatial Patterns

6.15. In the initial interview that was used to select the children, Jason could recognize the domino patterns, a triangular three, a row of four and a diamond four, and various arrangements of five items. Jason gave no indication that he used spatial patterns as figurative concepts at the time of this interview (cf. 6.02). He did not substitute a re-presentation of a spatial pattern for a hidden collection, after being told how many elements were hidden, without first seeing the collection.

Auditory Patterns

6.16. Tyrone used linear spatial patterns to monitor his counting activity and recognized two-through-five evenly spaced drum beats. We, therefore, formed the hypothesis that the two types of sequential patterns would emerge as perceptual preconcepts in the same time frame and that the integration operation might first be applied to sequential patterns. Jason's repertory of auditory patterns that he could recognize was on a par with Tyrone. He could recognize two-through-five evenly spaced drum beats and could also re-present and count a sequence of drum beats. For example, after hearing three pairs of drum beats, he first said that he did not know, and then spontaneously counted and said "six". For two pairs of three beats, he first said "seven" and then counted and said "six". He had connected both auditory and linear (i.e., rhythmic) spatial patterns of three and four elements with number words. However, he could not re-present a row of five dots and count it accurately (cf. 6.15). Linear spatial patterns were not as prominent as auditory patterns for Jason.

Finger Patterns for "Two" and "Ten"

6.17. Jason had constructed finger patterns for the number words "two" and "ten". He gave no indication of recognizing or using mobile finger patterns other than the finger pattern for "two".

T : (Presents two cloths that Jason took as covering squares) There are six here and five here. How many are there altogether?

J : (Sequentially moves fingers on his left hand, moving his index finger twice) 1-2-3-4-5-6. (Continues sequentially moving fingers on his left hand) 7-8, (middle finger and ring finger) -9-

10, (index finger and middle finger)-11-12 (moving no fingers).

Jason's attempt to count five more beyond counting to six indicated that he lacked a mobile finger pattern for "five". He completed two two-patterns and then said two more number words, which indicates a mobile finger pattern for "two". His initial count to "six" shows that he was quite capable of establishing finger patterns by counting his finger movements.

3 December 1980 Teaching Episode

Spatial Patterns for "Three" and "Four" as Figurative Concepts

6.18. Spatial patterns emerged as figurative concepts in this teaching episode. Jason could now use a spatial pattern to keep track of counting three times.

T : (Presents a cloth covering three felt squares, with four felt squares beside the cloth) There are three more squares under here (pointing to the cloth). How many squares are there altogether?

J : (Touches two visible squares) 1-2. (Moves to the cloth and touches it three times, his points of contact form a triangular three) 3-4-5. (Moves back to the visible squares and touches the remaining two) 6-7.

Jason did not see the three squares before he counted "3-4-5". This indicates that he re-presented a triangular three pattern before he touched the cloth and counted its elements. He behaved similarly when five squares were visible and four squares were hidden. He first counted all of the visible squares and then counted the hidden squares, and his points of contact completed a square four. "Five" did not seem to be connected to a re-presentation of a spatial pattern.

The Emergence of Finger Patterns for "Three"

6.19. Jason used his finger pattern as a substitute for a re-presented spatial pattern of three.

T : (Places three felt squares under each of two cloths while Jason has his eyes shut) Jason, open your eyes! There are three here and three here.

J : (Simultaneously extends three fingers on each hand, his index, middle, and ring fingers, and touches each finger while subvocally uttering number words. He then touches each cloth three times, his points of contact forming triangular patterns) 1-2-3--4-5-6.

This is the first finger pattern that we observed Jason using, other than his finger patterns for "two" and "ten". The manner in which he established the finger patterns provides no justification for a belief that he re-presented the finger patterns and then counted their elements. Rather, he seemed to create the finger patterns for the sole reason of having something to count in his visual field--his fingers. We do take the patterns, however, as substitutes for the covered items, because he touched the cloths as he counted. He eventually recognized finger patterns for "two" through "ten" (cf. 6.06).

21 January 1981 Teaching Episode

Spatio-Motor Patterns

6.20. In this and preceding teaching episodes, we tried to help Jason construct spatio-motor patterns. He spontaneously used the spatio-motor patterns to count the second hidden portion of a collection of items without first seeing it (cf. 6.05 and 6.18). This was in contrast to Tarus and James, whose spatio-motor patterns were restricted to the specific contexts from which they had been abstracted. He was the only one of these three children to develop spatio-motor patterns as we intended. This can be explained by his superior ability to re-present spatial patterns.

28 January 1981 Teaching Episode

Linear (Rhythmic) Spatial Patterns as Figurative Concepts

6.21. In this teaching episode, Jason used linear patterns in a way that surprised us. We tested the hypothesis that they were numerical patterns. Jason first completed a linear spatial pattern for "four" when he was told how many of a row of squares were hidden by a cloth.

T : (Presents a row of 11 squares and hides the fourth through the seventh while Jason has his eyes closed) OK, Jason. There are four squares under the cloth. Which one of the row is this one (points to the ninth square)?

J : (Starts counting over the cloth, touching it three times) 1-2-3. (Corrects himself and sequentially touches the first three squares of the row) 1-2-3 (Walks his index and middle finger along the cloth) 4-5-6-7 (touches the eighth and ninth squares) 8-9. This one is nine!

Jason behaved analogously in a task where there were five squares covered. However, he lost track of how many times he counted when six squares were covered, indicating that he could not spontaneously monitor his counting activity and construct a linear pattern for "six" on the spot. This is one of our strongest indications that Jason could re-present the linear spatial patterns he could recognize for the number words "two" through "five" at this point in the teaching experiment. However, his failure to construct a linear pattern for "six" without it being in his visual field indicates that he constructed the linear spatial patterns for "two" through "five" by re-presenting specific linear patterns that had occurred in his visual field.

4 March 1981 Teaching Episode

Mobile Finger Patterns as Figurative Concepts

6.22. Jason finally extended his re-presentational capacity to include finger patterns in this teaching episode. He had previously used his perceptual finger patterns on 3 December 1980 and 21 January 1981 to count a collection of items hidden by two cloths (cf. 6.06 and 6.14). His solutions in the following protocol indicate that he had constructed a mobile finger pattern for "four".

T : (Places "8 + 4 = " on a felt board) Do this one.

J : (Sequentially puts up eight fingers while subvocally uttering number words) 1-2-3-4-5-6-7-8. (He then continues putting up fingers while subvocally uttering number words, the two remaining on his left hand and two more on his right hand that he already had put up when counting to "eight") 9-10-11-12. Twelve!

To solve the 9 + 4 = ___ when it was presented immediately after the sentence in the above protocol, Jason simultaneously put up nine fingers for "9" and then put up the remaining finger on his right hand, closed his right hand, and then put up three more fingers on that hand to count four more. These two solutions indicate that any four fingers could be a finger pattern for "four". They also indicate that he re-presented a finger pattern for "four" before continuing to count, because he sequentially rather than simultaneously put up four fingers.

Dual Meaning of Number Words

6.23. Jason's finger patterns apparently embodied counting activity, because he continued to count beyond a finger pattern for "nine" that he had established by simultaneously putting up nine fingers. "Nine" seemed to have a dual meaning--finger pattern as well as counting. In fact, other solutions confirmed that any number word preceding and including "ten" had such a dual meaning. His meaning of number words and numerals in the "teens" is clearly indicated in the following protocol:

T : (Presents the sentence "12 + 4 = ___")
J : (Sequentially puts up ten fingers, completing an open hand, then closes his right hand and puts up his index and middle fingers. He continues by putting up the remaining three fingers on his right hand, closes it, and puts up his index finger again) 1-2-3- . . . -12--13-14-15-16.

Jason's meaning of "twelve" after he had counted seemed to be a specified collection of fingers. The resulting finger pattern for "twelve" was in the same category as his mobile finger pattern for "four" and consisted of a collection of fingers bounded by the beginning and end of the activity of counting them. Before he counted, his meaning for "twelve" seemed to be to count a re-presented plurality of fingers.

The Emergence of the Integration Operation

18 March 1981 Teaching Episode

Spatial Patterns

6.24. Jason had constructed linear and domino spatial patterns for the number words "one" through "six", at least as figurative concepts, as early as January 1981 (cf. 6.18 and 6.21). In this teaching episode, he displayed behavior that justified the inference that he could apply the uniting operation of integration to re-presented spatial patterns. The teacher presented Jason with a missing addend task, which Jason interpreted as a direct sum.

T : (Places a cloth in front of Jason) See those chocolate cookies under there (the teacher and Jason pretended that there were chocolate cookies under the cloth)? Put the number on the cloth that shows how many you want to be under there (hands Jason a box of felt numerals and Jason puts "8" on top of the cloth. The teacher lifts an adjacent cloth) See those chocolate cookies under there?
J : Uh-uh. (No.)
T : Well, let's put some under there (makes a shoving motion with his hand as though putting cookies under the cloth).

Now, there are ten chocolate cookies under both cloths (places the numeral "10" immediately above the cloths). How many are under here (the adjacent cloth)?

J : (Touches the cloth with the numeral "8" on it eight times) 1-2-3-4-5-6-7-8. (Continues touching the other cloth as if it hid ten cookies) 9-10-11-12 (completes a row of four points of contact and then continues touching the cloth immediately beneath the completed row) 13-14-15--16. (He looks up at his teacher while saying "sixteen" and then continues touching the cloth immediately beneath the two completed rows, continuing to look at the teacher) 17--18 (touches the cloth emphatically when saying "eighteen" to show that he was done).

As Jason counted over the second cloth, he segmented his counting acts into two linear patterns of four that he could recognize as "eight". Upon reaching "sixteen", he seemed to realize that he had completed a pattern for "eight", not "ten". At that point, we believe he took the two patterns of four as one thing, because he then changed from looking intently at the cloth in order to recognize completed patterns to looking intently at his teacher. This indicates that he reflected on his completed counting activity--he "took stock" of where he was and monitored his further counting activity (he did not seek, nor did he receive, nonverbal cues that would indicate to him when to stop counting). Although we know from past teaching episodes that Jason could recognize two rows of four as "eight", the way he proceeded beyond "sixteen" provides the necessary behavioral indication that he took these two rows of four as material of the integration operation. After establishing that he had counted eight times, he could count two more times to complete a pattern for "ten".

<u>Finger Patterns</u>

6.25. Jason could take finger patterns as well as spatial patterns as material of the integration operation.

T : (Places "8" on the cloth on which "8" was placed in the above protocol, and places "12" above both cloths) This time there are twelve. Can you find how many are under there (touching the adjacent cloth)?

J : (Sequentially puts up eight fingers, five on his left hand, and the index finger, ring finger, and middle fingers of his right hand) 1-2-3-4-5-6-7-8. (Continues, putting up the two remaining fingers of his right hand) 9-10 (Puts up the index finger of his right hand and then moves his middle finger), e-l-e-v-e-n--12. Four (after five seconds).

Jason separated his first eight counting acts from those he subsequently performed to count to "twelve". He reviewed the results of continuing to count beyond "eight" and recognized a mobile finger pattern--four. As there was no explicit perceptual record in his visual field, such recognition requires reflection--holding what he had done "at a distance", and taking it as an object to be operated on. We infer that he applied the integration operation to the finger pattern for "eight" and then to the records of continuing to count four more times. His ability to maintain the separation between the first eight counting acts and those of the continuation was a remarkable achievement for Jason at this time in the teaching experiment (cf. 6.11).

Limitation of Applying the Integration Operation to Patterns

6.26. At this point, Jason's counting scheme was still an enactive preconcept, and he was limited to counting motor unit items. He usually started counting from "one", even when the task was conducive to counting-on (cf. 6.09, 6.24, and 6.25). The novelty of taking his records of counting as material of the integration operation was dramatically displayed in a later task, when he counted beyond "five" until he reached "eleven" (he actually counted to "five" and the result was an open hand). He sat quietly for 25 seconds and then said "five" rather than "six", even though he had put up one more finger after he completed two open hands. This "mistake", coupled with the 25-second pause, shows that reviewing past counting activity to establish a specified collection of fingers was still novel to him. It was, however, a precursor of establishing his counting scheme as a numerical concept (cf. 6.15).

5 April 1981 Teaching Episode

6.27. Jason's teacher focused on his dual meanings of number words in an attempt to lead him to count-on.

T : I have nine cookies here (touching one of two adjacent cloths) and five cookies here (touching the other cloth). How many cookies are there altogether?

J : (Simultaneously puts up nine fingers) Nine--nine. (Closes his hands and opens a hand for "five". He does not recognize a finger pattern and re-establishes his finger pattern for "nine".)

T : Put those in your head. Pretend that you have nine in your head.

J : (After several exchanges where the teacher encouraged him to count beyond his finger pattern for "nine", he sequentially puts up five fingers) 10-11-12-13-14.

Jason solved a subsequent task where he counted four more, starting with "fifteen", by coordinating acts of putting up fingers with saying "16-17-18-19". The above protocol shows clearly that Jason did not independently count-on to solve tasks, even when the number words referred to finger patterns. His finger patterns could be used as material of the integration operation, but counting was something that he still had to carry out, if left to his own resources. He was successful in following his teacher's directives in the above protocol, primarily because his finger patterns embodied counting and could therefore be a substitute for counting.

The Period of Sequential Integration Operations

21 May 1981 Teaching Episode

The Counting Scheme as a Numerical Concept

6.28. Jason made rapid progress to his abstract stage. This confirms our claim that he applied the integration operation in the specific context of patterns while he was still in his motor period. In fact, he had no period that could be called verbal, even though he was observed creating verbal unit items in a teaching episode on 11 May 1981 (cf. 6.13). His use of counting in this teaching episode provides the basis for interpreting his counting scheme as a numerical concept. Jason convincingly modified his activity of counting in the following protocol to fit his interpretation of the task.

J : (Puts 14 checkers into a cup.)
T : (Puts more checkers into another cup) There are some more in here. Altogether, there are 20. How many are in here?
J : Oh! I was thinking there was six!
T : OK. I will take some out (takes three out and pours the rest into Jason's cup, which contains 14). There are seventeen in there. How many did I put in?
J : 15-16-17--three!

Like Tyrone (cf. 4.16) Jason seemed to reduce the initial task to a direct addition task--to fourteen and six make twenty. We infer that he applied the integration operation sequentially, just as when Tyrone estimated a missing addend (cf. 4.19). "Fourteen" and "six" seemed to refer to juxtaposed numerical composites, where "six" was an estimate of what the results of counting would be if it were actually carried out. This is indicated by his solution of the second task, where counting consisted of starting with "fifteen" and ending with "seventeen", and its results consisted of the numerosity of a numerical composite containing these counting acts.

6.29. Counting was a numerical concept, in the sense that "six" could refer to the results of starting to count with "fifteen" and ending with "twenty", without the activity actually being carried out. Jason could anticipate the results of counting starting with any number word.

6.30. Jason's abilities to re-present counting acts and to estimate the results of an actual count starting with any number word were consistent with how he solved the problems that he saw in number sentences. He could solve, say, "17 + __ = 21" by saying "18-19-20-21--four". At this point in the teaching experiment, the numeral "17" seemed to be a symbol for counting. It was the initial segment of the sequence "one" through "21" that he could materialize by counting-on, starting with "18".

6.31. Number words now seemed to refer to numerical composites. Moreover, he could construct numerical composites by applying the sequential integration system to completed forward or backward counting activity.

T : (After Jason places 16 poker chips in a cup) Take out four.
J : (Takes out four.)
T : How many are left in there?
J : (Places his hands on his lap and concentrates on manipulating the poker chips. The teacher cannot see what Jason is doing) There's twelve in there.
T : Tell me how you did that!
J : (Places the poker chips, one at a time, on the table) 16-15-14-13--there's twelve in there.

Jason went on to solve a similar task by counting 5 off from 19. In this example, he coordinated acts of putting up fingers with number words (cf. 6.12). In these solutions, the number words "sixteen" and "nineteen" did not seem to refer to just the poker chips or the marbles in the cup; rather, they referred to number sequences.

6.32. The elements of, say, 16 were linearly ordered, where the order was inherited from counting. Counting was reversible, in that the elements of a numerical composite could be expressed by counting either forward or backward--he could count up to a number to solve missing addend tasks, or count so many off from a number to solve subtraction tasks.

24 November 1981 Interview

Ten as a Numerical Composite

6.33. At the time of this interview, Jason's behavior suggests that he had constructed ten as a numerical composite. In fact, like Tyrone (cf. 4.22) and Scenetra (cf. 5.30), the indications are that Jason focused on the contents of the numerical composites he made, rather than on them as single entities. In the following protocol, "strips" refers to eight-inch strips of paper on which ten squares were glued.

T : (Places twenty squares under a cloth and three strips by the cloth) There are twenty little squares under the cloth. How many squares are there altogether?

J : (After a pause, Jason finally makes two sweeping gestures over the cloth with his index finger. He then sequentially puts up ten fingers) 31-32-33-34-35-36-37-38-39-40 (he again sequentially puts up ten fingers), 41-42-43-44-45-46-47-48-49-50.

We infer that Jason re-presented the hidden squares as two strips, because he made two sweeping gestures over the cloth before counting. The linguistic substitution of "two-tens" for "twenty" guided his re-presentation and "two-tens" served as a criterion for when to stop counting.

6.34. After Jason established two strips of ten squares each in visualized imagination, he spontaneously separated counting-on by one into modules of ten counting acts. This is a strong confirmation that he re-presented the elements of each of the two strips in his visualized imagination and counted these figural items. Our problem was now to determine whether Jason focused on each strip as one thing while maintaining its numerosity.

T : Shut your eyes (places four strips under a cloth and three visible strips by the cloth). Open them. There are seventy little squares altogether. How many strips are under the cloth?

J : Three (looks at the three visible strips), 4-5-6-7 (looking at the successive places on the cover that he took as hiding strips), four.

The key to Jason's solution is that he translated "seventy squares" to "seven strips". He obviously took a strip as one thing and counted-on by one. Although his solution of the first protocol gives us reason to believe that Jason might have maintained the composite quality of the strips when he counted their elements, there is no indication that he reflected on the numerical composites he re-presented. Our hypothesis was that he counted strips "4-5-6-7" as abstract units of one.

6.35. To test this hypothesis, we presented a task where it was not possible for Jason to use his linguistic rule that, say, "thirty squares" could be substituted for "three strips" (or vice versa). He became lost when he counted.

T : (Hides three strips and four extra squares. There are three strips visible) There are thirty-four little squares hidden. How many are there altogether?
J : T-h-i-r-t-y (in reference to the three visible strips). 31-32-33-. . . -45-46 (in synchrony with pointing to specific locations on the cloth). Forty--.
T : How many squares are under there?
J : Thirty-four--seventy --.
T : How did you find that out?
J : I don't know (shrugging his shoulders)!

Jason realized that he had lost track of the counting activity when he said "forty". There is absolutely no indication that he used a re-presentation of a strip of squares to organize counting, as he did in the protocol of paragraph 6.33. There, he could take two tens as a given because of his linguistic rules. In the above protocol, he did not seem to re-present a strip of ten before counting and intended to count 34 units past "thirty". These solutions indicate that he could re-present figurative patterns of ten that were materializations of numerical composites and whose elements symbolized counting. But there is no reason to believe that he could treat those figurative patterns of ten as one thing while maintaining their numerosity, and repeatedly count ten more by one, as Tyrone could at the same time in the teaching experiment (cf. 4.27, 4.28, and 4.31).

<u>Lack of Anticipation When Counting by Ten</u>

6.36. Our claim that Jason did not take ten ones as one ten and maintain its numerosity, even when there was perceptual material available, is consistent with his lack of anticipation of counting by ten and his inability to keep track of how many times he counted by ten.

T : (Places six strips in a pile in front of Jason) There are sixty little squares on these strips. How many strips are there?
J : Four!
T : There are sixty little squares! Can you count by ten to find out how many strips there are?
J : (Whispering) 10-20-30-40-50-60--sixty!

Counting by ten was not an anticipatory scheme that Jason could use to find how many units of ten there were in a collection, even in those cases where the collection had been prearranged into strips with ten squares per strip. When Jason was encouraged to count by ten, he did not keep track of how many times he counted, which again indicates that he did not take the units of ten as one thing. This behavior is consistent with his efforts in another task, to find how many rows of ten could be made using the 46 blocks in a bag. In this case, he had to actually make the rows and could not predict how many more he could make after the first two rows. The numeral "46" was present in his visual field during the solution.

The Period of Progressive Integration Operations

22 February 1982 Teaching Episode

<u>Progressive Integrations</u>

6.37. We searched for situations that would encourage Jason to apply the integration operation to the results of prior integrations. One involved repeatedly placing ten more blocks with an original collection of four.

T : (Asks Jason to count out four blocks and then gives him a pile of ten more blocks) How many blocks are there altogether now?
J : (Counts the pile of ten blocks) Four plus ten!
T : So, how many blocks?
J : (Points to each of the blocks in the pile of four) Fourteen.
T : (Places another pile of ten on the table so that the three piles form a row) and if I give you some more blocks, how many blocks would you have now?
J : (Counts the new pile of ten twice, touching the blocks while subvocally uttering number words) twenty-four.
T : (Touches the new pile of ten) How many have you here?
J : Ten.
T : Very good! If I gave you another ten blocks, how many would you have?

J : Thirty-four.
T : And another ten?
J : Forty-four (Jason went on, uttering), 54-64-74-84-94-104.

Jason's abstraction of the number word sequence in the protocol may have been based on isolating the number words he said last when he counted. There are indications, however, that he applied the integration operation to the results of prior integrations. Which inference is more plausible cannot be decided solely on the basis of the current protocol. Jason did count the second new pile of ten first to find its numerosity and then again, "15-16-. . . -24", to find the numerosity of the two piles. This indicates that he made two numerical composites, one corresponding to "fourteen" and one to "ten", and then took those results together. Further, his ease of abstracting the number word sequence "14-24-34- . . . "indicates that "fourteen" and "twenty-four" referred to single entities. He seemed to include the results of counting the fourteen blocks in the activity of counting the twenty-four blocks, and to take the results of each counting activity as one thing. These indications are strengthened by the very next task, where Jason first counted seven blocks and then uttered the number word sequence "7-17-27- . . . " without counting out any piles of ten blocks. The protocol of 6.38, however, provides the most convincing corroboration.

6.38. After Jason had constructed his new number word sequences, his teacher asked him what 23 plus 10 would be, with the intention that Jason would re-construct his number word sequences in situations different from the one in which he made the abstraction. But Jason used a computational algorithm to solve the task. Jason used his algorithm to solve what to him was a very specific task. His teacher then turned to using missing addend problems.

T : (Gives Jason a pile of blocks) There are fifty-three. I give you some more (places another pile in front of Jason), and now you have ninety-three. How many more did I give you?
J : (Sequentially puts up four fingers) Four more tens.
T : Can you count out loud?
J : I went 63-73-83-93 (sequentially putting up fingers).

Jason solved a subsequent task where he had a pile of 35 blocks, was given some more blocks, and was then told that he had 75 blocks. He coordinated "45-55-65-75" with the acts of putting up fingers.

6.39. We believe that Jason assimilated the task by using his number sequence that symbolized his newly constructed system of progressive integration operations. He could now take, say, the initial 35 blocks and the remaining blocks as abstract composite units that belonged to 75 because "75" pointed to his number sequence of which 35 was an initial segment. His solution to the task in 6.37 may have influenced his decision to count by ten to solve the missing addend tasks, in that he seemed to realize the possibility of making piles of blocks with ten per pile. However, the meaning of his results--"four tens"--is yet to be analyzed. Could he "unpack" them into their constituent unit items; in other words, did a counting by ten act signify ten more ones?

23 February 1982 Teaching Episode

Failure to Discriminate the Results of Counting-on by Ten and by One

6.40. In the context of its establishment, "four more tens" (cf. 6.38) seemed to be uttered with great clarity. However, on the very next day, Jason did not discriminate between solving a missing addend task by counting-on by one and solving a missing addend task by counting-on by ten.

T : (Places a pile of blocks in front of Jason) You have seventeen blocks. Now, I give you some more (places another pile of blocks in front of Jason) and now you have twenty-seven. How many more did I give you?

J : (Sequentially puts up ten fingers while subvocally uttering number words) ten more tens.

T : Seventeen and ten more is how many?

J : Twenty-seven.

T : You have twenty-seven. I give you some more. Now, you have thirty-seven (places a pile of blocks in front of Jason). How many more did I give you?

J : Ten more tens.

The results of counting-on by one had the same meaning for Jason as the results of counting-on by ten--he had counted so many times and his records, finger patterns, referred to singleton units, whether called "ten" or "one". In the immediately preceding teaching episode, Jason counted-on by ten and his answers were always "so many tens". Jason's failure to discriminate between the results of counting on by one and counting-on by ten was not a linguistic difficulty--he did not simply say the wrong word. He was in the initial stages of constructing a counting by ten scheme and he interpreted its results in terms of his counting by one scheme because of, we believe, the similarity of their assimilating operations--progressive integrations. As we see in the following protocol, Jason genuinely could not use the results of counting-on by ten to find what the results of counting-on by one would be.

6.41. After counting-on by ten, Jason had to actually count-on by one to answer a question concerning how many ones he had counted.

T : (Places 58 blocks in front of Jason) You have fifty-eight. I am going to give you some more (places a handful of blocks in front of Jason). Now you have seventy-eight. How many more did I give you?
J : That is two tens.
T : That is right. Two tens. How many ones did I give you?
J : (Sequentially puts up fingers while subvocally uttering number words) Thirteen ones.
T : How did you get that?!
J : I started with fifty and I worked up to seventy-eight (losing track of three open hands).

Although he made a tracking error, the important aspect of the protocol is that he counted-on by one to find how many ones he had counted after counting by ten. This indicates that Jason counted by one or counted by ten, depending on his intentions of finding how many more ones or how many more tens there were. Even though he seemed to use the same assimilating operations, the results of counting-on by ten and counting-on by one were not related. His counting unit of ten seemed to be repeatable, but not iterable. We know from some of Jason's other solutions that "ten ones" and "one ten" were related expressions (cf. 6.37) in situations where there was a pile of ten blocks he could use.

15 March 1982 Teaching Episode

Coordinating Counting-on by Ten and Counting-on by One

6.42. The coordination of counting-on by ten and counting-on by one means that a decision is made, prior to the actual counting activity to use two units in counting. In the protocol of paragraph 6.41, Jason counted-on by ten, but he was already in a "counting by ten" context, so no decision was necessary to use ten as a countable unit before counting. In his solution of the following protocol, there was no suggestion that he count-on by ten and then continue to count-on by one.

T : There are forty-two under here (touches a cloth under which there is nothing hidden). I put some more under here (pretends he is scooping something under the cloth). Do you see them (lifts the cloth and Jason playfully pretends that he takes a handful and puts them back)? Now we have seventy-six. How many more did I put under there?

J : 52-62-72 (sequentially puts up three fingers on his right hand) 73-74-75-76 (sequentially puts up four fingers on his left hand). There would be (reviewing his fingers) thirty-four!
T : That's just beautiful! Where are the tens?
J : Right here (shakes his right hand)!
T : Where are the ones?
J : Right here (shakes his left hand)! Three tens and four ones.
T : And how many is that altogether?
J : Thirty-four.

This solution is similar to Tyrone's solution that was excerpted from the November interviews (cf. 4.27). The primary difference (beyond the number word sequences) was the lack of obvious perceptual or figural material that could have supported Jason's construction of countable items. This lack of perceptual material, coupled with the coordination of counting-on by ten and then by one, indicates that each counting by ten act was a symbol for counting ten more by ones. In other words, ten now seemed to be an iterable unit.

6.43. The primary question at this point is whether "three tens and four ones is thirty-four" implied a juxtaposition of the tens and the ones, or a synthesis that resulted in a composite unit of 34 ones. The following protocol provides ample indication that the tens and ones were only juxtaposed, even though "thirty" could refer to thirty ones.

T : This time, we have 27 covered and we are going to go way up to 62 ("twenty-seven" referred to the imaginary items under the cloth).
J : Twenty-seven--37-47-57-67 (putting up fingers on his right hand).
T : Is 67 too far?
J : Uh-uh (no).
T : We want to go to sixty-two.
J : Oh! Take away five.
T : OK. Take away five. That is the five that you want to take away (Jason has his left hand open). How many have you here (pointing to Jason's right hand)?
J : Four tens.
T : How many ones?
J : Forty.
T : And you take away five. So, how many are left?
J : Four tens (closing his left hand)!
T : You have forty. Take five from four tens.
J : (Folds one finger down on his right hand and then puts it back up) Hm! (Looks perplexed.)

T : Do you know?
J : (Shakes his head "no".)

On a similar task, Jason had independently realized that counting by ten led to a number greater than, but in the same decade as, the number to which he was counting. He even counted backward by one five times to reach the number, but he did not know what to do with the counted units of one he had generated. He did not think of them as being included in the last unit of ten that he had created. Likewise, he did not include five ones in one of the four tens within the protocol above.

6.44. One could claim that the separation of Jason's records of tens and ones on different hands was the source of his difficulty. While it was perhaps a contributing factor, his primary source of difficulty seemed to be that he did not include the units of one he had created within the last unit of counting forward by ten. He did not "unpack" this unit of ten into its constituent unit items, take some of them away, and then apply the integration operation to those that remained. In short, he did not reversibly coordinate the units of ten and one.

The Period of Part-Whole Operations

29 March 1982 Teaching Episode

Extracting a Numerical Part from a Numerical Whole

6.45. The way in which Jason could solve missing addend tasks changed dramatically in this teaching episode. One strategy was to estimate the missing addend, add it to the first addend, and check the result to see if it was the sum.

T : (Places the sentence "27 + ___ = 36" in front of Jason) We have twenty-seven and some more and that is thirty-six.
J : Twenty-seven--(pause of about 20 seconds). Let me see--(another pause)--twenty-seven plus seven--it's nine more!
T : That's really good! Is there another way to solve that one?
J : Uh-uh (no).
T : How would you do it by counting backwards?
J : (Sequentially puts up fingers) 36-35- . . . - 27. Nine.

Jason seemed to view 27 as a number in its own right, as well as a part of 36. He did not simply make an estimate and then quit, as Tyrone had done earlier in the teaching experiment (cf. 4.16). Rather, after he made the estimate, he saw it as a possibility rather than as the answer. After estimating the missing number to be 7, he added it to 27, continued to 36, and then added the continuation to 7. These operations indicate that he used the units the numerals referred to as one thing, as well as composites. Moreover, 27 and 36 were related, in that 27 was a part that he had disembedded from 36. These claims are confirmed by the ease with which he counted from 36 down to 27. The teacher also tried his best to present "36 - 9 = ___" as a novel task immediately afterward.

T : I am going to give you another one. This time we are going to have something to take away (presents the sentence).
J : (Immediately) Twenty-seven.
T : How did you know?
J : Because we just did it!

Jason clearly viewed subtraction as the inversion of addition. In fact, the two problems involved identical parts of the same whole, and he merely had to recover the known missing part.

6 April 1982 Teaching Episode

Counting-Down-To by Ten When Solving Missing Minuend Problems

6.46. Previously, Jason coordinated his counting by ten and counting by one schemes in missing addend situations (cf. 6.43). He could also count-down-to by one in missing addend situations (cf. 6.45). A reorganization was observed in this teaching episode:

T : Can you give me a problem? (This was a question asked often of Jason.)
J : (Places "92 - ___ = 42" on the table) That's easy!
T : OK. (Starts to sequentially put up fingers) 92-91-(Jason shakes his head "no"), 90-89-88-87-86- . . . Gee, that is a long way to count!
J : (Nods his head "yes".)
T : Can you show me another way?
J : Fifty.
T : How did you do that?
J : (Sequentially puts up fingers) 92--82-72-62-52-42.

Jason was very amused by his teacher counting-down-to by one. It was obvious that he had another way to solve the problem, because he smiled and keenly watched the teacher count. He just couldn't wait to show the teacher his method. Immediately afterward, he counted from 42 up to 92 to demonstrate an alternate way to do the problem.

Discussion of Jason's Case Study

The Emergence of the Integration Operation

Initially, we thought it was plausible that if children could recognize auditory patterns, linear spatial patterns would be predominant for them because both patterns would be experiential contexts in which they could construct the integration operation. Like Tyrone, Jason could recognize two-through-five evenly spaced drum beats (cf. 6.16), but linear spatial patterns did not emerge as figurative concepts until late in January 1981 (cf. 6.21), when he used a linear spatial pattern to keep track of counting acts in the midst of counting. This ability to re-present a pattern and keep track of counting acts with it was not taken as indication of the integration operation, because Jason did not create a linear spatial pattern for "six" on the spot by monitoring his counting activity, as Tyrone did in the case of a linear spatial pattern for "five" (cf. 4.12).

Jason's failure to use linear spatial patterns as material for the integration operation implies that recognition of auditory patterns does not indicate the emergence of the integration operation, any more than recognition of nonlinear spatial patterns does. In fact, recognition of any type of pattern should not be taken as an indication of numerical concepts unless the child monitors their construction, as Tyrone did (cf. 4.13).

Finger patterns became a prominent feature of Jason's development. By March 1981, he had developed mobile finger patterns as figurative concepts (cf. 6.22). At this point in the teaching experiment, number words, at least through "twenty", had a dual meaning--a finger pattern meaning and a counting meaning (cf. 6.23). However, counting was still an enactive preconcept, which he had to carry out when he used it to give meaning to number words. The results of counting could also have a dual meaning for Jason. The activity of coordinating number word utterances with acts of putting up fingers was one meaning for "twelve"; the other meaning was the "finger pattern" that he established.

Jason first applied the integration operation to re-presented spatial patterns and finger patterns (cf. 6.24 - 6.25). (It is important to note that all three children were attempting either to keep track of counting activity or to specify the the second hidden portion of a collection when they were initially observed applying the integration operation. They were concentrating intensely on how to keep track of counting when the observed breakthroughs occurred.) Jason created a pattern for "ten" by extending a known pattern for "eight"--two rows of four. He used the pattern for "eight" as an object of reflection, and took it as a given intermediate step in his solution. This awareness of what he was doing while counting indicates reflection. Nevertheless, he was able to proceed in the way that he did because of a completed known pattern.

Jason could also review his counting activity after he put up eight, and then four, fingers to count to "twelve". One could argue that this is no more sophisticated than what Tarus did (cf. 2.20) at the beginning of his verbal period, when he recognized the number word sequence "8-9-10-11" as "four" after saying it. The difference is that Tarus capitalized on an experiential separation to recognize the pattern (i.e., he separated the items he counted first from those that he counted second). Since Jason reviewed his completed activity for five seconds before saying "four", this indicates that he did not simply recognize a pattern in immediate past experience, as Tarus did. Rather, he reviewed the records of his activity (there were no complete perceptual records) and isolated the mobile finger pattern that he had established in a continuation of counting. His ability to maintain the separation while reviewing his records of counting indicates reflection--he used his records of counting as material for further operating, which is quite beyond what Tarus did. To explain the difference, we attribute the uniting operation of integration to Jason.

The Period of Sequential Integration Operations

Two months after Jason was observed applying the integration operation in the context of patterns, his counting scheme became a numerical concept (cf. 6.28). This rather long lag can in part be attributed to our somewhat direct interventions into Jason's methods after he had constructed finger patterns. Jason attempted to conform to the directives of the teacher (cf. 6.27) and, as a result, little or no reorganization of his counting scheme occurred. In retrospect, our interventions may have hindered Jason in making applications of the integration operation, the sole source of progress to the abstract stage.

Upon entering the abstract stage, number words were symbols for numerical composites (cf. 6.28 and 6.33). Jason could take counting as a given and make estimates of its possible results (cf. 6.28). The elements of the numerical composites he made seemed to be symbols of individual counting acts, and appeared to be arranged in an ordered series (cf. 6.31). "Sixteen", for example, seemed to refer to the ordered composite units of the sequence "16-15- . . . -2-1" that he partitioned by counting backward. The particular unit items that a number word referred to were rather arbitrary (cf. 6.29), in that "six" could refer to the elements of a composite unit of unspecified numerosity such as "15-16- . . . -20" that Jason only estimated by saying "six". This first step toward the construction of an "unknown" was similar to the progress made by Tyrone and Scenetra.

Jason still considered numbers referred to by two-digit numerals as ordered composite units at the beginning of the second year of the teaching experiment (cf. 6.33). Number words and numerals that named decades, e.g., "30", could be translated into "three tens". However, this translation had not been established by keeping track of how many times he could count by ten to partition thirty into units of ten (cf. 6.36). Counting by ten was not an anticipatory scheme like counting by one, and he could not use it to find how many units of ten there were in a particular number. In other words, at this point in the teaching experiment, he could not take ten as a given prior to counting.

After he entered his abstract stage, Jason could apply the integration operation sequentially in the context of solving what were to us missing addend tasks (cf. 6.28), subtraction tasks (cf. 6.31), and direct addition tasks (cf. 6.33). The best indication that Jason focused on the elements of the numerical composites rather than on them as one thing occurred when he organized 20 hidden squares into two composite units of ten and then counted their elements, separating his counting acts into two modules of ten (cf. 6.33-6.34). He used his linguistic rule that "twenty makes two tens" because, when 34 squares were hidden, he became lost in counting (cf. 6.35). He did not treat the hidden strips of squares and the extra hidden squares as equivalent, in terms of their unity, and as distinct, in terms of their numerosity.

He did not count by ten and by one at this time in the teaching experiment, nor did he provide any indication that he could take ten as a given prior to counting (cf. 6.36), except in the special circumstances documented (cf. 6.33-6.34). He lacked anticipation when he counted by ten and failed to keep track of his counting by ten acts (cf. 6.33).

The Period of Progressive Integration Operations

Constructing number word sequences like "4-14-24- . . . " that occur in patterns by abstracting from the activity of repeatedly solving missing addend tasks is an indicator of progressive integration operations, if the construction is rapidly completed, and if the construction of like sequences is based on the abstracted pattern. Jason easily constructed the number word sequence "4-14-24- . . . " and could generate similar sequences without apparently engaging in problem-solving activity. After solving these tasks, he counted by ten to solve a missing addend task, which corroborates the fact that the construction of the number word sequences was based on progressive integrations.

The Period of Part-Whole Operations

Jason gave "seven" as an estimate to the missing addend sentence "27 + ___ = 36" in the 29 March 1982 teaching episode (cf. 6.45). But he did not quit, as Tyrone did when he made a similar estimate at the level of sequential integration operations (cf. 4.22). Tyrone took his estimate as being correct and responded to a prompt by the teacher to find out for sure by counting. Jason, on the other hand, viewed his estimate as a possibility rather than as a certainty, and added it to 27 to see if that was indeed the number he was looking for. He then continued from that sum to 36, added that continuation on to seven, and obtained the result, nine. This solution is clearly indicative of part-whole operations because twenty-seven was one part of 36 as well as a unit in its own right. Seven, his estimate, was potentially the other part of 36 as well as a unit in its own right. His understanding that these two parts had to constitute the whole led to his further operating. His estimate was a result of a system of reversible operations between the parts and the whole. Jason could now use the results of progressive integration operations as material for further operating. His view of subtraction as the inversion of addition (cf. 6.45) and his ability to count from the minuend down to the difference to find the subtrahend in a subtraction problem are also indications of part-whole operations (cf. 6.46).

Unit Types of the Unit of Ten

In contrast to Tyrone, Jason still worked with ten as a numerical composite at the time of the November 1981 interviews. He focused on what was in the unit, and not on the unit as one thing. One indication that he worked at the element level was that he counted-on by one rather than by ten after he organized twenty hidden items into two figural units of ten (cf. 6.33). A second indication was his inability to use a unit of ten to keep track of counting 34 beyond 30. Although it is possible that he had an inadequate linguistic rule for making a translation of two-digit numerals into "so many tens and so many ones", his performance on other tasks (cf. 6.40) suggests that he could not take units of ten and one as countable items in the same counting activity, as Tyrone could (cf. 4.27).

By late February 1982, Jason could take a numerical composite of ten as a unit (cf. 6.37) concomitantly with progressive integration operations. Another indication that he could make abstract composite units of ten is in the 15 March 1982 teaching episode, when he coordinated a count by ten and a count by one. Although he could differentiate a count by ten from a count by one in the same counting episode, he could not "unpack" the units of ten into their constituent individual units and assemble them into a new unit, even after counting. His records of counting so many tens and so many ones were not material for further operating. Not until the teaching episode on 6 April 1982 was there some indication that ten had emerged as an iterable unit. Jason first demonstrated that he had constructed part-whole operations just eight days earlier.

PERSPECTIVES ON THE CASE STUDIES

The Emergence of the Integration Operation

Early in their motor periods, all three children could re-present a spatial pattern they had been shown and count its elements if they could not recognize it. This provides another perspective on how children might connect spatial patterns and number words. In Chapter V, we argued that children can make such connections during immediate perceptual encounters with the patterns (cf. Discussion of Brenda's Case Study). In the case of auditory patterns, it can be argued that a child must be able to re-present a perceived pattern and count its elements in order to connect it with a number word, because the elements of the pattern are not "there" to be recognized. This argument is confirmed, because neither Brenda, Tarus, nor James associated auditory patterns with number words, even though they did so with spatial patterns. They connected number words with the spatial patterns that occurred in their visual field because they could not, in general, re-present those patterns.

On the other hand, Tyrone, Scenetra, and Jason could re-present and count the elements of spatial patterns they could not recognize and recognized a wider variety of spatial patterns than the other three children. Moreover, Tyrone and Jason could recognize auditory patterns up to five beats (although we did not document it, Scenetra made close estimates of such patterns without counting them). Consequently, it is plausible that their ability to recognize a wider variety of spatial patterns than the other three children was based on their re-presentational capacity. Although they may have been able to recognize some patterns that occurred in their visual field without re-presenting them at an earlier stage, the complexity of the spatial patterns they could now recognize indicated that they at least re-presented the more complex patterns and counted their elements while learning to recognize them. This is important, because the integration operation emerged in the context of patterns for these children. Figurative concepts of number words appear to play a crucial role in the construction of the integration operation.

Numerical Patterns

Although we found that the integration operation emerged in the context of patterns, we were surprised that sequential patterns seemed to play a prominent role only for Tyrone. Both finger patterns and nonlinear spatial patterns served as contexts for Scenetra and Jason. Upon the emergence of the integration operation, however, both of these children constructed sequential patterns and used them to keep track of counting. In retrospect, our observation that Tyrone first applied the integration operation to linear spatial patterns may be confounded. If a child applies the integration operation to patterns, that may "straighten out" the pattern (i.e., by disregarding the two-dimensional characteristics and focusing only on the rhythmic pattern involved), making it impossible to separate the material to which the operation is applied from the results, if those results are linear patterns. At any rate, because patterns in general served as a context for the emergence of the integration operation, emphasizing patterns in the construction of the meanings of number words and numerals can be justified.

There were profound differences between patterns as figurative concepts and as numerical concepts. As numerical concepts, the children were able to create patterns on the spot in order to monitor how many times they counted. They were also able to combine patterns and create new patterns, decompose patterns into subpatterns, and then recombine these subpatterns into new patterns. Finally, they were able to review the results of making an extension of counting and recognize a pattern, even in those cases where there were incomplete visual records. These behavioral indicators all justify our contention that the children used mental operations that were unavailable when the patterns were figurative concepts.

Number Sequences

Once the integration operation had emerged, number words could refer to numerical composites. The contents of the numerical composites were the elements of patterns that could symbolize counting. These numerical composites constituted number sequences because they were linearly ordered. Number word sequences were eventually interiorized and also became the content of numerical composites. The result of this interiorization is indicated by how a child records how many times he or she counts. Double counting is an indicator that the *number word sequence* has been interiorized and that the number words of the sequence are symbols for abstract unit items. That is, a number word sequence is reconstituted as a *number sequence*. A number sequence, therefore, can be constructed by applying the integration operation to patterns that embody counting activity. Counting backward to solve subtraction tasks also indicates that number word sequences have been interiorized. If a child only counts forward to solve missing addend and direct addition tasks without double counting, the child has probably interiorized figural patterns but not number word sequences.

Eventually the children's number sequences were not restricted to the number words preceding "twenty". The children became adept with the number words in the decades as symbols for number sequences, and quickly developed number sequences up to "one hundred" and then up to "one thousand". As a consequence of school instruction, however, the children (especially Scenetra) developed new meanings for the number words as "so many tens and so many ones". In fact, Scenetra typically re-presented patterns for the tens and the ones to give meaning to number words. She could also recognize so many perceptual or figurative units of ten and so many single perceptual or figurative units of one by saying the appropriate number word. These meanings were supported by her ability to make abstract composite units of ten (see 5.38). Nevertheless, these meanings were related to number sequence meanings only because they were connected to the same number words; they were not reorganizations of number sequences. We call them *figurative numbers* to highlight the role of patterns.

Whenever possible, Scenetra used number words and numerals to refer to figurative numbers. This retarded her construction of part-whole operations and of ten as an iterable unit. A special effort was made to change her view of what the number words and numerals in the decades might mean. It was necessary to devise rather novel (from the perspective of school mathematics) problem situations that would encourage her to give meaning to situations by using her available number sequences. She finally used her number sequence meanings when she solved what to us were addition and subtraction problems. Eventually, the children used counting by ten and by one to establish how many tens were in a number sequence referred to by a two- or three-digit numeral and then how many ones were left. The children felt quite powerful when they understood that 153 pennies, say, could be put into 15 piles with ten per pile, and three more piles with one per pile, because they could count by ten and by one, if necessary. We use the term "understood" because the children did not merely use a linguistic rule.

Although we did not report it in the case studies, we worked very hard with the children in an attempt to help them to further organize the 15 piles of ten. The question, "How many groups could you make with ten piles in each group?" was asked in a variety of situations. The children actually organized counting by ten acts into modules of ten. But they had a very difficult time finding how many pennies were in each group of ten, how many piles of ten pennies were left over, and how many pennies there were in all. Units of units of units were truly a novelty and a whole new sequence of constructions seemed to be necessary.

Stages in the Construction of the Numerical Counting Scheme

The most important result of the teaching experiment is that it was possible to isolate three periods in the construction of the counting scheme after Tyrone, Scenetra, and Jason entered what we then called their abstract stage, as documented in Chapter IV. In fact, we can no longer legitimately speak of the abstract stage because we claim that the identified periods constitute stages. We call these stages the stage of sequential integration operations, the stage of progressive integration operations, and the stage of part-whole operations. Figure 8 summarizes the stages of construction of the numerical counting scheme by the three children after they reorganized counting. We use "the numerical counting scheme" to highlight the number sequence.

Tyrone was in the stage of progressive integration operations on 1 December 1981, the beginning of the teaching experiment in the second year. He had entered that stage sometime after the end of the first year of the teaching experiment, so we do not indicate a period of sequential integration operations after that time. However, given Tyrone's performance on 1 December 1981, it is plausible that his stage of sequential integration operations extended well past 1 September 1981, the beginning of his second grade in school. In Scenetra's case, we are definitely justified in extending her stage of sequential integration operations up to 1 December because she created abstract composite units in the context of our interview. They were a novelty at the time. Jason, of course, did not create abstract composite units until 22 February 1982.

Figure 8

Stages in the Construction of the Numerical Counting Scheme

```
PART-  |                                         @@@@
WHOLE  |                                       ######
       |
PROG.  |                                     @@@@
INT.   |                                 $$$$$$$$$$$$$
       |                                 #######
       |
SEQ.   |         @@@@@@@@@@@@@@@@@@@@@
INT.   |     $$$$$$$$$$$$$$$$$$$$
       | ##########
       |._._._._._._._.__.__.__._._._._._.
        1 2 3 4 5 6 7 8 9 10 11 12 1 2 3 4 5 6
        ---------  1981  ---------  --  1982 --

        @: Jason   $: Scenetra   #: Tyrone
```

The emergence of the integration operation in the context of patterns and the stage of sequential integration operations are major findings of the teaching experiment and were not predicted at the outset of the experiment. In fact, we made no differentiation whatsoever then in the systems of integration operations. It was not until we were well into the teaching experiment that we realized that major changes occurred in the children which we could not explain as a result of either our teaching episodes or the children's classroom instruction.

The major insight that children are aware only of the material of numerical composites, the primary meaning of number words in the period of sequential integration operations, provides a powerful explanation for certain observations that are otherwise not explicable. For example, neither Tyrone, Scenetra, nor Jason could strategically find the pairs of numbers whose sum was, say, ten. They could find certain pairs, but could not use the pair they found to generate the next pair by compensating the addends. Also, they could not understand subtraction as the inversion of addition. Nevertheless, they could count-on to find what we take as sums and missing addends and could count-off-from to find what we take as differences.

The lack of taking a numerical composite as material of the integration operation prohibited the children from constructing a meaning of "ten" as one ten. This restriction in their meaning of "ten" prohibited them from constructing counting by ten as an anticipatory scheme and from using this scheme to establish how many units of ten could be made using a particular number sequence. For example, they could not independently count by ten, keeping track of how many times they counted, to find how many units of ten could be made from 59 blocks. They learned linguistic rules for separating "59" into five tens and nine ones, but that was unrelated to counting-by-ten, the operative method for establishing how many units of ten could be made from a particular number. Number words and numerals referred to units of one, not units of ten and units of one.

Another fundamental insight into the nature of the mathematics of these children is that whatever the terms "addition", "subtraction", and "missing addend" might mean to us as adults, the children's meaning was based on their sequential integration operations. What this means is that the children interpreted the problem situations in term of their number sequences--as counting problems. This is justified by how they solved a given problem independently of previously solved problems. Counting was symbolized by number words and it was the intention of the children to count to "twenty-one" to find, say, how many of a collection of 21 blocks were hidden. If the children counted the visible items, they could apply the integration operation to the counted items and then continue to count to "twenty-one", whereupon they could once again apply the integration operation to their records of continuing to count, creating a numerical composite whose numerosity could be established. If they were simply told how many items were visible, that number word could symbolize an integration operation and they could in this case again continue counting. This symbolizing function of number words permitted the children to appear to be able to perform more sophisticated operations than sequential integrations.

It is important to note that sequential integration operations were carried out during rather than before problem solution in those cases where they were not symbolized. In this sense, the children were in the process of constructing addition and subtraction as numerical operations by solving problems. This provides a viable model of children's numerical operations while they are in the stage of sequential integration operations. We turn now to a justification of our claim that the three periods constituted stages. In the justification, it is necessary to characterize the changes in the counting scheme in terms of the three parts of these schemes--the concepts; the activity of adding and subtracting; and the results of adding and subtracting.

Piaget's Invariant Sequence and Incorporation Criteria

Piaget's invariant sequence criterion seems to be satisfied because the systems of integration operations emerged in the same sequential periods for all three children, with the exception that Scenetra did not achieve the stage of part-whole operations. Sequential integration operations emerged in the context of patterns, and the progressive integration operations emerged when the children could apply the integration operation to numerical composites--the results of prior integrations--yielding abstract composite units. Part-whole operations emerged when the children became able to disembed an abstract composite unit from a containing abstract composite unit. Therefore, because each operation used the results of the operations of the preceding period, these systems satisfy Piaget's incorporation criterion.

The Reorganization Criterion

This criterion of stages seems to be satisfied, because the identified systems of integration operations were indicated by reorganizations of the children's counting schemes. The children could solve tasks in each identified period that they could not solve in a previous period, and could use methods that were not previously available. And, a task that could be solved in a previous period could be solved in ways that were not possible before. During their period of sequential integrations, for example, they could not "see" subtraction as the inversion of addition. When they were in their period of part-whole operations, however, it was quite natural for them to "see" subtraction in this way without being told by us or by their classroom teacher.

The children's construction of the progressive integration operations was indicated by counting-down-to to solve subtraction problems. The children's ability to decide when to count-down-to or to count-off-from was actually more important than the counting behavior itself, because it implied that the children could consider the subtrahend as either the first or last part of the minuend, depending upon the situation. This indicates that they could anticipate what and how they would count before counting, an especially strong indicator of new organization in the first part of their counting scheme.

Upon emergence of the disembedding operation in the first part of their counting scheme, a new sophistication was apparent in the way Tyrone and Jason viewed addition and subtraction problems and also their solutions. On occasion, subtraction was constructed as the inversion of addition. Here, it was understood that if two parts composed a whole, and if one of the two parts was taken away, the other part remained. It was also possible for missing subtrahend problems to be solved by either counting-down-to or counting-up-to. We found, too, that it was possible for estimates of missing addends to be made and used to find the required sum. Tyrone and Jason now had confident and independent attitudes toward solving the problems and monitored their own mathematical behavior.

Units of One

In the stage of sequential integration operations, units of one are what we have called abstract unit items (cf. Chapter I). They are the elements of numerical composites and are symbolized by number sequences. It is not until the stage of part-whole operations that one becomes iterable. For one to become iterable, it must be abstracted from number sequences--it must be viewed both as a unit in its own right and as part of a potential whole that can be constructed by repeating that part. Consequently, when one is iterable, a number word like "seven" can refer to an abstract unit (the potential whole) that contains a unit that can be iterated seven times (usually in either forward or backward directions) rather than to the specific number sequence indicated by 1-2-3-4-5-6-7. This added a new flexibility to the children's problem solutions that was manifested by counting-up-to or down-to when solving missing subtrahend problems.

The Unit of One in Sequential Integration Operations

Counting-off-from to solve subtraction problems does not require the unit of one to be iterable. At the stage of sequential integration operations, a minuend of, say, 12 can be taken as an ordered series of units--a number sequence such as 12-11- . . . -2-1. Using the elements of this ordered sequence, the child can make a partition by counting-off-from, by counting "12-11-10-9". The next number word is then a symbol for the number sequence 8-7- . . . -1, the established difference.

The Unit of One in Progressive Integration Operations

At the stage of progressive integration operations, the subtrahend can be taken as the initial segment of the minuend--as an ordered series of units--prior to counting. The numeral or number word that is for the adult the subtrahend symbolizes this initial segment. However, this segment is still in the minuend and is unexpressed. It cannot be treated as a unit in its own right. Similarly, the numeral or number word that corresponds to the minuend is used as a symbol for the number sequence in which the subtrahend is embedded. The child's understanding of the task is to count down to the subtrahend, starting with the minuend, to specify the numerosity of the remainder of the subtrahend in the minuend. The number sequence corresponding to the minuend serves as "background" for the operations of solution.

The number sequence that corresponds to the remainder can be materialized because the operations that are necessary to take the minuend and subtrahend as one thing are only symbolized. That is, the child's focus of attention is on the remainder, and the child must only re-present the items of the remainder and then keep track of uttering those number words. It is not necessary that the unit of one be iterable for a successful solution to be carried out. We could do a similar analysis for counting up to by simply changing the direction of the number sequence. The essential feature is that the child needs to focus on only the unknown part of the whole. This unknown part has meaning to the child because it is a composite unit whose numerosity *can* be specified by counting.

The Unit of One in Part-Whole Operations

Once the child has disembedded a number sequence from the one containing it, he or she can focus on the disembedded number sequence, as well as on its remainder in the containing number sequence. In this case, an unknown subtrahend can be taken as the remainder of a known difference in the minuend, where the known difference is taken as the initial segment of the minuend. Given a minuend and a difference, the child can count from the minuend down to the difference to specify the numerosity of the unknown subtrahend. This requires that the child think in terms of a whole and its two parts, taking each as an entity while maintaining them as number sequences. When one is iterable, this is facilitated, because the child can suppress the composite quality of the involved numbers.

Units of Ten

"Ten" referred to a numerical composite that is not different from any other numerical composite in the stage of sequential integration operations. In this stage, the unit of ten was a numerical pattern. The leap that must be made from ten as a numerical composite to ten as an iterable unit did not occur in one fell swoop for any of the three children. Ten emerged as an abstract composite unit as well as a unit which, for lack of a better term, we called "ten more". As an abstract composite unit, "ten" can be thought of as referring to that unit formed by taking a numerical composite of ten items as a unit.

The Stage of Sequential Integration Operations

In the stage of sequential integration operations, the children's counting by ten schemes were not anticipatory (cf. 6.36). These schemes were distinct from their counting by one schemes, and were essentially used in sensory-motor situations. The assimilating operations of the schemes seemed to be those operations necessary to construct pluralities and collections (cf. von Glasersfeld, 1981), and the integration operation. In particular, the children did not apply the integration operation sequentially to figurative material when counting by ten. They had learned the number word sequence "10-20-30-40-50- . . . " and could coordinate it with numerical patterns they believed contained ten items, when those numerical patterns were in their visual field. They could also coordinate the number word sequence with acts of putting up or folding down fingers where their fingers were symbolic substitutes for singleton units they named "ten"; this was nothing more than a modified counting by one scheme. However, they were obligated to count by one when placing ten more items with a particular collection (cf. 5.31), because they could not take the ten items as one ten and add it as a unit.

The Stage of Progressive Integration Operations

In the stage of progressive integration operations, the children's counting by ten schemes became anticipatory in situations where there was perceptual or figural material available that the children could take as an abstract composite unit of ten. The children had to *believe* there were collections of ten to count. By applying the integration operation *sequentially* to the figural material they took as a given, they could count by ten and keep track of their counting acts by putting up fingers (cf. 5.41). However, once they started to count, they seemed to lose their representation of the abstract composite unit of ten--their given--and a counting by ten act became equivalent to a counting by one act. This is understandable, because their counting by ten acts did not increment; the acts only repeated. Once the children started to count, they could easily isolate their sensory motor counting acts as substitutes for the operation of integration and stop performing that operation. This particular unit of ten is called a *repeatable* unit of ten.

Ten as a repeatable unit is restricted in important ways. For example, each counting act, "52, 62, 72", was a symbol for "ten" for Jason (cf. 6.48), but once he had created three tens and four ones, he did not "unpack" one of the units of ten and combine the result with the four ones. Although he could coordinate the two units of differing ranks, the results of repeating the units were not included in an encompassing unit whose constituent units were ones.

"Ten more" is a generic term like "one more"--it can have a variety of meanings. In this context, we use it to indicate that the child repeatedly counts ten more by one, and keeps track of those modules of ten counting acts. The child can review them and say how many more tens were counted. This unit provides valuable insight for teaching children to construct ten as an iterable unit, given they have constructed ten as an abstract composite unit.

The Stage of Part-Whole Operations

In the stage of part-whole operations, the children constructed ten as an iterable unit. To use ten as an iterable unit, the children must use it as they use the unit of one, once it has become iterable, and they must be able to coordinate it with the iterable unit of one. Essentially the two schemes, counting by ten and counting by one, merge into a single scheme we call counting by ten and one. The iterable unit of ten transforms this latter scheme into an *anticipatory* scheme, because the unit of ten is taken as a given along with the unit of one. When the unit of ten was an abstract composite unit, the children could *coordinate* a count by ten and a count by one whenever there were perceptual or figural units of ten that they could take as given. When the unit of ten is iterable, rather than coordinate the use of *two* separate schemes, the children use *one* scheme that contains two different units. Metaphorically, counting so many abstract composite units of ten is like jumping from one lattice of ten rungs to the next lattice, when the lattices are already in place. Iterating a unit of ten so many times is like repeatedly laying down a lattice of ten rungs end-to-end, with the intention of finding how many times it can be done.

Children can use this iterative scheme to find how many bags it would take to hold 170 pennies, if ten were put in each bag, by counting by ten, without actual bags or pennies being in their visual field. The part-whole operations are used to disembed an abstract composite unit of ten from the containing unit, and the iterative operation is used when the child counts by ten. An iterative operation includes repeating the abstract composite unit of ten and also integrating the result with the preceding results as indicated by a child counting, "1 is 10; 2 is 20; 3 is 30;. . . ". This is an indication that the number word sequence "10-20-30-40- . . . " has been interiorized, and that the unit of ten has become an iterable unit.

We found other uses for the counting scheme that are only *indicators* of the iterable unit of ten. When Jason solved a task where he was asked to pretend that there were 42 hidden items under one cloth and was asked to to put some more with them so that there would be 76 (cf. 6.48), he sequentially put up fingers in synchrony with uttering "52-62-72" and then continued putting up fingers on his other hand, uttering "73-74-75-76". He then intently reviewed his fingers and said "34". Double counting would not have been useful to Jason had he simply counted his number words, because he coordinated units of ten and units of one in the same counting episode. Coordinating counting-on by ten and by one when solving missing addend tasks can be an indicator of the iterable unit of ten. *If there are also indicators that a counting by ten act also increments by ten ones* (which wasn't the case for Jason), the inference that ten is an iterable unit would be plausible. Much stronger indicators are counting-down-to by ten and one to solve a missing minuend task or a direct subtraction task (cf. 4.38, 6.46).

The five unit types that we have hypothesized are as follows:

1. <u>Numerical composite</u>. Any pattern of ten items that is the result of applying the integration operation. The child focuses on elements of the patterns, and the pattern is not taken as one thing.

2. <u>Abstract composite unit</u>. The result of taking a numerical composite as a unit. It permits the coordination of a count by ten and a count by one when counting-on in certain situations.

3. <u>Ten more</u>. An abstract composite unit of ten whose elements are taken as extending beyond the elements of another abstract composite unit. The two abstract composite units are taken together in juxtaposition to form an encompassing composite unit.

4. <u>Repeatable unit</u>. A symbolic substitute for an abstract composite unit of ten that is repeated as an experiential chain. In its repetitions, the symbolic substitute can lose its composite quality.

5. Iterable unit. "Ten" as a conceptual structure that is available in the absence of particular collections of ten perceptual items, and makes possible the decision to count by ten prior to the actual activity of counting perceptual or hidden objects. A counting by ten act is a symbol for incrementing by ten more ones.

Other Perspectives

Our analysis of units is compatible with, but elaborates an analysis of, units provided by Russell (1903) and again by Herscovics (1983), eighty years later. Herscovics (1983) made a distinction among three mathematical interpretations of a unit: unit as component, unit as aggregate, and aggregate as counting component (p. 18). For Russell (1903, pp. 140-141), the term "unit" referred to a class consisting of a single member, which captures Herscovics's first distinction. Russell (1903) also provided an analysis of aggregates--they were wholes of a particular kind. "We regard[ed] the class as formed by all the terms, but usage seems to show no reason why the class should not equally be regarded as the whole composed of all the terms in those cases where there is such a whole. . . . The whole is, in this case, a whole of a particular kind, which I shall call aggregate" (p. 139). A class as "many" is a class of elements formed by all the terms and a class as "one" is what is meant by the term "aggregate". These distinctions are compatible with what we call a numerical composite and an abstract composite unit. In our analysis, however, these units are the results of mental acts.

> The "taking together". . . must become a purely conceptual operation. That is to say, several items, which are experientially . . . separate and discrete, must be considered as though they were one, and it is this mental act that creates the unitary composite. (von Glasersfeld & Richards, 1983, p. 3)

Herscovics's distinction of an aggregate as a counting unit is important, but it does not suggest the abstractions that seem to be necessary for a child to construct such a unit or the mental operations that make these abstractions possible.

As an abstract composite unit, ten is countable, in the normal sense of the term. Its limitations, however, were apparent in the case studies of the children. The construction of the iterable unit of ten was required before the children could understand the positional principle of the numeration system. We were surprised at how difficult it was for them to understand that each decade comprises a number sequence of numerosity ten and also that a counting by ten act could increment by ten more ones. Even if these constructions seemed to be made, there were still limitations in the uses of ten and one that were not overcome during the course of the teaching experiment (cf. 4.42 and 6.43), which suggests that an even more sophisticated system of mental operations than part-whole operations must be constructed before the children can use two units of different ranks to measure quantities (cf. 4.42).

Chapter VII

Strategies for Finding Sums and Differences

Brenda, Tarus, and James

Paul Cobb Leslie P. Steffe

From our point of view, strategies for finding sums and differences involve the coordination of arithmetic symbols that signify systems of integration operations and their products. Moreover, because mental operations (including integration operations) can be expressed in terms of action, the coordination of symbols implies a corresponding coordination of action that need not be carried out unless the need arises (Piaget, 1974b, p. 238). In general, a symbol can figure in a re-presentation and "point to" a signified structure, without the need to realize that structure through either sensory-motor action or re-presentation (von Glasersfeld, 1982a). At the level of operative thought, Piaget suggested that figural re-presentations are, in fact, nothing but "illustrations" that may accompany the performance of mental operations.

The coordination of symbols can involve using a known sum or difference to find an unknown sum or difference (Cifarelli & Wheatley, 1979a, 1979b; Rathmell, 1979; Steffe, 1979; Thornton, 1978, 1979). We call such coordinations thinking strategies to be consistent with the past literature on arithmetical thought.

As demonstrated in Chapter V, Brenda, Tarus, and James did not construct numerical concepts as the meaning of number words and numerals during the teaching experiment. Consequently, we hypothesized that they would not be able to make the coordinations that are required to construct thinking strategies, in spite of our best attempts as teachers. Numerous tasks were used to investigate this hypothesis. In all cases, the presentation of the tasks was guided by our current understanding of the children. Consequently, tasks were frequently sequenced so that the children might relate a current task to the results of solving a preceding task. For example, "12 + 6" might be presented immediately after "12 + 5". If the child solved the second task as a novel task unrelated to the first, the teacher conducting the session might present "12 + 7" and then ask the child if he or she could use the result "12 + 6 = 18". We sequenced tasks in this way and gave prompts to maximize the likelihood that the children would use the result of solving a task in the solution of a related task. It was hoped that the children would eventually realize that they did not have to rely solely on their counting methods.

In addition to arithmetical expressions involving numerals, we also presented tasks that involved collections of screened items. For example, a child might be asked to find out how many marbles there were in all, given that eight were in one cup and four were in another. Once the child had solved this task, he or she might be instructed to put two more marbles into the cup containing four marbles, and then to say how many marbles there were in all. If necessary, felt numerals would be placed beside the cups to help the child remember how many marbles there were in each cup originally. However, the objective was not to "impart knowledge" to the child. Rather, the objective was to focus on the child's interpretation of the situation, and on whatever methods the child might use to reach his or her goals. As Piaget (l974b) put it,

> To succeed is to grasp a given situation to a degree sufficient to achieve the proposed goals; to understand is to succeed in mastering the same situations in thought to the degree of being able to resolve the problems they pose, concerning the why and the how of the connections that have been noticed and used in action elsewhere. (p. 237)

Throughout our teaching episodes, we continually monitored the children's problem solutions for glimmers of the type of understanding alluded to by Piaget in the above quotation. The possibility that these children might construct thinking strategies was first investigated in March 1981, when Brenda and James were making progress toward their motor periods and Tarus had already entered that period. As the investigation continued, all three children made the transition to their verbal periods. In working with them, we found that it was necessary to distinguish between coordinations of symbols and coordinations of number words. This distinction is analogous to that between counting and reciting a sequence of number words. Counting involves coordinating each number word with an accompanying unit item of some type and, in the verbal period, the number words signify the unit items. In contrast, number words do not play a signifying role when a child merely recites a sequence of number words. Similarly, a child who coordinates symbols can perform the signified actions. In contrast, for the child who produces a number word coordination, the coordination does not point to or signify anything beyond itself.

BRENDA

By the end of the first year of the teaching experiment, Brenda was a counter of motor unit items and had constructed a figurative concept of addition (cf. Chapter V). During this first year, she was not observed making any type of coordination.

Independent Solutions

The teacher presented a sequence of tasks on 21 May 1981 by asking Brenda to pretend that a certain number of cookies were under each of two cloths and then asking her to find out how many there were in all. Successive tasks involved collections of eight and three, eight and five, eight and six, eight and seven, and eight and eight cookies. She correctly solved each problem, but did not use the results of previous solutions. In each case, she tapped on the first cloth synchronously with uttering "1-2-3- 4- . . . -8" and then continued by putting up fingers synchronous with uttering number words until she completed an appropriate finger pattern. This intuitive extension adding scheme was not an object of reflection for Brenda.

Brenda solved similar sequences of tasks independently on 26 and 28 May 1981, again by making intuitive extensions. She clearly did not use the result of solving one task to solve a subsequent one. The situation was no different at the beginning of the second year of the teaching experiment, when Brenda was still in her motor period. On 7 December 1981, the interviewer presented a sequence of tasks by adding blocks to one of two covered collections.

T : (Covers two collections of three blocks each with cloths, tells Brenda how many are under each cloth, and asks her to find out how many there are in all.)
B : Six (Brenda knew that "3 + 3 is 6").
T : Suppose I put two more with these (puts two more blocks under one of the cloths). How many would be there then?
B : Eight.
T : How many here (points to the cloth covering five blocks)?
B : . . . Five.
T : What's three plus five?
B : (Simultaneously puts up five fingers of one hand) 1-2-3-4-5 (sequentially puts up three on her other hand) -8.

Brenda was able to say that there were eight blocks in all after the interviewer had added two more. However, she considered that the two blocks had been added to the single collection of six covered blocks and recalled the phrase "six plus two is eight". This was not a symbolic coordination, because she failed to coordinate an increase in the blocks of one collection with an increase in the blocks of both collections.

Brenda's solutions to another sequence of tasks presented in the same teaching episode indicate that her failure to make symbolic coordinations should not be attributed to a belief that she was supposed to count. When she noticed a recurrent result of counting, she predicted what the result of counting would be in the next task. Successive tasks were presented by transferring a block from one of two covered collections to the other.

Initially, five blocks were under one cloth and three were under the other. After Brenda made an intuitive extension and said that there were eight in all, the interviewer moved one block from the collection of three to the collection of five. Brenda told the interviewer how many blocks were under each of the cloths when asked (six and two), but again made an intuitive extension to find out how many there were in all. The interviewer then moved one block from the collection of two to the collection of six. Brenda said that there were eight blocks in all without counting. She explained, "Cause every time I've been counting it's been eight, so there's got to be eight", and then, without counting, solved the subsequent problem in which two blocks were moved from one collection to the other. Brenda noticed that she arrived at the same number word each time she counted, but she did not attempt to explain why the answer was always eight. We infer that she abstracted (level 1) a recurrent result of counting rather than that she made a symbolic coordination. It can be noted, in passing, that Brenda's failure to make a coordination cannot be attributed to a limited capacity of "short-term or working memory" because she was able to say how many items were under each cloth, and she did abstract a recurrent result.

Number Word Coordinations

Brenda was not observed making any type of coordination during the remainder of her motor period. She was first classified as a counter of verbal unit items on the basis of observations made on 1 February 1982 (cf. 1.16). Brenda used the results of solving a previous task to solve related tasks in a teaching session conducted on the following day.

T : (Places 18 blocks in one cup, 6 in another, tells Brenda how many there are in each, and asks her to find out how many there are in all.)
B : 18-19- . . . -23 (sequentially puts up six fingers).
T : What's eighteen plus six, what did you say?
B : Twenty-three.

T : So what would eighteen plus seven be?
B : Twenty-four.
T : So eighteen plus seven is twenty-four; what would eighteen plus nine be?
B : 18-19- . . . -26 (sequentially puts up nine fingers).

Brenda's failure to make a coordination when she was presented with 18 plus 9 indicates that she might not have coordinated symbols when she found 18 plus 7. Alternatively, the teacher's prompts to use the result of her previous solution might have led her to notice that "seven" was the successor of "six", which led her to produce the successor of "twenty-three". As will be seen, her solutions to tasks presented in subsequent sessions indicate that this alternative interpretation is the more plausible.

In the following weeks, Brenda did not use the answer to a preceding task unless the teacher gave cues. For example, on 15 March 1982, she solved the following sequences of sums independently: 7 + 3, 7 + 4, and 7 + 5; 7 + 2 and 7 + 3; 7 + 8 and 7 + 9. Similarly, on 29 March 1982, she independently solved 7 + 7 and 7 + 8; 7 + 4, and 7 + 5; 7 + 4, 7 + 5, and 7 + 6. In each case, the teacher did not encourage Brenda to use the result of a preceding solution. Later in the same session, the teacher presented 7 + 9 immediately after Brenda had made an intuitive extension to solve 7 + 8, saying, "If seven plus eight is fifteen what's seven plus nine?" Brenda replied, "Sixteen", almost immediately. Brenda's non-counting solutions in this and in the 2 February teaching episode were highly contextual. She constructed and solved problems independently, unless she detected number word regularities in the teacher's statement of the task. She did not spontaneously search for number word patterns.

On 31 March 1982, the teacher gave Brenda opportunities to make coordinations that involved incrementing or decrementing an addend by one or two. He used felt numerals to present sequences of addition tasks and, for the first few minutes of the session, repeatedly indicated to Brenda that she should use the result of her preceding solution. The first sequence of tasks which involved decreasing an addend was 6 + 10, 6 + 9, 6 + 8, 6 + 7, and 6 + 6. Brenda solved the first three independently by counting, but related tasks to solve the last two.

T : So what's six plus seven?
B : Thirteen.
T : And what's six plus six?
B : Twelve--I go backwards.

Her final explanatory comment suggests that she had abstracted a number word pattern (she could not solve subtraction tasks by counting backward). At the very least, she had abstracted (level 1) "going backwards" from her sequence of answers. She may have also abstracted a coordination between the two backward number word sequences, "16-15- . . . - 12" and "10-9- . . . - 6." That is, she may have constructed a rule like, "If that goes backward by one, then so does the other". If this coordination involved substituting re-presented number word sequences or a finger pattern for actual counting activity, it would be a level 2 abstraction. Brenda's solutions to other sequences of problems in this teaching session allow us to decide whether she made a level 1 or a level 2 abstraction. Brenda certainly seemed rather pleased with herself after she had solved six plus seven and six plus six.

The following exchange occurred a few minutes later. Brenda had just found 7 + 8 independently of 7 + 7 = 14, by counting.

T : What's seven plus nine?
B : Sixteen?
T : Seven plus nine is sixteen.
B : Seventeen.
T : What's seventeen? Seven plus something is seventeen--what is going to be seventeen?
B : (Simultaneously puts up seven fingers, sequentially puts up her remaining three fingers, and then sequentially puts up seven fingers for a second time) Ten.
T : Seven plus ten is seventeen.
B : The next is eighteen.
T : Seven plus what is eighteen?
B : Eleven.
T : Seven plus eleven is eighteen.
B : And the next is going to be twelve--thirteen.
T : Wait a minute (makes 7 + 11 = 18 using felt numerals). Seven plus eleven is eighteen, so what's the next one going to be?
B : Seven plus twelve equals nineteen, and the next one's twenty, and the . . .

It will be recalled that Brenda had constructed sophisticated finger patterns for eleven through twenty. The seven fingers she initially put up when she solved the task corresponding to 7 + ___ = 17 could, for example, stand for either seven or seventeen; in the latter case, she re-presented an open hand. Her goal after making a finger pattern for "7" was to make one for "17". Consequently, she solved the task by counting from "one" beyond a finger pattern for seven. She completed two open hands by counting "1-2-3", and then continued "4-5-6-7-8-9-10", stopping when reaching a finger pattern for "seven", which now signified "seventeen".

Brenda repeatedly took the initiative in this exchange and in the remainder of the session. She had made a "discovery" and wanted to show the teacher what she could now do. This behavior was in contrast to that witnessed in the teaching episodes conducted in previous weeks. As the session progressed, she became increasingly alert and smiled more frequently. After Brenda had solved seven plus something is 17, she seemed to be aware of the coordination between two number word sequences; if one went forward by one, then so did the other. Consequently, it would seem that she made a level 2 abstraction after she used finger patterns to solve "seven plus something is seventeen". She now had a basis for making her abstraction. Her number words signified finger patterns, and her coordinations of number words reflected corresponding coordinations of finger patterns. Before this exchange, she only noticed regularities in the results of uttering number words--a level 1 abstraction. In the above protocol, her number word coordinations signified corresponding coordinations of finger patterns.

As this teaching session progressed, Brenda gradually came to realize that she did not necessarily have to solve problems independently, and she actively "searched" for patterns in her activity. Brenda's most advanced solution occurred near the end of the session.

T : Seven plus eight is fifteen, so what's seven plus six? Can you do that one by using seven plus eight?
B : . . .
T : Did I go forwards or backwards?
B : Backwards.
T : How much did I go backwards?
B : You went two times (holds up two fingers) because it's thirteen.

Brenda knew that the teacher had gone backward, indicating that she knew "six" came before "eight". Her failure to produce a coordination until she was prompted--"How much did I go backwards?"-- demonstrates her lack of a signified (contrast this with her initiative in the preceding protocol after she used her finger patterns). Her coordination did not refer to anything other than a specific "two-pattern". Once she found out how many times the teacher went backwards by recognizing a figural pattern formed by the number words "seven-six" (she held up two fingers), she made an appropriate coordination. In general, she produced number word coordinations only if an addend was changed by one; in other cases, she solved problems independently.

The fragile nature of Brenda's number word coordinations is illustrated by an exchange that occurred exactly a week later, on 6 April 1982. During this episode, the teacher gave Brenda the opportunity to compensate an increase in one collection by a decrease in the other. He told her that ten marbles were in one cup and five were in another, and asked her how many there were in all. After she had solved the problem, she transferred one marble from the cup containing ten to the other cup, as directed. The dialogue continued:

B : It's going to be six and it's going to be sixteen.
T : No, how many marbles in this one? (Points to the cup containing nine marbles.)
B : Nine.
T : So how many are there in all?
B : Sixteen.

The teacher indicated that her answer was incorrect. Brenda then counted and gave "fifteen" as her answer. She transferred another marble from the cup containing nine to the other.

B : Why does it have to be eight?
T : How many in this one now? (points to the cup containing eight marbles).
B : Eight.
T : And in this one? (Points to the cup containing seven marbles.)
B : Seven.
T : So how many are there altogether?
B : How many here? (Points to the cup containing seven marbles.)
T : Seven.
B : . . . fifteen.
T : If you don't like to do that one, we won't continue.

Initially, Brenda anticipated the teacher's questions and volunteered that there were six marbles in one cup and sixteen in all. However, she quickly seemed to lose confidence. Her aside, "Why does it have to be eight?" conveyed frustration. It seemed that she anticipated that she could make number word coordinations as soon as the teacher asked her to transfer a marble. From her perspective, adding a marble to one of two separate collections should correspond to saying the next number word. When the teacher intervened, she eventually realized that the other collection had decreased by one. Brenda realized that the number word coordination would not work and she could not find an alternative method to use.

Brenda did not reach the abstract stage in the remaining two months of the teaching experiment and, during this time, was not observed making more sophisticated number word coordinations.

TARUS

By 22 January 1982, Tarus could solve problems simply by uttering number words in sequence (cf. 2.34). Concomitantly, new flexibility emerged in counting.

Independent Solutions

Tarus did not make a number word coordination until he could count verbal unit items. Previously, there had been several occasions when he could have made such a coordination. But, each time, he solved the problems independently. On 19 March 1981, for example, when he was in the motor period, the teacher asked him to find out how many squares there were in all if five were under each of two cloths. Tarus made an intuitive extension by sequentially putting up all ten fingers as he uttered "1-2-3-4- . . . -10". The exchange continued:

T : Watch this (puts one more square under the first cloth). How many altogether now?
Ta : Five.
T : And how many over here? (Points to the cloth covering six squares.)
Ta : Six.
T : How many altogether? What is five and five?
Ta : Ten.
T : And I put one more with the five and how many do we have now?
Ta : Six.
T : Six under here (points to the appropriate cloth) and how many altogether?
Ta : Ten.

The teacher could hardly have given more blatant hints. Nevertheless, Tarus considered that the teacher had added one item to one of the two separate collections, rather than to a single collection comprising the original two. When he switched perspectives, viewing the screened items as one rather than two collections, he recalled that there were ten squares in all, ignoring the additional square that had been added. This indicates that his two perspectives were uncoordinated.

The teacher also investigated whether Tarus could compensate the decrease in one collection by an increase in another. On 24 March, 2 April, and 16 April, 1981, when he was still in the motor period, sequences of tasks were presented by transferring an item from one of two screened collections to the other. Tarus usually solved successive problems independently by using his intuitive extension scheme. There was no indication that he coordinated symbols to construct a compensating relationship.

Tarus first curtailed the motor component of his counting acts during a teaching session conducted on 12 May 1981. In the same session, he abstracted a recurrent result of counting when the teacher presented a sequence of tasks by transferring an item from one of two screened collections to the other. Initially, five poker chips were in one cup and four were in the other. To find out how many there were in all, Tarus uttered "1-2-3-4-5-6-7-8-9" without accompanying motor activity. He made an intuitive extension by counting verbal unit items. After he had transferred one chip from the cup containing four, Tarus correctly said that six chips were in one cup and three in the other. When asked how many there were in all, he again made an intuitive extension. Another chip was then transferred from the cup containing three. This time, Tarus was able to say how many chips there were in each cup and how many there were in all. He counted to solve a problem involving collections of seven and two items two weeks later, on 26 May 1981. This indicates that he did not recall a learned fact but instead noticed a recurrent result of counting--"nine". His behavior is similar to that which Brenda displayed just before she entered her verbal period.

Number Word Coordinations

Tarus's coordinations were not investigated until 7 January 1982, when he again produced behavior similar to that discussed above (12 May 1981). The teacher successively transferred marbles from one cup to another, and Tarus solved the first three problems by making intuitive extensions. He then gave the correct answer to all remaining tasks immediately, even in cases where four marbles were transferred. As on 12 May 1981, he abstracted the recurrence of a result, on this occasion after counting to solve three successive tasks.

On 28 January 1982, Tarus said the correct number word the first time an item was transferred from one collection to another, after he had initially counted to find how many items there were in all. He did not abstract a regularity from a sequence of results, but instead anticipated the regularity. The following day, the teacher asked him to find two more numbers that made eight, immediately after he had solved five plus three by counting. The teacher used felt numerals to present these tasks.

T : Can you find two more numbers which make eight?
Ta : . . . Six and two.
T : Can you find two more?
Ta : . . . Seven and one.

T : Two more?
Ta : . . . Four and four.

The order in which Tarus generated numeral pairs indicates that he coordinated successors and predecessors--giving the next number word after "six" was coordinated with giving the number word just before "two". These coordinations were supported by addition sentences like "5 + 3 = 8" that he formed using felt numerals.

Our claim that Tarus made a number word coordination is supported by two more pieces of evidence. First, Tarus always paused for several seconds before he answered. Each time, he had to do a lot of work before he could answer. He did not just "see" that the addends compensated. He generated pairs of number words by finding each one independently, finding first the successor of, say, "six", and then the predecessor of "two". The second indicator is that Tarus never attempted to justify why the answers were the same, despite repeated requests to do so. The number word coordination did not seem to signify anything for him.

During the experiment, several attempts were made to help him make other types of coordinations. On 16 April 1982, for example, the teacher orally presented a sequence of tasks by telling Tarus five items were hidden beneath one cloth, varying how many were under the second cloth, and asking him to find out how many there were in all. For collections of five and one, Tarus replied "six"; for five and two, "seven"; and for five and four, "eight". His answers indicate that he made a number word coordination by abstracting (level 1) a pattern from the sequence of results. This inference is even more plausible when one notes that on another occasion, having counted to solve five plus four, Tarus gave "ten" and then "eleven" as his answers when the second collection was increased by one item, and then by one more. He also solved a sequence of tasks in which one collection was decreased by relying on a number word pattern. Each time, he gave the number word immediately preceding his previous answer.

Tarus was also asked to solve sequences of arithmetic sentences in which one of the addends was successively increased or decreased (16 April and 28 May 1982). By this time, he could solve addition tasks by counting-on. His performance supports the contention that he made number word coordinations when he related successive tasks. Whenever the teacher hinted that he should use his previous solution, Tarus constructed what might be called a "numeral" context--he "looked for" patterns in arrays of numerals. Consider, for example, the following exchange, which also took place on 16 April 1982, in which numerals were used.

T : Remember, twenty-three plus seven is thirty. What do you think twenty-three plus eight would be?
Ta : Thirty.
T : Twenty-three plus seven is thirty, so what's twenty-three plus eight?
Ta : Um, 33-34-31.
T : If twenty-three plus eight is thirty-one, what's twenty- three plus nine?
Ta : Um, thirty-two.
T : OK.
Ta : Thirty-three.
T : What's going to be thirty-three? What am I going to have to put here? (Points above the "9".)
Ta : Ten.

Tarus might well have interpreted the teacher's frequent gestures at the numerals as cues to "look for" patterns. In the absence of such cues, he usually solved sentences independently. These cues and his failure to justify his responses indicate that the coordinations he made did not play a signifying function. At his most sophisticated, he spontaneously made number word coordinations with the teacher's guidance in situations similar to those in which they had first been constructed. In essence, the teacher's interventions had trained him to behave as though he was using a thinking strategy in certain very narrow contexts.

JAMES

Independent Solutions

During the second year of the teaching experiment, on several occasions we investigated whether James could make symbolic coordinations. He usually solved successive tasks independently. For example, on 8 December 1981, while he was in the motor period, the interviewer hid eight blocks under one cloth and five under another, and asked James how many there were in all. James answered "thirteen" after making an intuitive extension by putting up fingers. The interviewer presented each of the next four tasks by transferring one block from the cloth that originally covered eight to the other cloth. Each time, James was able to write an appropriate addition sentence on a chalk board when asked to do so (i.e., 9 + 4 = ___, 10 + 3 = ___, 11 + 2 = ___, 12 + 1 = ___). However, he used his intuitive extension scheme to solve each sentence, arriving at the answers "thirteen", "thirteen", "fifteen", and "thirteen".

Number Word Coordinations

Even when James could count-on, he usually solved problems independently. A rare exception occurred on 29 March 1982. James and the teacher were working on the basic addition facts, with seven as the first addend. At one point during the session, James had arranged the felt numerals "6", "3", "4", and "5" in a row. He had just solved the sentence "7 + 5 = ___" by using his intuitive extension scheme.

T : What was seven plus five? (Points to the "5" in the row.)
J : Twelve, (points to the four) eleven, (points to the three) ten.

After recalling the sum of seven and five, James volunteered answers to seven plus four and seven plus three. Because the numerals "3", "4", and "5" were arranged in order, they served as perceptual indices that supported his coordination of the backward number word sequence "five-four-three" with "twelve-eleven-ten".

Next, the teacher worked with James on the facts, with six as the first addend. After a few minutes, James systematically related successive tasks when an addend was increased or decreased by one. For example, he said that 6 plus 8 was 15, and then gave 14 as his answer to 6 plus 7. A few minutes later he said that 6 plus 6, 6 plus 7, and 6 plus 5 were 12, 13, and 11. These answers were not the result of James recalling a sum, because he had to count to find the sums when they were presented independently. As with the seven facts, James used the numerals as perceptual indices. His coordinations were highly contextual in that they were facilitated by the presence of a sequence of numerals.

As the session progressed, James began to take the initiative. He corrected the teacher if a sentence was presented for a second time, and told the teacher which sentences had not been presented. After he had worked on the six and seven facts, James asked to do the eight facts. However, the teacher presented the subsequent tasks so that the numerals were arranged in no particular order. James could not produce number word coordinations. Similar observations were made a few days later, on 6 April 1982. On that occasion, he made number word coordinations when he worked on the "six" facts. The teacher encouraged him to relate successive tasks when the second addend was increased by two or three. James was unable to do so and, after just a couple of minutes, said, "I don't want to do no more". In both of these cases, he had found a way to generate correct answers without counting, but experienced difficulties as soon as the tasks were altered. The number word coordinations that James made when he worked with basic facts were the most sophisticated that he produced during the entire teaching experiment. However, they were more restricted than those produced by Brenda and Tarus.

PERSPECTIVES ON THE CASE STUDIES

The most important finding of the three case studies was the children's failure to make symbolic coordinations. This occurred despite our attempts to provide the children with numerous opportunities to abstract the coordinations implicit in successive counting episodes. It was not until they reached the verbal periods that they constructed coordinations resembling what Brownell (1935) called a thinking strategy. Even then, the coordinations were, at best, coordinations of number word sequences that did not signify corresponding coordinations of either actual or re-presented sensory-motor action. These coordinations were made possible by the children's awareness of their utterances of number words and by their curtailment of the motor component of counting activity. In the motor period, the "noise" of the necessary motor activity seemed to preclude coordinations of the type that we observed in the verbal period.

When the children first entered their verbal periods, one result of counting was that the last number word uttered could now refer to the number word sequence. For example, a number word such as "eight" could refer to the number word sequence "one, two, . . . , eight" as well as to a counted collection (pattern) consisting of discrete unitary perceptual items. But "eight" could not refer to the number word sequence that the child would produce were he or she to count the collection. In other words, we have seen that when the children entered their verbal periods, they could re-enact counting a perceptual collection by subvocally re-uttering the number word sequence. This was the sense in which a number word referred to a collection of number words. However, it was not until late in their verbal periods that these children could take a number word as an index of a number word sequence before they counted. This indicates a dawning awareness that the number word sequence that ended with the given number word would be produced while counting the collection. This awareness, which was the result of a level 2 reflective abstraction, corresponds to the realization that no matter how a collection is counted, the activity yields the same terminal number word. The children were now becoming aware of how they counted.

The children's lack of awareness of how they counted was apparent when they entered the verbal period. Brenda solved sequentially presented tasks independently, unless she detected number word regularities in the teacher's statements of the tasks. When a sequence of tasks was presented by transferring a marble from one container to another, Tarus solved them independently before he abstracted the recurrent result. James abstracted regularities if the numerals had been placed in order when he solved a sequence of tasks, where one addend was held constant and the other varied by one. But if the numerals were arranged in no particular order, he could not make the coordinations that previously had seemed so easy.

Tarus, as a result of his abstraction of a recurrent result, may have become aware of the curtailed coordinations in that limited context. That is, he seemed to realize that transferring an item of one of two collections to the other did not change the result he would produce if he actually counted. This was especially plausible because 21 days later (28 January 1982) he counted only once in a sequence of the same type of tasks, thereafter answering immediately. However, this awareness was limited to specific situations. When arithmetical sentences were presented without perceptual material, changing "5" to "6" and "3" to "2" in the sentence "5 + 3 = 8" did not correspond to the transfer of an item from a collection of three items to a collection of five items. The explicit knowledge was that, if they were counted before and after the transfer, there would be eight, because the increase by one in one addend was compensated by a decrease by one in the other addend.

The highly specific "forward" and "backward" number word coordinations that Tarus made late in his verbal period indicate that he became aware of the coordinations between the production of sensory-motor unit items and the utterances of number words. While awareness of these coordinations should not be minimized, their generative power should not be overestimated. A coordination between two number word sequences (which itself is a coordination between two sensory-motor items) did not imply a corresponding coordination between the counted items that the individual number words of the sequences could signify. There was never any indication that the coordinations Tarus made referred to anything. We believe the primary reason was that number words were not symbols for composite units.

In Brenda's case (30 March 1982), the number word coordinations were based on her use of sophisticated finger patterns. Thereafter, Brenda initiated searches in her activity. However, this was only a temporary advance, specific to the particular situation in which she made the abstraction.

The limitations of number word coordinations are compatible with Piaget's (1974b) distinction between succeeding in action and understanding in thought.

> "To succeed in action" and "to understand in thought", both involved coordination, but the coordinations are qualitatively different: the first is material and causal in character, because it is a coordination of movements; the second is of

> implicative nature (in the sense of connections between significations. . .) even if, among its elements, there may be representations of movement. (p. 237-238)

If thought operates with symbols that signify actions, the coordinations produced by thought are coordinations of symbols and not of actions--but the coordination of symbols then implies the coordination of the signified actions. This type of coordination requires, in the numerical case, the mental operations of integration, whose results we observed in the subsequent abstract stage.

Number Facts

The question "Did these children learn the number facts in spite of their failure to use thinking strategies and the mental operation of integration?" is of practical interest. By March of 1982 the three children had learned less than half of the basic addition facts. For the most part, they had learned double facts (e.g., "4 + 4 = 8") and intuitive facts-- those that could be solved easily by using finger patterns because both addends were five or less. In March 1982, the project staff decided to document each child's attempt to learn the basic addition facts. All three children were counters of verbal unit items, and both Brenda and Tarus had, on occasion, made re-presentations of immediately prior counting activity. Ordinarily, all three children solved addition problems by making intuitive extensions. In several sessions, the teacher asked the children to solve sequences of addition sentences with the same first addend. Thus, during a session, the child might attempt to learn the addition facts whose first addend was 7, 6, or 3. The children were repeatedly told to try to remember, and to solve without counting. New sentences were often generated by repeatedly increasing or decreasing the second addend by one, and all three children occasionally produced solutions based on coordinations of number words.

After the teacher had presented each of a group of ten sentences two or three times, the children were usually able to answer correctly without counting. However, the children had to count to solve many of these sentences when they were presented in a teaching episode conducted within a week, often as soon as the following day. They could remember the facts for only a short period of time and had difficulty estimating or gauging the size of the sum; their guesses were often wildly inaccurate.

It would be easy to conclude from our emphases in the teaching episodes that we believe teachers should help counters of verbal unit items solve problems by using number word patterns. However, we have two reservations. First, the reorganizations the children made were ephemeral. The practice of helping children like Brenda, Tarus, and James produce number word coordinations seems to have few implications for enhancing their acquisition of mathematical knowledge while they remain in the verbal period. Second, such children might come to believe that mathematics involves finding "tricks" to produce answers. The three children, by necessity, regarded "number work" as counting. Looking for patterns and regularities in number words and numerals was not spontaneously generated, nor was the practice sustained.

Chapter VIII

Strategies for Finding Sums and Differences

Tyrone, Scenetra, and Jason

Paul Cobb   Leslie P. Steffe

Observations of children using thinking strategies to find sums and differences are reported in the literature (Brownell, 1928, 1935; Brownell & Chazal, 1935; Carpenter, 1980; Carpenter & Moser, 1982; Ginsburg, 1977; Hiebert, 1982; Hiebert, Carpenter, & Moser, 1982; Ilg & Ames, 1951: Rathmell, 1978; Smith, 1921; Steffe, Hirstein, & Spikes, 1976; Steffe, von Glasersfeld, Richards, & Cobb, 1983; Steinberg, 1985; Steiner, 1980). These reports indicate that children do use thinking strategies to solve addition and subtraction problems in novel, creative ways. Instead of using a well-established method, they relate the problem to a known sum or difference.

There is no generally accepted scheme to classify thinking strategies for finding basic facts. The types of strategies listed below represent a synthesis of previous analyses, particularly those of Brownell (l928), Carpenter (l980), Ilg and Ames (l951), Rathmell (l978), and Thornton (l978).

1. Addition

(a) The addend-increasing strategy. One of the addends is decomposed into two parts. The sum of one of these parts and the other addend is found. Finally, the remaining part is added to the partial sum. For example, "He himself noted his error with 9 + 6 and immediately corrected it by solving from 9 + 5: thus, '9 and 5 is 14, and one is 15'" (Brownell, 1928, p. 125).

(b) The addend-decreasing strategy. One of the addends of a sum is increased. The sum of the increased addend and the other addend is then found. Finally, this sum is decreased by the amount of increase. For example, "He first gave 14 for 9 + 6. He then solves thus, '9 and 8 is 17, less 1 is 16, less 1 is 15'" (Brownell, 1928, p. 30).

(c) The compensation strategy. One addend is increased and the other is decreased by the same amount. The sum of the resulting two addends is then found. For example, "He solved 7 + 3 as, '6 and 4 is 10, so 7 and 3 is 10'" (Brownell, 1928, p. 128).

For the most part, previous researchers have limited their investigations of thinking strategies to those used to find sums, Carpenter (l980) and Ilg and Ames (l951) being notable exceptions. Consequently, the types of thinking strategies for subtraction are based on a logical analysis as well as on examples of children's behavior.

2. Subtraction

(a) <u>The subtrahend variation strategy</u>. First, the subtrahend is increased or decreased. Next, the difference between the minuend and the altered subtrahend is found. Finally, this difference is altered by the amount of increase or decrease, the alteration being in the same direction. For example, 12 - 7 might be related to 12 - 9 = 3 by increasing 7 by 2, subtracting 9 from 12, and then increasing 3 by 2.

(b) <u>The minuend variation strategy</u>. First, the minuend is either increased or decreased. Next, the difference between the altered minuend and the subtrahend is found. Finally, this difference is altered by the amount of increase or decrease, but in the opposite direction. For example, 12 - 7 might be related to 14 - 7 = 7 by increasing 12 by 2, subtracting 7 from 14, and then subtracting 2 from 7. Alternatively, 12 - 7 might be related to 10 - 7 = 3 by decreasing 12 by 2, subtracting 7 from 10, and then increasing 3 by 2.

(c) <u>The inverse strategy</u>. First, the minuend is decomposed into the parts corresponding to the subtrahend and the unknown difference. The minuend is then viewed as the sum of the subtrahend and the unknown difference. Finally, the unknown addend is found. For example, "6 - 4 = 2 because 4 + ? = 6. 4 + 2, therefore the answer is 2" (Ilg & Ames, 1951, p. 8).

In analyzing the children's thinking strategies, we found it useful to distinguish between those in which children relate a current sum or difference to one just solved and to one known without solving. We call these local and spontaneous strategies, respectively. In both cases, we, as teachers, want children to be "on the lookout" for relationships among problems. This expectation is compatible with findings of a recent study conducted by Baroody, Ginsburg, and Waxman (l983), who made the following point when discussing third graders' solutions of the sequence of tasks 6 + 7, 6 + 8, . . . , 6 + 15.

> The third-grade students' use of this principle might have been depressed because of the cumulative effects of socialization. Use of the progression principle may be increased by instruction that fosters flexible problem-solving and searching for regularities. Failure to use a principle does not imply that the principle is not known. (p. 167)

In other words, one must consider more than the current state of a child's arithmetical knowledge when accounting for his or her failure to use a thinking strategy. The child's conception of the activity of doing arithmetic has to include an awareness of going beyond routinely solving unrelated problems. We call the child's general conception of doing arithmetic his or her arithmetical context. For this reason, the characterization we give of the relationship between concepts and thinking strategies is incomplete; although certain concepts might be necessary to a thinking strategy, they may not be sufficient.

We hypothesized that the children's meanings of addition and subtraction would place constraints on the thinking strategies they could construct. In particular, we speculated that the thinking strategies children constructed might be accounted for in terms of the mental operations that constitute their concepts of addition and subtraction. Consequently, we investigated the children's use of thinking strategies at the stages of sequential integration operations, progressive integration operations, and part-whole operations. In the following sections, we characterize the thinking strategies that Tyrone, Jason, and Scenetra constructed at the three stages.

Sequential Integration Operations

At the stage of sequential integration operation, the three children, with rare exceptions, did not use thinking strategies spontaneously in spite of our attempts to encourage them to do so. The exceptions involved either relating an unknown sum to a known doubles combination by increasing or decreasing an addend by one, or else increasing an addend of a sum from nine to ten when finding the sum. These strategies were intuitive and involved linkages between number words.

JASON

Jason was first observed constructing a local strategy on 14 December 1981.

T : (Makes the sentence "17 - 5 = " using felt numerals.)
J : 17-16-15-14-13--12.

T : What would 17 take away six be if 17 take away five is 12? (Removes the 5 and replaces it with a 6.)
J : 12--it would be eleven.
T : (Changes "17 - 6 = 12" to "17 - 6 = 11") If 17 take away six is eleven, what's 17 take away eight? (Replaces "6" with "8".)
J : 17-16-15-14-13-12-11-10 (sequentially puts up eight fingers), that would be nine.

Since "17 - 6 = " was only the second sentence presented, Jason did not have the opportunity to abstract a number word pattern from a sequence of answers. We infer that he coordinated the results of his counting-off-from scheme to solve the sentence "17 - 5 = " with his potential solution to the sentence "17 - 6 = " and realized he could count backward one more. This coordination, while dependent on actual counting activity, did not seem to be a number word coordination--rather, it had the quality of a thinking strategy. But it was limited to variations in the subtrahend by one.

The claim that Jason made a symbolic rather than a number word coordination is consistent with his next solution. After he had counted backward to solve the sentence "17 - 8 = ", the teacher asked the following question:

T : If take away eight is nine, what would nine plus eight be? (Makes "9 + 8 = " underneath 17 - 8 = 9.)
J : seventeen.
T : How did you do that one?
J : Nine plus nine would be eighteen, so nine plus eight would be seventeen.

The teacher's intention was to investigate whether Jason could relate addition and subtraction tasks. Instead, Jason related the sum to a known doubles combination.

A few minutes later, Jason again spontaneously used an addend decreasing strategy, this time relating the orally presented sum "nine plus seven" to the known sum "9 + 8 is 17". However, he failed to use a strategy if an addend was increased or decreased by two rather than by one. A similar observation was made when the strategy that he used to solve the sentence "17 - 6 = " was discussed. The most plausible explanation for this limitation in Jason's use of thinking strategies is that the symbolic coordinations he made involved number word linkages. For example, when he solved the sentence "17 - 6 = " by relating it to the solved sentence "17 - 5 = 12", he realized that he could count backward one more time because "six" immediately followed "five". In other words, the linkage "six-five" symbolized an additional counting backward act. However, he solved the sentence "17 - 8 = " independently of the solved sentence "17 - 6 = 11"; he did not "connect" the two number words "six" and "eight", and so could not make a symbolic coordination.

To summarize, the initial strategies that Jason used depended on linkages between adjacent number words. However, on 25 January 1982, he made coordinations that involved second as well as first successors. After he had solved the sentence "19 + 5 = 24", he explained his solution to the sentence "19 + 7 = " as follows (he said "27" rather than "26"):

T : OK., , so how did you do that one?
J : I don't know.
T : I saw you doing some counting there. Where did you start counting?
J : I started from five, then I counted two more.
T : So how did you count, can you do it out loud?
J : I started, I started . . .
T : Just a minute, you had nineteen and five is twenty-four, then what did you do?
J : It was twenty-four, I knew it was twenty-seven.

Jason realized that seven was two more than five, and he thought that 27 was two more than 24. Later in the same session, he solved the sentence "19 + 14 = " independently of the solved sentence "19 + 11 = 30". In general, the restricted and inconsistent way in which he used his strategies indicates that he did not explicitly decide to find out how much an addend had increased--he did not realize that the sum would increase by the same as-yet-unknown amount. Rather, he relied on linkages between number words in an intuitive manner. His failure to use the sentence "19 + 11 = 30" when solving the sentence "19 + 14 = " indicates that he did not "see" that "eleven" was linked to its third successor, "fourteen".

TYRONE

We did not attempt to help Tyrone construct strategies to find sums and differences until 4 March 1981, even though he had entered the stage of sequential integration operations in January. He used an addend-increasing strategy as soon as the teacher prompted him to do so. Specifically, he related the sentence "7 + 5 = " to "7 + 4 = 11", "8 + 6 = " to "8 + 5 = 13", and "13 + 5 = " to "13 + 4 = 17". A few days later, on 9 March 1981, Tyrone used an addend-increasing strategy spontaneously for the first time. He justified his answer to the sentence "5 + 6 = " by saying, "Five and five is ten and one more is eleven". However, his spontaneous use of strategies remained the exception rather than the rule for the rest of the first year of the experiment.

A few weeks after the session conducted on 9 March 1981, the teacher presented successive tasks by increasing an addend by two (on 15 April 1981). Almost invariably, Tyrone would increase the sum by three, thus making the same error that Jason frequently made when he was also in the stage of sequential integration operations. The teacher asked the following question immediately after Tyrone had found the sum of nine and five.

T : If I made five two bigger, what would that be over there (points to the 14)?
Ty : Seventeen.
T : How many?
Ty : Seventeen.
T : Five becomes only two bigger, so this has to become how much bigger?
Ty : Two (holds up two fingers.)
T : Two, so make fourteen two bigger.
Ty : Sixteen (seems uncertain).

Tyrone did not believe that the addend increased by three rather than by two. Instead, he probably re-presented each of "five", "six", and "seven", and proceeded to count starting with "fifteen" rather than "fourteen". This is reminiscent of a recurrent error that Piaget and Szeminska (l941) reported observing when children attempted to solve seriation tasks. Piaget argued that these errors indicated that the children did not realize that n objects precede the (n + 1)th position. In other words, they did not include the number n in the number n + 1. This is highly compatible with the inference that neither Jason nor Tyrone had constructed progressive integration operations.

In the same session (15 April 1981), Tyrone constructed an addend-decreasing strategy when sequences of tasks were presented by repeatedly decreasing an addend by one or two (e.g., the sentences "9 + 9 = ", "9 + 8 = ", "9 + 7 = ", "9 + 6 = ", "9 + 4 = "). On 25 May 1981, Tyrone used addend-increasing and -decreasing strategies to solve a sequence of missing addend sentences (e.g., "9 +   = 15", "9 +   = 16", "9 +   = 17", "9 +   = 19", "9 +   = 18", "9 +   = 16", "9 +   = 14"). As with Jason, we infer that he relied on a direct number word linkage between the given sums and then increased or decreased the appropriate addend accordingly.

In March and April 1981, several attempts were made to help Tyrone construct a compensation strategy. All were unsuccessful. In the last of these sessions, on 27 April 1981, Tyrone was told that there were seven cookies altogether under two cloths. He was asked how many he thought were under each cloth. After he had replied three and four he was asked, "Could you make it different?" This question was repeated each time he gave an appropriate answer. His responses, four and three, five and two, one and six, six and one, four and three, and two and four do not reflect successive compensations of the addends.

The teacher then said that there were eight in all. This time Tyrone answered three and five, zero and eight, six and two. The teacher then prompted, "You missed one, you had eight and zero and six and two", without success. Next, the teacher directed Tyrone to place eight marbles in one of two cups, and then to transfer a marble to the empty cup. When asked, Tyrone said that eight marbles were now in one cup and one was in the other. After he corrected himself when the teacher reminded him, "You took one away", he said that there were still eight marbles in all. Aided by the teacher's prompting, he answered correctly on the following two occasions, after he had transferred a marble. However, the next time he transferred a marble from the cup that now contained five to the one which now contained three, he said that four were in one and three were in the other. Like Jason, Tyrone's use of additive strategies was restricted to the addend-increasing and -decreasing strategies. Also, he seemed to construct symbolic coordinations by relying on number word linkages.

SCENETRA

In contrast to both Jason and Tyrone, Scenetra frequently failed to construct thinking strategies while she was in her stage of sequential integration operations. For example, on 6 April 1981, the teacher orally presented the sequence of sentences "5 + 5 = ", "5 + 6 = ", "5 + 7 = ", "5 + 8 = ", "5 + 9 = ", and "5 + 10 = ". Each time, Scenetra wrote the appropriate sentence on a chalkboard and then solved it, independently of the preceding sentence, by counting-on. In the same session, she solved a task in which collections of five and six items were covered by two cloths, independent of the preceding task in which two collections of five items were screened.

There appeared to be just one type of exception to her independent solutions: she would make coordinations if there was the suggestion that items had been added to or removed from a collection. On 6 April 1981, for instance, the following incident occurred immediately after she had failed to use either an addend-increasing or -decreasing strategy. First, the teacher covered six of a row of 14 squares, told Scenetra how many there were in all, and asked her to find out how many were covered. Scenetra made a numerical extension by first counting the eight visible squares and then continuing to 14 while putting up fingers before answering "Six".

T : OK., now close your eyes (lifts the cloth and puts one more square underneath; Scenetra cannot see what he is doing). Now there's fifteen.
S : Seven, you put one more under there.

On 27 April 1981, Scenetra counted-on to find how many cookies in all, after being told that seven were under one cloth and five were under another.

T : Suppose I made this one six (points to the cloth covering five cookies).
S : Thirteen.
T : Suppose I made this one seven (points to the same cloth).
S : Fourteen.

Most impressive of all, on 1 April 1981, she produced the following solution immediately after she had found that 16 squares were left when 5 had been removed from a covered collection of 21.

T : (Puts the five squares back under the cloth).
S : Twenty-one.
T : Now I'm going to take four away (removes four squares).
S : Seventeen.
T : How did you know that?
S : 'Cause the other time you took five away, and then you put one back, and then took away four.

Scenetra usually explained her strategies in terms of putting so many with or taking so many away. In contrast, both Jason and Tyrone usually referred to the preceding task, or spoke of a number going up or down when they explained their use of addend-increasing and -decreasing strategies. This suggests that Scenetra re-presented the action of adding or removing items when she made coordinations. The implied sense of direction in Jason's and Tyrone's explanations indicates that counting acts rather than collections were implicit in the numerical composites constructed when they used strategies.

An extensive investigation of Scenetra's strategies in situations with compensating changes in the addends was also conducted while she was at the stage of sequential integration operations. On 1 April 1981, Scenetra found that there were 11 marbles in all by counting-on after she had been told that seven were in one cup and four were in another. The teacher then transferred a marble from the cup containing seven marbles to the one containing four, and Scenetra said that six and five marbles were now in each cup. However, she again counted-on to find how many there were in all. The next two times a marble was transferred (seven and four marbles and eight and three marbles) she correctly said, without counting, how many were in each cup, and that there were eleven in all. She explained, "'Cause every time you say something, it'll still be eleven". A similar sequence of tasks was presented a week earlier (25 March), but with 16 rather than eleven items in all. Again, she counted to solve the first two tasks but not the third. Both sequences of solutions and her failure to explain why the sum remained unchanged indicate that she abstracted (level 1) recurrent results of counting.

Discussion: Sequential Integration Operations

All of the strategies that the children constructed occurred in the context of carefully sequenced interventions by the teacher. We termed strategies "spontaneous" only because they were alternatives to the strategies that we, as teachers, expected the children to use in that specific context.

The types of additive strategies that Jason and Tyrone used can be classified as addend-increasing or addend-decreasing strategies. These strategies were characterized at the beginning of this chapter without an analysis of the coordinations that are involved in their use. In the case of the addend-increasing strategy, the first assertion was that "one of the addends is decomposed into two parts". This is a possibility at the level of sequential integration operations, with the understanding that it is the figurative content of the numerical composite that is decomposed. Next, "The sum of one of these parts and the other addend is found". If "finding a sum" only means what the child does when finding the sum (i.e., count), then children at the stage of sequential integration operations should be able to do this. The counted items must then be taken together because the partial sum must be added to the other part. Again, the children at the stage of sequential integration operations should be able to do this last part of the strategy. But coordinating the stated sequence of conceptual operations using numerical composites as the material of the operations (as units), rather than what the numerical composites contained, would seem to be beyond the children at this stage. A similar conceptual analysis can be made for the other strategies that the children used.

The behavior of the three children fits this conceptual analysis well. Even in those cases where we termed a strategy "spontaneous", the children relied on number word linkages rather than on coordinations between conceptual operations. In each case, the child either related the sum to a known doubles combination by increasing or decreasing an addend by one, or else increased an addend from "nine" to "ten".

For all three children, the doubles were clearly special. In those rare instances when the children did use a doubles combination, they seemed to rely on a number word linkage. This is indicated by their failure to spontaneously use a doubles combination to find a sum when one of the addends varied from the double by more than one. On the basis of linkage between adjacent number words, they could coordinate an increase or decrease of one to a known fact. A similar explanation holds for the example where an addend was increased from nine to ten. It should be stressed that spontaneous strategies were the exception rather than the rule; the children did not usually relate a sum either to a known doubles combination or to a combination with an addend of ten when they had an opportunity to do so. Furthermore, they did not relate sums to any of the other combinations they had learned.

Progressive Integration Operations

Jason, Tyrone, and Scenetra used the transfer compensation strategy when they were in the stage of progressive integration operations. The children could, for example, use the sentence "12 + 8 = 20" to solve "13 + 7 = ", explaining that they had taken one from the eight and had given it to the twelve. When the children used this strategy, the transferred item could carry the significance of an abstract unit item, and "12" and "8" could signify abstract composite units. They could, therefore, "see" that decreasing eight by one and increasing 12 by the self-same unit were compensating acts because they were one level removed from the individual unit items. In short, the individual unit items could be objects of reflection. There was no indication that any of the three children could use this strategy while they were at the stage of sequential integration operations. This was true even when the teacher actually transferred an item from one collection to the other.

Children who are in the stage of progressive integration operations can apply the integration operation iteratively and construct a sequence of numbers, each included in its successor. This development is used to account for a notable advance in the use of strategies made by both Jason and Tyrone. In the second year of the experiment, 11 sessions were conducted with Jason and Tyrone to help them construct thinking strategies. As will be seen, this also involved helping them reorganize their general arithmetical contexts. Both children eventually differentiated between the contexts of doing arithmetic in class and doing arithmetic with the project staff. In contrast, only five teaching sessions were conducted with Scenetra between December 1981 and March 1982 to investigate her progress in the use of thinking strategies. The majority of her sessions during the second year focused on addition and subtraction algorithms and on her concept of ten. Unlike the other two children, Scenetra did not construct two alternative arithmetical contexts.

JASON

On 15 February 1982, the teacher investigated whether Jason could construct a compensation strategy. Jason first solved the open sentence "19 + 6 = " by counting-on. The session then continued:

T : (Makes 19 + 6 = 25 using felt numerals) Ok, Jason, can you find any more numbers that make twenty-five?
J : Twenty plus five.
T : Twenty plus five, any more?
J : Eighteen plus seven.
T : Eighteen plus seven, any more?
J : Seventeen plus eight.
T : Seventeen plus eight, any more?
J : Sixteen plus eight, Sixteen plus nine, I mean.
T : Keep going.
J : Fifteen plus ten.
T : Keep going.
J : Fourteen plus eleven.
T : Keep going.
J : Thirteen plus twelve.

The most striking feature of Jason's behavior was the seemingly effortless way in which he generated an appropriate sequence of addends. His performance was so smooth that the teacher did not even bother to make the successive sentences using felt numerals. In light of these observations, we infer that for the first time, Jason constructed a local compensation strategy. We call the type of strategy Jason used a transfer compensation strategy. By re-presenting the transfer of an item, Jason could create figural material to which he could progressively apply the integration operation.

The second noticeable advance in Jason's use of strategies in the teaching episode conducted on 15 February 1982 was his iterative use of addend-increasing and decreasing strategies. When he was in the stage of sequential integration operations, he used these strategies only when he recognized a pattern formed by a specific sequence of linked number words. Now, however, he could coordinate two number sequences.

T : (Makes "31 + 6 = 37" using felt numerals) Can you think of some other problems which are like that one, but where you keep the thirty-one the same?
J : No, I can't.
T : What would it be if it was seven instead of six?
J : Thirty-one plus seven equals thirty-thirty-eight.

T : (Makes 31 + 7 = 38 using felt numerals) Can you tell me some more?

J : Thirty-one plus nine is forty.

Jason then continued, giving the sentences "31 plus 10 is 41", . . . , "31 plus 15 is 46". Again, the ease was such that the teacher stopped making the successive sentences with the felt numerals and asked,

T : How far do you think you could keep going doing that?

J : 'Til one hundred.

In view of the striking ease with which Jason used his addend- increasing strategy and his apparent awareness that if an addend is iteratively increased by one, the sum will also iteratively increased by one, it is reasonable to conclude that there was a qualitative change in his use of thinking strategies. The coordinations that he made constitute what we call the iterative added-increasing strategy.

Arithmetical context. During the second year of the teaching experiment, Jason's classroom teacher had attempted to teach him to use standard addition and subtraction algorithms to find the sums and differences of two-digit numbers. Jason had reflected on his experience of doing arithmetic in class and thought of it as an activity in which one attempted to find correct answers by using prescribed methods. He was constantly on the lookout for opportunities to use his inflexible algorithms and would almost always do so if "regrouping" were not involved, even if he was prompted to use the result of solving a previous task. This problem became so acute that great care had to be taken with the selection of sequences of problems: the units part of the first addend was usually eight or nine, so that each of the problems involved carrying or borrowing. However, Jason still used his algorithms quite frequently. For example, on 15 February 1982, the teacher asked:

T : You know twenty plus twenty is forty, what's nineteen plus nineteen?

J : It seems like nineteen plus nineteen is one hundred and twenty- eight.

The speed with which Jason answered indicated that he did not attempt to use the result 20 plus 20 is 40. Instead he probably added by columns (i.e., 9 + 9 and 1 + 1) and put the one of "18" in the hundreds place. Jason also used his algorithm when he could easily have counted. In the same session, for example, he gave 97 as his answer to 31 + 6. He explained that he had added six to both the one and the three of 31. The teacher then instructed him to count, and he counted-on before answering "thirty-seven".

The general arithmetical context that Jason had constructed by reflecting on his classroom experiences greatly hampered the investigation of his construction of thinking strategies. Sometimes the investigation was reduced to the level of seeing whether Jason could relate two tasks when he was explicitly directed to do so. Care had to be taken when inferring the nature of any relationships that he might have constructed. From the beginning of the second year of the teaching experiment (October 1981) until 15 March 1982, many attempts were made to help Jason reconstruct his general arithmetical context. However, these efforts met with little success. From January until March he did not use a single spontaneous thinking strategy.

TYRONE

When Tyrone's strategies were first investigated at the beginning of the second year of the experiment, he appeared to have regressed. He frequently failed to use strategies in situations in which, at the end of the first year, he would have used addend-increasing or -decreasing strategies. The reasons for Tyrone's apparent regression became clear during a teaching session conducted on 15 December 1981. After saying that six plus eight was 14, he explained:

Ty : 'Cause I know the number group, I know the number group is six and eight and four.
T : Did your teacher teach you that?
Ty : (Nods.)
T : What's nine plus eleven?
Ty : Twenty.
T : How did you know that?
Ty : Because of my math book.
T : Fourteen plus eight?
Ty : Twenty-two.
T : How did you know that?
Ty : 'Cause I know the number group, two, four, and eight.

He was not always so successful when he used number groups.

T : What's fourteen take away seven?
Ty : . . . three.

Here, he used the number group three, four, and seven. His use of these groups involved recalling memorized triples and gauging the decade within which the answer would fall. When both addends were two-digit numbers, Tyrone usually attempted to use a standard algorithm. For example, when he was asked how he had solved the expression "17 + 12", Tyrone moved the 17 underneath the 12.

In view of these observations, it would seem that Tyrone's apparent regression in the use of thinking strategies reflected a change in his arithmetical context. As a consequence of doing arithmetic in class during the first quarter of second grade, the possibility of producing quick, efficient solutions by using a known result did not occur to him. For the most part, he attempted to get correct answers by using the prescribed methods and rules he had learned in class. This was illustrated when the teacher investigated whether he could construct an inverse relationship between addition and subtraction (14 December 1981). The teacher placed the sentence "12 - 4 =" directly beneath "8 + 4 = 12" and Tyrone completed it by selecting an 8. He explained, "It's the same, you supposed to use the same numbers on plus and take away". He elaborated, "You put the twelve and eight at the bottom (i.e., 12 - 8 =) and they go backwards". Next, the teacher placed the sentence "20 - 7 = " directly beneath "13 + 7 = 20". Tyrone selected 13 and explained, "They're supposed to go backwards. You put the twenty in front and the thirteen in back". Tyrone's explanations indicate that he used a rule stating that the order of the numerals should be reversed.

During the session conducted on 15 December 1981, we formulated the hypothesis that Tyrone might be able to reorganize his arithmetical context. Consequently, we continued to sequence tasks in the hope that Tyrone would use his addend-increasing and -decreasing strategies. We also urged Tyrone to think of a different way to do the problems. Much to our surprise, he suddenly started using unexpectedly sophisticated strategies. After Tyrone had found the sum of 13 and 6, we changed the sentence "13 + 6 = 19" to "(*)13 + 9 = 19", and Tyrone was asked to change "19". (Whenever we use an incorrect sentence in order to provoke a correction of one of the terms, we mark the sentence by a preceding asterisk.) Tyrone muttered quietly to himself for about 20 seconds and then changed the "19" to "22". He explained:

> Like that was six (changes "9" to "6") and that would be nineteen (points to the "22")--seven plus six would be twenty and eight plus six--eight plus six would be twenty-one and nine plus six would be twenty-two.

The teacher inferred from this explanation that Tyrone coordinated successive increases of an addend by one with successively increasing the sum by one, an iterative addend-increasing strategy. As the solution indicated that Tyrone was also in the process of reconstructing his arithmetical context, the teacher did not pressure him to give a more coherent explanation, but instead tried to be as encouraging as possible. The dialogue continued:

T : So I'm going to change this from thirteen to sixteen (changes "13 + 9 = 22" to "(*)16 + 9 = 22").

Ty : (During a pause of 30 seconds, he whispers) thirteen plus nine is sixteen, fourteen plus ten is seventeen . . . thirteen plus nine . . . (says aloud) thirteen plus nine?

T : Thirteen plus nine was twenty-two, so what's sixteen plus nine?

Ty : (Pause of 14 seconds during which he whispers) sixteen--thirteen plus nine is twenty-two, fourteen plus nine is twenty-three, sixteen plus . . . (changes "(*)16 + 9 = 22" to "16 + 9 = 25").

Tyrone again used an iterative strategy. The teacher then removed the "9" and changed "25" to "27" (i.e., "16 +   = 27").

Ty : Would be . . . (selects 11 and completes the sentence "16 + 11 = 27").

This time, he iteratively increased first the sum and then the addend, illustrating the flexibility of his strategy.

T : (Changes "16 + 11 = 27" to "(*)16 + 11 = 30") What's that got to be? (Points to 11).

Ty : (Whispers) Ten and eleven is twenty-one, eleven and eleven is twenty-two, twelve and eleven is twenty-three, thirteen and eleven is twenty-four, fourteen and eleven is twenty-five, fifteen and eleven is twenty-six, sixteen and eleven is twenty-seven, seventeen and eleven is twenty-eight, eighteen and eleven is twenty-nine, nineteen and eleven (selects 19 and completes the sentence 19 + 11 = 30).

As he did not use the previous result, this strategy is considered to be spontaneous. He was soon able to use his iterative strategy with relative ease.

Next, the teacher placed the felt numeral "20" over the "19" and the numeral "12" over the "11". Tyrone said, "One more . . . " and then changed 30 to 32. He explained, "One more up for this one would be thirty-one, and one more up for this one would be thirty-two". The teacher then investigated whether Tyrone could construct a compensation strategy by increasing one addend and decreasing the other.

19		13		
20	+	12	=	32

Ty : (Whispers) twenty plus twelve is thirty-two, so twenty plus thirteen is thirty-three (his utterances then become indistinct: points to 32).

T : Why's that?

Ty : 'Cause that one went one more up and that one went one more back.

Here, Tyrone used addend-increasing and -decreasing strategies. He constructed the problem in terms of the independent increase and decrease of the addends rather than in terms of the transfer of an item from one collection to the other.

The way in which Tyrone used iterative strategies to solve these tasks indicates that he had made a reorganization of his arithmetical context. He no longer attempted to use his number groups and his inflexible versions of standard algorithms, but instead actively strove to make coordinations. This was the last session conducted with him before the 1981-1982 Christmas vacation. When Tyrone's strategies were investigated in the new year, he again used his iterative strategies with little prompting.

In a teaching episode held on 27 January 1982, Tyrone used a compensation strategy spontaneously, again indicating that he had reorganized his arithmetical context. For example, he selected "24" when presented with the sentence "13 + 11 = ".

T : Why's that? That's right, it is twenty-four.

Ty : 'Cause you put one over there (motions from the "13" to the "11" with his hand), and that would be twelve, and you take one from there.

T : What's twelve plus twelve?

Ty : Twenty-four.

His explanation indicates that he used a transfer compensation strategy, where the transferred item carried the significance of an abstract unit item. Shortly afterwards, he spontaneously used an iterative addend-decreasing strategy to solve the sentence "11 + 14 = ". He related this to the double "14 + 14 = 28" and iteratively decreased the first addend and the sum by one.

The doubles in the low teens seemed to have a special significance for him. In the same session, he spontaneously used the double "13 + 13 = 26" to solve "13 + 15 = ", an iterative addend-increasing strategy. He also used the double "13 + 13 = 26" to solve the next task, "19 + 19 = ". Here, he iteratively increased each addend by one and the sum by two, whispering "thirteen and thirteen is twenty-six, fourteen and fourteen is twenty-eight, . . . , nineteen and nineteen is thirty-eight". We call this an iterative doubles strategy.

Tyrone's most sophisticated solution while he was apparently in the stage of progressive integration operations occurred a week later, on 2 February 1982. He spontaneously related 16 + 14 to 12 + 12 = 24 by first using a transfer compensation strategy, and then solving the equivalent problem 15 + 15 by using his iterative doubles strategy.

SCENETRA

When the strategies that Scenetra constructed during the second year are analyzed, it must be pointed out first that she relied on her algorithms and actively rejected any other method of solving addition and subtraction problems. Second, the possibility of counting did not occur to her once she had constructed her algorithms. Third, ten was a special number for her because she had patterns for ten.

The session conducted on 16 December 1981 was the only one during the second year of the experiment in which Scenetra spontaneously used strategies that were not related to her algorithm for finding sums and differences (cf. 5.37 and 5.38). For example, she explained that she had used a doubles strategy to solve nine plus nine:

S : 'Cause I added eight and eight and got eight and eight is sixteen, I added on two more and then eights are 16-17-18.

This strategy was unusual for her in that it did not involve ten. Two of the other spontaneous strategies she used were:

T : (Makes the sentence "9 + 8 = " using felt numerals) Nine plus eight.
S : . . . seventeen.
T : How did you do that one?
S : 'Cause ten and eight make eighteen, but ten's not there so I said nine and eight, and then it's seventeen.
T : (Makes "12 + 9 = " using felt numerals) Twelve plus nine.
S : Twenty-one.
T : How did you do that one?
S : 'Cause ten comes before eleven does, and twelve is after eleven.

The first was an addend-decreasing strategy, and the second was a transfer compensation strategy. Soon afterwards, she solved the open sentence "9 + 7 = " by relating it to the sentence "10 + 6 = 16". Her spontaneous use of this transfer compensation strategy corroborates the inference that she could use progressive integrations (cf. 5.39).

Discussion: Progressive Integration Operations

Jason's and Tyrone's iterative addend-increasing strategies were both what one might call decomposition strategies. However, "decomposition" implies that, given a number, the child separates it into two other numbers. This does not capture the essence of both children's mental operations. They coordinated two number sequences by iteratively increasing an addend and the sum by one, where each increase carried the significance of an additional counting act.

Both Jason and Tyrone could interpret addition sentences such as "31 + 6 = 37" in terms of progressive integration operations. This inference, which is based on their use of addend-increasing strategies, is also compatible with the analysis of their concepts of ten (cf. Chapter VI). For example, after Jason had given "97" as his answer to "31 + 6 = ", the teacher asked him to count, and Jason counted-on. When the teacher then asked him to find the sum of 31 and 7, Jason took the results of having counted 6 beyond 31 and the result, 37, as given and coordinated counting one more beyond the second addend with one more beyond the sum. Considering his use of iterative strategies, it is reasonable to infer that a counting act served a double function for Jason. For example, "seven" was both the seventh counting act of the sequence he could perform to build up the second addend and the 38th counting act of the sequence of acts he could perform to build up the sum. This double function was indicated in his comment "thirty-one plus seven equals thirty-eight", and by his freely generated but coordinated sequences of second addends and sums.

The explanation of the change in quality from the intuitive addend-increasing strategy to the iterative addend-increasing strategy requires the postulation of a new use of the integration operation--progressive integrations. Jason could create a new unit item by performing a counting act, "seven", and then integrate the units implied by "six" and the additional unit. He maintained a distinction between the first six units and the seventh. In effect, Jason double counted "7 is 38; 8 is 39; 9 is 40; 10 is 41; 11 is 42; 12 is 43; 13 is 44; 14 is 45; 15 is 46", where the constant addend "31" is understood. The words of the number sequences "38-39-40- . . . -46" and "7-8-9- . . . -15" were symbols for progressive integrations that he could carry out. Tyrone's explanation of the iterative addend-increasing strategy he used to relate "(*)13 + 9 = 19" to "13 + 6 = 19" (15 December 1981) is compatible with this analysis.

T : Like that was six (changes 9 to 6) and that would be nineteen (points to the 22 that he placed into the first sentence)--seven plus six would be twenty and eight plus six--eight plus six would be twenty-one and nine plus six would be twenty-two.

"Eight plus six", for example, implied the result of applying the integration operation progressively--six was included in eight. "Eight" was coordinated with 21--one more than 20 (i.e., "seven plus six") which, in turn, was one more than 19, the correspondent of six. Six and 19 were initially taken as given, 7 and 20 were the results of adding one more, 8 and 21 were the results of adding yet another, and 9 and 22 were the results of adding yet another. Each of these added units was included in the two preceding numbers, which themselves were taken as material for further operating.

Progressive integration operations introduced a new element into both Jason's and Tyrone's counting schemes, in that both children could now explicitly double count. This enabled them to construct an open-ended sequence of related addition sentences. An addition or missing addend problem could now imply a family of addition sentences produced by using the iterative addend-increasing strategy.

Tyrone seemed to be on the verge of disembedding a part from a whole, because he could coordinate sequential increases of the first addend of a sum by one with corresponding increases in the sum by one. When he was asked to change "11" in the sentence "(*)16 + 11 = 30", given that he had just solved "16 + = 27", he instead dropped back to a sum that he knew--"10 + 11 = 21"--and sequentially added one to 10, coordinating that with sequentially adding one to 21 until he reached 30. Then he changed "16" to "19". This indicates a dawning awareness of the relation of inclusion. At this point in the experiment, we did in fact infer that Tyrone's use of flexible iterative strategies indicated that he could disembed a part from a whole. If this was so, the teacher reasoned that Tyrone should be able to construct more efficient strategies with ease. In particular, he should become aware of the unidirectional variation of an addend and the sum, and thus anticipate that the sum would increase or decrease by the same unspecified amount that an addend increased or decreased. Once he had this awareness, he should have been able to use, say, 13 + 9 = 22 to solve the sentence "13 + 12 = " by first finding out how much the addend increased and then adding this increase to the known sum.

The teacher attempted to help Tyrone construct this strategy at the end of January 1982 by presenting successive tasks in which an addend was changed by three or four. He then asked Tyrone if he could find out by how much the addend had gone up or down. When he had done so, the teacher asked him what would happen to the sum. On occasion, the teacher varied the sum, and then asked Tyrone about changes in the sum and in one of the addends. Unfortunately, the first two of these sessions, which were conducted on 25 and 26 January 1982, were not completely video-recorded. The teacher noted in his diary that he only needed to ask the prompting questions described above when presenting the first few tasks on 25 January. Tyrone appeared to use the strategies with ease for the remainder of the session.

However, the following day, the teacher again had to give prompts when presenting the first few tasks; it was as if the previous teaching session had not taken place. The teacher concluded that Tyrone used the strategies with relative ease at the end of both sessions because he had inferred what he was supposed to do. In effect, the teacher had trained him to behave as though he was using the operative addend-increasing and -decreasing strategies. It seemed that Tyrone had no reason to find out how much the addend had changed. He did not anticipate that the sum would change by the same amount as the addend. This observation is compatible with the contention that Tyrone had constructed progressive integration operations, but not part-whole operations.

All three children eventually used a transfer compensation strategy. For example, Scenetra found the sum of 9 and 7 by relating it to the sentence "10 + 6 = 16"; Tyrone found the sum of 16 and 14 by relating it to the sum of 15 and 15 (which he then found by using the double "12 + 12 = 24"); and Jason generated a family of sentences after he had solved "19 + 6 = 25" by compensating an increase by one in one addend with a decrease by one in the other addend. The strategies the three children used to find differences were given little attention while they were in the stage of progressive integration operations. This was due in part to the relatively short period of time they stayed in this stage and in part to the need to examine their construction of other concepts and methods. The investigation of the relationships the three children constructed between addition and subtraction tasks while they were in this stage was also deferred for similar reasons. Neither Jason nor Tyrone were given the opportunity to use a previously solved addition or subtraction problem when they were solving what was, for the observer, an inverse subtraction or addition problem. Scenetra did have several such opportunities but, on each occasion, she solved the problems independently.

Part-Whole Operations

Once Jason and Tyrone disembedded a numerical part from a numerical whole, addition and subtraction no longer had a "do something" meaning for them, as Baroody (1982) and Labinowicz (1982) have suggested. Both numerical parts and the numerical whole were "out there" for the children in a specified relation. Psychologically, however, the children still had to do something when they found sums or differences. But the quality of their conceptual activities reflected the children's new awareness of the relation of the parts to the whole.

In the stage of part-whole operations, we were finally able to infer that the children used what we call operative strategies. We use the term "operative" to indicate that the children coordinated arithmetic symbols without involving actual or re-presented counting.

JASON

Jason's iterative addend-increasing strategy evolved into an operative addend-increasing strategy. On 29 March 1982, he produced the following solution several minutes after he had found the sum of 29 and 9:

J : Thirty-nine plus nine is . . . forty-eight.
T : How did you do that one without counting?
J : I don't know.
T : It just came into your head. Did you think at all?
J : I said because twenty-nine plus nine.
T : Because we did twenty-nine plus nine before. You remembered that one?
J : Uh-huh (yes).
T : What did you remember?
J : I remember that it was thirty-eight.

Jason realized that 39 was ten more than 29, and anticipated that the sum of 39 and 9 would be ten more than the sum of 29 and 9. This indicates that he was aware of the unidirectional variation between an addend and the sum. The strategy he used to find 39 + 9 is called the operative addend-increasing strategy.

Jason was absent from school for the two weeks preceding the session conducted with him on 29 March 1982. The teacher realized almost immediately during the session that Jason had made dramatic progress. From the teacher's perspective, it was as though he was teaching a different child. Not only did Jason display more sophisticated additive strategies, he also used sophisticated subtractive strategies. He was asked to find 32 - 6.

J : Twenty-six.
T : How did you do it, can you remember?
J : Uh-huh (yes). Like that, sort of (moves the 2 and the 6 of 32 - 6 together).
T : What do you mean, sort of?
J : Like thirty-two and then just take away three and then take away three more.
T : What did you get when you took away the first three?
J : The first? Thirty.
T : And then if you take away three more, what do you get?
J : Twenty-six.

This was the first time Jason spontaneously used a strategy to find a difference. (What Jason actually did was to take away two and then four.) The teacher then increased the minuend by one, changing 32 to 33. After a slight pause, Jason gave 27 as he explained, "I added another one from that right here", while pointing to the 33. The teacher next increased the subtrahend by one and asked him to find 33 - 7. Jason gave 26 as his answer almost immediately. He also used strategies when the minuend was increased by two (35 - 7) and when the subtrahend was increased by two (35 - 9). The teacher had attempted to confuse Jason by changing first the minuend and then the subtrahend. However, on each occasion, Jason answered promptly and without apparent difficulty. His third performance indicates that he was aware of the unidirectional variation between the minuend and the difference, and the variation in both opposite directions of the subtrahend and the difference. His awareness of these relationships between parts and wholes confirms the inference that he had constructed part-whole operations and could disembed a part from a whole. We call the strategies he used the operative minuend-increasing and -decreasing strategies and the operative subtrahend-increasing and -decreasing strategies.

Arithmetical context. The examples above convey the dramatic change witnessed in Jason's problem-solving behavior. It would, however, be misleading to attribute this change solely to his construction of part-whole operations. He also seemed to have reconstructed his arithmetical context. He actively searched for opportunities to use strategies and did not once attempt to use the algorithms that he had learned in class. A game seemed to develop between Jason and the teacher as the session progressed. The teacher attempted to pose problems that Jason could solve only by counting, and Jason attempted to construct a solution that did not involve counting. Even here, Jason did not resort to his classroom algorithm when he was stymied. Instead, he attempted to estimate or gauge the answer. Jason seemed to have developed what might be called a reflective attitude. He usually repeated the problem to himself and then paused before answering. Thus, when he used a strategy to solve 35 - 9, he said "thirty-five take away nine . . . equals . . . twenty-six". In general, he behaved as though he was searching for quick, nonroutine ways to solve the tasks.

Jason's reorganization of both his concepts of addition and subtraction and his general arithmetical context at about the same time would seem to be more than a coincidence. Jason finally became aware of his own arithmetical capabilities when he reorganized his arithmetical knowledge. His two-week absence from school might have been beneficial, in that he did not find himself in situations that seemed to call for the use of his algorithms. In any event, Jason seemed to have differentiated between the contexts of doing arithmetic in class and doing arithmetic with us. He maintained this distinction for the remaining two months of the teaching experiment and made rapid progress. This session (29 March 1982) was the last in which his thinking strategies to find sums and differences were investigated.

TYRONE

A change in Tyrone's use of local strategies occurred on 8 February 1982 when he was in transition to the stage of part-whole operations. On one occasion, for example, Tyrone had just used his iterative doubles strategy to solve the orally presented problem 23 plus 23 by relating it to 20 plus 20 is 40.

T : What's twenty-one plus twenty-three?
Ty : . . . fourty-four.
T : How did you do that?
Ty : 'Cause I know twenty-three plus twenty-three was forty-six, and you have to take away two, and that would be forty-four.
T : And why do you have to take away two?
Ty : Because it's twenty-two plus twenty-two.
T : But I asked you twenty-one plus twenty-three.
Ty : Because put one over there, and then it would be twenty-two.

He was operating within a thinking strategy context, and now used strategies to solve the few basic addition facts he still did not know. For example:

T : (Makes the sentence "6 + = 15".)
Ty : (Selects 9.)
T : What did your brain say?
Ty : I said six plus eight is fourteen, and I know that six plus nine is fifteen.

Although Tyrone used a variety of strategies in this session, he did not make further tries to use an iterative increasing or decreasing strategy. The teacher attempted to see if he could now use an operative addend-increasing strategy by asking him to solve the orally presented sentence 18 plus 16 immediately after he had found that 14 plus 16 was 30. However, as he spontaneously used a compensation strategy, relating 18 plus 16 to 17 plus 17 is 34, the outcome was inconclusive.

The following day (9 February 1982) the teacher again investigated whether Tyrone could use the operative addend-increasing strategy. To this end, he asked Tyrone to solve the sentence "26 + 19 = " immediately after he had found that "26 + 16 = 42".

Ty : (Selects 45.)
T : How did you do that one so fast?
Ty : How much was this (points to the 19), and it was three more bigger (holds up three fingers) and 43-44-45 (sequentially puts up three fingers).

The teacher then presented the task 26 plus 26 orally immediately after Tyrone had completed the addition sentence "26 + 22 = 48".

Ty : Fifty-four.
T : Why is it fifty-four.?
Ty : How much bigger is that than that (points to the 26 and then the 22?)
T : And how much bigger would it be?
Ty : (Simultaneously puts up four fingers) Four.
T : So . . .
Ty : It's fifty-four.

Tyrone seemed to anticipate that the addend and the sum would vary together, but failed to count-on from the known sum. As the teacher had not attempted to help him construct these kinds of strategies for two weeks (since 27 January), it is unlikely that he merely remembered a prescribed method. Three more pieces of evidence support this contention. First, Tyrone did not use these strategies on 27 January until he was prompted to "do this one another way". Second, he seemed to be operating in a strategy context rather than in what might be called a prescribed method context during this session. Immediately after he had produced the solutions described above, he related 26 plus 23 to the double "26 + 26 = 52", and "17 + = 35" to the sentence "17 + 14 = 31". Third, and most important, Tyrone demonstrated that he could use the operative addend-increasing and-decreasing strategies flexibly. During the next teaching session in which his strategies were investigated (22 February), the teacher changed "9" to "19" in 38 + 9 = 47 and asked Tyrone to find the sum. Tyrone changed the 47 to 57, explaining, "'Cause nineteen is ten bigger than nine!"

In a session on 30 March 1982, Tyrone demonstrated that he could use operative minuend and subtrahend strategies. The first task posed in this session was the sentence "43 - 8 = ".

Ty : (Completes 43 - 8 by selecting 35.)
T : (Changes "43 - 8 = 35" to "(*)44 - 8 = 35") What would it be if this was fourty-four?
Ty : (Changes "(*)44 - 8 = 35" to "44 - 8 = 36".)
T : And if this stayed at 35, what would it be? (Changes "36" back to "35".)

Ty : (Changes "8" to "9".)
T : (Changes "44 - 9 = 35" to "(*)44 - 11 = 35") What would that be?
Ty : (Changes "(*)44 - 11 = 35" to "44 - 11 = 33".)

Tyrone could use his local strategies for finding differences flexibly.

It might be argued that he did not use strategies in the last protocol, but instead solved the problems independently by using a classroom subtraction algorithm. However, his attempts to solve the following problems indicate that he was operating in a strategy context. The teacher changed the sentence "44 - 11 = 33" to "(*)46 - 13 = 33", and Tyrone gave first 35 and then 31 as his answers. He could not coordinate minuend-increasing and subtrahend-increasing strategies. The teacher then placed the sentence "45 - 12 = " between "44 - 11 = 33" and "46 - 13 = 33" and Tyrone replied, "thirty-four". Again, Tyrone did not coordinate the two strategies. He focused on the increase in the minuend from 43 to 44, and increased the difference accordingly.

At this point in the session, Tyrone realized that he did not really understand what he was doing--he could give two alternative answers, depending on which change he focused on. His following attempts to resolve the conflict were independently executed.

T : Do you want some multiplication problems?
Ty : No (motions for the teacher to leave the subtraction sentences). 45-44- . . . -33 (sequentially puts up fingers), it's the same thing (he solved 46-13).
T : Do you know why it's the same thing?
Ty : (Shakes his head.)
T : What would fourty-five take away twelve be?
Ty : 44-43- . . . -33 (sequentially puts up fingers).
T : They're all thirty-three.
Ty : Why?

Tyrone rejected the option of starting another activity and instead spontaneously counted backward to find one of the differences. This, coupled with wondering why they were all the same, indicates an explicit awareness that 11 was part of 44 as well as was 33. What he was yet to understand was that an increase of the whole and one of the parts by the same amount left the other part unchanged. His persistent behavior was not unusual; it had become a characteristic of his arithmetical activity. On other occasions he told the teacher, "You don't help me now", when the teacher attempted to intervene because he thought that Tyrone was having difficulties.

Perspectives on the Case Studies

Arithmetical Context

Scenetra's case study contrasts sharply with those of Jason and Tyrone. Unlike Jason and Tyrone, Scenetra did not reorganize her general arithmetical context and differentiate between the context of doing arithmetic in class and that of doing arithmetic with us. She searched for opportunities to use her algorithms and, in general, thought of arithmetic as an activity in which one used prescribed methods. Another difference was that Jason and Tyrone often re-presented sequences of counting acts when they expressed numbers. Scenetra, on the other hand, always seemed to re-present collections of items.

A final important difference between these children during the final months of the experiment was the way in which they reacted when things went wrong. Tyrone's independence, his desire to understand, and the way in which he tried to think things through for himself have already been documented. Jason displayed these same characteristics, though to a lesser extent. He did not try to infer how the teacher expected him to behave, nor did he merely strive to produce correct answers. Instead, he attempted to solve the problems he constructed by modifying his methods, and did not become upset or frustrated if he did not succeed immediately. Like Tyrone, he was persistent and could cope with failure. Both children were very easy to work with. This was not the case, however, with Scenetra. She often became upset and resentful when things did not work out immediately, frequently blaming the teacher as the cause of her unpleasant experience. She readily gave up and took her failure very personally. In Wertime's (1979) terminology, she had a limited courage span. Further, she was far more dependent on the teacher for assistance than the others and frequently had to be cajoled and enticed to continue working. In many respects, she did not seem to regard the problems she created as her own; it was as if they were, for her, obstacles which the teacher placed in her path.

Thinking Strategies and Integration Operations

It was possible to link the use of various kinds of thinking strategies to the construction of increasingly sophisticated concepts of addition and subtraction. However, two important caveats are in order. First, a particular concept of addition or subtraction does not guarantee the use of a particular type of thinking strategy. These concepts are best thought of as cognitive correlates. If the children regarded arithmetic as a rule-governed activity or as an activity in which one uses prescribed methods, they did not use thinking strategies spontaneously. We found that it was crucial to consider their arithmetical contexts as well as their addition and subtraction concepts when accounting for their use or nonuse of a particular kind of strategy.

Second, it is not claimed that the thinking strategies observed constitute a complete list of the various kinds of strategies a child might use. In fact, no list of strategies can ever be complete. There is always the possibility that a child will construct a thinking strategy or coordinate strategies in a novel way that he or she has used previously. Having acknowledged the creativity with which children construct strategies, the framework of increasingly sophisticated concepts can be used to develop explanations of innovative observations.

Thinking Strategies and the Basic Facts

The thinking strategies Tyrone and Jason used at the stage of part-whole operations are compatible with the strategies to find basic facts that were elaborated at the beginning of the chapter. This observation is revealing, because the strategies that we observed at the stage of part-whole operations were used to find sums and differences beyond the range of the basic facts. This suggests that thinking strategies characterized by other researchers do require the construction of part-whole operations, a suggestion that finds corroboration in the work of Brownell (1928) and Ilg and Ames (1951). Brownell (l928) observed five methods that he claimed emerged in developmental sequence.

1. Counting (e.g., solving 4 + 3 by counting "1-2-3-4-5-6-7").
2. Partially counting or counting-on (e.g., solving 4 + 3 by counting-on "4-5-6-7").
3. Grouping (e.g., solving 4 + 3 by breaking up the second addend, "4 and 2 is 6 and one is 7").
4. Multiplication and conversion (e.g., solving 4 + 3 by relating it to a known combination such as 4 + 4, 5 + 2).
5. Meaningful habituation.

Brownell's findings are compatible with those of Ilg and Ames (1951), who interviewed 30 children at half-yearly intervals, from the age of five until the age of nine. They reported the following "developmental gradient" in children's methods for finding sums: counting, counting-on, and thinking strategies. They also identified two levels of complexity in children's use of thinking strategies to find sums.

1. "Figure it out", "think it out in your head": 7-8 years. Breaks harder ones down into simple combinations: 18 + 5 = 19 + 4 = 20 + 3 = 23: 7 years.
2. Same thing but more complex: 8 years. 8 + 5 = 13; because 7 + 5 = 12+ one more = 13; 9 + 6 = I can always tell 10 + 6, 9 is one less

= 15; 6 + 8 = take 1 from 6 and make 8 into 9, 9 + 5 = 14; 7 + 6 = 7 + 7 and then subtract 1. (p. 8)

The strategy of breaking harder ones down into simple combinations corresponds to Brownell's methods of grouping. According to Ilg and Ames, this strategy emerges before the more complex strategies that correspond to Brownell's methods of multiplication and conversion.

Without our careful interventions, we would not have observed the intuitive strategies when the children were in the stage of sequential integration operations. Consequently, that stage would seem to correspond to Brownell's counting-on. The local iterative strategies were also a product of our interventions and were not discussed by either Brownell or Ilg and Ames. The more sophisticated strategies at the stage of part-whole operations correspond to grouping and multiplication and conversion. But we do not claim any perfect correspondence for several reasons. It is possible for thinking strategies to emerge first for numbers with small numerosity, say, less than 15; or just the opposite may be true. Children might construct thinking strategies for numbers whose numerosities are in the decades and then use the strategies with numbers of lesser numerosity. Both scenarios are quite feasible, and are related to a child's arithmetical context. If the child learns the basic facts without using strategies, the latter scenario would be more plausible and is, in fact, what happened in the case of the three children with whom we worked.

Jason, Tyrone, and Scenetra learned most of their basic facts before we observed them using thinking strategies consistently. Jason had done so by January 1982, when he was in the stage of sequential integration operations. Since he had constructed only the intuitive increasing and decreasing strategies and did not use them spontaneously, it cannot be claimed that strategies facilitated his learning of these facts. Instead, he probably learned the facts while working on them in class and using his algorithms to solve two-digit addition and subtraction problems. Scenetra also learned the basic addition facts while she was engaged in this kind of activity. By the middle of February 1982, she did not have to count when she used her algorithms, demonstrating that she had learned both addition and subtraction facts. It will be recalled that she did not use a single thinking strategy spontaneously during January and February of 1982.

As a result of classroom instruction during his first quarter in second grade, Tyrone used what he called number groups to solve basic addition facts in December 1981. These were associated triples such as 2, 4, and 6 or 3, 5, and 8. Since he did not use thinking strategies spontaneously until he reorganized his general arithmetical context in January 1982, it would seem that strategies contributed little, if anything, to his learning of these facts.

Even though we have observed that children can and do learn their basic facts without using thinking strategies, one can argue that children might find learning the basic facts more enjoyable if they are encouraged to use thinking strategies. Moreover, they might learn them in a quite different way, as Brownell (1945) has suggested.

> Activities and experiences containing the new fact 7 + 5 = 12 are multiplied. Furthermore, the child is not left at the primitive level of counting as the only means of understanding the relationships. Instead, he is soon shown how to complete the first number (7) to 10 by taking from the second number (5), and thus to translate the new fact into a familiar one (10 + 2 = 12). (p. 24)

Stressing relationships among the basic facts is consistent with what we take to be the primary reason for teaching thinking strategies. They can contribute to the children's understanding of what it means to do arithmetic.

Thinking Strategies and the Construction of Part-Whole Operations

In our teaching episodes, emphasizing local thinking strategies seemed to facilitate the construction of part-whole operations for numbers whose numerosities were in the decades. Tyrone was in the stage of progressive integration operations at the beginning of the second year of the experiment, and reached the stage of part-whole operations sometime during March of 1982. In the latter part of January, the teacher had attempted to help him construct the operative addend-increasing and -decreasing strategies. Successive tasks were presented by changing an addend by three or four. The teacher asked prompting questions when he presented the first few tasks, and Tyrone soon appeared to use both strategies with ease. However, on the basis of Tyrone's performance the following day, the teacher concluded that he had trained Tyrone to behave as though he was using these strategies.

At the end of the first week of February, the teacher again presented successive addition tasks by changing an addend by three or four. This time, Tyrone immediately used local non-iterative addend-increasing and -decreasing strategies without prompting. His explanations also indicated that he was aware of what he was doing; he was not merely attempting to behave appropriately. The teacher inferred that Tyrone had constructed the part-whole operations, but in retrospect that was problematical (cf. 4.35-4.37). Tyrone had made progress, but he was still using the results of an immediately solved problem to solve his current problem. By 9 March 1982, part-whole operations were explicitly displayed (cf. 4.38).

Tyrone's construction of part-whole operations was based on his experiences of constructing and using local thinking strategies. In particular, the episodes in which the teacher had attempted to help him construct operative addend-increasing and -decreasing strategies may have been particularly significant to him.

The observation of delays between local and general conceptual reorganizations is an especially important one. When a child makes a local reorganization, he or she initially constructs the problem in terms of current concepts of addition and subtraction and then reorganizes the concepts while attempting to solve the problem. In doing so, the child goes beyond current concepts and procedures and reorganizes his or her activity at a higher level in this problem-specific situation. However, the reorganization is local and only temporary. To make a general reorganization of current concepts, the child has to interiorize particular features of the local reorganization. The lag between the local and general reorganizations suggests that the local reorganizations serve in the adaptation of currently held concepts.

It would seem that Tyrone made general reorganizations between teaching episodes. Similar delays were also observed between Jason's local and general reorganizations. At the beginning of the second year of the experiment, in December 1981, Jason was in the stage of sequential integration operations. The first indications that he could make progressive integrations were observed on 15 February 1982. Three weeks earlier, on 26 January 1982, the teacher investigated whether he could construct a transfer compensation strategy by transferring a block from one row of blocks to another. During this session, Jason experienced conflict between two answers, one resulting from the use of a thinking strategy. Jason again worked with blocks a week later, on 1 February 1982. In this session, he could explain why 13 + 8 and 12 + 9 both equaled 21 after he had solved both tasks. However, he did not anticipate the equality before task solution. Jason was absent from school for the following two weeks. In the next teaching session, conducted on 15 February 1982, he was asked to find more numbers which made 25 after he had solved 19 + 6 = . He immediately generated a sequence of sentences with apparent ease by using a compensation strategy.

The first indications that Jason had constructed part-whole operations were also made immediately after he returned from a two-week absence from school. In the last session before his absence (15 March 1982) the teacher investigated both his thinking strategies and the flexibility of his operative counting schemes. Jason appeared to make several local reorganizations, but frequently experienced difficulty when he attempted to solve problems. In the first session conducted after his absence (29 March 1982), Jason demonstrated that he had made considerable advances. The indicators that he had constructed part-whole operations are documented in paragraph 6.50.

From Jason's and Tyrone's case studies, it can be argued that experiences involving the construction and use of thinking strategies can serve as the material from which children abstract when reorganizing their concepts of addition and subtraction. Their conceptual reorganizations were indicated by novel uses of counting (e.g., counting-down-to to solve subtraction problems) as well as by the use of novel thinking strategies.

Goals for Teaching Thinking Strategies

The contention that children should be encouraged to use thinking strategies has been debated for over fifty years. Early protagonists addressed the question from differing psychological and pedagogical viewpoints, the two most prominent being the connectionist and drill theory perspective and the meaning theory perspective. The meaning theorists, Brownell (1928, 1935), Swenson (1949), and Thiele (1938) supported the contention forcefully, while the connectionist Thorndike (1922) and the drill theorists Knight (1930) and Smith (1921) had considerable reservations. Each side, given certain psychological assumptions, regarded its own position as rational and the opposition's as irrational, and interpreted the empirical findings to support its stand.

In recent years, interest in the teaching of thinking strategies was revived. A lively interchange in the Journal for Research in Mathematics Education indicates that the issue was still far from settled (Cifarelli & Wheatley, 1979a, 1979b; Rathmell, 1979; Steffe, 1979; Thornton, 1978, 1979). For the most part, the analyses of more contemporary researchers and pedagogues were conducted, intentionally or not, within either the meaning theory or connectionist paradigms. Rathmell (1978) and Thornton (1978), for example, reiterated many of the arguments of the earlier meaning theorists. Moreover, like their predecessors, the current researchers offered different interpretations of the empirical evidence. Both Rathmell (l978) and Cifarelli and Wheatley (1978b) cite the results of Brownell and Chazal's (1935) study to support their divergent positions.

The failure of both sides of the debate to extend the analyses of the early protagonists suggests that research on thinking strategies was no longer in a progressive phase (Lakatos, 1970). A similar conclusion is reached if one applies Laudan's (1977) more liberal criteria. The lack of progress was in part the result of restricting the investigation of thinking strategies to the learning of the basic facts for addition and subtraction. This was a particularly unfortunate restriction, because it masked far more profound reasons for stressing thinking strategies in school arithmetic. We found the children's construction of thinking strategies was inextricably connected to their arithmetical contexts. In particular, they rarely used spontaneous thinking strategies if they thought that arithmetic was a rule-governed activity in which one attempts to use prescribed methods.

The analysis of the children's arithmetical contexts, which is a new feature in the investigation of thinking strategies, has important pedagogical implications. The two children who reorganized their arithmetical contexts and searched for opportunities to relate tasks made more rapid progress than the child who did not. This suggests that the practice of helping children construct thinking strategies should be viewed as an end in itself--the goal is for children to use a variety of strategies spontaneously which, in turn, contributes to the development of part-whole operations. In contrast, previous advocates of the teaching of thinking strategies regarded them only as a means to an end and the goal was to learn the basic facts rather than part-whole operations. Our findings indicate that the role that thinking strategies could play in the elementary school curriculum should be radically revised. By helping children construct thinking strategies once they reach the abstract stage, the teacher can simultaneously help them become aware of their developed arithmetical capabilities. This dawning awareness represents an understanding of the self doing arithmetic. As Wertime (l979) said in his analysis of the activity of attempting to solve problems, "the problems which we tackle are deeply involved with our self-esteem" (p. 193). "Thus we might say: a problem is, to some extent, a project for the future we commit ourselves to by an act of will. This means by implication that a problem entails risk" (p. 192). In other words, "a problem, once realized, and once pursued, no matter how little, has become a part of us" (p. 196). As we have seen in the case studies, Scenetra never seemed to fully accept her problems; she seemed to distance herself from them and to view them as externally imposed obstacles. Consequently, she readily gave up. In general, if students "lack persistence, it is not because they are lazy, or cowardly, or docile; it is much rather because they have never had a knowledge of their persistence revealed to them" (Wertime, 1979, p. 195). By helping young children construct thinking strategies, the teacher can help them develop some of the attitudes that characterize the activity of successful problem-solvers.

Chapter IX

Modifications of the Counting Scheme

Leslie P. Steffe

Children's mathematics encompasses the evolving schemes of action and operation of children. We emphasize "evolving", because children's mathematics is not static; it includes the mathematics that children construct under the influence of adult teaching. The children's mathematics that we specified in the preceding chapters is the result of our *retrospective* interpretations of the language and actions of the six involved children, using the schemes we could infer. Some of their mathematics was not known to us before the teaching experiment and its specification was the primary purpose for doing the experiment.

Predicting Modifications of the Counting Scheme

At the beginning of the teaching experiment, it was difficult to predict what modifications the children might make in their counting schemes. One of our critical decisions was made in the preliminary interviews, when we classified Brenda, Tarus, and James as counters of perceptual unit items and Tyrone, Scenetra, and Jason as counters of motor unit items. Although the observations we made (cf. 1.02, 2.01, 3.01, 4.01, 5.01, and 6.01) might seem to be insignificant, the counting types model allowed us to "see" a vital difference that was manifest in the progress the children made over the duration of the teaching experiment. The independent construction of motor unit items by Tyrone, Scenetra, and Jason was a forerunner of their construction of the numerical operation of integration and the systems of integration that followed--sequential integration operations, progressive integration operations, and part-whole operations. On the other hand, the inability of Brenda, Tarus, and James to count anything but perceptual unit items signaled a long figurative stage in the development of their counting schemes.

These differences are especially dramatic when considering that we intentionally did not select first-grade children who were counters of abstract unit items for participation in the teaching experiment. We would expect these children to make even greater progress than Tyrone, Scenetra, and Jason did (cf. Thompson, 1982). There are *three* major categories of six-year-old children, then, with respect to the development of the counting scheme: children who are in the perceptual stage, children in the figurative stage, and children in the stage of sequential integrations. These categories can be used by teachers to anticipate the cognitive constructions of six-year-old children for as long as a two-year period.

When we started teaching the children, we had a limited understanding of what we could do to facilitate modifications of their counting schemes. In all cases, but especially for Brenda, Tarus, and James, it was critical that we decentered and separated our knowledge from the children's knowledge because we found that we could not cause the children to change or not to change in a particular way. For example, in spite of our efforts, neither Brenda, Tarus, nor James gave numerical meaning to number words. Although it is legitimate to ask whether what we did constrained these children in their efforts to construct the integration operation, it is important to point out that Tyrone, Scenetra, and Jason did construct it before they left the first grade. We cannot say that the work we did with the latter three children *caused* them to construct the integration operation, any more than we can say the work we did with the former three children *constrained* their efforts to construct it. All we can say is that the tasks we posed were designed to challenge the involved child while being within the realm of a possible solution.

Whenever we felt we had understood the mathematical knowledge of a particular child in a teaching episode, we formulated hypotheses about how the child might modify his or her currently available counting schemes under our guidance. These hypotheses constituted a model of what Vygotsky (1956) has called the child's zone of potential development--that which the child is capable of learning with the help of a teacher. Such a model can never be uniquely specified, if for no other reason than that there is more than one direction in which a teacher might decide to take a child. The hypotheses we formulated in the teaching experiment are implicit in the specification of children's mathematics in the preceding chapters but there are no exact correspondences.

After formulating a particular hypothesis, we tested it on the spot by presenting a problem situation. We cannot stress enough that our interactive communication with the children, along with their problem solutions, constituted the context for observation in the teaching episodes. Each teaching episode and interview took its own course as the teacher formulated and tested hypotheses concerning the children's counting schemes. For example, in paragraphs 1.02 and 1.03 of Chapter II, the goal of the interviewer was to find the most sophisticated unit item that Brenda could create and count. To achieve the goal, the interviewer tested the hypothesis that Brenda did not generate the intention to count hidden as well as visible squares. Four of seven squares were hidden, and Brenda uncovered two of the four when attempting to count the visible squares. The interviewer then said, "OK, I'll show you two of them", and folded the cloth covering the four hidden squares to reveal the two Brenda had counted. The interviewer then said, "There's two more under here". More blatant hints could hardly have been given. In other words, the interviewer went as far as possible with indirect suggestions that Brenda was to count the hidden as well as the visible items. But still Brenda did not count the hidden items.

We could only infer that Brenda had indeed interpreted the message that she was to count the visible and hidden items, because she did try to uncover the hidden squares to count them and eventually counted the hidden squares that were revealed. That she was not able to count the squares while they were hidden indicated to us that she could not act on the message; she could not create alternative sensory items as substitute countable items. After the problem-solving attempt, we made the decision that Brenda was a counter of perceptual unit items, a decision that was confirmed over the duration of the teaching experiment.

Mathematical Learning

To explain how Brenda made progress to the figurative stage of her counting scheme, we isolated modifications that she made in the first part of her scheme. Such modifications are part of mathematical learning. In essence, mathematical learning is based on Piaget's notion of assimilation and accommodation in the context of schemes. At a conference on cognitive studies and curriculum development held at Cornell University in 1964, Piaget stated,

> The fundamental relation involved in all . . . learning is not association. . . . I think that the fundamental relation is one of assimilation . . . the integration of any sort of reality into a structure . . . which seems to me to be the fundamental relation from the point of view of pedagogical or didactic applications. (p. 18)

Assimilation can manifest the results of learning as well as precede learning, but it cannot produce those results. Mathematical learning consists in the *adaptations* that children make as a result of their experiences. In other words, the *accommodations* of current schemes that serve in neutralizing perturbations account for learning.

Over the course of the teaching experiment, two basic types of accommodations were isolated--functional and metamorphic. A *functional accommodation* of a counting scheme is any modification as a result of reflective abstraction that occurs in the context of using the scheme. The functional accommodations are called procedural, engendering, and retrospective.

Procedural accommodations are essentially of two types--those arising as a result of reflective abstraction using conceptual elements or operations internal to a counting scheme and those arising as a result of reflective abstraction using conceptual elements or operations external as well as internal to the scheme. In each type there can be a modification of the activity of counting or a novel way to view the results of counting. In either case, a modification of the first part of the scheme follows.

The engendering accommodations are also of two types--those involving a modification of the first part of a counting scheme prior to the activity and those that are procedural. For a functional accommodation to be engendering, it must occur independently, involve reflective abstraction using conceptual elements or operations external as well as internal to a counting scheme, lead to further accommodations, and involve or lead to a structural reorganization. Retrospective accommodations are procedural, occur independently, and involve using conceptual elements constructed in an earlier application of a counting scheme.

Modifications of the counting scheme as a result of reflective abstraction that occur independently but not in any particular application of the scheme are called *metamorphic* accommodations. They too were involved in the transitions from one stage of the counting scheme to the next, starting with the figurative counting scheme. The transition from the perceptual to the figurative stage involved an engendering accommodation.

How these types of accommodations were linked to our models of the children's zones of potential development are illustrated in the following sections. We start with the perceptual stage. The first example is taken from an interview with James, conducted at the beginning of the experiment (cf. 3.05, Chapter II). It illustrates what we found to be a common occurrence--a child might make what seemed to be a modification of a scheme but, in retrospect, was only temporary and could not be classified as an accommodation.

The Perceptual Stage

Temporary Modifications

Motor unit items. In paragraph 3.05 of Chapter II, we pointed out that, after James counted five marbles in a cup (three other visible marbles were lying by the cup), the interviewer placed his hand over the cup in an attempt to test the hypothesis that James was a counter of perceptual unit items. From the dialogue in the protocol, we can see that James intended to count all of the marbles, because he initially pointed to the interviewer's fingers and started to count them as perceptual replacements for the marbles. To discourage James from counting his fingers (the interviewer already knew that James could create and count perceptual replacements), the interviewer removed his hand from the cup. James then immediately started to count the marbles in the cup. The interviewer took the cup from James and exclaimed, "Don't count them! Don't count my fingers either!", to provide a critical test of the most advanced item James could create and count. Clearly, James was actively involved in attempting to count the marbles, and we inferred that he understood what he was to do. James then made what seemed to be a major modification of his counting scheme--he pointed sequentially in one place over the aperture of the cup, synchronously with uttering "one, two, three, four, five", and went on counting the visible marbles, "six, seven, eight", pointing to each in turn.

Although we could look to the interviewer's actions for what caused James to make this modification, there was nothing to suggest to James that he was to point over the aperture of the cup, creating experiential countable items in the kinesthetic channel rather than in the visual channel. The interviewer did everything he could to limit James's search for countable items to channels other than the visual channel, but he could not cause James to turn to his kinesthetic channel. For the modification to occur, it was necessary that James actively search for countable items and find none immediately available. This in turn led him to isolate the pointing acts involved in counting visual perceptual items and take them as countable--a level 1 abstraction.

James experienced the perturbation created by having no perceptual items to count in the context of interactive communication with the interviewer. Eventually, the usual response of his counting scheme--coordinating visual perceptual items with his number word sequence--was constrained. His goal was to specify a collection but he had no way to reach that goal. This is compatible with what Polya (1962) meant when he stated that to have a problem means "to search consciously for some action appropriate to attain a clearly conceived, but not immediately attainable, aim" (p. 117). It is only compatible because we believe that James did not *consciously* search for alternative countable items. Although there is no question that he engaged in search activity, from James's point of view, he simply counted the marbles, and seemed only momentarily aware that he had counted his pointing acts.

Our assertion that James was not aware of solving a problem and creating a novel countable item is justified because we did not observe James do anything similar in the teaching episodes during March, April, and May. Nevertheless, we now had a good reason to include motor unit items in our model of James's zone of potential development. We believe that the elements of a child's zone of potential development must be, at least temporarily, constructed by the child and represent possible advances in currently available schemes. The job of the teacher is to help the child abstract these items of knowledge from his or her activity, and to reorganize the child's current knowledge, in a modification of old schemes, to include the novel item. In order to help the child make a further abstraction (accommodation), the teacher must have a model such as we have presented in the preceding chapters that indicates *where the child might go*.

Perceptual replacements. The perceptual replacements made by Brenda and James (cf. 1.04 and 3.03) also qualify as temporary modifications. They occurred fortuitously in the children's visual field as they searched for perceptual items to count. It is one thing for children accidentally to find perceptual items to count, and quite another intentionally to create sensory motor items as substitutes for hidden perceptual items. The latter situation involves a more or less permanent modification of the counting scheme that we have isolated as the figurative stage.

Figural patterns and figural collections. The figural items that Tarus and James (cf. 2.03 and 3.04) created and counted occurred in quite different situations. Tarus's counting scheme had been activated in an immediately preceding task, when he counted the elements of two visible spatial patterns. Before he counted the elements of the two patterns, they had been hidden to test the hypothesis that Tarus could re-present spatial patterns and count their elements. After they were hidden, he seemed to re-present the patterns, but they did not activate his counting scheme. They were then uncovered and he was allowed to count them. In doing so, he apparently isolated counting as being relevant (a level 1 abstraction) because, in the immediately succeeding task, he counted the elements of two spatial patterns *after* they were hidden. However, spatial patterns did not become an assimilatory structure of his counting scheme at this time, even where he could recognize them (cf. 2.26). The apparent progress was only transitory. Nevertheless, we had reason to include the re-presentation of spatial patterns within our model of his zone of potential development of his counting scheme.

Spatial patterns were not involved in the example of James's creation of figural unit items. After counting four visible marbles, he attempted to continue counting the remaining hidden marbles. Since he pointed to specific places on the interviewer's hand while counting, we had good reason to include the creation of figural unit items in our model of James's zone of potential development. It seemed to be important for James to first count a homogeneous collection of perceptual unit items before he could continue on, counting figural unit items of the same kind. Our goal for him was to be able to start his count with figural unit items, which would necessitate the re-presentation of perceptual items prior to counting. We also had reason to include re-presentation of spatial patterns in our model of James's zone of potential development (cf. 3.21). In Brenda's case, we were limited to including recognition of spatial patterns.

Procedural Accommodations

All the children established connections between finger patterns or spatial patterns and number words by counting the elements of the patterns (cf. Chapter V, Discussion of Brenda's Case Study). If a child counts the elements of a pattern, say, "1-2-3", connecting the specified collection of items with the last number word said, that is an act of reflective abstraction--what Piaget (1980) calls a pseudo-empirical abstraction.

> Reflective abstraction . . . in its elementary forms, is accessible to the subject only when it is embodied in external objects . . . the embodiment is merely a matter of temporary characteristics, introduced and imposed upon the objects by the subject himself. (p. 92)

Counting can be curtailed because the pattern embodies its results. The pattern provides an opportunity for the child to construct a dual meaning of a number word--unitary and, at the same time, composite--because the elements of the pattern seem to co-occur. The pattern provides an "object" for reflection and abstraction without which the connection might not be made. If a child isolates a pattern in his or her visual field on some future occasion, the assimilation could lead the child to utter the number word previously connected to the pattern without any intervening counting activity. This procedural accommodation was important for the engendering accommodations that propelled the children to the figurative stage of their counting schemes.

This completes the discussion of our models for the zones of potential development for Brenda, Tarus, and James at the beginning of the teaching experiment, when they were in rather early perceptual stages. Although our model for Brenda contained fewer elements than those for Tarus and James, we posed many of the same tasks to her in a search for elements we could use to upgrade her model. From her case study, we see that our search was in vain, at least in terms of spatial patterns. We now examine a different type of accommodation made by these three children while they were in their perceptual stages.

Engendering Accommodations

In paragraph 2.06, we see that Tarus introduced what we took as a novelty in the assimilatory structures of his counting scheme. Finger patterns were not included in our model of his zone of potential development, and his use of them was a surprise to us. In retrospect, we should have been more sensitive, because there was one undocumented teaching episode in which Tarus did try to use finger patterns. Nevertheless, it seemed to occur quite abruptly, and did not appear as a result of carefully sequenced tasks (as his counting the elements of hidden spatial patterns did, cf. 2.03). This was a permanent modification that Tarus spontaneously introduced, and it led to further modifications.

Two features of Tarus's accommodation were vital in his progress. First, he was able to re-present his available perceptual finger patterns (cf. 2.28 and Perspectives on the Case Studies in Chapter V), and second, he counted his fingers as perceptual items to *complete*, in perception and action, the finger patterns he had previously re-presented. While he was in his motor period, he continued to re-present finger patterns before he counted the acts of putting up fingers. In fact, counting to complete his figural finger patterns by sequentially putting up fingers led to his isolation of the motor acts of putting up fingers as countable items and to his motor period (cf. 2.09-2.12).

Both James (cf. 3.22 and 3.26) and, to a lesser extent, Brenda (cf. 1.05, 1.27, and 1.28) independently introduced their finger patterns in a search for perceptual items to count. However, Brenda's use of her finger patterns could have been a temporary modification, like her perceptual replacements (cf. 1.05). In spite of her initial use of them as perceptual preconcepts, her use of finger patterns proved to be an engendering accommodation and served a primary role in her future accommodations of her counting scheme (cf. 1.29-1.31). There was nothing about her perceptual finger patterns by themselves that would serve as an engendering accommodation. But combined with re-presentation, they became crucial assimilatory structures of her counting scheme. James's case was similar, although he could re-present a wider variety of patterns than Brenda.

Isolated Procedural Accommodations

Tarus developed spatio-motor patterns (cf. *Spatial Patterns*, Chapter I) while he was in his perceptual stage (cf. 2.05 and 2.28). We then thought that re-presentation of spatial patterns had become an assimilatory function of his counting scheme. However, it turned out that his spatio-motor patterns were restricted to the situations from which they were abstracted; hidden spatial patterns. Destroying the patterns led to his use of his more available finger patterns (cf. 2.28), which presented a dilemma for us, because spatio-motor patterns were definitely included in our model of Tarus's zone of potential development at the time. Because of our observation that Tarus could re-present spatial patterns in the preliminary interviews, we felt that our teaching was in harmony with his re-presentations of spatial patterns. In retrospect, however, we now believe that Tarus did not re-present spatial patterns when he constructed spatio-motor patterns. Consequently, the spatio-motor patterns proved to be not engendering; they were isolated procedural accommodations.

Upon re-evaluating our teaching methods, a possible reason why Tarus's spatio-motor patterns were isolated could be our decision to emphasize them while he was in his perceptual period. Unlike finger patterns, Tarus did not independently introduce spatio-motor patterns as an element of his problem solutions. Consequently, we now believe that more indirect teaching methods are called for in the case of spatial patterns when children are in their perceptual stage, where the *children* are left to introduce spatial patterns independently in the context of solving problems (cf. Labinowicz, 1985, for a discussion of indirect methods).

Our methods were appropriate, however, for *Jason* (cf. 6.04 and 6.20) when he was in his motor period, because he independently used his spatio-motor patterns to keep track of counting the second hidden portion of a collection when the hidden items were not prearranged into spatial patterns. The spatio-motor patterns represented an engendering accommodation. In retrospect, we believe the difference resides in Jason's pointing scheme as well as in his ability to re-present spatial patterns. He was already aware of his pointing acts as substitute countable items and easily isolated a square spatio-motor pattern as an enactive preconcept of "four". In fact, a square four became an assimilatory structure of his counting scheme, because it was his intention to count the re-presented spatial pattern. Consequently, he could substitute the pattern for a collection of four perceptual items and count the elements of the pattern rather than the hidden perceptual items. In other words, Jason's spatio-motor patterns were a part of his more general counting scheme that could be used in appropriate situations. For Tarus, however, counting was carried out to enact the patterns, not to count them. It was a means of establishing the spatial patterns.

James independently introduced spatio-motor patterns for the number words, up to and including "four", as an element of his problem solutions (cf. 3.06) in a manner analogous to Jason, demonstrating that it is quite possible for children in the perceptual stage to introduce spatio-motor patterns as well as finger patterns as engendering accommodations in transition to their *motor* period. As a result, we included spatio-motor patterns in our model of James's zone of potential development. However, emphasizing spatio-motor patterns in the teaching episodes led James to use them without first re-presenting spatial patterns (cf. 3.23 and 3.24). He connected the number words with the motor pattern that constituted the response of the scheme, essentially creating a modified scheme, where the assimilatory function of re-presenting spatial patterns was curtailed. Nevertheless, re-presentation of spatial patterns returned upon his curtailment of the motor patterns (cf. 3.25). In retrospect, these modifications in his spatio-motor patterns were isolated procedural accommodations. We see no reason to emphasize spatio-motor patterns in teaching episodes when children are in their perceptual stages.

The Figurative Stage

We did not observe an engendering accommodation while Brenda, Tarus, and James were in their figurative stages. Most of the accommodations seemed to be procedural, because they occurred as a direct result of using current schemes in an attempt to solve the problem situations we posed. The children seemed to be on a plateau.

Procedural Accommodations

Sophisticated finger patterns. Brenda's construction of sophisticated finger patterns (cf. 1.15) seemed to occur as a result of her specifying the collection of fingers generated by counting to complete two finger patterns in succession. They were not in our model of her zone of potential development and seemed to occur when Brenda was asked to find sums greater than ten in her schoolwork. We never presented Brenda with a problem situation where we intended for her to use her sophisticated finger patterns. Through our observation of Brenda's problem solutions, we isolated sophisticated finger patterns as part of children's mathematics in general. They are not restricted to Brenda, because we have observed their use in field work other than this teaching experiment.

Brenda's sophisticated finger patterns were the result of a procedural accommodation of the figurative finger pattern scheme she had constructed to find indicated sums of ten or less (cf. 1.29). In case of the latter scheme, sequentially putting up fingers to complete figurative finger patterns provided Brenda with an opportunity to connect number words with the finger patterns. This was a new possibility for constructing finger patterns for the number words up to and including "ten" and, eventually, upon hearing a number word spoken, counting, as well as a finger pattern, was signaled. Upon hearing "thirteen plus four", counting to "thirteen" was signaled. In this way, Brenda could establish sophisticated finger pattern meanings for the number words up to and including "fifteen" by counting fingers she had already used (cf. 1.09 and 1.10). The result of counting to "thirteen", for example, could be an open hand and three more fingers extended on her other hand as well as "thirteen". Another possibility was for Brenda to count until completing a finger pattern for "eight" upon hearing "eight plus seven", say, and then continue counting "1-2- . . . -7" until completing a finger pattern using fingers she had already counted. She then could count all of the fingers she had already counted until reaching "fifteen". In this way, "fifteen" could be connected to two open hands.

Once she had a rather wide range of sophisticated finger patterns available (up to "fifteen"), she reactivated and modified an earlier finger pattern adding scheme to find indicated sums whose addends were "five" or preceding "five". Earlier, she had counted from "one" to establish each perceptual finger pattern and then counted all of her extended fingers as a single collection, again starting from "one". In her sophisticated finger pattern adding scheme, the last count was unnecessary because she could recognize the involved finger pattern. She also developed this facility with her more primitive perceptual finger pattern adding scheme.

These procedural accommodations can be summarized as follows. Using her figurative finger pattern scheme led to the isolation of putting up fingers as well as to the completed finger pattern as a meaning of the number word said last when counting. This led to two changes in her finger patterns. First, a wider variety of finger patterns became available for re-presentation and, second, these figurative concepts of number words contained records of the motor activity used in their establishment. As new assimilating structures, they in turn led Brenda to construct sophisticated finger patterns, to modify her earlier perceptual adding scheme, and to isolate the number word sequence involved in counting (cf. 1.16-1.24). This in turn led to dual concepts of number words (cf. 1.33-1.36).

<u>Intuitive extension and mobile finger patterns</u>. The construction of the intuitive extension adding scheme also involved a procedural accommodation (cf. 1.16, 2.09-2.12, 3.01-3.02), which included modifications of the response of the counting scheme as well as of its assimilatory structures. While the children were in their perceptual stages, we noted the engendering accommodation of re-presenting finger patterns. This engendering accommodation led to the construction of the intuitive extension scheme, but not without a necessary procedural accommodation.

After the engendering accommodation occurred, the children counted their fingers as perceptual items, although they either put up or folded down fingers. At this point in the teaching experiment, intuitive extensions and mobile finger patterns definitely were in our model of the children's zone of potential development. In fact, we carefully sequenced the problem situations so that the children would develop mobile finger patterns, overcoming the inclusion of part of a completed finger pattern in the completion of the one following (cf. 2.07). We systematically varied the elements of the first hidden portion of a collection while keeping the elements of the second hidden portion within the range of figurative finger patterns (e.g., "seven" and "two"; "eight" and "one"; "eight" and "three"). Upon isolating their motor acts, Tarus and James modified their previous schemes, developing mobile finger patterns (cf. 2.09-2.12 and 3.28). But Brenda did not develop mobile finger patterns until she was in her verbal period (cf. 3.28). When they appeared, however, Brenda had two adding schemes that she used appropriately, her intuitive extension scheme and her sophisticated finger pattern adding scheme (cf. 1.16).

Counting-on. Although we did not document it, we experimented with counting-on in teaching episodes while the children were in their motor periods. Not until they were in their verbal periods, however, were our efforts "successful" (cf. 1.37, 2.24, and 3.18). It was our goal to find when counting-on *could* be included in our models of the children's zone of potential development.

Counting-on involved a substitution of a finger pattern for the activity of counting. This use of substitution would have qualified as an engendering accommodation, had the children independently introduced it as an element of their problem-solving behavior. However, it was introduced by all three children in the context of carefully choreographed interactive communication in problem-solving situations. Of course, the children actually made the substitution, but the timing of the messages we sent to them seemed to be critical. We believe this was not the case when the children introduced re-presentations of finger patterns into their problem-solving behavior. Re-presentation was something they introduced from "outside" their currently available schemes, and seemed to be independent of interactive communication.

The dual nature of the meaning of number words--a pattern meaning and a counting meaning--was itself the result of a procedural accommodation that involved abstracting the counting meaning from the pattern meaning. Because a number word referred to both, our intensive interactive communication with the children could spawn the substitution of the pattern meaning for the counting meaning. In the absence of awareness of the dual meaning, though, the substitution would not have occurred. The failure of all three children to independently introduce counting-on reflected the procedural accommodation that gave rise to the substitution.

Temporary Modifications

One of the most dramatic modifications that occurred in the figural period was temporary. It occurred when James (cf. 3.28 and 3.29) anticipated the result of completing two juxtaposed figural finger patterns by sequentially putting up fingers. Had we been able to infer that his finger patterns were objects of reflection, we would have taken them as being numerical finger patterns. However, in the midst of completing the patterns by counting, he could curtail the remaining activity because the mobile finger pattern for "four" could be a thumb, which completed two open hands, and three more fingers. This is the only indication that

James *could* form a sophisticated finger pattern, and it was therefore taken as a *temporary* modification.

We had not included curtailment of counting to complete two finger patterns in our model of James's zone of potential development and it came as a surprise. In retrospect, we now have a good reason for including it. We did not then attach the significance to the problem solution that it may have warranted and it is quite possible that, had we taken advantage of James's temporary accommodation, he would have developed numerical finger patterns before the end of the teaching experiment, because the integration operation involves a recursion of the operations he already had available at the level of re-presentation.

Other temporary modifications occurred when Tarus solved a missing addend problem (cf. 2.19-2.23), James and Tarus created spatio-auditory patterns (cf. 2.13-2.15, 2.19, and 3.11), and Brenda counted backward in subtraction (cf. 1.17-1.19). The spatio-auditory patterns occurred as a result of curtailing the motor activity in spatio-motor patterns. For example, James and Tarus could coordinate uttering any three number words, with making three points of visual focus in a triangular pattern while they visually scanned a spatial region. Apparently, substituting the involved spatial pattern for the second hidden portion of a collection being counted instigated the curtailment of putting up fingers when they completed the finger pattern that had been substituted for the first hidden portion of the collection. Although mixing two pattern types when making a substitution of patterns for hidden portions of collections was fortuitous, it was possible because the children had used both pattern types before the modification.

Retrospective Accommodations

The accommodations that Brenda and James made in the construction of "ten" as a countable motor unit differs enough from other functional accommodations to deserve a special name, because both children independently projected the motor items they had constructed in their counting-by-one scheme into a current counting-by-ten activity. It certainly was not a temporary modification because it persisted, in some form, over several teaching episodes. The independent way in which it was introduced by the children (cf. 1.44 and 3.32) might qualify it as an engendering accommodation. But the children did not make further accommodations that should have been within the realm of possibility, had the modifications been engendering (cf. 1.45-1.46 and 3.35). Consequently, "retrospective" is a better term than "engendering".

Re-presentation and Review of Prior Activity

The closest that Brenda, Tarus, and James came to an engendering accommodation in their figurative stages was when they re-presented or reviewed records of prior activity (cf. 1.20-1.24, 2.25, and 3.19-3.20). This ability to re-present and reflect on their immediate past experience (or to re-present a number word that signified a number word sequence) fostered a *contextual* reorganization of their counting scheme. Because this occurred at the end of the teaching experiment, we were not able to observe whether it was an engendering accommodation or a procedural accommodation. If it was engendering, we would expect that a major reorganization of their counting schemes would emerge, like those of Tyrone, Scenetra, and Jason when they entered the stage of sequential integration operations (cf. Chapter IV). The accommodation was similar to that made by Tyrone at the beginning of the teaching experiment, when we first observed the emergence of integration (cf. 4.12-4.13). It was, therefore, *possible* that Brenda, Tarus, and James made integrations in these isolated contexts, but we have no other observations to confirm or refute the conjecture. Although this is one of the unresolved issues of the teaching experiment, we will gain insight into it in the next section.

The Figurative Stage: Tyrone, Scenetra, and Jason

We now turn to an analysis of the accommodations made by Tyrone, Scenetra, and Jason over the duration of the teaching experiment. At the beginning of the experiment, we did not make any observations to indicate that we should include integration in our model of their zones of potential development. Not until we conducted the retrospective analysis did it become apparent we should have included it. The counting types model was essentially not encompassing enough to inform our model of the zones of potential development of the three children. We did include the re-presentation of spatial patterns the children could not recognize as well as the curtailment of the coordination involved in counting. In Jason's case, it was necessary to include the intuitive extension scheme. As it turned out, our models of the children's zones of potential development were too conservative.

Procedural Engendering Accommodations

Although Jason used his spatio-motor patterns in a variety of situations (cf. 6.20, 6.21, and 6.24), his finger patterns proved to be even more significant (cf. 6.22, 6.23, and 6.25). The specific perceptual finger patterns were products of procedural accommodations, in that they were the results of counting his fingers as perceptual items. Re-presentation of these patterns changed their nature, and Jason's figurative patterns, in contrast to Brenda, Tarus, and James, served as material for integrations. In subsequent accommodations involving the integration operation, Jason's use of his counting scheme led to results that induced a perturbation he could resolve only through reflection on his records of using the scheme.

This type of reflection was a characteristic of all three children. For example, Tyrone (cf. 4.12-4.13) lost track of counting over a cloth covering the second hidden portion of a collection because he did not recognize touching the cloth five times with his finger. He started counting again *without suggestion from the teacher* and monitored the nonvisual records of his counting acts; this is the engendering accommodation, a solid indication that he was aware of an uncertainty in the results of counting--he had not specified the hidden collection.

We take his starting over and counting again as his attempt to resolve the uncertainty, especially because he created a linear spatial pattern for "five" on the spot. This indicates that he created numerical composites using the nonvisual records of his counting acts (which consisted of pointing acts) which were novel results of counting.

Scenetra, like Tyrone, provided an indication that she could re-present patterns and reflect on the results of completing these patterns at the beginning of the teaching experiment (cf. 5.17). The independence she exemplified in resolving the conflict created by not having enough fingers left to make a finger pattern for "five" after making a finger pattern for "six" was quite similar to the independence Tyrone exemplified when he monitored his counting activity. However, her initial modification was temporary, and similar modifications did not reappear until more than three months later (cf. 5.03-5.06, and 5.18-5.25).

Upon their reappearance, Scenetra used integration in the context of patterns to neutralize perturbations she experienced in assimilation (cf. 5.05). In the context of counting a collection of eleven squares, five of which were hidden, Scenetra first tried to use her finger patterns, as she did in a previous task (cf. 5.04). Not having enough fingers created a perturbation she neutralized by changing her scheme of operating from finger patterns to counting. She could then take the six counted squares as material of an integration, register the results "in her head", and continue to count. The independence she exemplified in switching from one scheme to another indicates a deliberate choice and reflection on her actions. We believe these were made possible by her creating numerical composites using her finger patterns and her visual records of counting the six squares. Like Tyrone's, the accommodations she made were harbingers of her abstract period.

The critical observations of Jason's initial integrations also involved reinitializing his counting scheme as a result of a perturbation. First, he monitored his counting acts (cf. 6.24), and second, he reviewed the records of past counting activity (cf. 6.25). In the latter case, after counting over a cloth that hid the last four of a row of chips, "7-8-9-10", Jason had no visible records of touching the cloth four times. Like Tyrone (cf. 4.12-4.13), he reinitialized his counting scheme without any suggestion from his teacher. Counting had produced an ambiguous result, and so he switched to putting up fingers rather than touching the cloth to make records of counting.

In the former case, out of necessity Jason also organized ten counting acts of a continuation of a count to eight into two patterns of four and two additional acts (cf. 6.24). He seemed to appreciate that simply touching the second cloth while counting beyond his count to "eight" would have led to an ambiguous result. In another situation (cf. 6.25), he continued to count up to "twelve" after his count to "eight" but did not know how many items were hidden until he independently reviewed and organized the results of counting into a pattern he could recognize.

The engendering accommodation of independently operating on the records of an immediate past experience was a characteristic of all three children. It was an operation that came from "outside" the involved scheme, and its independent use represented a quality that was lacking in the re-presentations and review of the records of prior activity made by Brenda, Tarus, and James at the end of the teaching experiment. Although this should not be taken as a refutation that the second three children used the integration operation, it does lead to interpreting their accommodations using the composite wholes constituted by figural patterns.

Re-presentation and reflection certainly are not limited to children who can apply the integration operation, nor is conscious awareness. Nevertheless, when the operation of integration emerged, we saw the self-initiated modifications of the results of using schemes. We believe the independence of the modifications was no accident, because reflection implies an object of reflection. Integration is the operation children can use to create such an object (a numerical composite) in their experiential field. In retrospect, it isn't surprising that integration emerged in the context of patterns, because a pattern provides the children with an experiential unity whose elements seem to co-occur, an immediate apprehension of a specific numerosity. The accommodations were engendering, because they led to the reorganizations of counting we took as indicators of the abstract stage.

Temporary Modifications

The engendering accommodations that we have identified were signs for the onset of major changes in the children's counting and pattern schemes. We also observed various modifications that turned out to be only temporary products of integration and re-presentation, the constructive mechanisms of numerical composites.

One of the most interesting temporary modifications occurred when Scenetra made contextual records of her backward counting acts (cf. 5.07-5.09). This modification occurred as a result of her applying the integration operation to the records of backward counting acts. Although double counting can be taken as prima facie indication that a child has reorganized counting, our observation is consistent with the notion that children use their conceptual operations in local contexts before they interiorize the sensory-motor objects that served in the use of the operations.

Another interesting but temporary accommodation occurred when Tyrone curtailed the coordinations involved in counting (cf. 4.04). Although this modification of the response of the counting scheme was not as dramatic as Scenetra's double counting, Tyrone did make the modification with ease. He seemed to be able to abstract the involved number words from acts of counting by re-presenting counting. Without Tyrone's capacity to take the records of counting as material of integrations, he would not have shown sensitivity to a statement made by the teacher that he did not have to point if he did not want to.

Curtailing the coordinations involved in counting occurred ten days before Jason's reorganization of counting (cf. 6.09-6.10). In the same counting episode, he created a linear spatial pattern for "seven" to keep track of counting. The presence of the linear pattern for "seven", together with previous indicators of the integration operation, justify our contention that integration was instrumental in Jason's curtailment.

Metamorphic Accommodations

The engendering accommodations and temporary modifications identified above can now be taken as an indication that major reorganizations of the counting scheme were under way for all three children (cf. 4.07-4.11, 5.10-5.14, 6.11-6.14). We call these reorganizations metamorphic accommodations for three reasons. First, there was a preceding period of engendering accommodations (approximately two months for each child) during which the counting scheme and patterns were being assimilated by the operation of integration and thereby interiorized; second, there were changes in the structure and function of the counting scheme; and third, the accommodations occurred in no specific application of the counting scheme.

The changes in the structure and function of the counting scheme were manifested by the children using their counting schemes in concert with their pattern schemes during the assimilation of a variety of problem situations, and then accommodating those schemes in creative and unusual ways to "fit" the situations. It was especially significant that all three children were able to count backward to find how many of a collection of perceptual items were hidden, and to count forward to accomplish a similar goal, regardless of the numerosity of the hidden collection (there were practical limitations, but the children were not limited to recognition of a pattern when specifying the numerosity of the hidden collection).

These counting solutions cannot be passed off as functional accommodations that occurred in a specific application of a scheme, because we had not presented Tyrone with either of these two types of problem situations, except on the rare occasions when we probed his available conceptual operations. We had never observed him using counting-on, counting-up-to, or counting-off-from before the documented observations, nor did we observe him reorganizing his counting scheme in any particular problem situation to neutralize some perturbation. Rather, Tyrone reorganized his counting scheme over the Christmas holidays, when it was very unlikely that he solved missing addend problems. The other two children reorganized their counting schemes while school was in session, but we have reason to believe that, like Tyrone's, their reorganizations "broke through" during a short time period, even though there were preceding periods when the changes were under way (cf. 5.10-5.14, 6.28-6.32). We never modeled counting-off-from to solve take-away subtraction problems for the children, nor did we observe them solving such problems in that way before our documented observation of their using counting-up-to as a generalized scheme in the abstract periods.

Neither Tyrone nor Jason counted-on before they reorganized their counting schemes, although we had encouraged Jason to do so (cf. 6.09). Scenetra had counted-on in the period preceding her reorganization, but it was only a temporary modification (cf. 5.05). This is in contrast to the three other children, for whom counting-on was the result of a procedural accommodation. Since Tyrone, Scenetra, and Jason had no verbal periods like those of Brenda, Tarus, and James, they had no opportunity to develop counting-on as a procedural accommodation. For them, counting-on can be considered an indication that a number word could, by itself, be taken to imply the number word sequence from "one" up to and including the given number word, as well as a collection of discrete unitary items that could be coordinated with that sequence (cf. *Abstract Unit Items*, Chapter I). What made this possible was the interiorization of counting (cf. Perspectives on the Case Studies, Chapter IV).

Certain records of counting acts became contained in the abstract unit items of the numerical composite produced by an integration. As such, counting was part and parcel of the assimilatory structures of the counting scheme, and could be taken as a given in appropriate situations. The function of the counting scheme changed from specifying a collection to being an assimilatory numerical concept (cf. 4.16, 5.28, and 6.28). As a numerical concept, the counting scheme was transformed into a constructive mechanism the children used in numerical situations throughout the remainder of the teaching experiment. As a scheme, then, counting-on (and certainly counting-up-to and counting-off-from) is more complex than the schemes and operations used in its construction.

Stages in the Construction of Part-Whole Operations

Upon the reorganization of their counting schemes, our models of the children's zones of potential development shifted to include the following:

1. Counting-down-to in subtraction.
2. The construction of subtraction as the inversion of addition.
3. The construction of the iterable unit of ten and its coordination with the unit of one in counting when solving problems.
4. The construction of the place value, the face value, and the total value of numerals in two-digit numerals by counting by ten and one.
5. Strategies for finding one- and two-digit sums and differences.

Our models turned out to be too optimistic, because the stage of sequential integration operations that followed the reorganizations of counting for the three children lasted for approximately eight months (cf. 4.16-4.25, 5.26-5.32, and 6.28-6.36). During this period, most of the above items proved to be too far removed from the children's current schemes to be learned. However, they did make noteworthy procedural accommodations in the stage of sequential integration operations.

Sequential Integration Operations

Procedural Accommodations

All three children learned most of the basic facts of addition and subtraction during the stage of sequential integration operations--before they used thinking strategies spontaneously (cf. Thinking Strategies and the Basic Facts, Chapter VIII). This is in marked contrast to the inability of Brenda, Tarus, and James to learn their basic facts (cf. Number Facts, Chapter VII) and it countermanded any belief that thinking strategies might be necessary for children to learn basic facts. Tyrone, Scenetra, and Jason apparently learned their basic facts by making procedural accommodations in their numerical counting and pattern schemes.

A "basic fact" is nothing more than a connection between a particular sum and a response, not unlike the functional connections in Thorndike's connectionism.

> The term *connection* . . . refers to a functional relation between a situation and a response. (Gates, 1942, p. 145)

However, we have to consider carefully what "response" refers to in the context of a scheme. For a connectionist, "one connects the . . . response '9' with the stimuli '3x3' and so on" (Brownell, 1935, p. 5). In a counting scheme, "9" is the *result*, or third part, of the scheme. The connection, then, between a situation and a result is initially a functional connection only in the sense that the result follows upon the response (counting).

Addition facts. The crucial differences in the two groups of children when learning basic addition facts were in the assimilating operations of their counting schemes. When the assimilating operations were sequential integrations, the counting scheme had been reconstituted as a numerical concept. It was anticipatory and the children could start with an *explicit intention* of finding the numerosity ("how many" or "how much") of, say, five and four more. We have seen that such anticipation was only a temporary modification on the part of James, and we never observed it in Brenda and Tarus.

Further insight can be gained into how Tyrone, Scenetra, and Jason learned their basic facts by analyzing procedural accommodations that are documented in the stages of their sequential integration operations. When finding how many squares were in a collection where eight were visible and 11 hidden, Tyrone created numerical composites for "eight", "eleven", and "nineteen" in his immediate experience as solution to a problem. The chance of the connection being strong is quite good because Tyrone monitored the activity of continuing to count 11 times beyond his count to eight. His reflective awareness of the successive results of counting provided an occasion for the establishment of a connection among "eight", "eleven", and "nineteen". If it was a strong numerical connection, upon meeting a similar situation he might simply use that connection to produce the result. It certainly wouldn't have taken much for the connection to become permanent.

Estimates of the numerosity of a numerical composite whose elements contain the records of the counting acts in a continuation of counting provides an opportunity for children to learn their basic facts (cf. 4.16-4.19 and 6.28-6.30). Both Tyrone and Jason independently made such estimates in what normally would be considered difficult tasks for six-year-olds, and counted-up-to in verification of their estimates. These estimates were not wild guesses and were close to being correct, if they were not actually correct. They provide one of our strongest indications that records of counting were implicit in the unit items of numerical composites, because the children could envision the results of counting without actually finding how many times they did or would count. The crowning confirmation that their estimates were made as a result of contemplating how many times they did or would count resides in their independent verifications of their estimates by recording counting. These estimates show that children can be in complete control of their intentions and actions in the context of learning the basic facts.

Establishing connections by construction (reflection and abstraction) is different from and better than establishing connections by rote learning. In the former case, the connections are operative and can be easily reestablished by children in situations that differ from those that served in their construction. In the latter case, the connections are figurative in nature and it is not a question of their re-establishment in novel situations. These connections are essentially sentences of the form "five and six are eleven", where the sentences do not symbolize sequential integration operations or counting. If the novel situation does not include an incomplete sentence like "five and six are ___", the connection cannot be relevant because it does not symbolize the conceptual operations the child performs to solve the problem presented by the situation. If the sentence did symbolize the conceptual operations, their performance (or incomplete performance) might trigger or point to the sentence.

Subtraction facts. The children learned their subtraction facts independently of their addition facts, because they did not view subtraction as the inversion of addition while they were in the stage of sequential integration operations (cf. 4.25-4.26; 5.35-5.36; 6.13 and Sequential Integration Operations: JASON, Chapter VIII). How the children might have learned their subtraction facts is indicated in the case where Tyrone and Jason counted-off-from. For collections of ten or less, their finger patterns were at least implicitly involved, because they sequentially put up fingers when counting. Scenetra, on the other hand, used her numerical finger patterns without counting. She even developed an ingenious subtracting scheme to use when the minuend was in the teens and the subtrahend was less than ten (cf. 5.35-5.36) that included her more primitive finger pattern subtracting scheme as a subscheme. Upon encountering differences like 16 - 8, she could assimilate the problem as taking eight away from 16 but, lacking 16 fingers, she could not perform subtracting actions. Her concept of "sixteen" as two open hands and six more fingers opened up new possibilities, because she could take eight fingers away from the finger pattern for ten simply by folding down eight fingers. She then recognized the incomplete result as addition and used her adding scheme, thus developing a novel subtracting scheme that worked in a wider variety of problem situations. Scenetra's creative power certainly is consistent with our assumption that she could establish numerical connections by using her schemes.

Engendering Accommodations

At the culmination of the stage of sequential integration operations, there was a shift in the material of integrations from collections and patterns to numerical composites. The resulting accommodations were not unlike the engendering accommodations involving integrations that occurred while the children were in the figurative stage of their counting scheme. During our first observation of Tyrone in the second year of the teaching experiment, he solved an addition problem and a missing addend problem (cf. 4.07, 4.11) in such a way that we included taking a numerical composite as one thing as part of his assimilatory operations, and as part of the operations he performed in his solutions (cf. 4.26-4.33). We did not have an opportunity to observe a more primitive solution in which Tyrone modified the results of counting, creating an abstract composite unit in the process.

Scenetra had modified her finger pattern subtracting scheme by the beginning of the second year of the teaching experiment (cf. 5.35). We were fortunate to observe how she again modified her subtracting scheme to solve problems involving a decade as minuend (cf. 5.36-5.37). In finding how many of 23 blocks would be left after she removed six, she partitioned two numerical composites of ten (finger patterns), put one of them "in her head", and established a finger pattern for the other. She then folded six fingers and counted as before, "Ten; 11-12-13-14". This was itself an independent modification of her previous scheme. Through intensive interactive communication, Scenetra made another modification that we believed would be possible only if she took each numerical composite of ten as one compound thing. This new way of using integration apparently led to a general subtracting scheme she could use to solve problems like "62 - 7 = ____" (cf. 5.38). Because of the intensive interactive communication, neither of Scenetra's two accommodations was spontaneous; however, each was made independently of any suggestion about how she should proceed. In fact, although it is not documented, in the first case the particular accommodation was not the one the interviewer intended. He was working toward Scenetra putting "thirteen" in her head and ten on her fingers.

Scenetra's first accommodation was engendering, because she assimilated a wide variety of novel subtraction problems using the modified scheme, an assimilating generalization. Unfortunately, this subtraction scheme was a basis neither for constructing ten as an iterable unit nor for constructing reversible part-whole operations. Rather, it constrained these constructions, because Scenetra had a scheme that worked for a wide variety of problems and she soon developed standard paper-and-pencil schemes for finding sums and differences. Nevertheless, applying the integration operation to numerical composites was essential for her future progress. What was missing was the application of the integration operation in situations where she re-presented her number sequences (cf. 5.44-5.48). That she could apply her integration operation to number sequences has been documented (cf. 5.39), but she preferred not to solve problems in this way.

Jason also applied the integration operation to the results of prior integrations in the context of solving a problem (cf. 6.37). By taking the results of counting as one thing, he abstracted the number word sequence "4-14-24- . . . ". The accommodation was engendering, because he quickly isolated new number word sequences like "7-17-27- . . . " (cf. 6.37) and found how many of 93 blocks were hidden when 53 were visible by uttering "63-73-83-93" synchronously with putting up fingers. His assimilatory operations seemed to include taking a segment of a number sequence as one thing, as did Tyrone (cf. 4.31-4.33).

Although the observed accommodation was not immediately coordinated with Jason's current counting scheme (cf. 6.40-6.41), a modified counting scheme appeared (cf. 6.42) less than one month later. In retrospect, the type of problems that we presented to Tyrone (cf. 4.31) or to Scenetra (cf. 5.49) are preferable to repeatedly adding collections of ten, as we did in Jason's case (cf. 6.37), to encourage a shift in the material of integration. The former problems encourage the child to *organize* the task and to reflect on counting in immediate past experience. Repeatedly adding a collection of ten encourages the child to isolate a recurrent number word pattern even though the initial abstraction might have been based on reflecting on counting in immediate past experience. It essentially turns the problem situation into a number word situation. This was a reason for the lag in Jason's reorganizing his counting scheme to include "ten". He had established novel number word sequences in the context of his current assimilating operations, and these operations were now connected to the novel sequences. So, upon assimilating a new problem where he counted-on by one, the results of saying these novel number word sequences in similar problems interfered with the results of his using more established counting by one schemes. His two responses were not differentiated and coordinated. But having two responses did turn out to be a source of progress, because he soon coordinated counting-on by ten and counting-on by one (cf. 6.42-6.44). Nevertheless, Tyrone's path to the same result is preferable and should be encouraged, if counting by ten is encouraged before the construction of reversible part-whole operations.

Progressive Integration Operations

The shift from sequential integration operations to progressive integration operations is difficult to explain solely on the basis of the children making engendering accommodations when using their schemes. Nevertheless, the crucial product of the stage of sequential integration operations was the re-emergence of the integration operation in the context of number sequences. It is quite plausible that the children extended the integration operation to include the results of prior integrations in the context of using their schemes. In fact, we isolated these modifications as engendering accommodations for the construction of progressive integration operations.

The *reorganizations* of their counting schemes engendered by the integration operations being applied to the results of prior integrations, however, cannot be as readily explained (cf. 4.31, 4.33, 4.35, 5.39, and 6.42). Our technique of hiding part of a collection of perceptual items and then asking the children to find how many were hidden contributed to the extension of integration to number sequences, because all three children solved these types of problems. However, this is not the same as the children using progressive integration operations as assimilating operations *prior* to actually counting. In fact, the difference is profound. Scenetra independently made a choice between using counting-down-to and counting-off-from the first time we observed her using counting-down-to in subtraction (cf. 5.39), and we had not worked on counting-down-to in subtraction with her in teaching episodes. The solution episode was quite dramatic and occurred in the same way for Tyrone (cf. 4.35). His use of counting-down-to to solve a subtraction problem was a surprise to us because we had not worked with him in solving a subtraction problem in that way. Jason's solution of a missing addend problem by counting-on by ten and by one was also a rather sudden shift, although it had its precursors (cf. 6.42-6.44).

Our explanation of the rather sudden shifts in the way the children conceptualized the problems is predicated on the assumption that the children did, on previous occasions, re-present a number sequence and take the re-presented sequence as one thing in the context of solving problems. Thus, records of integrations became embedded in the number sequences. This is analogous to the interiorization of counting that precipitated the reorganization of the children's counting schemes when they entered their stages of sequential integration operations (cf. Steffe, et al., 1983, Chapter II). There, the records of counting had become embedded in spatial and finger patterns when the children counted to specify them. When integration emerged in the context of the re-presented patterns, the records of counting (as well as the figural items) became contained in the abstract units of the resulting numerical composites, creating an interiorized number word sequence, or a number sequence. The children could then re-present a numerical composite of specific numerosity by re-presenting an interiorized number word sequence, implying a collection of unit items with which the words of the sequence could be coordinated. It is important to observe that these initial number sequences were not inclusive, in the sense that one is included in two, two is included in three, three is included in four, etc., as

Piaget's model of the development of number would have us believe (Sinclair, 1971), for that is the work of progressive integration operations. The initial number sequence is just that for children--a sequence.

Initial number sequences, then, were themselves the work of prior integrations. Nevertheless, the children were yet to construct *nested* number sequences. A number word was yet to symbolize the number sequence up to and including that number word as one thing. It could symbolize the individual number words in sequence, but it was yet to symbolize a unit containing that sequence. When records of integrations became embedded in the initial number sequences, an internal reorganization occurred and number sequences emerged that were *tacitly* nested. A number word was now a symbol for a unit containing a number sequence from one up to and including that number word (or any other segment of a number sequence of specific numerosity indicated by the number word). A number word preceding another symbolized an inclusion relation that remained implicit throughout the stage of progressive integration operations. In short, the children were unaware of the inclusion relation symbolized by the relation of precedence.

A unit might contain, say, the segment 30, 29, 28, 27, 26, 25, 24, 23, and the children fully understood that the numerosity of this segment could be specified by counting these elements. The advantage of the children developing number sequences in reverse order should be apparent, for this enabled them to perform conceptual operations on backward sequences as well as forward sequences, and eventually to count-down-to to solve problems.

Internal Reorganizations

The internal reorganizations that yielded the initial and tacitly nested number sequences led to what appeared to an observer to be novel solutions of problems. They were the work of reflective abstraction, as pointed out by Piaget (1977): "Reflective abstraction must necessarily reconstruct on the new level B whatever it picked up on the level A from which it started . . ." (p. 6). An essential difference in reflective abstraction and re-presentation is that re-presentation is current--it is happening or it has just happened. In this sense, re-presentation is how children might start to go from what Piaget calls level A to level B. It does not complete the shift in levels, because the act of taking the results of re-presenting a pattern (a figurative pattern) or an initial number sequence (a figurative number sequence) as one thing "lifts" the involved figurative structure, at least momentarily, and transforms it into an abstract sequence of "slots" that contain the records of the figurative structure.

Tyrone's engendering accommodation that preceded sequential and progressive integration operations is diagramed in Figure 9 (cf. 4.12-4.13). The engendering accommodation should be thought of as the operations

Figure 9

Tyrone's Engendering Accommodations

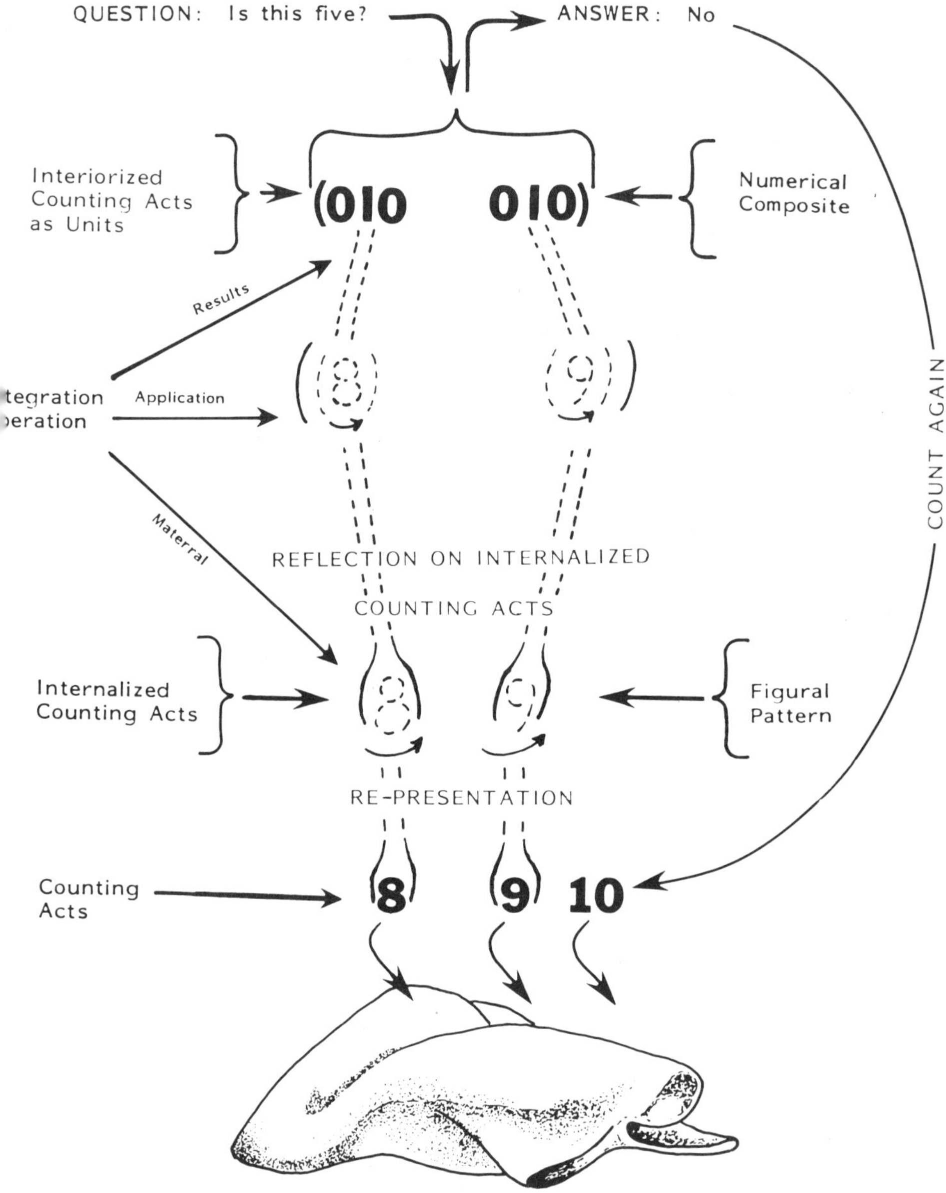

NOTE. Numerals rather than number words are used to simplify the figure.

↘ Denotes pointing acts.

involved in transforming two or more counting acts into a numerical composite. In Figure 9 the operations are diagramed in that case after Tyrone had counted "8-9" and where it was his intention to count until establishing meaning for "five". Because of the lack of perceptual records, it is necessary to include a re-presentation of the two counting acts. But re-presentation alone is insufficient to explain the accommodation because Tyrone monitored his counting activity, taking stock of where he was after each count. We know from the case studies of Brenda, Tarus, and James that children can create figurative patterns by re-presenting perceptual patterns and use these figurative patterns to keep track of counting without monitoring their activity. To monitor counting activity, there must be an explicit awareness of the material in re-presentation, an awareness that is indicated by "Reflection on Internalized Counting Acts" in Figure 9.

There is no intention to reify reflective awareness, because it is a corollary of the operations of unitizing the internalized counting acts, indicated by the parentheses around "8" and "9" and uniting the result, indicated by the outermost parentheses. The unitizing operation separates the two counting acts as abstract entities and the uniting operation binds them together as a pair--as a numerical composite. These operations repeated themselves until Tyrone constructed a numerical composite for "five".

Although the engendering accommodations made by Scenetra and Jason (cf. 5.04 and 6.25) would be diagramed differently than those of Tyrone, the accommodations involved the same conceptual operations. We refer to them as "disembedding operations", because part of the number word sequence was extracted from the sequence. For example, in Scenetra's case, there is justification that she took the records of counting to "six" as material for the integration operation. However, rather than concentrate on diagraming the engendering accommodations of Scenetra and Jason, we turn to the metamorphic accommodations that were engendered.

In the engendering accommodations diagramed in Figure 9, we hypothesize that the *number word sequence* that served as material of the operation of integration became permanently recorded. These permanent records were only temporarily limited to the number word sequences that were embedded in the patterns of the initial integrations because, upon the reorganization of counting, the children used number words up into the teens as symbols for number sequences. In fact, approximately two months elapsed between our observation of integration in the context of patterns and the reorganization of counting for the three involved children and, during this period, number word sequences up to at least twenty became permanently recorded. *The reorganizations of counting appeared when the children became able to re-present these initial number sequences and use their elements as symbols of segments of number sequences* (cf. 4.07-4.11).

To explain the metamorphic accommodation, we hypothesize that a disturbance in the children's internalized number word sequence was created by the engendering accommodations. The disturbance was the result of part of the number word sequence being interiorized and the rest of it being only internalized. We hypothesize that this perturbation was neutralized by a reapplication of the integration operation to elements of the figurative number word sequence in a way that was quite analogous to the engendering accommodations, with the exception that the integration operation was applied in no particular application of the counting scheme. From the observer's perspective, the child was "at rest". There is no assumption that the child *intentionally* reapplied the integration operation, only that it was reapplied. Moreover, there are no assumptions made concerning how many times it was reapplied or how many adjacent number words might have served as material for a particular integration. The only assumption we make is that the integration operation was reapplied enough times to interiorize the child's number word sequence.

The relevance of experience in permanently recording number word sequences is incontestable because Tyrone, for example, created a numerical composite using "8-9-10-11-12" as material when he monitored counting in one of our *initial* observations before the reorganization of counting (cf. 4.12). Records of these number words, then, as well as any other such sequence could become contained in the sequence of slots of the numerical composite that was the result of the integration. Although we did not document it, the children also created patterns for the number words up to "ten", and they could re-present these patterns. This experience also provided the children with opportunities for progress.

In the case of the construction of progressive integration operations, the engendering integrations used re-presentations of the initial number sequences (figurative sequences) as material and disembedded these number sequences from themselves, leaving them "behind" and creating an abstract sequence of "slots" that contained the records of the figurative sequence. We hypothesize that this process created a disturbance. The source of the disturbance resided in the two objects that an interiorized number word involved in such an integration (e.g., "six") symbolized. As a member of the initial number sequence, "six" was a term of the sequence. It now also referred to an abstract composite unit containing six elements. In restoring equilibrium, the initial number sequence was transformed into a tacitly nested sequence--e.g., "six" was still a term of a number sequence but it now also referred to the first six terms taken as one thing. The children could unpack six into an ordered sequence and make a distinction between, say, the first four terms and the last two. But, as a current in a river can be separated into its eddies and rapids but cannot be separated from the river, the first four and the last two terms could be distinguished from each other but neither could be simultaneously taken as series in its own right while being left in the series of six terms. When the records of the tacitly nested number sequence were re-presented, an element of a re-presented number sequence (a number word) served as a symbol for an integration operation that would yield a composite unit containing a number sequence of which the involved number word was last. In other words, a figurative sequence, as a symbol of the records that made it possible in the first place, was a carrier of the operations recorded in those records.

The claim that the children created a tacitly nested number sequence as a reorganization of their initial number sequence finds justification in the strategies the children were able to construct during their stages of progressive and sequential integration operations. The children operated sequentially in the stage of progressive integration operations (cf. Progressive Integrations, Chapter VIII). They constructed iterative strategies for finding sums and differences and, for the first time, engaged in double counting. They could iteratively coordinate two number sequences, where the words of the involved number sequences were symbols for progressive integrations (cf. Discussion of the Case Studies: Sequential Integration Operations, Chapter VIII). On the other hand, when they were in the stages of sequential integration operations, even the strategies they used spontaneously depended upon number word linkages between adjacent number words (cf. Sequential Integration Operations, Chapter VIII). They could only coordinate an increase or a decrease of one with a known combination. With few exceptions, the strategies they constructed were local and occurred in the context of carefully sequenced interventions by the teacher. They did not use thinking strategies spontaneously, except in the isolated cases noted.

Part-Whole Operations

The stage of progressive integration operations that we isolated was a preparatory period for the emergence of reversible part-whole operations (cf. 4.38-4.44, 5.51-5.52, 6.45-6.46). As a result of the internal reorganization, the children still had only one number sequence of which they were aware. From their point of view, they could solve problems in a way not possible before, although they had no idea why. They were simply more powerful. There were still problems, however, they could not solve, and operations they could not perform. To solve these problems and to create these operations, it would be necessary for the children to disembed a segment of a tacitly nested number sequence from the sequence, a conceptual operation they had already used to create the initial and the nested number sequences. It seemed inevitable that, given the problems we posed to the children (especially where we encouraged thinking strategies), they would eventually perform one or more such operations (cf. Thinking Strategies and the Construction of Part-Whole, Chapter VIII).

Applying the integration operation to a figurative segment of the tacitly nested sequence lifts it to a new plane, creating a unit that contains a nested number sequence. Again, there seems to be an internal reorganization of the tacitly nested sequence. The new operations allow the child to operate in a way that is no longer only sequential. A number word can now be a symbol for a unit that contains the nested sequence, where that number is the last element and the sequential operations are symbolized (cf. Units of One, Chapter VI). The sequential operations can be carried out, of course, but the child finds new power in leaving them implicit.

An important result is that the inclusion relation that was implicit in the tacitly nested number sequence is now made explicit. The child can "see" the inclusion relation in the reorganized number sequence, because it is symbolized by the sequence and can therefore intentionally disembed a segment of an explicitly nested number sequence from its inclusion in the containing sequence, and treat it as a unit in its own right. The child can also actually perform these operations using units for which there is no explicit symbol (like the remainder of 23 in 49). Moreover, he or she can replace what was extracted, which is another way of saying the children do not destroy the records of the original number sequence by performing their operations. They can now have two number sequences side by side, and understand that one of them can be included in the other, whereas before, they could only coordinate two different number sequences. As a result, they can extract an initial segment from an explicitly nested number sequence, take the remaining segment of the number sequence as a unit, find its numerosity, and recombine it with the initial segment to re-form the original explicitly nested number sequence. They can also interchange the order of the two parts. These sophisticated operations we call reversible part-whole operations.

The claim that the children reorganized their tacitly nested sequences, thereby creating an explicitly nested number sequence that implied part-whole operations, finds justification in the strategies Jason and Tyrone were able to construct in their periods of part-whole operations (cf. Part-Whole Operations, Chapter VIII). Scenetra seemed to be reorganizing her tacitly nested number sequence, but lagged behind the other two children for reasons that we have discussed (cf. 5.41-5.52). Jason and Tyrone constructed operative strategies for finding sums and differences and, for the first time, constructed subtraction as the inversion of addition. In fact, the children reorganized their addition and subtraction operations into part-whole operations.

We also find justification for the claim that Tyrone and Jason reorganized their tacitly nested number sequences in the shift of the unit of ten from an abstract unit to an iterable unit (cf. 4.40, 4.44, 5.51, 6.46). This shift occurred in the same period within which the children created operative strategies and subtraction as the inversion of addition (cf. 6.45-6.46). Such remarkable consistency indicates an underlying general reorganization of the children's tacitly nested number sequences.

Phylogenetic Perspectives

Five stages in the ontogenetic development of the number sequence have been isolated: the perceptual counting scheme, the figurative counting scheme, the initial number sequence, the tacitly nested number sequence, and the explicitly nested number sequence. There are important parallels to this ontogenetic construction of the number sequence in its cultural history. It is particularly striking that the role patterns played in the construction of the integration operation is compatible with Menninger's (1969) historical analysis of the development of the numbers two, three, and four. Even more striking is Menninger's finding that the number sequence evolved with the development of language itself because, in our ontogenetic analysis of the development of number sequences, number word sequences play a fundamental role. However, the number sequence did not spring forth as a strong, exact mental process in the mind of man and then remain fairly constant over the millennia.

> The number sequence was not created or "made", it did not spring more or less fully formed from the mind of a single man of genius--it grew up and evolved slowly and randomly with man himself and his various languages. Like a frail plant, it grew and budded timidly, going from "I--You" to "one--two" and then on to three and four, which was the first of the early limits of counting. (p. 189)

Menninger provides convincing evidence for this very important claim. First, he distinguishes between two as dual and two as unity. The analysis of two as dual is a prenumerical analysis and, as such, is quite consistent with Brouwer's (1913) analysis of "two-oneness".

> This neo-intuitionism considers the falling apart of moments of life into qualitatively different parts, to be reunited only while remaining separated by time as the fundamental phenomenon of the human intellect, passing by abstracting from its emotional content into the fundamental phenomenon of mathematical thinking, the intuition of the bare two-oneness, the basal intuition of mathematics. (p. 85)

This "falling apart of moments of life into qualitatively different parts" is caught by Menninger as an awakening of consciousness--the isolation of self in an environment--"The I is opposed to and distinct from what is not I, the thou, the other" (p. 13). In two as a unity, "We experience the very essence of number more intensely than in other numbers, that essence being to bind many together into one, to equate plurality and unity" (Menninger, p. 13).

The operations of unifying the divided and dividing the unity have been fixed by languages in compounds formed from the word "two", as in the English "twin" (Menninger, p. 14). In the early developments, neither two as dual nor two as unity were separated from their sensory contents and thus were not the abstract two, a noun. Two was used as an adjective--two cows or two men.

Second, in the step to three, a new element appears in the dichotomy of I--You, namely, what lies beyond them, it. According to Menninger, the it is the third, the many, the universe.

> This statement, in which psychological, linguistic, and numerical elements come together, may perhaps roughly paraphrase early man's thinking about numbers. "One--two--many": a curious counting pattern, but it is mirrored in the grammatical number forms of the noun, singular--dual--plural." (pp. 16-17)

Menninger shows how the writing of the Egyptians perpetuated the early conceptual stage of three as many. For example, water was symbolized as three waves. He takes the step to three as the decisive one in the development of the number sequence, because it introduced (but did not complete) infinite progression. It was a first step in the abstraction of the number sequence from the things counted, an abstraction characterized by Menninger (1969, p. 7) as creating great difficulties for the human mind.

Menninger also found "four" as an old limit of counting. He gave two reasons in answer to, "Why does the break come just after Four?" First, "The hand has four fingers, not counting the thumb. What happened to the thumb here was like what happened to One--it was not regarded as being equal, it was not a "finger" like the others. . . . A second reason might be that a quantity larger than four, or even three, can no longer be apprehended" (p. 22).

Menninger's analysis of the evolution of two, three, and four is particularly compatible with the engendering accommodations of the figurative counting scheme preceding the metamorphic accommodation that yielded the initial number sequence. Both Menninger and Brouwer explicitly identified the operation of integration, although they did not name it as such--"the very essence of number . . . being to bind many together into one, to equate plurality and unity" (Menninger, p. 13) and "the falling apart of moments of life. . . . [T]o be reunited only while remaining separated by time [is] the fundamental phenomenon of the human intellect" (Brouwer, 1913). We found that this uniting operation of the mind emerged in the context of patterns, and made the engendering accommodations possible. However, is there anything in the cultural history of the number sequence that corresponds to the metamorphic accommodation which yielded the initial number sequence? Menninger (1969) paints a clear and unequivocal picture.

> All these pieces of evidence show that Four was a very ancient limit in counting. Will Five be the next such boundary? Five, of course, is practically offered by the human hand with its fingers. No, surprisingly enough, in our Indo-European culture this was not the case. Five was not a limit in counting but rather one of the essential members of the number sequence. This very knowledge of how to arrange the numbers following after five is, indeed, the reason why beyond Five the number sequence no longer pauses but runs on continuously. The first four numbers are not members of the sequence; they are the first steps forward, made gropingly and without any sense of a general plan, which--although it too contains numerical breaks--was finally attained with the number Five. (p. 26)

In the cultural history of the number sequence, there is an obvious discontinuity between the first four numbers and the number sequence, which began with the abstraction of the number five. This historical development is recapitulated by Tyrone's initial engendering accommodation of his figurative counting scheme. Although we do not claim that every child makes this particular reflective abstraction, we do claim that patterns, whatever they might be, play an incontestable functional role in the engendering accommodations that precede children's metamorphic accommodations, which yield their initial number sequence.

The cultural history of the number sequence also contains suggestions of the distinctions that have been made between the explicitly nested and the initial number sequences. Menninger (1969) found that "early concepts of grouping *lead* to gradation" (p. 46).

> The number sequence is graduated. This is achieved by giving names to the elements of the sequence; those

> elements no longer remain anonymous and undifferentiated, but form the steps of a stair-case: Seven is "higher" than three. (p. 45)

The initial number sequence is not graduated. Seven, for example, is a particular term in a sequence, and does not refer to seven individual unit items in that position. It does refer to the number sequence from one, up to and including seven. This is why children who are in the stage of the initial number sequence focus on the individual unit items in a numerical composite. In an explicitly nested number sequence, seven is still a particular term in the sequence. But it can also refer to an abstract unit that contains a unit of one that can be iterated seven times--to an iterable unit of one.

Zones of Potential Development in Retrospect

The analysis of the types of accommodations made by Tyrone, Scenetra, and Jason provides a perspective on the elements that might be included in a model of the zone of potential development for children who are in their figurative stage at or near the beginning of the first grade. We have already pointed out that the elements included in such a model should at least be temporary modifications of the counting scheme. However, temporary modifications may be observable only in retrospect, as they were for us, so it is quite important to be aware of possible accommodations at the outset.

Figurative Stage

Other than the figurative concepts of number words that patterns of all types make possible, reflection on the records of using the counting scheme should be an element in the model. We noted that the critical engendering accommodation for the reorganization of counting occurred in counting a collection of items where at least a portion was hidden. If the children counted a hidden portion as a continuation of counting the first portion (hidden or not), and if they had no figurative concept of the number word that referred to the second (hidden) portion, they became lost in counting. The resulting perturbation led to the children *monitoring* their counting acts and taking their records, visible or not, as material for applying the integration operation. These findings provide a solid rationale for including applying the integration operation to the records of making intuitive extensions, as well as reflection on and re-presentation of patterns, in the model.

The reorganization of counting that marked the children's entry into their stages of sequential integrations should be also included in the model. This metamorphic accommodation is, however, at least as difficult to influence as the engendering accommodation on which it is based. Because the metamorphic accommodation is not functional, it can be only indirectly encouraged by an adult. Nevertheless, experience plays an incontestable role in its occurrence and both types of accommodations should be thought of as by-products of the children's problem-solving attempts. An adult can create problematic situations for children and encourage them to reflect on their activity, resolving the conflicts and neutralizing the perturbations that arise through reflection. Although there are no guarantees that the children will perform integration operations and create initial number sequences, teachers should understand that these are the primary reasons for encouraging children to reflect on the results of their problem-solving activity while they are in their figurative stage.

Sequential Integration Operations

Entry into the stage of sequential integration operations is one of the major events in children's early mathematical education. In an important sense, it is an endpoint of a period where the children constructed the initial number sequence, and the beginning of a period where the children constructed part-whole operations. But, at the beginning of the teaching experiment, we didn't anticipate the long periods of sequential integration operations (at least eight months) nor did we differentiate between a numerical composite and an abstract composite unit. We also did not fully understand the initial number sequence and the role it would play in further numerical development.

Beyond the procedural accommodations the children made in their schemes while learning the basic facts, we now include abstract composite units in our model of the children's zone of potential development at the point when they first enter the stage of sequential integration operations. One of Scenetra's first abstract composite units consisted of a numerical finger pattern (cf. 5.36-5.37). Tyrone and Jason also used numerical finger patterns as material of integrations. However, none of the three children were *limited* to numerical patterns when they made numerical composites, primarily because their initial number sequences *implied* a collection of items. "Fourteen", for example, denoted the number sequence from "one" up to and including "fourteen", as well as a collection of perceptual items the child could count. In the stage of sequential integration operations, the children's focus of attention seemed to be on the elements of the implied collections, whatever they might consist of.

However, we found that a number word which referred to a collection also referred to the elements of the number sequence, from "one" up to and including the given number word. We thought the children would actually take the collections as material of integrations. But, because this number sequence was itself a product of integrations, it symbolized an integration, and the children could view the collection as a numerical composite without making an integration.

The children could view a pile of marbles, so many fingers, or any other collection of perceptual items from the perspective of their number sequence, and did not actually have to count the collection for it to be considered a numerical composite. It was sufficient for them to be told that there were, say, fourteen marbles in the bag, because "fourteen" symbolized the necessary operations for them to constitute a collection of marbles as a numerical composite of specific numerosity fourteen. The difference between Scenetra and the two other children was that it was more difficult for her to focus her attention on the number sequence implied by a number word. She continued to focus on the implied collection, and operated with its elements rather than with the elements of the number sequence. Although we would never discourage re-presentation of patterns or collections whose elements do not co-occur in patterns, we feel that it is important for children also to re-present their number sequences and segment them, for that proved to be the essential element in their progress to higher order operations.

The type of problem that might be presented to children to encourage the segmentation of a number sequence would be to ask how many twos would be counted if they counted to twelve without there being perceptual items to count. Of course, the same type of question could be asked of a child while counting out twelve marbles. When asked to count, say, twelve marbles by twos, children often will count "1-2" while taking two, then "3-4" when taking two more, etc., but they will have no idea how many pairs of marbles they counted. Asking them to make records encourages them to focus on a pair of marbles as one countable item, and encourages taking a numerical composite as one thing--as an abstract composite unit. This encourages engendering accommodations in their counting schemes, the creation of abstract composite units, and the construction of talicitly nested number sequences.

There are many other problems and activities that can be used to encourage a child to take a re-presentation of a number sequence as one thing. McLellan & Dewey (1908) went so far as to say number springs from the need to measure things. Although we do not go so far as to claim that number must necessarily spring from the need to measure things, number sequences *can* be constructed in the context of measuring activity. A child might measure the length of a table and find it to be one hundred centimeters long. Finding how many decimeter strips it would take to cover the same table length, without actually placing them on the table, is the type of problem-solving activity that should be encouraged if the child counts by one and records each module of ten counting acts. The major work during the stage of sequential integration operations is the construction of progressive integration operations, and counting in measurement contexts provides the child with a fundamental experience on which he or she can reflect.

Progressive Integration Operations

This is the stage where children should be encouraged to reason strategically to find sums or differences, including counting-down-to when finding differences. In fact, the reason Scenetra did not construct an explicitly nested number sequence is that she essentially refused to reason strategically even though she could do so. She preferred to use her standard algorithms that she had learned in her mathematics class. The explicitly nested number sequence was constructed by both Jason and Tyrone as a result of their strategic reasoning to find sums and differences. The primary goal of this stage is for the children to advance to the next stage because it is transitional.

Part-Whole Operations

Children do construct the part-whole operations when learning the explicitly nested number sequence. These symbolized numerical operations should be used when encouraging children to count by ten and by one to solve problems, modifying their schemes counting-on, counting-up-to, counting-off-from, and counting-down-to to include the unit of ten. These modified schemes are included in the *child generated algorithms* (Steffe, 1983) that should be encouraged in this stage. The children should also construct the decimal system of numeration and concepts of place value and total value of a digit in a multiple-digit number. Because counting by ten and by one is an anticipatory scheme in this stage, the children can use it to find how many dimes can be traded for a pile of, say, 72 pennies and how many pennies would be left over. Such activities can be also used to learn the place value and total value of the digits in two-digit numbers and can be extended to three-digit numbers if counting by hundred is developed.

Operative strategies, including reversibility of addition and subtraction, should be included in the model for children's zone of potential development. Other possibilities are ten and one hundred as iterable units; counting by units other than ten to find sums and differences; counting by a composite unit (e.g., three) to find how many individual units are in so many of those composite units or how many of those composite units can be made from the elements of a containing composite unit.

Final Comments

There are several current practices in early childhood mathematics education that we found counter-productive for the children while they were in their stage of sequential integration operations. Among the most debilitating were the work with ten and place value, and the work with algorithms for finding sums and differences of two- and three-digit numbers. We must remember that the sequence of number words in a given culture was built up long before a mature system of numerals became established.

> Our researches thus far have shown us that the laws that govern early numerals, ordering and grouping, do not in fact correspond to the rule of the sequence, which is stepwise gradation. Hence, the writing of the numerals is *not* merely the representation of the number-word sequence. (Menninger, 1969, p. 53)

Menninger's observation that Roman and Indo-European number sequences differ only in minor details, but that their systems of numeration differ radically, demonstrates the independence of verbal and written systems. It also provides a perspective on why, in school mathematics, there is an unresolved tension between children's verbal number sequences and written numerals. Whatever numerical operations are available to children are initially symbolized by their verbal number sequences and these operations do not serve as a basis for the written system. That is, children are asked to learn the written system without using their verbal number sequences, a practice that might constrain the construction of part-whole operations, as we have documented in Scenetra's case study. Unfortunately, the decimal system of numeration cannot be understood if part-whole operations are not available (Kamii, 1986). An information processing model has been written that specifies part-whole operations apart from the number sequence, but it does not specify how the operations might be constructed (Resnick, 1983a, pp. 114-15).

In particular, the work with the standard paper-and-pencil algorithms should be abandoned and replaced with work on the schemes counting-on, counting-up-to, and counting-down-to. Children's mathematics should be stressed where there is an emphasis on the creativity of children in problem-solving contexts of the type already mentioned. Engendering accommodations must be sought and, when found, capitalized on.

We also feel that the children should not be drilled on their basic addition and subtraction facts while they are in the stage of sequential integration operations. Remembering certain connections should not be discouraged, but the children should not develop the concept that arithmetic is devoted to answer getting rather than to problem solving and strategic reasoning.

Our view of mathematical teaching and learning in the teaching experiment implies a major shift in the normative curriculum. Conventional phrases like "second-grade arithmetic" imply almost universal consensus about their meaning, and elementary schools proceed on that assumption, which is repeatedly confirmed with each new release of a textbook series, state and local achievement tests and guidelines, or standards for mathematical education. The conventional language, concepts, and assumptions concerning school mathematics overwhelm what conceptual progress has been made. "Second grade arithmetic", for example, could be redefined as the collective mathematical experiences of children at the age of seven years, where no a priori assumptions need to be made about what those mathematical experiences should be for any particular child. The experiences would be operationally defined by the interactive communication between teachers and children, as well as among children themselves. If schools were viewed as adaptive institutions and teachers as adaptive decision makers, we feel the children would be far better off, because mathematics would then be viewed as something that children do or construct in the course of problem-solving activities.

References

Adler, M. J. (1982). The paideia proposal: An educational manifesto. New York: Macmillan.

Bamberger, J. (1975). The development of musical intelligence: Children's representation of simple rhythms (Artificial Intelligence Memo 342). Cambridge, MA.: The MIT Press

Bamberger, J. (1978). Intuitive and formal musical knowing: Parables of cognitive dissonance. In S. S. Madeja (Ed.), The arts, cognition, and basic skills: Second yearbook on research in the arts and aesthetic education (pp. 173-206). CEMREL.

Baroody, A. J. (1982, March). The effects of instruction on children's understanding of the "equals" sign. Paper presented at the Annual Meeting of the American Educational Research Association, New York, NY.

Baroody, A. J., Ginsburg, H. P., & Waxman, B. (1983). Children's use of mathematical structure. Journal for Research in Mathematics Education, 14, 156-168.

Bernstein, R. J. (1983). Beyond objectivism and relativism: Science, hermeneutics, and praxis. Philadelphia: University of Pennsylvania Press.

Beth, E. W., & Piaget, J. (1966). Mathematical epistemology and psychology. (W. Mays, Trans.). Dordrecht, Holland: D. Reidel.

Bridgman, P. W. (1927). The logic of modern physics. New York: Macmillan Co.

Bridgman, P. W. (1934). A physicist's second reaction to mengenlehre. Scripta Mathematica, 2, 101-117 and 224-234.

Brouwer, L. E. J. (1913). Intuitionism and formalism. Bulletin of the American Mathematical Society, 20, 81-96.

Brownell, W. A. (1928). The development of children's number ideas in the primary grades. Chicago: University of Chicago Press.

Brownell, W. A. (1935). Psychological considerations in the learning and teaching of arithmetic. In W. D. Reeve, (Ed.), Teaching of arithmetic: Tenth yearbook of the NCTM (pp. 1-31). New York: Bureau of Publications, Teachers College, Columbia University.

Brownell, W. A. (1945). When is arithmetic meaningful? Journal of Educational Research, 38, 481-498.

Brownell, W. A., & Chazel, C. B. (1935). The effects of premature drill on third grade arithmetic. Journal of Educational Research, 29, 17-28.

Campbell, R. L., & Bickhard, M. H. (1986). Knowing levels and developmental stages. New York: Karger.

Caramuel, J. (1977). Meditatio prooemialis, mathesis biceps. In A. Parea, P. Soriano, & P. Terzi (Eds.) L'aritmetica binaria e le altre aritmetiche di Giovanni Caramuel, Vescovo di Vigevano. Vigevano, Italy: Academia Tiberina. (Original work published 1670)

Carpenter, T. P. (1980). Heuristic strategies used to solve addition and subtraction problems. In R. Karplus (Ed.), Proceedings of the Fourth International Conference for the Psychology of Mathematics Education (pp. 317-321). Berkeley, CA: University of California.

Carpenter, T. P., & Moser, J. M. (1982). The development of addition and subtraction problem solving skills. In T. P. Carpenter, J. M. Moser, & T. A. Romberg (Eds.), Addition and subtraction: A cognitive perspective (pp. 9-24). Hillsdale, NJ: Erlbaum.

Cifarelli, V. V., & Wheatley, G. H. (1979a). Critique of the Thornton study. Journal for Research in Mathematics Education, 10, 233-234.

Cifarelli, V. V., & Wheatley, G. H. (1979b). Formal thinking strategies: A prerequisite for learning basic facts? Journal for Research in Mathematics Education, 10, 368-370.

Davydov, F. V., & Andronov, V. P. (1981). The psychological conditions of the organization of ideal actions (Project Paper No. 81-2). Madison: Wisconsin Research and Development Center for Individualizing Schooling.

de Saussure, F. (1959). Course in general linguistics. New York: The Philosophical Library.

DiSibio, M. (1982). Memory for connected discourse: A constructivist view. Review of Educational Research, 52, 149-174.

Dooley, G. B., & Gill, T. (1977). Mathematical capabilities of Lana chimpanzee. In G. H. Bourne (Ed.), Progress in ape research (pp. 133-142). New York: Academic Press.

Ferster, C. B. (1964). Arithmetic behavior in chimpanzees. Scientific American, 1964, 210(5), 98-106.

Fischer, J. P. (1981). L'enfant et le courtage. Unpublished manuscript, Ecole Normal; 16, rue dila Victorie. 57158 Montigue-lis-metz.

Flavell, J. H. (1963). The developmental psychology of Jean Piaget. New York: D. Van Nostrand Company, Inc.

Frege, G. (1974). Die grundlagen der arithmetik. Oxford, England: Blackwell. (Originally published, 1884)

Fuson, K. C., & Richards, J. (1980, April). Children's construction of the counting numbers: From a spew to a bidirectional chain. Paper presented at the annual meeting of the American Educational Research Association, Boston.

Gates, A. I. (1942). Connectionism: Present concepts and interpretations. In N. B. Henry (Ed.), The psychology of learning: Forty-first yearbook of the NSSE (pp. 141-164). Chicago: University of Chicago Press.

Gelman, R., & Gallistel, C. R. (1978). The child's understanding of number. Cambridge: Harvard University Press.

Ginsburg, H. (1977). Children's arithmetic: The learning process. New York: D. Van Nostrand Company.

Greeno, J. G. (1983). Conceptual entities. In D. Gentner & A. L. Stevens (Eds.), Mental models. Hillsdale, NJ: Erlbaum.

Hatano, G. (1982). Learning to add and subtract: A Japanese perspective. In T. Carpenter, J. Moser, & T. Romberg (Eds.), Addition and subtraction: A cognitive perspective (pp. 211-223). Hillsdale, NJ: Erlbaum.

Hayes, K. J., & Nissen, C. H. (1971). Higher mental functions of a home-raised chimpanzee. In A. M. Schrier & F. Sollnitz (Eds.), Behavior of nonhuman primates (pp. 60-115). (Vol. 4), New York: Academic Press.

Herscovics, N. (1983). In: Comments and notes to chapter I. In L. P. Steffe, E. von Glasersfeld, J. Richards, & P. Cobb, Children's counting types: Philosophy, theory, and application (pp. 12-21). New York: Praeger Scientific.

Hiebert, J. (1982). The position of the unknown set and children's solutions of verbal arithmetic problems. Journal for Research in Mathematics Education, 13, 341-349.

Hiebert, J., Carpenter, T. P., & Moser, J. M. (1982). Cognitive development and children's solutions to verbal arithmetic problems. Journal for Research in Mathematics Education, 13, 83-98.

Husserl, E. (1970). Philosophie der arithmetik. Den Haag: Martinus Nijhoff. (Originally published 1887)

Ilg, F., & Ames, L. B. (1951). Developmental trends in arithmetic. Journal of Genetic Psychology, 79, 3-28.

Inhelder, B., Sinclair, H., & Bovet, M. (1974). Learning and the development of cognition. (S. Wedgwood, Trans.). Cambridge: Harvard University Press.

Judd, C. H. (1927). Psychological analysis of the fundamentals of arithmetic (Supplementary Education Monograph). Chicago: University of Chicago Press.

Kamii, C. (1986). Place value: An explanation of its difficulty and educational implications for the primary grades. Journal of Research in Childhood Education, 1(2), 75-86.

Knight, F. B. (1930). Some considerations of method. In G. M. Whipple (Ed.), Report of the society's committee on arithmetic: Twenty-ninth yearbook of the NSSE (pp. 145-268). Bloomington, IL: Public School Publishing Company.

Labinowicz, E. (1982, March). Children's intellectual autonomy and the construction of bi-directional equality. Paper presented at the Annual meeting of the American Educational Research Association, New York City.

Labinowicz, E. (1985). Learning from children. Menlo Park: Addison-Wesley Publishing Company.

Lakatos, I. (1970). Falsification and the methodology of scientific research programmes. In I. Lakatos & A. Musgrave (Eds.), Criticism and the growth of knowledge (pp. 91-196). Cambridge, England: Cambridge University Press.

Laudan, L. (1977). Progress and its problems. Berkeley: University of California Press.

Menchinskaya, N. A. (1969). The psychology of mastering concepts: Fundamental problems and methods of research. In J. Kilpatrick & I. Wirszup (Eds.). Soviet Studies in the psychology of learning and teaching mathematics (Vol. 1, pp. 13-38). Stanford: School Mathematics Study Group.

Menninger, K. (1969). Number words and number symbols: A cultural history of numbers. Cambridge: The MIT Press

McLellan, J. A., & Dewey, J. (1908). The psychology of number. New York: Appleton.

Piaget, J. (1936). La naissance de l'intelligence chez l'enfant'. Neuchatel: Delachaux et Niestle.

Piaget, J. (1937). La construction du reel chez l'enfant. Neuchatel: Delachaux et Niestle.

Piaget, J. (1945). La formation du symbole chez l'enfant. Neuchatel: Delachaux et Niestle.

Piaget, J. (1950). The psychology of intelligence. London: Routledge & Kegan Paul Ltd.

Piaget, J. (1964). Development and learning. In R. E. Ripple & V. N. Rockcastle (Eds.), Piaget rediscovered: A report of the conference on cognitive studies and curriculum development (pp. 7-20). Ithaca, NY: Cornell University Press.

Piaget, J. (1970). Genetic epistemology. New York: Columbia University Press.

Piaget, J. (1971). Biology and knowledge. Chicago: University of Chicago Press.

Piaget, J. (1974a). La prise de conscience. Paris: Presses Universitaires de France.

Piaget, J. (1974b). Reussir et comprendre. Paris: Presses Universitaires de France.

Piaget, J., & Collaborators (1977). Recherches sur l'abstraction reflechissante. Paris: Presses Universitaires de France.

Piaget, J. (1980). Adaptation and intelligence: Organic selection and phenocopy. Chicago: University of Chicago Press.

Piaget, J., & Szeminska, A. (1941). La genese du nombre chez l'enfant. Neuchatel: Delachaux et Niestle.

Polya, G. (1962). Mathematical discovery: On understanding, learning, teaching problem solving. New York: John Wiley & Sons.

Rathmell, E. C. (1978). Using thinking strategies to teach the basic facts. In M. Suydam & R. Reys (Eds.), Developing computational skills (pp. 13-38). Reston, VA: National Council of Teachers of Mathematics.

Rathmell, E. C. (1979). A reply to "Formal thinking strategies: A prerequisite for learning basic facts?" Journal for Research in Mathematics Education, 10, 374-377.

Resnick, L. B. (1983a). A developmental theory of number understanding. In H. P. Ginsburg (Ed.), The development of mathematical thinking (pp. 110-151). New York: Academic Press.

Resnick, L. B. (1983b). Towards a cognitive theory of instruction. In S. G. Paris, G. M. Olson, & W. H. Stevenson (Eds.), Learning and motivation in the classroom (pp. 5-38). Hillsdale, NJ: Erlbaum.

Rumelhart, D. E., & Norman, D. A. (1981). Analogical processes in learning. In J. R. Anderson (Ed.), Cognitive skills and their acquisition (pp. 335-359). Hillsdale, NJ: Erlbaum.

Russell, B. (1903). Principles of mathematics. New York: Norton.

Sinclair, H. (1971). Number and measurement. In M. F. Rosskopf, L. P. Steffe, & S. Taback (Eds.), Piagetian cognitive development research and mathematical education (pp. 149-159). Washington, DC: NCTM.

Smith, J. H. (1921). Arithmetical combinations. Elementary School Journal, 16, 762-770.

Starkey, P. & Cooper, R. J. (1980). Perception of numbers by human infants. Science, 210, 1033-1030.

Steffe, L. P. (1979). A reply to "Formal thinking strategies: A prerequisite for learning basic facts?" Journal for Research in Mathematics Education, 10, 370-374.

Steffe, L. P. (1983). Children's algorithms as schemes. Educational Studies in Mathematics, 14, 233-249.

Steffe, L. P., Cobb, P., & Richards, J. (1983). An analysis of children's creation of countable items while counting. In L. P. Steffe, E. von Glasersfeld, J. Richards, & P. Cobb, Children's counting types: Philosophy, theory, and application (pp. 43-74). New York: Praeger Scientific.

Steffe, L. P., Firth, D., & Cobb, P. (1981). On the nature of counting activity: Perceptual unit items. For the Learning of Mathematics, 1(2), 13-21.

Steffe, L. P., Hirstein, J. J., & Spikes, W. C. (1976). Quantitative comparisons and class inclusions as readiness variables for learning first-grade arithmetical content (Technical Report No. 9). Tallahassee, FL: Project for the Mathematical Development of Children. (Eric Document Reproduction Service No. ED 144808)

Steffe, L. P., Richards, J., & von Glasersfeld, E. (1978). Experimental models for the child's acquisition of counting and of addition and subtraction. In K. C. Fuson & W. E. Geeslin (Eds.), Explorations in the modeling of the learning of mathematics (pp. 27-44). Columbus, OH: ERIC/SMEAC Center for Science, Mathematics, and Environmental Education.

Steffe, L. P., Thompson, P., & Richards, J. (1982). Children's counting in arithmetical problem solving. In T. Carpenter, J. Moser, & T. Romberg (Eds.), Addition and subtraction: A cognitive perspective (pp. 211-223). Hillsdale, NJ: Erlbaum.

Steffe, L. P., von Glasersfeld, E., Richards, J., & Cobb, P. (1983). Children's counting types: Philosophy, theory, and application. New York Praeger Scientific.

Steinberg, R. M. (1985). Instruction on derived fact strategies in addition and subtraction. Journal for Research in Mathematics Education, 16, 337-355.

Steiner, H. G. (1980). Introduction. In H. G. Steiner (Ed.), Comparative studies of mathematics curricula: Change and stability, 1960-1980. Bielefeld, West Germany: Institut fur Didaktik der Mathematik der Universitat Bielefeld.

Swenson, E. J. (1949). Organization and generalization as factors in learning, transfer, and retroactive inhibition. In Learning theory in school situations (pp. 9-39). University of Minnesota Studies in Education, No. 2. Minneapolis: University of Minnesota Press.

Thiele, C. L. (1938). The contribution of generalization to the learning of addition facts. New York: Bureau of Publications, Teachers College, Columbia University.

Thom, R. (1973). Modern mathematics: Does it exist? In A. G. Howson (Ed.), Developments in Mathematics Education. Proceedings of the Second International Congress on Mathematical Education (pp. 194-209). Cambridge: Cambridge University Press.

Thomas, R. K., Fowlkes, D., & Vickery, J. D. (1980). Conceptual numerousness judgments by squirrel monkeys. American Journal of Psychology, 93(2), 247-257.

Thompson, P. (1982). A theoretical framework for understanding young children's concepts of whole number numeration. (Doctoral dissertation, University of Georgia, 1962). Dissertation Abstracts International, 43, 1868A.

Thorndike, E. L. (1922). The psychology of arithmetic. New York: MacMillan.

Thornton, C. A. (1978). Emphasizing thinking strategies in basic fact instruction. Journal for Research in Mathematics Education, 9, 214-227.

Thornton, C. A. (1979). Emphasis on thinking strategies in basic fact instruction - A response. Journal for Research in Mathematics Education, 10, 235-237.

Toulmin, S. (1963). Foresight and understanding. New York: Harper Torchbooks.

Van den Brink, J. (1981). Queries around the number concept. In Psychology of mathematics education: Proceedings of the fifth conference of the international group (pp. 56-62). Grenoble, France: Laboratoire Institut Mathematiques Appliques.

Van Engen, H. (1949). An analysis of meaning in arithmetic. Elementary School Journal, 49, 321-29, 395-400.

Van Engen, H., & Gibb, E. G. (1956). General mental functions associated with division. Cedar Falls: Town State Teachers College.

von Glasersfeld, E. (1980). The concept of equilibration in a constructivist theory of knowledge. In F. Benseler, P. M. Hejl, & W. K. Kock (Eds.), Autopoiesis, communication, and society (pp. 75-85). Frankfurt, West Germany: Campus Verlag.

von Glasersfeld, E. (1981). An attentional model for the conceptual construction of units and number. Journal for Research in Mathematics Education, 12, 83-94.

von Glasersfeld, E. (1982a). On reflection and abstraction. Unpublished manuscript, The University of Georgia, Athens.

von Glasersfeld, E. (1982b). Subitizing - The role of figural patterns in the development of numerical concepts. Archives de Psychologie, 50, 191-218.

von Glasersfeld, E., & Kelly, M. (1983). On the concepts of period, phase, stage, and level. Human Development, 25, 152-160.

von Glasersfeld, E., & Richards, J. (1983). The creation of units as a prerequisite for number: A philosophical review. In L. P. Steffe, E. von Glasersfeld, J. Richards, & P. Cobb, Children's counting types: Philosophy, theory, and application (pp. 1-20). New York: Praeger Scientific.

von Glasersfeld, E., Steffe, L. P., & Richards, J. (1983). An analysis of counting and what is counted. In L. P. Steffe, E. von Glasersfeld, J. Richards, & P. Cobb, Children's counting types: Philosophy, theory, and application (pp. 21-44). New York: Praeger Scientific.

Vygotsky, L. S. (1956). Learning and mental development at school age. In A. N. Leontiev & A. R. Luria (Eds.), Selected psychological works. Moscow, 438-452 (Article written in 1934).

Vygotsky, L. S. (1965). Thought and language (E. Haufmamn & G. Vakar, Trans.). Cambridge: MIT Press.

Wertime, R. (1979). Students, problems, and "courage spans." In J. Lochhead & J. Clement (Eds.), Cognitive process instruction (pp. 191-200). Philadelphia: Franklin Institute Press.

Glossary

ABSTRACTION

EMPIRICAL ABSTRACTION: concerns a perceptual (sensory) experience and results in a TEMPLATE that serves to recognize further experiences as similar or equivalent to the past one; eventually the abstracted template turns into a CONCEPT and can be re-presented as an INTERNALIZED item without the presence of the sensory material in actual perception.

REFLECTIVE ABSTRACTION is divided into three types:

1. PSEUDO-EMPIRICAL ABSTRACTION: concerns a motor (kinesthetic or attentional) action, something the subject does, and results in a pattern that serves to recognize further kinesthetic or attentional actions as similar or equivalent to the past one; eventually the pattern may turn into an INTERNALIZED action and can then be reenacted whenever sensory material suitable for the execution of the activity is perceived.
2. REFLECTING ABSTRACTION: derives from a PSEUDO-EMPIRICAL ABSTRACTION and produces an INTERIORIZED action or operation that can now be carried out "in thought", i.e. with re-presented sensory material when that material is not perceptually available.
3. REFLECTED ABSTRACTION: derives a rule from several PSEUDO-EMPIRICAL or REFLECTING ABSTRACTIONS and produces an "operation with operations" that no longer requires any specific perceptual or re-presented sensory material to be carried out in thought.

ACCOMMODATIONS OF COUNTING SCHEMES

ENGENDERING ACCOMMODATION: a FUNCTIONAL ACCOMMODATION that occurs independently, involves using conceptual elements external as well as internal to a counting scheme, leads to further accommodations, and involves or leads to a structural reorganization of the scheme.

FUNCTIONAL ACCOMMODATION: modification of a counting scheme as a result of REFLECTIVE ABSTRACTION that occurs in the context of using the scheme.

METAMORPHIC ACCOMMODATION: a modification of a counting scheme as a result of REFLECTIVE ABSTRACTION that occurs independently but not in any particular application of the scheme.

PROCEDURAL ACCOMMODATION: a FUNCTIONAL ACCOMMODATION that involves a modification of the activity of counting or a novel way of viewing the results of counting. In either case, a modification of the first part of the scheme follows.

RETROSPECTIVE ACCOMMODATION: a FUNCTIONAL ACCOMMODATION that occurs independently and involves using conceptual elements constructed in an earlier application of the scheme.

AWARENESS OF PLURALITY: requires the production of a visualized image of a PERCEPTUAL UNIT ITEM along with its repetitions or repeatability. It is an indefinite awareness of more than one PERCEPTUAL UNIT ITEM.

COMPOSITE WHOLES

ABSTRACT COMPOSITE UNIT: the result of applying the INTEGRATION OPERATION to a NUMERICAL COMPOSITE or to a symbolized NUMERICAL COMPOSITE. The child focuses on the unit structure of a NUMERICAL COMPOSITE--e.g., one ten--rather than on the unit items--e.g. ten ones.

COLLECTION: an experientially bounded PLURALITY.

COMPOSITE UNIT: the result of applying the INTEGRATION OPERATION to any COLLECTION or PATTERN of sensory-motor or ABSTRACT UNIT ITEMS.

COUNTABLE FIGURAL UNIT OF TEN: any FIGURAL PATTERN or ENACTIVE CONCEPT of ten that is coordinated with a number word of the sequence "10-20-30-...".

COUNTABLE MOTOR UNIT OF TEN: any MOTOR UNIT ITEM that is coordinated with a number word of the sequence "10-20-30-..." and that constitutes a SUBSTITUTE for a FIGURAL UNIT OF TEN.

FIGURAL COLLECTION: experientially bounded results of repeatedly re-presenting a FIGURAL UNIT ITEM.

FIGURAL PLURALITY: the results of repeatedly re-presenting a FIGURAL UNIT ITEM.

ITERABLE UNIT OF TEN: "ten" as a conceptual structure that is available in the absence of particular collections of ten perceptual items, and makes possible the decision to count by ten prior to the actual activity of counting perceptual or hidden objects. A counting by ten act is an indicator for incrementing by ten more ones.

NUMERICAL COMPOSITE: any NUMERICAL PATTERN of ABSTRACT UNIT ITEMS of one. The child focuses on the unit items of the PATTERN and not on the PATTERN as one thing. The ABSTRACT UNIT ITEMS can be symbolized and a NUMBER SEQUENCE like "one, two, three, four, five, six, seven" can symbolize a NUMERICAL COMPOSITE.

PLURALITY: an unbounded sequence of sensory-motor unit items.

REPEATABLE UNIT OF TEN: a symbolic SUBSTITUTE for an ABSTRACT COMPOSITE UNIT of ten that is repeated as an experiential chain. In its repetitions, the symbolic SUBSTITUTE can lose its composite quality.

SYMBOLIC MOTOR UNIT OF TEN: a MOTOR UNIT ITEM that is a SUBSTITUTE for an ABSTRACT COMPOSITE UNIT of ten.

TEN MORE: an ABSTRACT COMPOSITE UNIT of ten whose elements are taken to extend beyond the elements of another ABSTRACT COMPOSITE UNIT.

CONCEPTS

CONCEPT: any conceptual structure that can be re-presented in the absence of perceptual material (see EMPIRICAL ABSTRACTION).

ENACTIVE CONCEPT: the results of re-presenting a perceptual SUBSTITUTE for an ENACTIVE PRECONCEPT.

ENACTIVE PRECONCEPT: a PRECONCEPT whose use requires kinesthetic signals--e.g., a rhythmic pattern.

FIGURATIVE CONCEPT: the results of re-presenting a PERCEPTUAL PRECONCEPT in the absence of perceptual material.

FIGURATIVE PRECONCEPT: any PERCEPTUAL PRECONCEPT that can be re- presented only after it is used in recognition of a perceptual situation.

NUMERICAL CONCEPT: a result (possibly symbolized) of applying the INTEGRATION OPERATION.

PERCEPTUAL PRECONCEPT: a PRECONCEPT whose use does not involve kinesthetic material.

PRECONCEPT: any conceptual structure whose use requires sensory material of some type (see EMPIRICAL and PSEUDO-EMPIRICAL ABSTRACTION).

COUNTING SCHEMES

ANTICIPATORY SCHEME: a SCHEME is anticipatory when recognition of an experiential situation (1st part of a specific SCHEME) leads to a re- presentation of the associated activity and/or result.

FIGURATIVE COUNTING SCHEME: a counting SCHEME whose first part consists of FIGURAL COLLECTIONS or PATTERNS, whose second part consists of counting MOTOR or VERBAL UNIT ITEMS, and whose third part consists of the records of counting. Repetition of the last number word can be an INDEX of the records.

NUMERICAL COUNTING SCHEME: (cf. NUMBER SEQUENCES).

PERCEPTUAL COUNTING SCHEME: a counting SCHEME whose first part consists of perceptual collections or patterns, whose second part consist of counting PERCEPTUAL UNIT ITEMS, and whose third part usually consists of a SPECIFIED COLLECTION and the arrival at a last item of the collection.

SCHEME: a SCHEME is goal-directed and consists of three parts: first is the child's recognition of an experiential situation as one that has been experienced before; second is the activity the child has come to associate with the situation; and third, is a result the child has come to expect of the activity.

INDEFINITE AWARENESS OF NUMEROSITY: requires the review of a COLLECTION (or FIGURAL COLLECTION) and the awareness of the repeated use of the abstract unit pattern. It is an indefinite awareness of more than one ABSTRACT UNIT ITEM.

INDEX: part of a sequence of experiences that has been causally connected to the others; perception of the "cause" may indicate the "effect", perception of the "effect" may indicate the "cause" (e.g., smoke is an INDEX of fire; "six" can be an INDEX of "one, two, three, four, five, six").

INTERIORIZATION: the most general form of ABSTRACTION; it leads to the isolation of structure (form), pattern (coordination), and operations (actions) from experiential things and activities; an INTERIORIZED entity is purged of its sensory-motor material.

INTERNALIZATION: the process that results either in the ability to re-present a sensory item without the relevant sensory signals being available in actual perception or in the ability to reenact a motor activity without the presence of the kinesthetic signals from actual physical movement. INTERNALIZATION leads to "visualization" in all sensory modalities.

LEXICAL MEANING: whatever MEANING is associated with a single word.

MEANING (of number words or a combination of number words): whatever aspects of one or more schemes that are associated with a word or words within the awareness of the child.

NUMBER SEQUENCES (NUMERICAL COUNTING SCHEMES)

EXPLICITLY NESTED NUMBER SEQUENCE: the essential difference in the TACITLY and the EXPLICITLY NESTED NUMBER SEQUENCE is that the number words of an EXPLICITLY NESTED NUMBER SEQUENCE symbolize an ABSTRACT UNIT containing an ITERABLE UNIT that can be iterated as indicated by the number word. A number word of the sequence can now refer to an ABSTRACT COMPOSITE UNIT apart from the sequence as well as to the ABSTRACT COMPOSITE UNIT containing the number sequence from one up to and including the given number word.

INITIAL NUMBER SEQUENCE: an INTERIORIZED NUMBER WORD SEQUENCE that can be re-presented when assimilating situations involving COLLECTIONS. The actual counting activity that follows is an instantiation of the counting activity symbolized by the re-presented number sequence and is referred to as counting ABSTRACT UNIT ITEMS. The number words of an INITIAL NUMBER SEQUENCE can symbolize NUMERICAL COMPOSITES as well as the INITIAL NUMBER SEQUENCE from one up to and including a given number word.

NUMBER SEQUENCE: any composite unit whose elements symbolize counting acts.

TACITLY NESTED NUMBER SEQUENCE: the essential difference in the INITIAL and the TACITLY NESTED NUMBER SEQUENCES is that the number words of a TACITLY NESTED NUMBER SEQUENCE symbolize ABSTRACT COMPOSITE units as well as NUMERICAL COMPOSITES. In particular, they can symbolize an ABSTRACT COMPOSITE UNIT containing the number sequence from one up to and including a given number word.

NUMEROSITY: can be formed by repeatedly instantiating an ABSTRACT UNIT ITEM in an experiential situation synchronously with uttering number words in sequence. The INDEFINITE AWARENESS OF NUMEROSITY that led to counting is made definite and it is this INDEFINITE AWARENESS OF NUMEROSITY plus the assignation of number words that constitutes a NUMEROSITY of a COMPOSITE UNIT. A NUMEROSITY can be symbolized by a number word if the number word stands for (or implies) a count using all number words preceding the given number word in a number sequence.

OBJECT CONCEPT: a template that has become available for spontaneous RE-PRESENTATION.

OPERATIONS

DISEMBEDDING OPERATION: the application of the INTEGRATION OPERATION to only part of a NUMBER WORD SEQUENCE, a NUMBER SEQUENCE, or the elements of a COMPOSITE UNIT.

INTEGRATION OPERATION: the conceptual act of uniting what one may also consider distinct unitary items.

PART-WHOLE OPERATIONS: those operations made possible by disembedding an ABSTRACT COMPOSITE UNIT from a containing COMPOSITE UNIT. They include comparing the disembedded unit to the containing unit, exhaustively disembedding two ABSTRACT COMPOSITE UNITS from a containing unit while remaining aware of the containing unit, and combining the two disembedded ABSTRACT COMPOSITE UNITS to form the containing COMPOSITE UNIT.

PROGRESSIVE INTEGRATION OPERATIONS: the application of the INTEGRATION OPERATION to material that includes the results of a previous application of the INTEGRATION OPERATION.

SEQUENTIAL INTEGRATION OPERATIONS: repeated application of the INTEGRATION operation to sensory-motor material.

UNITIZING OPERATION: the application of the INTEGRATION OPERATION to a complex of sensory-motor signals or to a sensory-motor item.

PATTERNS

FIGURAL PATTERN: the results of re-presenting a PATTERN of any type.

FINGER PATTERN: the result of putting two or more fingers up simultaneously. In this sense, finger patterns are motor programs whose result can appear in the visual field or actual field.

MOBILE FINGER PATTERN: a specified sequence of finger movements.

NUMERICAL PATTERN: the result of applying the INTEGRATION OPERATION to a PATTERN, including FIGURAL PATTERNS.

PATTERN: a collection of elements that can be characterized (and recognized) by the spatial and/or temporal relations that connect them.

RHYTHMIC PATTERN: a sequence of "beats" that recurs with unchanged intervals.

SEQUENTIAL OR TEMPORAL PATTERN: a sequence of "beats" that seem to co-occur in RE-PRESENTATION.

SOPHISTICATED FINGER PATTERN: FINGER PATTERNS for the number words after "ten" and including "fifteen", formed by one open hand standing for "ten" and the other showing fingers for the units above ten.

SPATIAL PATTERN (discrete): a constellation of perceptual items that seem to co-occur.

SPATIO-AUDITORY PATTERN: a sequence of auditory items that are coordinated with the elements of a SPATIAL PATTERN.

SPATIO-MOTOR PATTERN: motor activity that traces an identifiable SPATIAL PATTERN--e.g., pointing acts that trace a triangular pattern.

PERMANENT OBJECT: an experiential thing of which the subject has an OBJECT CONCEPT and the successive experiences of which the subject has linked by the attribution of "individual identity"; a PERMANENT OBJECT is believed to "exist" somewhere even when it is not within the subject's perceptual field.

PROTONUMEROSITY: can be formed by repeatedly instantiating a TEMPLATE in an experiential situation synchronous with uttering number words in sequence. It can be formed also by re-presenting the involved number word sequence if the number words signify the experiential unit items. The AWARENESS OF PLURALITY that led to counting is made definite and it is this definite awareness of a bounded plurality that constitutes a PROTONUMEROSITY. This does not yield a numerosity in the abstract sense.

RE-PRESENTATION: re-creation of a perceptual or motor experience without actual sensory-motor material; one is in it and, in a very real sense, one acts again. It is like a playback

SOUND IMAGE: the term derives from de Saussure and refers to the auditory TEMPLATE that allows a subject to recognize sound patterns as proper words of the language. In a competent speaker of the language, SOUND IMAGES must also have the status of CONCEPTS so that they can be freely re-presented for the purpose of actively producing the respective words in speech.

SPECIFIED COLLECTION: a COLLECTION that has been counted (counting here refers only to the assignation of number words with no implication of NUMEROSITY).

STRATEGIES

> **ADDEND-INCREASING or -DECREASING STRATEGY**: finding an unknown sum by altering one of the addends to create a known sum. The known sum is then altered by the amount of change in the original addend but in the opposite direction. The strategy is called "addend increasing" or "addend decreasing" depending on whether the known sum is increased or decreased, respectively. Finding the sum of 8 and 7 by using the known sum of 8 and 5 and then increasing 13 by 2 is an example of an ADDEND-INCREASING STRATEGY.
>
> **COMPENSATION STRATEGY**: finding an unknown sum by altering the two addends by the same amount but in opposite directions to create a known sum. Finding the sum of 9 and 7 by using the known sum of 8 and 8 is an example.
>
> **INVERSE STRATEGY**: finding an unknown difference by using the subtrahend as one of two addends whose sum is the minuend. Finding the difference of 12 and 7 by finding what added to 7 yields 12 is an example.
>
> **LOCAL THINKING STRATEGY**: a THINKING STRATEGY that involves finding an unknown sum or difference using a sum or difference just found.

MINUEND OR SUBTRAHEND VARIATION STRATEGY: finding an unknown difference by altering the minuend or subtrahend to create a known difference. The known difference is then altered by the same amount, the alteration being in the same direction in the case of alteration of the subtrahend and in the opposite direction in the case of alteration of the minuend. Finding the difference of 11 and 5 by using the known difference of 10 and 5 and then increasing the difference 5 by 1 is an example of the MINUEND VARIATION STRATEGY.

SPONTANEOUS THINKING STRATEGY: a THINKING STRATEGY that involves finding an unknown sum or difference using a sum or difference known without solving.

THINKING STRATEGY: a coordination of arithmetic symbols that involves using a known sum or difference to find an unknown sum or difference.

SUBSTITUTE: an item that can play the part of a specific other item in a specific situation or context.

SYMBOL: a perceptual or re-presentational item that has been linked to another and has the power to call forth a re-presentation of that other.

SYNTACTICAL MEANING: those MEANINGS that arise out of a combination of words.

TEMPLATE: result of an EMPIRICAL ABSTRACTION from an experiential "thing"; the template serves for the recognition (assimilation) of further experiential things as repetitions of things already experienced; the formation of a template leads to a CONCEPT and to categorization.

UNIT ITEMS OF ONE

ABSTRACT UNIT ITEM: a unit pattern that is the result of UNITIZING one of the sensory-motor unit items (see REFLECTING ABSTRACTION).

FIGURAL UNIT ITEM: a re-presented PERCEPTUAL UNIT ITEM (see EMPIRICAL ABSTRACTION).

ITERABLE UNIT: a unit pattern that has been abstracted from a NUMBER SEQUENCE that can be iterated so many times (see REFLECTED ABSTRACTION).

MOTOR UNIT ITEM: a motor action that has been UNITIZED and thereby isolated as a specific motor pattern. In counting, a motor unit item is a SUBSTITUTE for a PERCEPTUAL UNIT ITEM or its figural representative (see PSEUDO-EMPIRICAL ABSTRACTION).

PERCEPTUAL UNIT ITEM: a complex of sensory-motor signals that have been ABSTRACTED and UNITIZED as a specific experiential "thing" (see EMPIRICAL ABSTRACTION).

VERBAL UNIT ITEM: an utterance of a number word that signifies a PERCEPTUAL, FIGURAL, or MOTOR UNIT ITEM (see PSEUDO-EMPIRICAL ABSTRACTION).